POLITICS IN THE PLAYGROUND

.

HELEN MAY

Politics in the Playground

The world of early childhood in Aotearoa New Zealand

OTAGO UNIVERSITY PRESS
Te Whare Tā o Te Wānanga o Ōtākou

Published by Otago University Press
PO Box 56 / Level 1, 398 Cumberland St,
Dunedin, New Zealand
Email university.press@otago.ac.nz

First published 2001 by Bridget Williams Books Ltd
Copyright © Helen May 2001, 2009, 2019
Revised editions 2009, 2019

ISBN 978-1-98-853181-6

Cover design by Nell May
Printed in China through Asia Pacific Offset

MIX
Paper from
responsible sources
FSC
www.fsc.org
FSC® C136333

CONTENTS

Investing in the Early Years: third edition

This third edition of *Politics in the Playground* continues the swings and roundabouts story of early childhood education in Aotearoa New Zealand. The first edition concluded in the early years of the Labour government 1999–2008. The second edition concluded soon after the election of a National government in 2008. This third edition is written in the aftermath of the election of a Labour-led coalition government in 2017.

Broadly, the story from the late 1940s concerned the growth of part-day preschool education with increasing government oversight and funding. From the 1970s–90s the story was shaped by the advocacy for more diverse early childhood services including childcare and initiatives for Māori and Pasifika communities. Early childhood policy during the past 20 years has been characterised by policies around equitable funding, the infrastructure of quality and qualifications and extending participation rates, but rationales for this investment at the time have been linked to the political dogma of the party in power. Updated editions of *Politics in the Playground* have been framed around the nine-year government terms for Labour and National respectively, each time concluding with the promise of radical shifts in direction as a new government takes office.

The 2000s were a rollercoaster of change for the early childhood education sector, with early childhood policy high on the government's agenda and the reputation of New Zealand's early childhood curriculum and policy evident on the international stage. Representatives of the sector were tasked with developing a strategic plan and positioning some 'blue skies' aspirations around the rights of children on the agenda. By 2008 the key tenets of the plan were in place and the impact of these policies, including some 'blue skies' elements, were evident in the lives of children and families. The National government of

2008–17 was characterised by cutting back the costs of quality and aligning early childhood with a targeted social investment policy framed around families at risk and vulnerable children. In its first year in office, over 2017–18, the Labour-led coalition government promised to 'turn the tide' and negotiate a new strategic plan with the sector. In 2019 the direction ahead is agreed, but its implementation is dependent on Labour being re-elected in 2020.

A new chapter has been added in this third edition, with a selection of stories that collectively illustrate the wider politics shaping the era. The selection is personal, linked to various campaigns and endeavours I was associated with or examined. The New Zealand early childhood story has continued to attract international interest as well as national interrogation, and parts of this new chapter were first considered in invited presentations and publications, across both national and international arenas. Other scholars and advocates have also documented the early childhood story, and the new chapter frames up a range of research, writing and commentary to provide a broad insight and a collective analysis of the times.

HISTORICAL CONTEXTS

Twentieth-century social policy was characterised by campaigns calling for the state to support the health, welfare and education of children. A worldwide industry surrounding childhood was the result. *Politics in the Playground* addresses the campaign in New Zealand for the state support of preschool education, or early childhood education (ECE) as it is now known. At the heart of this campaign are the see-saws, swings and roundabouts in a seeming playground of political, educational and social opinion on the best place for the care and education of young children, and a century of emancipation of women from the confines of the home. The story provides insights into the social, ideological, economic and political changes that characterised the latter half of the twentieth century and the early years of the twenty-first century.

My book *The Discovery of Early Childhood* outlined the emergence of the idea of institutions for the care and education of very young children in Europe and then New Zealand.[1] This sequel picks up the story after the Second World War, when education and welfare policies were blueprinted to create a fairer and better world for children and families. Equal opportunities for all was the dream. The disorder of war became a catalyst for new ideas such as early childhood education, and opinion swung to the view that governments should directly support preschool education at kindergarten, as a benefit both for children and for their mothers.

Before the war, charitable kindergarten associations worked primarily with the inner-city poor. A few private kindergartens catered for the children of the middle classes. After the war, kindergartens emerged from their philanthropic umbrella to become an acceptable preschool education service for all children. By the 1950s those children not attending preschool came to be regarded as unfortunate, by the 1960s as disadvantaged, by the 1970s–1980s as disenfranchised. By the new millennium there was an emerging discourse on entitlement as a citizen child, but overlaid by discourses of the 'risks' of not participating. This book investigates the political and pedagogical rationales for these shifts that began with understandings of social progress and the mental health of the nation, came to include principles of equity and rights, and then incorporated views for a more instrumental investment in the economy.

The postwar years were characterised by policy to both contain and/or manage the growth of the early childhood provision. In 1944 there were 2301 children attending the 49 free kindergartens that received a government subsidy, representing 3.4% of three- and four-year-olds. In 2017 there were 202,772 children from birth to five years of age attending 5527 early childhood services.[2]

The pattern of provision had changed greatly. Kindergartens catered for only 15% of children, with 65% of children attending education and care centres that provide childcare. There were licensed services such as Playcentres, kōhanga reo, Pacific Islands centres and home-based family daycare, offering a range of full-day and part-day programmes, including specialist groups such as Montessori, Steiner, and bilingual or language immersion centres. Other services included hospital play programmes, unlicensed playgroups and/or language groups, and parent support programmes. Each service had emerged to meet a new need. Each brought a new rationale for broadening the state's investment in the early years. Some challenged the dominant ideology of the time before their ideas were incorporated into the mainstream.

CONSTRUCTING EUROPEAN CHILDHOOD

The Century of the Child is the title of a bestselling book published in 1900 by Ellen Key, an early Swedish feminist.[3] Key attributed the ills of the 'modern world' to failures in childrearing. She envisaged a more moral society if the state supported a childhood where children were expertly reared by mothers. To Key, the nineteenth-century discovery of the crèche, kindergarten and nursery were second best. Key would not have approved of the widespread education of preschool children in state-supported institutions. Throughout the 70 years spanned by my book, the rationale for investing in the early years shifted to accommodate new perceptions of childhood, education and welfare. Early childhood institutions were at the forefront of pioneering the new, as well as being agents in regulating the accepted views of the time.

Halfway through 'the century of the child', in the 1950s, childhood had been intricately mapped out. Sociologists Allison James and Alan Prout outline how the concept of childhood as a distinct stage crystallised in nineteenth-century Western thought, and how, during the twentieth century, this 'theoretical space [was] elaborated and filled out'.[4] Nurseries and kindergartens in Europe and the United States were the laboratories for much of the research creating developmental norms and stages that Western society then constructed as 'normal' for the bodies and minds of all children. These understandings brought the lives of children and their parents under increasing scrutiny. British sociologist Nikolas Rose is critical of the 'gaze of the psychologist', which caused childhood to become 'the most intensively governed sector of personal existence'. This was justified by an intensifying quest for the best ways to protect the modern child from danger, to ensure 'normal' development, and to promote certain attributes such as intelligence, educability and emotional stability.[5]

James, Jenks and Prout argue that 'Developmental psychology colonised childhood in a pact with medicine, education and government agencies.'[6] The developmental map of the preschool child was the most intricate and vulnerable, justifying more intensive oversight. According to Berry Mayall, health visitors, preschool staff and social workers intervene in private lives to regulate what goes on in the family mainly by co-opting mothers towards their own professional understanding of the 'normal' child:

> The preschool child is defined in certain ways through the teaching of these professionals, acting as agents of the state. For instance the model preschooler is co-operative, friendly, alert and obedient. Mothers must learn that they must school their child to be fit to engage with school social and academic norms by the time they reach the age of five; the school entrant should be able to manage dressing, know her colours and numbers, be accustomed to behaving socially as a member of a group.[7]

The Discovery of Early Childhood detailed how the systematic mapping of childhood in the first half of the century affected the curriculum in kindergartens and also in other institutions, such as nursery schools and Playcentres, established to demonstrate the benefits of new understandings of children's development. The implications for school-aged children were also far reaching. In *Teachers Talk Teaching* (1997) Sue Middleton and Helen May described how, in what was termed 'new education', progressive or child-centred approaches to learning and teaching were trialled and practised in a few New Zealand schools and preschools before the Second World War.[8]

The 'gaze' of the state, however, had been focused on the physical needs of young children, with state investment acceptable through the frames of health and welfare. By mid-century, researchers, educators, welfare reformers and policy makers were sufficiently convinced that the mainstream institutions of childhood should incorporate psychological insights into child development. Their vision was one of socialised and happier children and better-adjusted adults in a saner world. C.E. Beeby, a key architect of New Zealand education policy from the 1930s to the 1960s, claimed that 'if schools could turn out the right kind of individuals, they could surely help to produce a more just society'.[9] During the postwar years, reforms spearheading these ideas swept through all education institutions and welfare services for children.

CONSTRUCTING MĀORI CHILDHOOD

A key difference between the period covered in *The Discovery of Early Childhood* and this postwar sequel is the visibility of Māori children and their families in early childhood institutions. However, as I argued in *Discovery*, the absence of Māori from nineteenth- and early twentieth-century kindergartens, crèches and nurseries should not imply that the roots of Māori early childhood education history were located only in the postwar world. In the period covered by this book Māori families completed a rapid urban migration.

Māori children were perceived as a problem when they started school and as educational failures when they left, and Māori communities eventually established their own early childhood institutions. These phenomena had their origins in the European settlement of New Zealand, and the Treaty of Waitangi – signed in 1840 but still in dispute. I stated in *Discovery*:

> Colonial society created both the need and the impetus for charitable and educational services for European children; but for Māori, it brought about the

loss of population, land, mana and language. These factors are at the crux of later early childhood services.[10]

For the Māori child 'the century of the child' was not the same as it was for the Pākehā child. In 1900 the life chances of Māori infants were considerably lower than those of Pākehā infants, and they lived primarily in separate communities. Māori preschoolers came to Pākehā attention only when they arrived at school, possibly at five but often older, speaking only Māori. Rapid and sometimes harsh Europeanisation was deemed the solution to the 'problem'. During the postwar years Māori preschoolers became increasingly visible in suburbs and cities and in the occasional kindergarten. They became the focus of educational intervention by both Māori and Pākehā. Early childhood institutions established over the latter part of the century both for and by Māori were at the forefront of the wider politics of struggles over power and powerlessness, land, language and culture for Māori and Pākehā. Issues of European colonisation and tino rangatiratanga were still at the heart of the argument.

POLICY FRAMES

The postwar years have been framed by a sequence of reviews of the government investment in early childhood services. In 1947 the government released its postwar blueprint, the *Report of the Consultative Committee on Preschool Education Services*, known as the Bailey report after the chair, Colin Bailey.[11] In 1988 *Before Five*[12] was released as government's response to *Education to be More*, known as the Meade report after the chair of the working group, Anne Meade.[13] There were two key differences between these reports:

- The Bailey report called for the state to take over early childhood education, in line with the view that 'The voluntary principle is generally repugnant in that it carries overtones of charity.'[14] By contrast, the Meade report was linked to moves by the state to draw back from educational management in favour of the 'self-managing school'.
- The Bailey report was primarily concerned with part-day preschool education for three- and four-year-olds in kindergartens. The Meade report focused on a policy framework for a diverse range of early childhood services from birth to five years.

Despite the 40-year time difference, there were also similarities:

- Early childhood was positioned as a political priority for social policy. Both reports were optimistic about the effect of the state's investment in individuals, families and the nation as a whole.
- However, neither report's recommendations were fully implemented. Moreover, as a return on their investment, the respective governments sought to increase state scrutiny of programmes for children, administration of services and quality of teachers. This was not always welcome.
- Both initiatives came under Labour governments and were linked to welfare and employment policies for supporting women and families. When National governments came to power soon afterwards, in 1949 and 1990, the impetus for action was slowed.

In the years between these reports the ongoing pattern was broadly one of consolidation (but sometimes cutbacks) under National, with change (and sometimes chaos) under Labour. Numerous innovations and increasing participation in early childhood education in that period demonstrate that much was achieved. The frustration for those in the early childhood sector was managing the delivery of services with insufficient funding, as well as coping with incomplete and, for some groups, restrictive policies.

In 2000 a Labour-led government embarked on developing a new strategic plan for early childhood, after a decade of dissatisfaction concerning the implementation of the 'Before Five' policies. Anne Meade was again asked to chair the working group, which made recommendations to the government for *Pathways to the Future – Ngā Huarahi Arataki*, a 10-year strategic plan for early childhood education published in 2002.[15] After nine years of Labour government, and part-way through the implementation of the plan, in 2008 there was a change of government. In the midst of a global economic crisis the incoming National government determined not only to contain the costs of Labour's policy, but to frame (for the first time) its own policy agenda for early childhood education. In 2011 a small taskforce published *An Agenda for Amazing Children*, with a policy blueprint that prioritised participation in early childhood education by 'priority children'.[16] The more radical elements of this approach languished, but so too did recommendations to improve quality in particular for under-three-year-olds. This latest edition of *Politics in the Playground* concludes with the Labour-led coalition government updating its early strategic plan for new political times,[17] while Prime Minister Jacinda Ardern takes maternity leave and gives birth to Neve Te Aroha.

Social and political change has been the impetus for many early childhood initiatives. Establishment of services, however, brought the world of early childhood under the 'gaze' of political patronage. The contradiction between the dream and the political reality has been mediated as early childhood services have negotiated state funding, and governments have increased regulation and extended their scrutiny.

Part One of this book, *Growth and Expectation*, explores the psychological paradigm underpinning investment in early childhood services from the late 1940s to the 1960s. By mid-century, developmental psychology was shifting its gaze from the laboratory to the home. Preschool institutions were a support for mothers and a site of expert advice and backup where mothers failed in their task. Socialisation theories saw childhood primarily as the domain of psychology, with mothers, preschool institutions and schools as the key agents socialising children into becoming acceptable citizens. Perceived disruptions such as illegitimacy, delinquency, educational failure and working mothers were 'understood' as part of a cycle of psychological ills.[18] Various kinds of early childhood provision were classified by the state as acceptable or unacceptable, according to whether they were deemed at the time to cause or cure such ills.[19] The ideal of an orderly socialisation of children proved unsustainable. The diversity of cultures and lifestyles, behaviours and experiences of families could not always fit within the defined boundaries of normality and adjustment.

Part Two, *Challenge and Constraint*, covers the period from the late 1960s to the early 1980s. Older understandings of childhood were overlaid by sociological and political insights, particularly in relation to the rights of Māori, women and children.[20] New understandings of education generated radical critiques of schooling and highlighted the inadequacies of older views. Educational institutions were perceived by some as tools of an oppressive state, but by others as possible sites for liberation. It was argued that programmes and institutions for children should be empowering, not just for themselves but also for their families and/or their cultures. Again, early childhood institutions were at the forefront, as a testing site for the possibilities of intervention and investment. There was again optimism that oppression and inequity in society could be overcome. The state, however, was a more cautious participant, as the gaze shifted to find the cause of disempowerment within the colonial, capitalist and patriarchal structures of the state itself.

Part Three, *State Interest and Devolution*, appraises the years from the 1980s to the end of the century. The state was again persuaded that substantive investment in early childhood was warranted. Ironically, this was paralleled by government seeking to downsize and 'out-source' its earlier 'cradle to grave' welfare policies in favour of new codes of individual and family responsibility.[21] Devolving responsibility in the education sector did not, however, mean less scrutiny. National curricula across the education sector were promulgated, with 'learning outcomes' and 'essential skills' required in order to participate in a new 'enterprise society'. A culture of audit and assurance, from the world of business management, became operative throughout all government agencies,[22] inevitably affecting early childhood centres. Audit trails required surveillance and evidence. The early childhood tools of child observation and supervision were used to discern measurable outcomes of learning in the minutiae of children's daily activities.

Part Four, *Strategic Directions*, contains new chapters for the second and third editions respectively, now covering almost two decades of the new millennium. There was the promise of a more supportive state that would play a more 'hands-on' role in the support of early childhood education. There were issues of rights in relation to pay parity for teachers, free early childhood and access to early childhood services for children alongside the growing presence of big business as a provider of services attracted by the increasing investment in the sector. A final chapter outlines the curtailment of these initiatives, with a political gaze framed by social investment policies and the almost compulsory participation of vulnerable children in early childhood education.[23] The landscape of services continued to shift with private-for-profit provision ascendant over the decline of community-based services. The Labour government promised to 'turn the tide' towards the principle of free public education. This was a bold agenda, the outcome of which is still uncertain.

The material environment of early childhood education stayed remarkably consistent over the 70 years of this study, involving stories, puzzles, blocks, paints, dough, water, sand, junk and outdoor climbing equipment, although by the 2000s the 'ICT child' was evident, and by the 2010s there was much emphasis on environmental sustainability. The assumption that young children learn through play remained the dominating discourse, but the rationales for the benefits of play were periodically realigned, explained initially in terms of the emotional and social well-being of the child. Issues to do with children's rights and power relationships between children and adults later impacted in various ways on the environment for playful learning. By the end of the century, play and progressive education in schools were under attack as having failed too many children. National standards, which assessed every child in primary school every year in their 3Rs, were introduced by National then removed by Labour. The benefits of play survived in early childhood but the child at play was subject to more rigorous scrutiny, as was the teacher. The state demanded evidence that future workplace skills were an outcome of play.

Early childhood has always been the Cinderella of the education sector. Childcare was once the Cinderella of early childhood education. My quest to know and understand the history of early childhood began during my days in childcare, as a parent and worker, when childcare was clearly outside the acceptable. When political activism seemed to fail, I wrote my first book, *Mind That Child* (1985), which traced the hidden history and politics of childcare provision in New Zealand. I came to see that the issues underlying the lack of support for childcare were enmeshed in the contradictions and conflicts in the lives of women in relation to men, children and work. This became the focus of doctoral research, later published in the book *Minding Children, Managing Men* (1992). *The Discovery of Early Childhood* sought to position the story of early childhood in New Zealand alongside the history of education as an integral but distinctive part of it, both nationally and internationally. The revised edition of this book continues the story of early childhood but is accompanied by a parallel story of early education at school spanning two books and two centuries, *School Beginnings* (2005) and *'I am five and I go to school'* (2011).[24]

In *Politics in the Playground*, selective scenarios from the spectrum of early childhood services are used to detail experiments, curricula, campaigns, issues, research and ideas; to highlight children, politicians, teachers, mothers and researchers; and to comment on centres, the workplace, home, schools and government. Collectively, these scenarios map the dynamics of early childhood education in this country, but they do not fill the landscape. Many histories and herstories make up the full picture. Some have been told or written by individuals and organisations. These have been a resource in constructing my story. So too have the archives of government departments, early childhood organisations and individuals, along with conversations with many people over the years. There are many more stories still to be told.

PART ONE

Growth and Expectation
1940s–1960s

CHAPTER ONE

Psychology of Freedom

In the immediate postwar years advocates of progressive education practices in New Zealand preschools and permissive childrearing at home saw benefits for all young children in 'free play'. This was play undirected by adults, which provided opportunities for creativity and exploration in a range of mediums. Adult observation and support of this play was believed to provide clues towards understanding children's psychological and developmental needs. The belief that psychologically healthy children were the first step towards a saner society became the key tenet of the Western world view of early childhood education, a view summarised by Swedish educator Alva Myrdal in 1948:

> The world is sick and troubled ... We know that if children were given the right opportunities and handled with the right educational care, so much of the mental ill-health which is now crippling individuals should be prevented, and so many of the conflicts and tensions which are harassing the world could be turned into productive forces.[1]

A decade later *NZ Parent and Child* magazine (May–June 1958) claimed: 'There has never been a more watched, spied-upon and dissected generation of New Zealand youth than this.' The psychological 'gaze' focused not only on children but also on teachers and, in particular, on mothers. This chapter explores various sites of this gaze in the kindergarten, Playcentre (originally play centre), home and school. Though there were advocates and opponents of progressive and permissive ideas in all sites, the appearance and focus of early childhood care and education in New Zealand was transformed as a consequence of these ideas. It goes on to appraise the 'problems' that psychological explanation could both cause and cure, and the emergence of the idea of preschool as a solution to the 'problems' of Māori children.

The drive to 'understand' children is at the core of the child-centred pedagogy that came to dominate practice in early childhood institutions, schools and homes during the second half of the twentieth century. Its themes saturated the media. James Hymes' *Understanding Your Child* (1952) was a popular book from the US translating new developmental theories into usable ideas for parents and teachers.[2] New Zealand psychologist Quentin Brew's 1958 radio series, 'Understanding Children', was based on talks to mothers at Parents' Centre, an advocacy organisation founded in 1951. Beverley Morris's popular book *Understanding Children* (1967) was based on her child development lectures for Playcentre supervisors.[3] Erica Burman defines the main tenets of child-centred pedagogy as:

> readiness: concerning the child's maturity to learn,
>
> needs: implying that all children have fundamental needs which if not met will cause problems later,
>
> choice: highlighting how learning should be directed towards the interest of the child,
>
> play: suggesting that learning should be enjoyable and self directed,
>
> discovery: meaning that learning is a personal experience.[4]

The pedagogy viewed knowledge of child development as the foundation of curriculum (in institutions) and of child management (in homes). In the early childhood sector there was a particularly strong correlation between curriculum and developmental psychology.[5] In the early school sector there was also the view that formal teaching of the traditional '3Rs' should be delayed and incorporated into a developmental framework. Knowledge mapped out a detailed path for development which, with the appropriate interventions by parents, teachers and other professionals, would create a 'normal' child. To 'understand' children also required adults to be observers of children, to collect evidence and clues, so that each individual child could be supported through the various developmental stages. Critiques of developmentalism, as it is often called, have claimed that this child-centred pedagogy brought about more regulation of children, as every detail of their lives became subject to scrutiny.[6] Secondly, individuals, groups and cultures whose patterns seemed different were labelled as retarded, backward, abnormal, deprived or even deviant.[7]

The ideas of two important theorists from the US, Arnold Gesell and Erik Erikson, underpinned education policy, curriculum practice and advice to parents in New Zealand during the 1950s. Their theories promoted a pedagogy for learning and development through the medium of play within a climate of motherly (or mother-like substitute) love and attention.

By mid-century Gesell's mapping of the milestones of infant development was influential. In *Infant and Child in the Culture Today* (1943) Gesell and Frances Ilg linked each age level with a behaviour profile and behaviour day, along with suggested activities for mothers at home. For children from the age of 18 months they outlined a nursery behaviour profile, and suggested techniques for nursery teachers.[8] Gesell and Ilg's ages, stages and advice were disseminated widely. Most childrearing advice, including the manuals of New Zealand's main infant and child health organisation, Plunket, contained milestone charts for measuring individual children alongside prescribed norms developed from observational data collected at the Yale Clinic of Child Development where they worked.

Gesell envisaged a 'democratic culture for the psychological welfare of infants and young children'.[9] To this end, democracy supported individuals developing 'naturally', but with guidance, along the developmental path. He depicted the increasing 'social control' of the 'welfare of the preschool child' through '(1) Medical supervision of child development, (2) Parental and preparental education, and (3) Readaptation of the kindergarten and nursery school'.[10] In New Zealand, Plunket, parent education and preschool were, as Gesell envisaged, an integral part of the postwar blueprint for the right environment. Nikolas Rose, however, describes the work of Gesell and his colleagues as 'an exemplary demonstration of the techniques for the disciplining of human difference' ... [which introduced] 'a new division in the lives of small children, a division between normal and abnormal'.[11] Esther Thelen and Karen Adolph write that Gesell's 'typical child living his typical life was clearly male, white, native born, middle class, and in an intact family, with a virtually invisible father and a devoted but strangely passive mother'.[12] This critical perception was not common at the time.

A second psychological map was provided by Erikson. His book *Childhood and Society* (1950) expanded Sigmund Freud's psychoanalytic theory of psychosexual stages into eight psychosocial stages from infancy to adulthood.[13] Psychoanalytic theory had constructed a view of the child as vulnerable and filled with urges that were difficult to control. A pedagogy of learning, derived from the work of Sigmund Freud, brought self-expression to the fore. Educators such as Susan Isaacs in Britain and Anna Freud in Vienna and later Britain had already pioneered nursery school programmes that provided opportunities for expression of feelings and conflict resolution through the creative arts, dramatic and social play.[14]

Each of Erikson's stages was a potential crisis involving conflicts to be resolved. Unlike Freud, Erikson's arena of struggle was not within the individual, but in relation to society. A satisfactory outcome was a healthy personality. To Erikson, play was a means for the child to deal with the complexities of life. To early childhood educators who interpreted his work, play allowed the child to maintain equilibrium and develop a sense of self.[15]

Erikson shifted from Vienna to the US during the 1930s. He first presented his theory of personality development at the 1950 White House Conference on Children and Youth.[16] In contrast to earlier psychoanalytic theories, he was concerned to present a less pathological view of development, in which it was generally possible for individuals to triumph over the psychological hazards along the way. Like Freud, however, he saw the reasons for children and adults having problems in adjusting to society as located in the early years of childhood. This placed the institutions and practices of childrearing under scrutiny.

BENEFITS OF PLAY

The play of children has long been a focus of attention for child-centred approaches to education.[17] At the birth of the twentieth century John Dewey encouraged reforming kindergarteners to create a free-play environment with real-life reconstructions such as the 'family corner'. The rationale was that co-operative free play would provide children with the social skills for democratic living.[18] Advances in psychology, outlined previously, focused attention on mental health. The medium of play in the early years was deemed the key for normal adjustment and development.[19]

By the 1940s short periods of free play were occurring in some New Zealand infant classrooms, kindergartens and new nursery Playcentres. New understandings of the importance of the early years as a foundation for later learning and development were taken on board at the highest political level.[20] By mid-century belief in the benefits of learning through play for young children was sufficiently strong to convince educational policy makers to promote further reform. The Director of Education from 1940 to 1960 was C.E. Beeby. With his wife Beatrice Beeby (a founder of Playcentre) he had long been interested in the benefits of play.[21]

Publicity for the 1944 Ministerial Education Conference, attributed to the Minister of Education, H.G.R. (Rex) Mason, but penned by Beeby, strongly endorsed progressive classroom practice and psychological understanding. Alongside a photograph of children engaged in free-play activities, Mason wrote:

> Nothing short of a revolution has taken place in the infant room during the past twenty years. It has my full support ... we must all agree that in the infant room the learning of formal intellectual skills is of secondary importance. What is of supreme importance is that the young child should be healthy and happy, that he should learn to work and play with other children, that his mind should be kept lively and eager and full of wonder, and that he should lay the basis of good habits and attitudes from which all healthy growth in later life must spring.[22]

Preschool education was to provide the foundation for learning in the infant room. It received prominent attention at the conference. The benefits of preschool education, later outlined in the 1947 Bailey report, were to provide companionship for children, stimulating play environments, and parent education. Preschool education would also assist with the transition to school and with health supervision. However, the benefits were not just for children. It would also provide relief for mothers from the emotional strain of full-time parenting, give them time for shopping and appointments, and encourage them to have more children. Overall, the 'stabilising' life of the kindergarten was viewed as enhancing the mental and physical health of the community.[23]

The government's new focus on preschool education was shared in international arenas. In 1948 Beeby became the Assistant Director General of Unesco, which organised the first world early childhood conference for the Organisation Mondiale pour l'Education Préscholaire (OMEP) in Prague. Opening the conference, Beeby described how:

> The spirit of education through understanding the child, which is so typical of pre-school education, [is now] overthrowing the 'academic tyranny of ... [earlier] forms of instruction' ... [24]

Alva Myrdal from Sweden, also attending, defined a blueprint for part-day early childhood provision:

> The basic need for security can only be satisfied by the home. But above that, children need a place where they can cultivate independence and learn to rely on themselves in a wider environment ... In this world organised for adults there is a need for a 'children's world', where they can learn to be citizens among equals, independent and self-reliant, courageous and resourceful in thought and action ...[25]

This was a vision for childhood in a Western democracy. The eastern bloc countries were also expanding preschool education, but full-day care was their preference, as it released mothers for employment and allowed more opportunity for socialisation in collective communist values.

Myrdal identified the pivotal role for early childhood professionals in promoting the benefits of psychological understanding in the postwar world:

> We are in a way the middlemen between those who make the advances in science, finding out how the unhappy developments can be forestalled … We are the ones who dig it out of the laboratories. The nursery school, kindergartens and infant classes have taken on this pioneering work. Wherever a nursery school is, there is a living force right in the community working towards a greater understanding of the educational rights of the young.[26]

Such optimism continued and, although the grand dream was never realised, many individuals, families and communities did feel the benefits. In New Zealand, realisation was delayed by an unexpected baby boom, whose impact was first felt in the hospitals from 1946 on, then upward through the education sector for the next 20 years. While policy makers were keen to see teachers implement new child-centred methods, day-to-day survival, rather than grand dreams, was most teachers' main preoccupation.[27]

FREE PLAY AT KINDERGARTEN

Transforming the older charitable ethic of kindergarten into a preschool service for all was the postwar challenge. Moira Gallagher was a New Zealand school adviser known for her progressive practice in infant classrooms.[28] She was appointed as secretary to the Bailey committee, and in 1946 became the first Supervisor of Preschool Services in the Department of Education, a position she held until 1965.

Gallagher's brief was to manage the government's policy of expansion and support to preschool education. Unofficially, her brief was to 'free up the kindergartens', which both Beeby and Gallagher considered to be kindly but too regimented.[29] Neither task was simple. The low salaries of kindergarten teachers, the sometimes conservative kindergarten associations and the poor physical conditions of many kindergartens all prevented rapid change.

In 1948 the government began paying kindergarten teachers' salaries, and student allowances were increased. Conditions were attached, the most significant being that the director (head teacher) had to be trained. All associations had difficulty complying, and not everyone welcomed the government's new role. As Gallagher recalled: 'Panic set in – [some saw this as] government

Gwen Somerset was a long-time advocate and practitioner of progressive education in schools through running her nursery school in Feilding. In the 1930s with her husband Crawford she had travelled to many sites of progressive thinking in Europe and the US. In 1948 the couple shifted to Wellington and Somerset became a staunch advocate of a free-play philosophy in Playcentre. In 1949 she wrote *I Play and I Grow* as a practical guide. Early nursery Playcentres were often run along timetabled kindergarten lines. Her instructions were:

> At a Play Centre concentrated and interested play should have nothing or no one to interrupt it … FREE CHOICE OF OCCUPATION IS FUNDAMENTAL … His play must be free and spontaneous and there must be sufficient play material for him to feel that he is making a real choice according to his own feelings and his own needs. The afternoon must not be divided into 'set periods' where adults decide it is time for special occupations.[51]

Somerset set about persuading Playcentres that free play was a good idea. This was not always successful. In 1951 the Avondale Playcentre was nearly disaffiliated from the Auckland association for putting these ideas into practice.[52]

I Play and I Grow was the first publication written for the federation. With four editions it grew in size and scope over the years, as did Playcentre. For many years Moira Gallagher issued *I Play and I Grow* as a 'departmental' handout to kindergartens and visitors.

Though Playcentre had connections in the highest academic and political echelons, this did not translate into financial support. Playcentre's annual grant in 1954 was £2635, whereas £247,000 went to kindergartens that year. Policy makers found dealing with two organisations complex. At a meeting with the Play Centre Federation on 7 May 1954, the Assistant Director of Education, D.G. (Douglas) Ball, stated bluntly that the government was not happy about preschool education, and urged better co-operation between Playcentre and kindergarten.[53] He warned Playcentre that the government would not increase its funding if there was 'overlap, competition or conflict with the kindergarten movement'. Playcentre responded strongly:

> To be regarded as stepping stones to kindergartens or as makeshift and cheap substitutes is not acceptable … We would regret to see the day when only one type of pre-school service was available in New Zealand. We need more preschool centres in New Zealand if more than 11% of the population is to be catered for … unless NPCs [Playcentres] were functioning, these children and their parents would receive no pre-school experience at all.[54]

Competition was inevitable, particularly in smaller towns. In Taihape in 1960, for example, a Playcentre with 20 children already existed. A proposed kindergarten needed 60 names on the roll to proceed, which would have put the Playcentre out of business. Such spats caused the Director of Education, Arnold Campbell, to write to the Kindergarten Union warning that 'wasteful overlapping of services' was unacceptable and that such clashes undermined the ability of the 'two movements … to work side by side'.[55] Public arguments over the differences between the two organisations fuelled the conflict. In the *Wairoa Star* (2 April 1962) an anonymous writer with Playcentre sympathies asked, 'How does a play centre differ from a kindergarten?' and gave this answer:

> At a kindergarten children are taught, at a play centre they learn by themselves; at a kindergarten there is discipline, at a play centre children are not forced to do anything but are gently persuaded; at kindergarten all the children are engaged in one activity, at play centres they amuse themselves for most of the time at various activities of their own choice.

This brought a heated reply (4 April 1962) from an 'ex-kindergarten director':

> I would like to point out that children at kindergarten are free to choose their own activities from any of the out or inside activities. They are not taught as stated but learn through play. Kindergarten discipline is not like that of a school classroom as [implied], but the children are controlled as unobtrusively as possible. At times for the welfare of everyone, it is essential that children do as they are asked; how bad for a child always to do as it pleases! In some kindergartens there is never a time when all the children are engaged in the one activity … kindergartens are run by more qualified staff who cater for more children, for longer periods and at far lower cost to parents …

The distinctiveness of Playcentre was that it was operated and supervised primarily by mothers.[56] Positioning the mother on a level with the trained kindergarten teacher was a bold move, dictated partly by pragmatics: there was no other source of teachers, and no money. Somerset, who was a key architect of this thinking, fused supervisor (i.e. teacher) training and parent education. This was a successful recipe, but the perception that Playcentre training was lightweight remained. Somerset later wrote: 'The acceptance of parents as co-workers in education was too new a concept in 1948 for it to be regarded as a serious area for academic concern.'[57]

Lex Grey was another key person in shaping the philosophy of Playcentre. He saw it as a political community for parents,[58] describing the Playcentre movement as 'an experiment in better community living'.[59] Amidst the rhetoric of the Somerset and Grey perspectives, Playcentre was able to craft some distinctive messages. Playcentre was a 'family affair', which met the mental health needs of parents as well as their children. Educationist Jack Shallcrass later described Playcentre as one of the 'divergers' in education and 'ahead of its time', in that 'it had an organic view of the child, his family and his society'.[60]

Both kindergartens and Playcentres were attempting to redefine the role of the adult in children's play. *I Play and I Grow* dictated a clear stand:

> The principle followed in supervision is that of standing by and watching, rather than actively 'helping' a child to play. Except in special circumstances where a child is diffident about beginning to play. At times a child will need guidance, or a new point of view may need to be presented.[61]

Geraldine McDonald later recalled that:

> Play became a sacred kind of activity not to be interfered with … Of course the emphasis on a child's self-directed play moved the gaze away from what teachers can do for children. This made it easier for mothers to play a professional role in playcentre.[62]

Free play also had a political context, as Val Burns, teacher and Playcentre parent, explained:

> You've got to see it in terms of the 1950s still reacting to the war and the importance of freedom … New Zealand was emerging from Victoriana and you've got to remember that all of us were brought up in strictly authoritarian situations where as children you were seen and not heard. So this is a philosophy which actually says that children are human beings. It makes sense. It treats children like thinking human beings. It just gave me so much hope for children.

Freedom had wider contexts:

> We were fighting to have our husbands there at the birth of our children. We were busy fighting for rooming-in. I was revolutionary because my husband would change naps; my husband would push the pram. I got a lot of criticism for all those things … Playcentre was another one where you were breaking boundaries.[63]

Playcentre's free play environment, however, did have its rules, particularly for mothers. The research of British psychiatrist John Bowlby promoted full-time mothering as optimal for young children (see Chapter Two).[64] This was backed by Playcentre, which could demonstrate that their particular kind of early childhood service strengthened the mother–child bond. Introductory literature for Auckland parents, written by Grey, was stern:

> Playcentre does not cater for mothers who want to be free of their children. It exists for families who want to expand and deepen the warmth of relationship with their children … Children need their mothers. She is their world in the early years. She represents their faith and trust. You are there in the centre as a helper because your child needs you.[65]

Betty Armstrong was a committed Playcentre parent, but she also needed relief from a sometimes 'clingy' child:

> Some kind of childcare would have been the salvation for me with him. I can remember people from playcentre saying, 'Oh, no! Mothers should be at home with their children.' They knocked the idea. I nursed it for years. We all needed childcare, as it was a strain on all of us.[66]

These conflicts continued to simmer. The claim that Playcentres benefited both children and mothers was true, but only in the context of placing first the psychological needs of their children for full-time maternal attention.

TEACHING MOTHERS AND MOTHERLY TEACHERS

During the 1950s–60s both Playcentre and kindergarten organisations created a workforce of women in preschool education who 'understood' children. Playcentre mothers and kindergarten teachers were, to a degree, also successful in gaining increased recognition and status for their work with children. This was encouraged by the maternalist belief, now strengthened by psychology, that mothers perform a service to the state by raising children.[67] Maternalist belief, however, also limited activism to arenas that supported assumptions that children were psychologically safest when men and women had separate spheres.[68] The image of the Playcentre mother who could have a career rearing her children, and the unmarried kindergarten teacher with professional teacher training, were both based on assumptions that young children benefited from mothers with parent education and/or potential mothers who had teacher training. The training of both mothers and teachers as experts in understanding the preschool child was carefully positioned alongside the psychological benefits of full-time mothering at home.

By the 1950s Playcentre had created an accepted and popular preschool institution on the premise that 'the basis of successful *child* education is the continuing education of the *parents*'.[69] Grey's training workbook, *Parents and*

Children: Partners in Learning, sums up the ethos. There were tensions in this task. In 1958 a male correspondent to the *Playcentre Journal* wrote:

> Do we continue trying to educate our mothers still further so that in our zeal we make them specialists or psychology students of them? This may undermine a mother's opinion of her own capacity to handle her children and even cause feelings of inadequacy ...[70]

Beverley Morris interpreted this concern differently.

> We would get a bit of a backlash at playcentre when women would say that they couldn't come [to training] any more because their husbands wouldn't let them. There was a lot of that. The same with taking office in playcentre – 'My husband doesn't like me going out at nights.' A lot of women began to get ahead of their husbands in education and awareness. That broke up some marriages that I know of.[71]

Empowerment was the theme of Grey's philosophy of emergent leadership.[72] 'All are experts – all are learners.'[73] This caused Playcentre to be seen as troublesome. Historian Frances Porter relates:

> [The Education Department] was geared to teacher trainees, and Mums and Dads were right in the background ... but here were these stroppy women who were saying that they could look after their own preschool centres and wanted government funding ... it was tricky, keeping on side with Moira Gallagher, even keeping on side with Beeby. We weren't really popular with the Education Department.[74]

Women did feel empowered by Playcentre. Future Governor General Cath Tizard claimed:

> Playcentre is responsible for 'My Glorious Career'. It was certainly the first committee I ever sat on ... Forty-odd years ago when my children were young, playcentres were still relatively new and, to some people, somewhat controversial. The concept of parent involvement in the management of the centre was very strange and the ideas coming out of the training courses highly suspect to many of those of the authoritarian Truby King generation.[75]

The training of mothers by Playcentre benefited their children and allowed Playcentre to operate as a preschool institution. Playcentre was an acceptable career for mothers, but when they sought to transfer their new skills to employment for themselves, they were stepping outside maternalist boundaries. In 1967 Geraldine McDonald interviewed 58 women about their experiences at Playcentre. They strongly supported the view that mothers should be at home with their children. McDonald points out that while the Playcentre movement was able to mediate 'arrangements both for the care of children and [for] the training of mothers as staff', it could not 'resolve the psychological conflict between duty as a mother and desire for status and recognition'.[76] Playcentre saw itself as feminist, but feminism of the 1960s and 1970s caused more women to seek alternatives to the Playcentre dictum that kept mother and child linked so closely.

The ethos of kindergarten teaching was different to Playcentre work. The report on the *Recruitment, Education and Training of Teachers* (1951) recommended that kindergarten training move into the teachers' colleges alongside primary training. This did not happen until 22 years later. Nevertheless, the content of the training was upgraded, entry qualifications raised and working conditions for teachers improved. Despite considerable pressure and ad hoc measures, the Department of Education held to a standard that required at least a trained director in each kindergarten. In 1954 the Minister of Education, Ronald Algie, admitted that he had once wondered whether kindergarten teachers needed training, until 'Mr Beeby took me to an afternoon party for about forty to fifty children and told me to run it. After that I saw that special training was needed!'[77] It was not until 1965 that the Wellington Kindergarten Teachers' Association could announce: 'All kindergartens staffed with TRAINED TEACHERS. First time in many years.'[78]

In a study of postwar women teachers Kerry Bethell details the ambivalent status of kindergarten teachers:

> Bolstered by the postwar reconstruction of a society battered from the stresses and deprivations of a world war and the earlier depression, kindergarten teaching gained status. Young children and early childhood education became part of the new reconstruction and reform of the education system. Women with their gender-defined special nurturing characteristics were to play a considerable role towards attainment of this goal.[79]

Nevertheless, the older charitable ethic of kindergarten remained. Class was still a factor in the selection of prospective trainees. Peggy Dalmer, former principal of Christchurch Kindergarten College, recalled that even during the 1960s:

> Quite a few of our girls came from small, private schools and from well-off families. Kindergarten training was considered a nice thing for girls like that to do. These girls had grown up in well-run homes … [and] had a style of their own, very gentle and polite but firm underneath.[80]

Recruitment material stated that 'Play is the Work of Kindy' and emphasised the benefits of kindergarten training for a 'mother of the future'.[81] However, with the average marriage age during the 1950s being 21, most kindergarten teachers worked for only a few years. Minister Algie blamed kindergarten staffing difficulties on the popularity of marriage, stating that 'the arrow of Cupid has a special poison for you people'.[82]

Bethell's study presents a picture of conformity to dominant codes of femininity. Kindergarten associations advocated the role of full-time wives and mothers for women, and were reluctant to sanction exceptions officially; nevertheless, there is considerable evidence of associations pleading for married women to stay on or return to teaching.[83] In 1961 the first married women were accepted into primary and kindergarten training, but it was many years before all discriminatory practices were removed for married kindergarten teachers.

A significant initiative towards professionalism in kindergarten teaching was the formation of the New Zealand Free Kindergarten Teachers' Association (KTA) in 1954. In 1958 this association began to negotiate employment conditions. In keeping with an ethos of ladylike femininity and maternalist priorities, the president, Phyllis Varcoe, reminded teachers not to permit '… the desire for more salary to overshadow the paramount aim – to advance the cause of education amongst preschool children'.[84]

Kindergartens, like Playcentre, saw themselves as involved in parent education, although it was a less cohesive connection. Gallagher's visits to kindergartens reported on the parent education programme and the involvement of mothers. She was less than satisfied at times, which is not surprising, given that teachers were often young and inexperienced compared with mothers.[85] Kindergartens advertised themselves as complementing the home, but in a different way from Playcentres, which drew no boundaries between home, parents and centre. In an oft repeated talk Gallagher told the audience that:

> I see the kindergarten as the pooling of the resources of an area to provide for children things that cannot be provided in the home … but we do not attempt to replace the home and mother … Authorities throughout the world have come to believe that the most important years in the life of a child are the first – broadly the first five. We must ensure that the total environment is as good as we can make it.[86]

Kindergarten teachers were positioned as a repository of psychological knowledge through specialist training with which to support and educate mothers, who carried the main responsibility for the mental health of children.

Kindergarteners were told that, 'It was the duty of teacher and parent to combine in helping the child find his status in the home and the community'.[87] In earlier years kindergartens had advertised their work as creating useful citizens of the future through 'moral training' and 'habit training'. This belief was still present, but the terminology had changed. Kindergartens now described themselves as 'workshops of democracy', where citizenship training began under the guidance of a trained teacher, who understood about the psychological importance of mental health – the key to 'stable living' and the 'foundation of a democracy'.[88]

PLAYWAY AT SCHOOL

The benefits of learning though hands-on activity were also promoted in schools. The Department of Education promoted a seamless transition from preschool as a preparation for school. 'Playway' was the school equivalent of free play, but more contentious; it became a newsworthy catchphrase, used by critics as evidence that children were now only playing and no longer learning at school. The perceived consequences of playway ranged from a decline in education standards to increased moral decadence among the young. The *NZ Woman's Weekly* (26 June 1947) wished the term had never been coined:

> How much tragic understanding hinges upon this term … Modern teaching practice recognises the need for activity – and makes use of it, works through it, directs it. Old-fashioned methods with their 'sit still on your seat' tactics checked and thwarted it, condemning the child to long years of boredom and frustration.

By the 1950s teachers in the early years of school were expected to include a period of free-play activity. A widely available British booklet, *Activity and Experience in the Infant Classroom* (1951), provided teachers with useful advice:

> Children who have played … at activities of their own choosing, for the first hour of the morning, are very ready to settle down to somewhat more formal, less self-directed, work afterwards … there is no doubt that children come to their … '3R work' … with far more zest and interest, with more ideas and better concentration, when it follows the activity period.[89]

Teachers were told that they 'no longer had to force the child to learn' because 'the impulse to learn comes from the child'. The young child 'learns under his own steam'.[90] The benefit of play was linked to psychological 'readiness' for learning. The concept of 'readiness' had first surfaced in the 1940 Department of Education report to parliament, with the statement that '… this early formal instruction is unnecessary, if not harmful. There should be a postponement until readiness is reached.'[91] Providing a 'wise environment' for play best supported Gesell's maturational approach to development and allowed children naturally to develop 'readiness' for the next stage.[92] Classroom play came to be known as 'developmental' and was a time for teachers to observe and support children's development.

A letter sent to Moira Gallagher in 1946, when she was an Infant Adviser, from D. Veale, a teacher at Henderson, provides some insight into the changes:

> Thank you so much for the Readiness Test and also the catalogue of apparatus. May I say how grateful we are for all the help and encouragement you gave me last Monday. I just wish you could see our rooms. You would hardly recognise them. I took your advice and got rid of half my tables. This leaves quite a lot of floor space at one side in which we have set up a fine shop and we have a community table, and a Wendy House, which arrived on Tuesday. I am thrilled with the improvement. The children are having a lovely time collecting acorns and buttons and bringing in things for the shop.[93]

In 1951 Marie (Metekingi) Bell returned from England, where she had studied with some of the leaders in progressive education. 'England at that time was right into the brave new world and everybody was going to have freedom,' she recalled. After working briefly in kindergarten she was appointed to Mount Cook School, Wellington:

> The British all-day activity school was the big thing. In the developmental programme you had play from 9 to 10 and then you just went on with your ordinary programme. In the activity programme everything pivoted on what emerged during play. You followed the children's interests through and you had your maths, your reading and your writing all linked into that. Myrtle Simpson had just been made a woman inspector and she was full of these ideas and she was interested in what I was doing.[94]

The role of the teacher during 'developmental' was ambivalent. Early advice to teachers was to stand back:

> The teacher's role at the time is a subtle one. She must restrain all impulse to teach and direct – in other words she must cultivate a capacity for passive watchfulness. She is the security for the group. Her advice is only given when asked; her treatment in all situations is a positive one and in each case the onus is thrown on the child.[95]

The emphasis on child observation was at the core of the 'new education'. The teacher analysed behaviour or observed readiness for moving to the next stage of learning. Developmental theories emphasising the role of observation assumed the need to understand the child's point of view.

Department of Education advice promoted progressive ideas, but translating such ideas into practice was not easy, with large class sizes, poorly equipped classrooms and inexperienced teachers. Older teachers were not always motivated to change, and public debate continued to place the idea of play at school under scrutiny. In Wellington a series of public meetings on playway education gained media attention. The 'Playway Revolt in Wellington' reported in *NZ Parent and Child* (May–June 1958), began with a letter to the *Evening Post*. Mr Parkes felt 'betrayed by the educationalists of this country' when he looked at the 'spelling, writing and arithmetic' of his children. He argued at a series of public debates that 'free expression in the classroom had gone too far'. Debates on playway also surfaced in parliament. Beeby himself emphasised the lack of evidence for any drop in educational standards, and pointed to the greatly increased opportunities children had in the education system.

In 1960 a Commission of Education was set up to review the postwar reforms and to plan for the future. The submissions provided an opportunity to debate the merits and pitfalls of the new education ideas in schools. There was a claim that 'the 3Rs have been thrown away and the three Ps rule – psychology, phys-ed and the playway'.[96] In contrast, Kelburn Normal School supported playway. They described how they now delayed the teaching of reading, writing and arithmetic until children were ready, and claimed that by Standard Two there were no children with severe reading difficulties.[97] Auckland Playcentre supervisors went further, calling for an extension of the current developmental period to the upper school, with a view that outdoor adventure activities should also be allowed. 'We believe this time must really allow children to be free to choose and develop their activities for as long as they need ... children should be observed by trained observers.'[98]

In New Zealand key individuals were active in several contexts related to the psychological 'gaze'. For example Lex Grey, active in Playcentre, was appointed to the Auckland Teachers' College in 1952. He recalled the impact of new psychological ideas on schools:

> Arnold Campbell, who later became Director of Education, had been instru-mental in introducing child development into training college for the first time ... [It was] too successful in that it caught on with the students but it threatened

the older teachers, so there was a strong kick-back against it. Instead of students stopping fights in the playground by punishing the kids, they'd be looking more at what the feelings were that were operating and dealing with the feelings of both the children.[99]

In Wellington, Marie Bell became a beacon for progressive ideas. She was appointed to teach child development at Wellington Teachers' College in 1953. She introduced a 'baby study', where each trainee followed the development of a baby. Val Burns had begun her long career in early childhood education as a primary trainee:

> Marie Bell took me for child development. We had to read Spock [1946], who was very revolutionary in those days. I was fascinated … We also had [Edna] Mellor in a book called *Education Through Experience* [1950].[100] Marie was certainly pushing deeper into learning.[101]

Bell later taught at the Wellington Kindergarten College and was active in both Playcentre and Parents' Centre organisations.

The developmental principle of understanding through experience also guided initiatives in the teaching of reading and mathematics during the 1950s–60s. Prior to this, progressive ideas were in the realm of the experimental, but the postwar goal of the Department of Education was to develop curriculum approaches and materials that could be applied *en masse* in the mainstream. The infant rooms were at the forefront of this endeavour in the compulsory sector.

In 1960 Beeby retired as Director of Education. There was much left to do, but New Zealand infant classrooms were livelier and happier places of learning than they had dared be in 1940 when his programme of reform had begun. The foundations for this came from the work of kindergarten and Playcentre, as well as from growing expectations by parents that teachers be more understanding of their children.

PERMISSIVE MESSAGES TO MOTHERS

Parent education was the other cornerstone of the healthy democracy envisaged by Arnold Gesell. New understandings of children moved from the laboratory, the university and the teachers' college into the childrearing manuals and magazines as advice to mothers. The message that parents should be more permissive in managing their children was different from earlier expectations of child control and moral supervision. New ideas, and resistance to them, created debate and confusion.[102] Playcentre in the 1940s and Parents' Centre in the 1950s were established as advocates of the new. Government education, welfare agencies and voluntary organisations such as kindergarten and Plunket cautiously moved their thinking and advice in new directions.[103]

The most comprehensive advice came via Plunket. By the 1950s, 87% of Pākehā babies were under its oversight. In rural areas the health of Māori families was the responsibility of district health nurses, who promoted the 'Plunket way'. Truby King, the founder of Plunket, had died in 1938, but his ideas held sway.[104] King had advocated that regularity of feeding, sleeping and toileting in infants could be achieved through time-scheduled training. A child was not to be spoilt with playful attention from his or her mother. King's message to mothers was that their instincts must be curbed and trained. If mothers followed the Plunket routine their baby would be 'a joy in the home – not a source of anxiety and worry'. But he warned that 'any baby can be easily spoilt and made a cross and fretful tyrant'.[105] King was influenced by the behaviourist school of thought, which believed in the malleability of the infant to fit a prescribed regimen.[106] Freudian psychology blamed this regimentation and repression during infancy as the *cause* of the same disorders. Now motherly instincts and unconditional love were being rehabilitated.

Pioneering the new was not easy. In 1939 Dr Helen Deem had been appointed medical adviser to Plunket. *Modern Mothercraft* (1945, 1953), written by Deem and Nora Fitzgibbon, updated King's advice and softened the strictness of his rules, advising common sense and showing more empathy with mothers.[107] Parents were still not encouraged to play with their babies, apart from a daily 30-minute 'social hour'. For the 1953 edition, however, Deem asked Gallagher to write a chapter. Gallagher provided psychological insight into the 'problems' of childhood, beginning with the statement: 'A balanced personality is as important as physical fitness … Warm human relationships are essential for healthy development.'[108] Gallagher emphasised the importance of play and understanding individual differences. Her message, however, was positioned alongside Plunket's timetabled day for baby, and charts standardising the 'normal' baby's development.[109]

The giant in advice to parents was Benjamin Spock's *Common Sense Book of Baby and Child Care* (1946), which became an immediate bestseller. In New Zealand it was a text at some teachers' colleges and widely promoted by education and parent organisations. More accessible were the radio talks, *NZ Woman's Weekly* articles and advice columns whose presenters and authors adopted Spock's approach. His message to mothers was to remain cheerful and calm. The first sentence of *Baby and Childcare* read: 'Trust yourself. You know more than you think you do.'

Spock's ideas were a product of the political and social disorder of the interwar years. He envisaged an American nation of well-adjusted adults, who were reared according to the freedoms of the 'free world', not the totalitarian repression of fascism and communism. The 'free' adult had inner discipline and control. Spock's ideas came from several intellectual schools. First came progressive educational theory and John Dewey's emphasis on democracy. Spock sought to encourage parents to allow the child an opportunity to participate in his or her own upbringing.[110] Secondly came the influence of Freud; like Erik Erikson, Spock wanted to promote an understanding of the child's psychological need for security, identity and self-esteem. New Zealand writer Elsie Locke, then the mother of a young family, ironically noted the alliance between mothers and psychology:

> The psychologists at the moment are very kind to us mothers. Self-effacing creatures that we are, mere Jills-of-all-trades … we have been so accustomed to laying our judgement aside in defence of those who know better. Who are we to ask questions of Sir this or Dr. that M.B., Ch.B., M.R.C.P., or whatever? … It is a glorious time for mothers. All the things we have wanted in our heart to do, turn out to be the right things … mothers go up the social scale. She puts her shoulders back and lifts her head and looks the experts straight in the eye. They may have letters to their names, but SHE has instincts.[111]

Mother–child relationships were the crux. To Spock, the child would be happier and more secure if the mother 'had an air of self-confidence and steered him in a friendly automatic way through the routines of the day'.[112] The general kindliness and tolerance of childlike whims was labelled permissive by many. He encouraged parents to be playmates with their children. His sub-headings sought to reassure: 'Let him get dirty', 'Is punishment necessary?', 'How much sleep does a child need anyway?'[113] In terms of 'discipline', Spock's headlines read: 'Keeping bedtime happy', 'Let him enjoy his duties', 'You can be both firm and friendly', 'A boy needs a friendly, accepting father'. This approach avoided the need for repressive discipline, and presented fun and play as preventing the new ills of child 'loneliness' and 'boredom'. In 1951 American anthropologist Martha Wolfenstein commented on the emergence of a 'fun morality' in American childrearing advice: 'Fun having been suspect if not taboo, has [now] tended to become obligatory.' Giving the baby pleasure was meeting a legitimate demand.[114]

In New Zealand the Plunket message remained dominant, but not without criticism. An article in the *NZ Woman's Weekly* (8 December 1949) entitled 'Do New Zealand Babies Get the Best Care?' referred to Spock, and claimed that advice from Plunket nurses increased tension in young mothers by advocating a hospital standard of sterility, by spreading the myth that babies could be 'trained', by urging parents to mould their lives to a strict schedule in which the baby must co-operate, and by insisting that mother and baby sleep in separate rooms right from birth. R.S. Glasson replied (5 January 1950):

> I agree entirely with all the writer says. Anyone acquainted with overseas methods, or who reads overseas works on the subject of mothers and babies, is well aware that Plunket theories lag far behind.

But 'Primapara' disagreed and wondered whether the writer had been 'unlucky', claiming that 'Plunket nurses do keep up with advances in theories about infant care' and that her nurse had 'approved cordially when I adopted variations from the strict four-hour [feeding] routine'.

Old ideas died hard. Eight years later an article in the Christchurch *Star Sun* reported a talk to parents on 'permissive methods of discipline' in which Elizabeth Bailey warned of the 'unhealthy consequences' of harsh discipline and argued that 'discipline involved an inner freedom that would lead the individual to control himself when necessary'. Responses poured in, for example:[115]

> A great many parents of my acquaintance are beginning to feel that the whole business of bringing up children is becoming so complicated that only trained psychologists could hope to achieve success ... 'Confused Mother' (22 October 1958)

> I have been rushing into print on this subject or similar ones having first been advanced in the 1920s. In that time I have seen the behaviour of the young deteriorate considerably ... 'Sumac' (28 October 1958)

> I feel it a pity that 'Sumac' has hurried into print on the subject of child discipline. We get plenty of uninhibited little savages in our schools, but we get them from the homes where they have been very strictly brought up ... Parent–Teacher (October 1958)

By the 1960s Dr Spock was being accused of raising a generation of American children on an 'inadequate and harmful diet of permissiveness'. Spock's defence was that poor results in childrearing came not only from 'strictness that comes from harsh feelings but also permissiveness that is timid or vacillating'.[116] In later editions he clarified his position on discipline, but continued to blame the failures of freedom on the application rather than the substance of his message. Parents then felt they were to blame when permissiveness did not feel like fun, or did not create a manageable child. Spock reassured parents that 'discipline, good behaviour, and pleasant manners' were a natural 'part of the unfolding of the child's nature', but he warned that 'the process was liable to go wrong at any point if parents don't handle it right'.[117] Understanding your child required parents to have a repertoire of child development knowledge for every situation, which Spock and other experts readily supplied.

PARENT CAMPAIGNS

By the 1950s the 'new' ideas supporting the psychological well-being of the preschool child at kindergarten and Playcentre were becoming mainstream educational practice. Although the specific focus of this book is on early childhood education, advocates of these new ideas saw a cumulative continuum of practice from birth to adulthood, across homes, schools and hospitals.

The history of Parents' Centre is told elsewhere.[118] Its link to the postwar growth of early childhood education is the interchange of people, ideas and radicalism. Mothers were successful in overturning entrenched expert opinion on some issues. In effect they 'replaced' the medical expert with the psychological expert. That the foundations of mental health began with mothers and babies was a powerful political message with broad application: for example, that mothers are empowered by knowledge and control of their bodies; that babies require full-time love and attention; that young children develop optimally in an environment of free play; and that playway in the early school years enhances learning.

Parents' Centre was established in 1951 by a small group of women, backed by some influential men, to campaign against the excessive medicalisation of childbirth and to promote natural childbirth, the involvement of fathers at birth, rooming-in of infants with mothers, demand feeding of infants, and new views about the separation of children from their mothers in hospital. Parents' Centre clashed headlong with the medical profession, including midwives, doctors and Plunket. Dr T.F. Corkill, the senior obstetrician at Wellington Hospital, like many doctors, did not approve of a lay organisation interfering in medical matters. He was outraged when, in 1952, a delegation asked whether men could attend their wives in the first stage of labour, calling them 'nothing but a bunch of communists'.[119] The leaders of Parents' Centre, such as foundation members Helen Brew, her husband Quentin, and Christine Cole, were advocates of progressive education ideas. There was a crossover with Playcentre: Lex Grey, Beverley Morris and Marie Bell worked tirelessly across both organisations. The psychological well-being of mothers, infants and preschoolers were paramount in both contexts.

Morris became a tutor for Parents' Centre and for many years wrote on child development issues for the *Parents' Centre Bulletin*. For her first childbirth experience in 1947, like most women, she did as she was told: she left her husband at the door, was left alone to labour for five hours, anaesthetised for the birth, then left alone again. She did not see the baby or even know its sex for nine hours. The child was brought to her only for feeds, then returned to the nursery.[120] In preparation for her third child, born in 1951, Morris read British obstetrician Grantly Dick-Read's classic on natural childbirth, *The Revelations of Natural Childbirth* (1942). She persuaded the matron of a Wellington private hospital to support her:

> I had had no contact with other people doing it and Helen Brew was getting such bad press and such bad vibes from the doctors that it was a bit tricky even to be known to be interested. But things were starting to move fast in terms of better communication and we were getting stuff from America. Up until then we had felt really cut off because of the war.[121]

In her history of Parents' Centre, *The Trouble With Women* (1990), Mary Dobbie explains how:

> Wellington, when the Brews arrived there, was experiencing an upsurge in liberal thinking in education. Dr C.E. Beeby, Director of Education, had provided a climate benign to growth and change. It brought together some vigorous and creative minds … A new attitude towards mental health was abroad … offering some kind of balance against the intractable conservatism of the health services … [It was] a world where interesting and important things were happening. A generation of young mothers was being introduced to a new concept of pre-school education, the idea that play could be a learning process in which mothers have a significant role.[122]

Parents' Centre gave women knowledge that encouraged control of their own bodies during childbirth.[123] The weapon for women was psychology. Dick-Read emphasised that emotional factors in childbirth profoundly affected the physical aspects of labour. Helen Brew quoted Hazel Corbin, the director of the New York Maternity Centre:

> Lack of consideration for the mother herself, for her emotional security, her human dignity … all these would tend to cause tension, and tension causes pain, and pain creates a demand for deep anaesthesia, which often makes surgery necessary.[124]

Most women did not find pain so easy to eliminate, but the concept of preparation for childbirth through relaxation and breathing was tried by many. However, it was some years before the hospitals supported such ideas.

The Christchurch Psychological Society had been promoting alternative ideas on childbirth since the early 1940s. Its founders, Enid Cook, Frank Cook and Maurice Bevan-Brown, had worked overseas. Bevan-Brown had been a psychiatrist for 17 years at the Tavistock Clinic in London, the base for Bowlby and James Robertson (see Chapter Five), both of whom worked on issues concerning children and separation. Bevan-Brown, like many others in the fields of psychiatry and psychoanalysis, saw mental health as the key to an ordered society. Most of the emotional disorders that currently plagued society could be prevented, and the ability to do this rested with parents. 'The child needs to feel loved from the first hour – even minutes – of extra-uterine life.'[125]

Bevan-Brown and Enid Cook were keen to promote natural childbirth in New Zealand. In 1948 they published a booklet, *The Psychological Preparation for Childbirth*. In 1950 Bevan-Brown published *The Sources of Love and Fear*, in which Helen Brew described the joy of her natural birth experience. This was the crux of the issue: the heightened sense of emotional feeling after natural childbirth was the catalyst to cement the love between mother and child and thus lay the foundation for the future mental health of the child. Bevan-Brown's views were promoted by Parents' Centre activists campaigning among doctors, midwives and politicians. They listed the neuroses and disorders that could be avoided if the right psychological climate surrounded the first five years. The main person responsible was the mother, whose 'good nurture … will favour the development and establishment of a healthy, stable, personality. "Bad" nurture will interfere with this, and may produce an unhealthy and unstable personality.'[126] Bevan-Brown warned of the dangers of 'personality disorder' if a newborn baby experienced fear through lack of attention to his or her needs. He argued that the cries of hungry babies waiting for the clock to strike time for the next feed caused the fear from which profound disturbances occured. Bowlby's research outlined the detrimental consequences for infants from the absence of continuous loving maternal attention.[127] Parents' Centre used this as evidence to argue their case for rooming-in of mothers and babies in hospital, as well as for open visiting of children in hospital.

By the 1970s the position of Parents' Centre and indeed Playcentre as radical groups had waned, and on some issues they were now conservative.

The challenge came from women who did not view their own interests as so closely aligned with those of their children. Heather Knox has argued that Parents' Centre and Playcentre were radical only insofar as they operated within the dominant constructions of femininity in the 1950s.[128] This defined being a mother and wife within the nuclear family, with a husband as breadwinner, as a woman's ultimate destiny. The success of these groups, however, lay in their ability to harness and shape the accepted constructions of motherhood in order to forge change in the name of psychology. This was also a feature of kindergartens and schools, which, with government sanction, used psychological understanding to alter the shape and content of learning in the early years.

CHAPTER TWO

Psychology of Disorder

The postwar years were characterised by a quest for order, security and prosperity.[1] These goals were pervasive in many dimensions of life. Globally, the Western world sought to uphold democracy and capitalism against totalitarianism and communism. Nationally, new welfare state policies provided various forms of support for nuclear families, such as family benefits and housing assistance. New Zealand politicians reasoned that this would encourage women to have more children, and families who were home-owners would be less vulnerable to communist dogma.[2] Individuals, too, would benefit from the planned suburban environments of homes, kindergartens and schools. They would help to keep abnormality at bay. The abnormal was characterised as deviant, dysfunctional or maladjusted. The label was ascribed to whatever did not fit normal prescriptions of child development, family life, cultural perspective or political viewpoint.

There was a belief that education, science and psychology could transform the abnormal into the normal, and therefore disorder into order. The paradigm of order was operative within the wider political and economic sphere, in terms of collective security and material prosperity; in family relationships, in terms of marriage and separate spheres for men and women; and in individuals, who could be socialised into well-adjusted citizens through psychological management.

Yet although psychological management was seen as a preventative measure against disorder, in fact the psychological 'gaze' created its own disorder. A 1956 Department of Education preschool officer's report on a kindergarten teacher indicates the subjectivity of the boundary between the two:

> Miss K—— has started her parent work but with no real understanding. She
> has visited parents but has discussed their children with so little tact that many

of them have been given the impression that their children are psychological problems ... I am worried about her. She has an ill-judged knowledge of psychology (although all the fashionable jargon off pat) which makes her see problems where none exist and worries mothers into believing that their children are abnormal.[3]

This chapter explores some of the wider dimensions of disorder that impacted on early childhood services. While kindergarten and playcentre basked in being accepted as a good idea, the growth of childcare and the increasing numbers of working mothers were deemed less acceptable, while the increase in illegitimacy was unacceptable. The ills of teenage delinquency and sexuality hit the headlines, and psychological rationales were used to apportion blame. Good mothers and acceptable forms of preschool could prevent such ills, but bad mothers and the use of childcare were likely to cause them. The most damaging potential circumstance for the child was single motherhood.

During the 1960s such rationales began to crack. The boundaries of normality were challenged and there was growing disaffection with the view that psychology could cure all. The key story, although it is often elusive, is the increasing visibility of childcare and the rhetoric, mainly of concern, surrounding its growth. This is threaded through broader insights on aspects of family dysfunction and its likely causes.

During the 1940s–1960s childcare was positioned as harmful. By the end of the century it was the main provider of early childhood services in New Zealand. The seeds of this transformation emerged during these years.

(DYS)FUNCTIONAL FAMILIES

Family life was deemed to be the cradle of the ordered society as well as the cause of its disorder. A statement of beliefs on the 'value of parenthood and family life' in an introductory booklet for playcentre parents summed this up:

> ... a well-adjusted society depends on good family relationships within the home. Through better understanding between parents and children, and between parents themselves, later difficulties of adjustment to work, authority and society are reduced.

> ... the seeds of mental ill health, showing later in life as delinquency, physical or ill health, or general instability are sown in the early years, the years when personality is in the making.[4]

In a 1953 radio series, 'The Foundations of Mental Health', Maurice Bevan-Brown claimed that 50,000 New Zealand adults suffered from a mental illness, and estimated that one-third of these cases were preventable disorders. Listeners were told: 'All authorities now agree that these disorders have their origin in the first five years of life.'[5] The American sociologist Talcott Parsons espoused a powerful paradigm of the nuclear family which was increasingly child centred, particularly through the function of mother–child relationships. By mid-century many of the traditional functions of the Western family had been transferred into the care of experts and institutions.[6] In New Zealand the state subsidised Parsons' ideal family with a raft of welfare policies supported by a buoyant economy and backed by full employment. Families that did not function as a 'good family' were judged to be deficient. If the children exhibited so-called problem behaviour, state scrutiny was justified.

Child welfare services moved to step up preventative policies focusing on the broader frame of family welfare. In her history of New Zealand child welfare Bronwyn Dalley suggests that 'Family background was seen as crucial to children's welfare; maladjusted home conditions could precipitate drastic consequences.'[7] Heredity was no longer considered to be the basis of a child's social ills, although such explanations did not disappear. Psychological management placed new demands on welfare services. Dalley refers to the explosion in child welfare cases. She notes that annual reports 'conveyed a mounting sense of dismay' that delinquency and crime was increasing rather than waning as expected.[8] Family breakdown was blamed. However, a more analytical penetrative 'gaze' could itself be seen as creating the concern.[9] Explanations for social order or disorder were primarily psychological in construction. Sociology was a much newer discipline. Berry Mayall writes:

> Childhood was the province of psychology, and its unexplored, uncontested theories could be relied on by sociologists as a basis for defining children as objects of socialization in the family and the education system. The mother, whose natural place was in the private domain of the home, had the task of teaching her young children basic social morality; socialization of older children took place within the education system and aimed at the production of the young adult as a useful and acceptable citizen.[10]

Socialisation theory, popular during the 1950s and 1960s, concerned itself with how a child becomes 'adjusted to' society. Parsons' model relied on the notion of developmental stages through which mothers and teachers assist the child:

The term socialization ... refers primarily to the process of child development. However, there is another reason for singling out the socialization of the child; there is reason to believe that, among the learned elements of personality in certain respects the stablest and most enduring are the major value-orientation patterns and there is much evidence that these are 'laid down' in childhood and are not on large scale subject to drastic alteration during adult life.[11]

The child, however, was seen as immature, irrational, incompetent and asocial – all potentially dangerous and deviant characteristics, unless proper socialisation occurred. At issue was the transformation of what Parsons termed the 'basic personality structure' of the child. However, as child welfare staff discovered, socialisation of children into acceptable adults was not always successful. As so-called abnormal situations (such as broken homes, illegitimacy and working mothers) grew in number, the boundary between acceptable and unacceptable was forced to shift. By the late 1970s the state was starting to respond to all these situations with policy that was less judgmental. New explanations for individual and family ills were sought. For example, in the early 1960s it began to be argued that society itself was sick.[12] In the late 1960s women's liberation began to seek political explanations for the ills of women within the patriarchal state.

WORKING MOTHERS AND MATERNAL DEPRIVATION

The demand for childcare was caused mainly by increasing numbers of women joining or returning to the workforce. This trend, however, was in conflict with the strengthening views, backed by research, that children under five years needed the almost full-time attention of their mothers. Full employment and a shortage of labour during the postwar years had encouraged married women into paid work, and neither social sanctions against working mothers nor research evidence were sufficient to prevent many New Zealand mothers moving quietly back into employment with increasingly younger children. The war had been a watershed in women's employment patterns, but other patterns were emerging: a declining birth rate, improvements in domestic technology, more educational opportunities and new aspirations for independence. The 'problem of the working mother' was a subject frequently aired by the public.

The boundary shifted quite rapidly during the 1950s. By the 1960s the accepted code was that women could have a 'dual role'. Mothers whose children were at school could benefit themselves and their family with part-time work, provided it took place within school hours, did not disrupt family life, and did not overturn the husband's role as chief breadwinner and head of the household.[13]

My study of Pākehā women with children during the 1950s, *Minding Children, Managing Men* (1992), showed that most of the women did have employment, but they were not sufficiently visible to attract the label of 'working mother' or to threaten the appearance of separate spheres. Statistics on married women in the workforce demonstrate the trend, but not the extent, and there are no separate statistics for working mothers. In 1945, 7.7% of married women of all ages were employed for over 20 hours a week. By 1971 this had risen to 26%.[14] Graphs compiled from census figures show a drop in workforce participation during the prime childbearing years between 21 and 29, with participation rising again from age 30. In 1945 only 10% of 25- to 29-year-old married women and 8% of 30- to 34-year-old married women were in employment. By 1971 these percentages had risen to 21% and 24%.

Oswald Mazengarb QC, who had chaired the government's commission on juvenile delinquency, described the 'problem' in *NZ Parent and Child* (August 1956):

> Any father who let his wife go out working for a refrigerator need not be at all surprised if his own son ended up in the 'cooler' … Bleak homes and working mothers [are] listed among the most potent causes of delinquency … Only a small proportion of married women need to work … The pity of it is that many of these married women do not pause to consider the possible effects on their children.

The issue of 'working mothers' was frequently debated in parliament. A lengthy 1954 budget debate kept returning to the issue. D. Rae, an Auckland MP, supported working mothers:

> I believe that within limits a woman's place is in the house, but she has a choice in the matter, and if she goes out to work because she wants to do so, that is all right.
>
> P.G. Connelly: It is not; the children are running on the street.
>
> D. Rae: How would we get on if some of our married women didn't work? We owe a great debt of gratitude to them for the work they are doing. I hope that the homes are not suffering … Married women are getting some of the amenities that they should have around their homes, and they are making their lives happier …[15]

However, H.L.J. May, MP for Onslow, argued in patriotic terms:

> When I was at school … it was understood that the womenfolk of the British Empire, and of New Zealand in particular, were in a class removed from the

womenfolk of other countries ... we were secure in the knowledge that when we returned home we would find our mothers there, but today I venture to say there are thousands of children who go home from school to find their mothers still out at work.[16]

Dunedin MP Ethel McMillan, one of only four women in parliament, was concerned that in a time of 'peace and prosperity' there were even more women working than during the war. 'There are mortgages on homes that wives have to work to wipe off ... the whole thing is irrational.'[17]

The message that mothers were selfish and neglecting their children by going out to work was promoted by Plunket, Parents' Centre, Playcentre and kindergarten. As the focus on family background increased, kindergarten teachers kept records of 'special home circumstances', which were filed in preschool officers' reports to the Department of Education during the mid-1950s.[18] 'Mother works', 'mother works at home', 'mother works parttime' or 'mother works in family business' were most frequently mentioned. Also noted was 'broken home' or 'mother divorced'. This was even less acceptable, but it was sometimes the reason that mothers were employed. These lists are useful indicators of the boundaries of 'normality'.

Bowlby's study of the effects of maternal separation on young children was heavily influential in shaping opinion on mother–child relationships. His report *Maternal Care and Mental Health* (1951) documented his investigation into the mental health of children in institutions in the aftermath of the war. Bowlby's subsequent theory of maternal deprivation became a dominant discourse in Western countries, and was used to attack working mothers and childcare provision. Bowlby claimed that 'Deprived children, whether in their homes or out of them, are a source of social infection as real or serious as are the carriers of diphtheria or typhoid.'[19] He tuned into anxieties concerning social order, and his hypothesis that 'restoration of families is restoration of the nation' was soothing.[20]

Bowlby concluded that the institutionalised children he observed were mentally and emotionally retarded. He also reviewed retrospective studies of juvenile delinquents showing that these children had experienced a disruption in maternal relationships during infancy. Bowlby was influenced by the psychoanalytic thinking of Melanie Klein, who believed infants were controlled by innate and conflicting emotions of love and hate towards their mothers.[21] It was during separation from the mother that the infant's feeling became unbearable and potentially destructive. Bowlby's view of motherhood was as a 'psychic organiser' of the infant's emotions.[22] He also hypothesised that children could suffer from maternal deprivation in homes where they did not 'experience a warm, intimate and continuous relationship with their mothers (or permanent mother substitute)'.[23] He warned that:

> The mothering of a child is not something which can be arranged by rota; it is a loving human relationship which alters the characters of both partners ... The provision of constant attention night and day, seven days a week and 365 days in the year, is only possible for a woman who derives profound satisfaction from seeing her child grow from babyhood, through the many phases of childhood, to become an independent man or woman.[24]

Bowlby's recipe for full-time motherhood gave mothers new value, which many women appreciated. But not all women were able or wanted to mother with such intensity. The consequences of separation, or a lack of mothering, were grim. Bowlby once claimed that the full-time employment of a mother 'is on a par with the death of a parent, imprisonment of a parent, war, or famine' as 'reasons for family failure'.[25]

Bowlby's thinking became a 'scientific truth' passed on from meeting to meeting, country to country. Mrs A.F. Johnson, president of the NZFKU, addressed kindergarteners after returning from a conference at which Bowlby was a speaker:

> The view that a child deprived of mothering in the early years of life will grow up to be a criminal was expressed at the Melbourne conference by Dr Bowlby. Partial deprivation, he had said, on the part of the child led to anxiety, guilt, depression, and excessive craving for attention, adulation and affection and to anti-social, uncontrolled behaviour.[26]

In 1977 Geraldine McDonald examined the impact of Bowlby's ideas in New Zealand, claiming that maternal deprivation was still being presented 'as if it were a scientific fact':

> [They] were accepted ... by Government departments and other bodies having to do with the health of children and with the provision of care and welfare. The net result was that whether or not women knew of Bowlby's ideas they were likely to be affected by them.[27]

Maternal deprivation was not laid to rest politically in New Zealand until the 1988 Meade report, citing McDonald, labelled it a myth, stating: 'John Bowlby's theories have long been debunked, but their influence has lingered on and is reflected in mythology and policy.'[28]

Bowlby's ideas were criticised at the time. Anthropologist Margaret Mead dismissed them as a 'new and subtle form of anti-feminism, in which men under the guise of exalting the importance of maternity, are tying women more tightly to their children'.[29] Child psychologist Bruno Bettelheim, who was studying kibbutz-reared children in Israel, could not accept Bowlby's reasoning that a bad family was always better than a good institution.[30] Cath Tizard recalls her own scepticism when rearing three children:

> I accepted a lot of what he said about the importance of bonding at an early stage, but I didn't accept that I had to be with my child every minute, morning, noon and night, and that was the only way to salvation … so I was suspicious about his theory even though it was so influential in those days.[31]

It is likely that many women felt similarly. Bowlby's views did not restrict preschool expansion in New Zealand, but did provide evidence to justify part-time preschool attendance as best for three-year-olds and over.

Occasional debates about preschool provided clues to the range of opinion. In *Here and Now* (June 1952) 'Mrs La Lone', a visiting American Fulbright Scholar, was critical of:

> New Zealand [for] moving in the direction of an earlier break in the tie between mother and child … The most common mistake made by today's mothers, both here and in America, is the belief that all important things lie outside the home.

'M.L.D.' (Mary Dobbie) supported La Lone:

> The mistake of this kindergarten movement in New Zealand is in providing a service that takes the child out of his home and encouraging mothers to believe that this is good for him … The views coming from an American source will cause both kindergarten teachers and mothers to take umbrage, but the same things are being said in many parts of the world and by men and women qualified by long experience in child guidance work to know the full implications of their advice.

Elsie Locke's reply (*Here and Now*, August 1952) reflected a more mainstream view:

> … the postwar era will be known in the future as the era of the rediscovery of the home … On the other hand, these institutions have been built after many years of hard work and struggle against prejudice; we can't have them thrown out lightly … Take a look inside any kindergarten or playcentre and you can't deny that most of the children are having a fine time … The mother's claim to be a complete person and an active citizen as well as a housewife cannot be overlooked … the housewife narrowed to her four walls is not a good mother.

Issues of separation generated increasing research attention and advocacy. James Robertson was a colleague of Bowlby's at the London Tavistock Clinic. He promoted Bowlby's ideas to persuade hospitals not to separate children from their mothers. Robertson, like Bowlby, also portrayed the ideal mother as ever attentive to her child: 'She is his whole world.'[32] Marie Bell was a postgraduate student at the London Institute of Education during 1949–51. She met Robertson and Bowlby and saw early clips of Robertson's famous film *A Two Year Old Goes to Hospital* (1953). Back in New Zealand she got an advanced copy to 'show around nurses' groups and teachers' colleges'.[33] The film, one of a series on separation, documented the traumatic psychological effect that separation had on a young child. It became a key weapon for Parents' Centre in their campaign to persuade hospitals to change their policy on restricting visits by mothers, and later to persuade the public against childcare. In the 1970s both Bowlby and Robertson visited New Zealand to add their voices to campaigns against childcare.

THE BACKYARD GROWTH OF CHILDCARE

During these early post-war years some form of childcare was still needed for mothers of preschoolers who worked outside the home. Most used informal (and thus invisible) arrangements – with family, friends or paid minders. Before the Second World War the only acceptable contexts for formal childcare provision were a few charitable or church centres for 'cases of misfortune', a few community shoppers' crèches 'for the assistance of mothers in town', and several nursery schools, which provided an educational programme of play and 'time off for mother'.[34] During the war there was a small increase in the number of centres offering childcare for working mothers, but government initiatives were minimal. Nevertheless, the war was effective in making debates on childcare visible. For several years, calls for more 'crèches, kindergartens and nurseries' became a combined chorus by women's organisations.

At war's end, reconstruction was the focus. Calls for childcare were still heard. For example, the submission by the Family Planning Association to the Parliamentary Select Committee on Dominion Population in 1946 stated that more nurseries would encourage women to have more babies.[35] Magazines printed letters highlighting the difficulties of mothers:

> Have we creches which can relieve the mother's troubles? There is much talk about the need for increased population, but years have passed and the young mother in this country is still an absolute captive of her babies. (*NZ Woman's Weekly*, 26 April 1945)

If babies are worthwhile, why – for example – put so many obstacles in the way of their transport on trams, trains and buses? … No shops offer an easy parking place for prams or a playroom where children may be left under supervision while mother makes her purchases in peace. (Mary Dobbie, *Here and Now*, October 1949)

'Emancipated Wife' in a letter entitled 'A Creche in Your Department' (*PSA Journal*, February 1945) argued that some women were 'determined not to return to economic dependence and a docile acceptance of home life'. She proposed workplace support for maternity leave, childrearing leave and the provision of crèches, nursery schools, Playcentres and kindergartens.

Two government initiatives tempered the childcare demand. A universal Family Allowance was introduced in 1946. This was paid directly to mothers; at 10 shillings per week per child it was close to 9% of the average weekly wage. The 1947 Bailey report recognised the need for a limited service for 'the sake of those mothers who for various reasons must go out to work and those whom ill health prevents from undertaking the normal responsibilities of the home', but concluded that:

> Young children spending the whole day from Monday to Friday in a nursery school are deprived of the vital experiences that only a normal home can provide … Further, the all-day school would be a costly institution, because of the special equipment for meals, and of the extra staff required.[36]

The report stated that there had been 'very strong opposition' to nursery schools and 'little demand' for them during the war. It recommended that limited extended-day kindergartens be available in the major cities for use in 'exceptional circumstances'. This did not happen. The three extended-day kindergartens, one in Dunedin and two in Wellington, operated from 9 am to 3 pm and did not see their role as supporting working mothers. In the submissions responding to the Bailey report, the lack of advocacy for childcare is evident. One of only two references to the report's opposition to childcare came from the Catholic Education Service:

> One cannot but commend Recommendation 9 that the standard pre-school institution should be the kindergarten type and not the all-day nursery school. This was a point which was made very emphatically in our memorandum, for no light danger exists in the nursery school as regards the weakening of the bond between mother and child.[37]

Childcare as an acceptable demand soon faded from public debate. The growing use of childcare was portrayed as 'dumping' by 'selfish' mothers, and thus damaging to the child. There is no paper trail to help the historian document the expansion of childcare during the 1950s. References to it are fleeting, and people and places elusive. But all the evidence points to quiet growth alongside often shrill condemnation.[38]

A few reports provide some clues to the issues. The Motherhood of Man Movement was established in Auckland in 1942 to provide a maternity home and other services for unmarried mothers. A day nursery was established alongside the home in 1946:

> This nursery will aid the wives of men who are on a sick pension or low wages. It will help widows to eke out their miserable pensions. It will help unmarried mothers to keep their little ones with them.[39]

There were 56,000 daily attendances between 1946 and 1952. An article called *They Collect and Deliver* pictured a van packed with children and noted that the nursery had:

> … proved a blessing to many mothers who cannot support themselves or their children unless they work, yet are faced with the problem of finding somebody to look after their children while they are away.[40]

An article about a creche in Sandringham, Auckland, entitled 'Boon to Young Mothers' (*NZ Woman's Weekly*, 24 January 1946), stated:

> Prior to its inception, one young mother who has taken advantage of the crèche had not been able to leave the children for a single day or night for over a period of two years and there are many others like her.

This crèche operated with voluntary staff, and it was hoped that a rota system might overcome staffing problems. The *New Zealand Herald* (30 September 1950) reported the Mother Superior, of the Order of the Good Shepherd Creche, as saying that 'hundreds of children are turned away every year'. In Christchurch the Canterbury Housewives' Union 'discovered that scores of toddlers are sent to backyard nurseries' and planned to sponsor a scheme for a local day nursery.[41] This did not eventuate. A few factories also set up childcare to assist their labour supply. A 1954 National Film Unit clip entitled 'Factory Kindergarten' showed Auckland children eating, exercising and sleeping while their mothers worked. The few photographic images of children in childcare during the 1950s have nurses, not teachers, as staff, and there is little evidence of the planned free-play programmes promoted in the mainstream preschool settings.

In 1946 a fledgling Day Nurseries Association was established in Auckland with the mayoress, Mrs J.A.C. Allum, as patroness.[42] Her husband was the president of the Auckland Kindergarten Association, which had strongly resisted the government's request for some Auckland kindergartens to run extended hours during the war.[43] It is unclear whether this association was connected to a Day Nursery Association which joined forces with the first Auckland Nursery Play Centre Association, established in 1945.

No day nurseries were established under the auspices of Playcentre, although some day nurseries and the Salvation Army 'Nest' in Hamilton (a residential nursery) had a long-term association with the Auckland Playcentre Association.[44] The original plan had been to establish Playcentres in the suburbs and a day nursery in the city.

In the absence of government recognition, childcare became the domain of a few charitable/church institutions and small-scale private enterprise in private homes. Social Welfare officer Anne Frizelle recalled how 'in the late '50s some New Zealanders awoke to find their neighbours looking after other people's children'.[45] This 'backyard' visibility further fuelled the spectre of 'maternal deprivation'. In earlier years Elsie Locke had used childcare:

> It is not really a question of 'should the children have a day nursery?' but 'what would be the alternative?' Let no one imagine that the provision of nurseries would entice unwilling mothers into factories. Do you think this is an attractive prospect? ... To dress Junior at 7 am, rush off to the nursery with him (changing trams on route to the factory), toil all day at the bench, shop furiously in the lunch hour, rush home about 5 pm, cook dinner and bundle the poor child into bed ... She feels the maternal deprivation as much as the child. But the child will survive that ... if he knows in his bones that he is wanted, loved, cared for, yes and worked for.[46]

In an article entitled 'Danger! Mothers at Work' (*NZ Parent and Child*, May 1955) one mother, a widow whose son had attended a day nursery for three years, explained that 'it need not be tragedy for the child'. The mother acknowledged the psychological difficulties of separation, but argued that other factors were also important. If the child's welfare was carefully attended to and the 'choice of environment' carefully selected, the mother argued:

> Attendance at a day nursery, all things being equal, can ensure the *continuity* which is so essential to the sense of security I have stressed ... Of the actual conditions under which my son has been cared for, I cannot speak too highly. I feel that he has had all the benefits of an organisation expertly designed to meet the needs of children in his situation – combined with human contacts giving everything that could be desired of kindliness and intelligent understanding ... He is an extremely happy child. I believe that he has escaped much

of the loneliness which an only child, particularly a boy, could experience in a fatherless household.

This two-page positive description of childcare was a rare find.

Public opinion mainly attacked mothers as selfish. Auckland MP Warren Freer worked with the Motherhood of Man organisation. In 1951 he told parliament:

> Although the majority of children are there because their mothers are either widows or deserted wives ... there is a growing and damaging trend in the country today for young people to shirk their responsibility to their family, and pass that responsibility on to someone else in order that they might go out and earn something ... no matter how good the institution be ... they can never replace the interest and the proper affection and guidance that can come from the parents themselves ... Too often after a wife has been at work for a while in order to pay off a second mortgage, or to buy a refrigerator, or a motor car or something else, she finds she enjoys the companionship of her job ... I see no personal, moral or cultural risk in the mother working when her child has reached the age or fifteen or sixteen ... but I believe there is a grave social and moral risk in the community when people look forward to the day when their youngsters go out to school so they themselves can go to work. [47]

The childcare centres themselves became a public concern only through crisis and scandal. In 1958 police, welfare and medical officers removed 29 children from an Auckland home. The issue was debated in parliament. Freer questioned the Minister of Child Welfare, Mabel Howard, concerning the state of the children who had been removed due to 'neglect and ill treatment', and asked whether the government was considering some kind of legislation to prevent 'this kind of person from operating a day nursery'.[48] Howard declared that the case was 'too shocking to give full details'. She told parliament that the owner, Mrs Fulham, had been circumventing the requirements of the Infant Life Protection Act, which governed the boarding of infants in homes, by running a day nursery. She did not know the names of the children. One of the children had a fracture of the leg. Most of the children had skin diseases and one baby was in a poor physical state. They were taken to hospital. The nursery itself was 'badly run and dirty'.[49]

Three weeks later Howard reported that 'the Government is examining the question of promoting legislation to place day nurseries under supervision'.[50] The 1958–59 annual report to parliament from the Superintendent of Child Welfare, C.E. Peek, announced that the formulation of minimum standards was under way. He located the problem with parents, not the centres themselves, and viewed the 'irresponsibility' of some parents who 'appear oblivious to the effect on the mental health of their children by attendance day after day at understaffed centres' as a 'major difficulty'.[51] This tension over the responsibility for monitoring childcare standards was ongoing. The government was reluctant to become involved.

REGULATING CHILDCARE

The Childcare Centre Regulations 1960 came into effect in the twilight months of the 1957–60 Labour government. Regulation did not mean financial support. Government interest was restricted to 'the enforcement of minimum standards and practices (which) should go a long way towards reducing the danger of neglect or exploitation of children'.[52] Only two of the 41 applicants for licences in 1961 were successful. These first controls reflected the preoccupation with the earlier scandal; they emphasised health and safety and keeping children from harm. Centres were required to have 'suitable play-things' but trained staff were not a requirement, although centres whose staff had nursing or teaching qualifications could display an 'A' licence. There is no indication of concern about 'maternal deprivation' in the regulations, although 'in house' guidelines for child welfare officers inspecting the centres asked, for example, 'Have staff time and opportunity for "mothering" a disturbed child?', and 'Can the children obtain reasonable adult attention?'[53]

Despite the barriers created by the new regulations, childcare provision grew during the 1960s. The economy was buoyant and there was a continuing demand for female labour. By 1966 there were 6336 child places available – 1430 full-day and 4906 part-day. This had risen to 8948 places by 1971 – 2807 full-day and 6141 part-day – although a significant proportion of the latter were in private kindergartens which were now covered by the regulations.[54] The overall growth, however, was regarded with concern. Responsibility for childcare was placed within the Child Welfare Division of the Department of Education, not the preschool section. This divided services for 'care' and 'education' of young children. The distance between the two increased when Child Welfare was transferred to the new Department of Social Welfare in 1972. This division never fitted the realities of the early childhood services; as Geraldine McDonald wrote, it served to perpetuate 'childcare … as something aberrant … [whose] existence did not threaten the "natural" law that mothers should care for their own children at home'.[55]

Nevertheless, regulation galvanised action towards a childcare movement.

The regulatory demands for licensing required most centres to be upgraded. There was unhappiness about the cost of this. Some wondered why Playcentres were not required to meet the same standards.[56] Trade unionist Sonja Davies was involved in the Nelson Day Nursery. Another toilet was required but the owner of the building, the Nelson City Council, refused to pay.

> I made an appointment to see the Minister of Social Welfare, the Hon D. McKay … he remarked that I was the fifth person to call on him that month with a problem! 'If you were all joined together in one group,' he grumbled, 'it would be easier for everyone.' Feeling he had dealt suitably with me, he saw me out. He did not know me.[57]

In 1963 Davies organised the inaugural meeting of the New Zealand Association of Childcare Centres (NZACCC) in Nelson. After approaching both the Free Kindergarten Union and the Playcentre Federation about affiliation and being turned down, Davies told members that standing alone 'would not only result in a better deal for the children, but also for those who had the responsibility for administering centres'.[58] It was due to Davies' 'up front' political style during her 15-year term as president, and the dedication of a small group of core members, that childcare emerged from the underside. Davies' language and analysis were outside the frames of psychology, located instead in issues of rights for women and children. From the beginning the association set about improving the quality of childcare through training and better regulations, and calling for government funding, more care for babies and after-school care.[59]

It was an uphill battle. As Davies has said, 'Childcare was not a polite topic for conversation.'[60]

> The whole question of childcare in this country is extremely controversial and emotive. For a lively experience try introducing the subject at a gathering of strangers. The battle lines will be clearly defined in two seconds flat.[61]

> We had to cope with antagonism and suspicion from the other two pre-school organisations and almost total opposition from Members of Parliament of both parties.[62]

After a North Island tour of centres during 1963, with Jessie Donald from the Lower Hutt Civic Day Nursery, Davies wrote:

> The people running them were not badly intentioned, but they obviously had no idea of children's needs in a properly run day care centre. [The centres]

had no education programme and little or no play equipment, [and] as a result the children seemed listless or lacklustre. After visiting about ten of these duds [in Auckland] Jessie and I stood on the pavement and asked ourselves whether we were doing the right thing – might the anti-childcare lobbyists have some justification? And then we remembered the good centres we had seen and knew that our struggle must be to ensure that there were more of those.[63]

Former Prime Minister Walter Nash spoke at the first conference and quoted from a World Health Organisation publication, *Care of Children in Day Centres.* It addressed the international trend of 'modern women' to be active outside the home, and the growing role of crèches and kindergartens to support this. Nash expressed doubt whether such institutions could replace the home. Davies was quick to advise that 'childcare was meant to supplement home life, and not replace it'.[64] Not everyone was convinced.

A key issue was childcare training. The government's suggestion was Playcentre supervisor training. At the inaugural meeting Jessie Donald referred to this as 'the main cause of unhappiness'. Those present were unanimously opposed to Playcentre, whose programmes they perceived to be 'free expression and no discipline'.[65] However, some childcare staff were accepted into Playcentre training. Marge Williams did a correspondence course with Lex Grey through the Auckland Playcentre Association, although she too felt that 'He let free play go too far'.[66] Key people from both kindergarten and Playcentre gave support. Williams recalled: 'I learnt a lot from Marie Bell – each child is an individual and whatever its disability or its ability, it's a child first.' In Wellington Beverley Morris was supportive too. In 1969, due to the lack of success in persuading government or any institution to establish a childcare qualification, the association arranged for childcare workers to sit the Royal Society of Health Certificate of Childcare from London.

The childcare regulations covered a diverse range of services, including factory nurseries, shoppers' crèches, private kindergartens, community and private day nurseries and residential nurseries. It is a tribute to Davies' skill that she welded such diverse interests into a cohesive group, determined to position childcare alongside kindergarten and Playcentre as a good place for children and a benefit for families. The early stalwarts of the association included women such as Marge Williams, who had opened a centre in Taupo in 1959, originally because she needed economic security for herself and her children. 'We started with eleven children but the need got greater and greater.'[67] In 1961 Williams was approached by the mother of a child with

Down's Syndrome, and thereafter she included many children with special needs in the programme. Williams stated that 'I saw myself as a kindergarten', but she became a strong advocate for childcare after attending the second conference with eight others at a private centre in Tauranga:

> It was amazing the things we discussed: the need for training, the need for much higher standards of hygiene ... Of course we heard the horror stories too about the daycare centres that were being run very badly.[68]

Like a number of other early childcare activists, Williams was ambivalent about her role: 'I've never been particularly political, but I felt strongly about certain issues.' These women believed that children who attended childcare should have the same rights to trained staff and government funding as those attending Playcentre and kindergarten.

Another early stalwart was Joan Kennett from Palmerston North. Kennett's introduction to childcare was through her employment in a private kindergarten run by the Young Women's Christian Association (YWCA). 'The desks were in rows. I had very little equipment. It wasn't long before I changed that.'[69] Her background was in Playcentre, which she recalled as

> very anti-childcare and there was quite a bit of conflict about what I was doing ... It was the time of John Bowlby and his maternal deprivation theory which did a lot of harm.[70]

Kennett later called her own centre a preschool. 'People didn't have to say that their child went to childcare. I know that [at first] I didn't like telling people that I ran a childcare centre.' Running a private centre was a small, although rarely profitable, business for women.

These private 'kindergartens' and 'preschools' brought respectability and strength to the childcare movement. In response to the huge waiting list at the local kindergarten, Margaret Lamb established a private kindergarten in her Auckland home. Parents who could afford to pay often preferred the better staffing ratios, smaller group size and more personal touch that some private kindergartens offered:

> People respected me because I had been a teacher. It sounds snobby now, but you were looked up to. You were respected. The mood was really very strong that we should get out of Child Welfare. The only way we would get recognition was through training and being seen as education.[71]

But when Lamb started going to NZACCC conferences in the 1960s she found that she was enthused by the 'vision for something better' and the strength of working together.

Like Williams, both Kennett and Lamb also discovered the darker side of childcare. The soft approach taken by the association was generally one of quiet encouragement to change and to become a member. This was at odds with an association making a hard political case for quality childcare. Kennett's description summarises the concerns:

> I was quite horrified at what I saw. I found that most [staff] were untrained and were doing all the wrong things. They were organising children. I saw children queuing up to go to the toilet and queuing up for everything … They had very little equipment and the children just looked forlorn. I saw a lot of thumb sucking and children looking as if they were bored. They fought a lot … Children quarrelling and tearing around aimlessly to me is an inadequate preschool.

Davies, meanwhile, continued to address the wider issues, lobbying government to address the concerns of working mothers positively, rather than attack them. Her 1967 president's report opened with this statement:

> New Zealand has been for some years in a rapid state of transition, and this state has had an effect on our social life which has caught us by surprise. No longer does our welfare system fit our needs. It falls far short … At a time when mothers and children are more particularly in need our society has lagged behind in the provision of care for them.[72]

In reviewing the work of the decade, the 1970 president's report emphasised the uphill battle to change attitudes that constrained the growth of support and acceptance for childcare:

> Only too often this opposition was reflected in the attitude of those who occupy public office … We spent a lot of years planning for a situation that we knew already existed and suspected would develop swiftly. We were handicapped by a society that generally would not admit that social change was happening in its midst, accelerated as it was by the rapid growth of women in the New Zealand work force and the unfolding of the technological era.[73]

The first concession was announced by the Minister of Finance, Robert Muldoon, in the 1969–70 budget. It introduced tax allowances for working wives, who could claim up to $240 per annum for housekeeping or day nursery fees. The tide was slowly beginning to turn.

BLAMING MOTHERS

Little is recorded from mothers who used childcare during these years. There were no mothers' clubs or committees like the ones that were the backbone of Playcentre and kindergarten. To leave a child in childcare was deemed harmful. Mothers were warned of the consequences.

'One Ordinary Devoted Mother and her Baby' was the title of a popular radio series and book by British psychiatrist Donald Winnicott, a close colleague of Klein and Bowlby. The talks were reprinted and broadcast in New Zealand. Parents' Centre bought multiple copies to pass around parent groups. Winnicott, like Spock in the US, addressed mothers directly. In his opening talk in 1949 he began:

> You will be relieved to know that I am not going to be telling you what to do. I am a man, and so I can never really know what it is like to see wrapped up over there in the cot a bit of my own self … In the ordinary things you do you are quite naturally doing important things, and the beauty of it is that you do not have to be clever. But all this does not matter, and it hasn't anything to do with whether you will be a good mother or not. If a child can play with a doll, you can be an ordinary devoted mother, and I believe you are just this most of the time. Isn't it strange that such a tremendously important thing should depend so little on exceptional intelligence?[74]

In the second talk Winnicott told mothers that they should concentrate on the enjoyment of motherhood, but also told them that an 'ordinary devoted mother', 'simply by being devoted to her infant', is 'making an immense contribution to mankind' because the home is 'the only factory for the democratic tendency in a country's social system'.[75] However, Winnicott's talks, which aimed to reassure mothers, also had a darker side. Mothers were warned that mismanagement of childrearing would have long-term consequences. Antisocial behaviour and delinquency were psychological illnesses resulting from a 'deprivation of home life'.[76] Placing a child in a childcare centre fitted this theory. The heightened scrutiny of motherhood as both the cause and cure of all ills caused strain for many mothers. 'Guilty Mother' wrote to the *NZ Woman's Weekly* (29 June 1954):

> All those lectures and articles about the mistakes made by mothers have had me worrying about whether I've done the right thing with my children. I've been so afraid I've given them complexes or hurt them too deeply for them ever to forget.

The term 'delinquency' was a mid-century import to New Zealand, but the problem was not new. Concerns over hooliganism and larrikinism stretched back to early colonial days. *NZ Parent and Child* (May–June 1958) ran the headline '12,000 New Zealand Children Emotionally Unstable'. This 'conservative' estimate was also quoted in a New Zealand Educational Institute (NZEI) investigation into maladjustment in school children.[77] The causes were located in early rearing that was regulated and harsh. Parents were warned that mother–child relationships needed to be 'warm, loving, permissive and accepting'. As *NZ Parent and Child* noted somewhat ironically:

> To be young in our country today is to be suspect. To be young means that you might be tainted by special germs which may evolve into the dread social disease of Delinquency, Bodgieism, Anti Socialism, Irresponsibility. Or if you're even younger than that, a worse disease may already be devouring your body and soul – you might be 'playway' educated.

The appearance of 'bodgies', 'widgies', 'teddy boys' and 'milk-bar cowboys' provided a rich field for studies such as *Street Society in Christchurch* (1957) and *The Bodgie: A Study in Abnormal Psychology* (1958). According to Sandra Coney, delinquency in the 1950s 'was a moral rebellion', generated 'by the sons and daughters of solid suburbia'.[78]

In 1954 the nation was shocked when Pauline Parker and Juliet Hulme, two girls from Christchurch Girls' High School, murdered Parker's mother amidst overtones of teenage lesbianism, linked to marital infidelity (in the Hulme family), and marital irregularity (in the Parker family). That Hulme was the daughter of a university professor, and the murder originated in the established suburbs of Christchurch, defied belief. There was public soul-searching for the reason, although the details seemed too sordid to address explicitly. Bevan-Brown applied some Freudian psychology to the crime:

> It is a tragic demonstration of what can happen as a result of a generally inadequate nurture … This case shows that the resulting delinquency can proceed to the extreme length of matricide and murder.[79]

Regarding the issue of homosexuality, he wrote:

> What is contended here is that in this crime love was the driving force – love no doubt of an immature and even infantile type and dating back to their own intense infantile needs … I would suggest that if one seeks the ultimate origin of this crime, it could be expressed as 'Deprivation of love in childhood'.[80]

Moral panic regarding delinquency came even closer to home after a much publicised sex scandal involving 65 school children in the Hutt Valley, who used their homes for 'organised sex' after school. The government appointed a committee, chaired by Oswald Mazengarb QC, to investigate. The resulting *Report on Moral Delinquency in Children and Adolescents* (1954) was posted to every household with children in the country and listed the possible causes for the perceived moral decay: co-education, playway education, new housing developments, contraceptives, broadening of divorce laws, high wages for adolescents, self-expression in children, new views on morality, materialism and parental neglect (as one-third of the mothers of the 65 children were employed).[81]

C.E. Beeby worked to deflect blame from his education reforms:

> We cannot expect the profession as of right to teach with conviction practices and principles that are not firmly in normal, decent citizens in the adult world. So a community that hopes to use the schools as a principal agent of moral revolution is fooling itself, unless it is prepared at the same time to make a strong attack on adult moral standards.[82]

Beeby argued further that 'The teacher can strongly reinforce the influence of a good home, but he has limited powers of counteracting the influence of a bad one.'[83] The problem rested with parents. 'Broken homes' were blamed, but working mothers were the prime target. There were pleas for women to return home. R.A. Keeling, MP for Gisborne, claimed that 'Every magistrate in this country has positive proof that many cases of juvenile delinquency have been brought about because mothers have been forced to go out to work in order to provide for the needs of the family.'[84]

The report of the later 'Currie' Commission on Education (1962) also addressed concerns of delinquency. Asserting that the critical factors lay in the emotional relationships of childhood, the report recommended more preschool services (such as kindergartens and Playcentres) and more guidance and psychological services.[85] Both services had expanded during the years of the discovery of 'delinquency'. According to Dugald McDonald:

> Despite this diversity of child-centred services (some cynics may say 'because of') New Zealand has seen little reduction in problems related to parental ill treatment or neglect of children and steady rise in delinquent behaviours coming to official notice.[86]

Fathers were seen to have little responsibility for delinquent behaviour. There is little mention of fathers in the political rhetoric or childrearing advice. Popular psychology portrayed fathers as 'symbolising the great world beyond [the home]' (*NZ Woman's Weekly*, 4 December 1952). However, Playcentre and Parents' Centre worked hard to create role models of hands-on fatherhood. In these groups fathers were encouraged to play and have fun with their children and to assist their wives with everyday childrearing. Winnicott, Bowlby and Spock all emphasised the role of the father as a breadwinner and an emotional support for his wife, but there was little condemnation of fathers when this support failed and women had to manage alone.

Elly Singer was to later write of this period in Western society that 'Through the child, the mother was made responsible for violence and social chaos in the world outside the family, a world from which she was more or less excluded.'[87] Preschool institutions such as Playcentre and kindergarten were portrayed as mediators in relieving the problems of bad or destructive mothering, as well as supporting mothers to provide the 'ordinary devotion' children required. Childcare centres were evidence of less than devoted mothers, although they were tolerated if mothers were genuinely forced to work.

ILLEGITIMATE SOLUTIONS

Concern about the causes and consequences of delinquency, premarital sexuality, mother–child separation and back-yard childcare brought increased scrutiny of unmarried mothers and their children. The fate of illegitimate babies during the twentieth century is a story of slow improvement in their life chances, with increasing state interest through Child Welfare surveil-lance.[88] In 1969 the Status of Children Act removed the legal stigma of illegitimacy and in 1973 the introduction of a statutory Domestic Purposes Benefit (DPB) enabled single mothers to support themselves and their babies. These initiatives mark a boundary in time, before which unmarried mothers and their illegitimate babies were unacceptable and kept hidden.

Anne Else's study of adoption details the growth of illegitimate births in the postwar years.[89] In 1950, 3.99% of births were illegitimate. By 1970 this had risen to 13.34%. The preferred solution was still to facilitate stranger adoption, but more unmarried mothers were quietly keeping their babies.[90] Prior to the 1970s few were able to manage a viable existence, from either an economic or a moral point of view. Of interest to this study were the consequent connections between maternity homes for unmarried mothers, charitable baby homes, fostering homes licensed under the Infant Life Protection Act, and day nurseries. They were the underside of early childhood institutions, providing a service in often desperate, and sometimes unsafe, circumstances, far removed from the acceptable Playcentre and kindergarten images of play and motherly 'understanding'. The regulation of childcare centres from 1960 provided increased oversight, closed some legal loopholes and dealt with the worst abuses. After the advent of the DPB, hidden back-yard childcare arrangements were gradually transformed into the newly visible but only reluctantly acknowledged 'problem' of the 'solo' mother and her child(ren).

The pervasiveness of Bowlby is again evident. In 1953 he detailed a cycle of illegitimate birth, unstable early rearing arrangements and potential delinquency.[91] He was concerned with both punitive and overly sentimental attitudes. One view justified taking the baby from the mother as a punishment; the other insisted that the mother look after the baby that she had irresponsibly produced. Both resulted in babies being reared in unsatisfactory fostering and minding arrangements. Bowlby called for 'fresh directions'. In weighing up the psychological issues of separating the mother and her baby, Bowlby came to the view that 'in skilled hands adoption can give the child nearly as good a chance of a happy home life as that of the child brought up in his own home'.[92] Fostering or group care should be only for emergency purposes.

In New Zealand, along with other Western countries, the emphasis on child-centred nuclear families led to an increase in childless couples seeking to adopt babies. This coincided with an upsurge in the illegitimacy rate. For 20 years demand and supply were carefully balanced, supported by the consensus view that it was best for the illegitimate child to become a member of a 'normal' family. If the adoption transaction occurred discreetly and quickly, the birth mother could resume her place in society untainted by stigma. The figures for 1960 give an indication of the arrangements. There were 3445 known illegitimate babies, of whom 50 died. Of the others, 1142 babies were adopted, and 819 stayed with their mothers in de facto relationships. It was the remainder whom Child Welfare saw as 'difficult', because the 'mother hopes to keep her baby' or has 'not decided what to do'.[93] Of these, 558 stayed with their single mothers, 20 were placed in hospitals or long-term residential care, and eight were committed to the care of the state.

During the 1950s–1960s attitudes to unmarried mothers began to shift. A more sympathetic understanding of the plight of both mother and child emerged in some quarters. Major Thelma Smith began work at the Salvation Army's Bethany Home and Hospital in Auckland in the early 1950s:

> Parents were still absolutely shamed by a daughter who became pregnant out of wedlock. I can remember some girls who came to us as early as two to three months pregnant, because they lived in small towns and the shame was so great that they had to be hidden.[94]

Smith reformed the Home, turning it into a place of emotional support for the prospective mother and a welcoming environment where families and prospective fathers could visit. Smith made contact with Parents' Centre, and Bethany became the first hospital to introduce antenatal classes. This was exceptional. In 1958 Smith completed Victoria University's new social work qualification, which provided the latest psychological explanations for the 'purpose behind an out of wedlock pregnancy … There were all these sorts of theories and I came back fired up.' More understanding of the unmarried mother did start to emerge, although some institutions for unmarried mothers persisted in an attitude and regime that regarded the unmarried mother as a 'fallen woman'.[95]

But a more permissive and 'understanding' society was also blamed for the increase in illegitimacy, a view summed up by a panel member in a radio series called 'Out of Wedlock':

> The trouble begins, say, with nine- and 10-year old children who are left unsupervised from the time school ends until the evening meal time. Today's society is permissive. The chaperone is an antiquity; couples have unlimited opportunity to be alone – in cars, at parties, even in their own homes.[96]

The superintendent of Child Welfare, L. Anderson, blamed the media for encouraging young children 'to be anti-adult, anti-authority, and immoral … Our illegitimate birth rate does give cause for concern.'[97]

Homes for unmarried mothers focused on brokering adoptions. In a study of the Motherhood of Man organisation, Else wrote:

> They quickly came to see adoption as best for everyone concerned and operated on that assumption. In order for adoption to be widely accepted by prospective parents and the public in general, single mothers had to be presented and treated as nice but foolish girls who had merely slipped, rather than as fallen women. However, this worked two ways; maintaining one's status as a nice girl depended on agreeing to adoption and never seeing the child again.[98]

This was expedited by the 1955 Adoption Act, which allowed a legal transfer of the baby to its new parents 10 days after birth. Secrecy and swiftness were the aim, converting the disorder of illegitimacy into the order of normal family life for the infant. In the 1960s Major Eunice Eichler of the Salvation Army initiated the first steps towards open adoptions, where birth mothers and the adoptive parents met one another. This was opposed by other agencies and Child Welfare, but Eichler, like Smith, was trying to break down the taboos and secrecy surrounding the event. Prior to that, 'the staff would make sure all the girls were in the dormitory and then a member of staff would whisk the baby down to the office, sometimes under a coat, to be shown to the parents. It was awful.'[99]

Child Welfare claimed that welfare officers did not persuade mothers to give up their babies. 'They are not allowed and must offer impartial advice on the advantages and disadvantages. She makes her own decision,' reported Anderson in 1964.[100] However, the available options were limited. Smith recalled:

> You tried to help the girls to look at all the avenues because in the 1950s there was still quite a lot of fostering. But if a girl didn't relinquish her child and wanted to take it home there was very little available to her and often no possibility of keeping the child. I think it was one of the main reasons for adoption.[101]

But some mothers did keep their babies. They boarded them out or found a childcare place so they could earn. All illegitimate births were required by law to be investigated by Child Welfare, who had an 'obligation to ensure that illegitimate babies are not neglected, abandoned or subjected to … an unsatisfactory environment'.[102] Part of this role involved the oversight of the adoption process. Another part was the licensing and oversight of homes that boarded infants under the Infant Life Protection Act, first enacted in the nineteenth century to deal with baby farming scandals.[103] The discreet boarding of infants was no longer called baby farming, but the practice continued, and was sometimes a means of delaying or preventing adoption. Its extent can be partly gauged by Child Welfare statistics. For example, the half-yearly returns for 1959 show that Child Welfare investigated 1189 illegitimate births; there were 1310 babies in licensed Infant Life Protection homes, and 765 new placements were undertaken.[104] The extent to which Child Welfare could supervise these children was limited. The records not only indicate the kinds of abuses that occurred, but also the existence of even more children in placements outside Child Welfare surveillance or control.

In one New Plymouth case Mrs S, who was licensed to have four children boarding, also took children by day. This was 1952 and there were no childcare regulations. Mrs S had six children coming daily from 8 am to 5.30 pm, plus six grandchildren living with her. The inspector reported: 'The day children were having to sleep on the beds and cots of the boarders and the grandchildren. There are far too many children for one elderly woman to look after, especially as two were babies.' The report also noted: 'Child Welfare has no jurisdiction over the number of day children taken in … I think the development needs looking into.' The follow-up suggestion was to limit the number of infants that Mrs S could board, and to 'keep an eye on the over-crowding'.[105] The licence for the four boarders was not revoked. A case where a licence was withdrawn was that of Mrs T, from Auckland, in 1958. Mrs T was licensed for two children, but was found to have nine children in her care, plus three of her own. Their ages were: 14 years, 11 years, nine years, four years, three aged three years, two 19-month-olds, and three under one year. There had been up to 16 children. The house was undergoing renovations, and on the inspection visit it was found that:

> Children kept popping up from all directions some with pants half mast from having 'been' and some safely closeted in plastic. All had matted unkempt hair and did not appear to have had even a sketchy wash. The children milled around upstairs and downstairs and outside amidst the carpenter's jumble. We went up to the nursery and found three babies in bed. Their toilet had been unattended to. One had a bottle in bed and needed changing and washing. It would appear that the children are washed in the wash-house or the sink. There is no evidence of individual towels or toothbrushes. Mrs T said she only had one registered child. The other eight boarders returned to their mothers at the weekend.[106]

The report noted that Mrs T was circumventing the act by boarding children for five successive nights, then readmitting them. Child Welfare decided that the case did not warrant police involvement, but persuaded Mrs T to surrender her licence due to the renovations. 'Mrs T was most compliant', but the report noted that she would apply again.

This was the kind of home that caused the 1958 scandal noted earlier. The subsequent 1960 childcare regulations blocked the loophole regarding the daytime care of children. The connections between illegitimacy and childcare are twofold. A number of the early applicants for childcare centre licences were from women who boarded infants under the act. A few childcare centres also gained licences for limited overnight care. The links nevertheless remain elusive; not only were such centres and homes discreet, but their existence was often short term. The issues of illegitimacy and childcare became more explicitly entwined as more single mothers started to keep their babies.

During the 1960s the numbers of prospective adopters failed to keep pace with the increasing numbers of illegitimate children. There were more children for whom alternative arrangements had to be made, particularly if the baby had some disability or was not of full European ethnicity.[107] Newspaper headlines such as 'Need for Adoptions is Desperate' caused Child Welfare to reassure the public that 'thousands' of unwanted babies were not languishing in institutions, and that none had ended up as state wards due to the shortage.[108] To increase the pool of adoptive parents there was less surveillance of their suitability, but imperceptibly public opinion swung towards the view that mothers should be able to keep their babies. A letter to the *Gisborne Herald* (12 October 1964) from a once unmarried mother was headlined 'Unmarried Mothers Want to Keep Their Babies':

> Having your baby adopted is not like giving away a puppy. It is a vital limb or organ taken away for someone else's benefit and to be made happy at your expense. A huge payment for a common and not so criminal mistake.

Organisations such as the Motherhood of Man softened their preference for adoption. In 1966 a new secretary, Mrs Bailey, acknowledged that 'many girls would prefer to, and are capable of, caring for their babies if they had sufficient moral and practical support'.[109]

From 1965 the term 'single mother' was more frequently used and the plight of the 'single mother and her baby' started to become the subject of investigation and advocacy. The assumption shifted from that of facilitating an expedient adoption to ways of supporting the mother who chose to keep her baby. Before 1973 those mothers that did keep their babies had financial support only for as long as they were breastfeeding. Afterwards, their possibilities of support were getting help from their families, working as housekeepers where they could take their children, or using boarding or daycare arrangements for their babies while they worked. Several religious organisations operated residential baby homes, and boarded the babies of unmarried mothers for a fee, but they were generally reluctant to accept long-term placements, as their priority work was emergency care.[110]

A groundbreaking report, *The Unmarried Mother, Problems Involved in Keeping Her Child* (1969), noted that few 'solo parents' used registered childcare services, due to the cost. 'The alternative of "backyarding" or informal arrangements [was] more likely for unmarried mothers.'[111] The report also noted the issues of accommodation and referred to the 'accommodation–childcare–employment' cycle that needed to be addressed. This was preparing the ground for new policies in the 1970s, which gave childcare subsidies to parents 'in need' and introduced the DPB. Illegitimacy, once a condemned and hidden problem, had in a few short years become visible. A growing concern with back-yard childcare arrangements was part of the rationale for change. Postwar attempts to rationalise and contain 'problems' such as illegitimacy, working mothers and childcare as hidden and unacceptable had failed. They all became too visible for containment. But it was going to take considerable advocacy for what psychology had labelled 'ills' to become mainstream options. This transformation forms the focus of Part Two.

CHAPTER THREE

Getting Ahead

During the early postwar years Māori migrations brought Māori and Pākehā into closer proximity. In 1936 only 9% of Māori lived in urban areas. By 1956 this had risen to 24%, increasing to 68% by 1971.[1] Economic necessity and opportunity were the major causes. Full employment provided jobs. The writer of a government publicity book, *The Maori Today* (1949), euphorically described:

> … a growing exodus from the tribal villages of Maori youths seeking horizons beyond their ancestral homes. The basis of this spirit of progress and adventure which is drawing the Maori of the younger generation towards the pakeha way of life is largely economic … The younger generation of Maori people have become cramped for living space, for the ancestral lands can no longer give them the fuller life that is rightfully theirs.[2]

That this land now belonged to Pākehā was acknowledged, but the government was optimistic that urbanisation would provide the solution, completing the processes of assimilation begun a century earlier. No inkling of Māori grievance was suggested, and there was pride that 'Today the people of New Zealand, Maori and Pakeha, live on terms of complete unity and equality. Social standing in this country has no relation to colour.'[3] The Minister of Maori Affairs, Peter Fraser, stated:

> There is a youthfulness of spirit, an eagerness, a haste to grasp the opportunities, rights and privileges which they fully share with their fellow New Zealanders, the pakeha. There is an urge to embrace all that is best in the pakeha way of life … At the same time there is also the desire to retain all the best features of the Maori way of life.[4]

Statistics revealed significant differences in life chances, health, housing and economic well-being between Māori and Pākehā. For example, in 1946 life expectancy for Māori males was 48.8 years, compared with 67.2 years for Pākehā males.[5] Geographic mobility and occupational changes did not lead automatically to social or economic mobility.[6] Strengthening ideals of equal opportunity seeded views that such statistical disparities were less acceptable. More proactive intervention was needed. As a consequence, statistical gaps did narrow considerably by the 1960s, but they did not close.

This chapter explores the implications of 'getting ahead' for Māori in the Pākehā world, in relation to early education. The dynamics of new initiatives for Māori preschoolers, taken by both Māori and Pākehā, were complex. The early years of Māori childrearing came under scrutiny, due to new expectations of Pākehā codes for Māori parenting; changing measures of school success and failure for Māori children; an international discourse on economic and educational 'disadvantage' and 'cultural deprivation;'[7] research on the language 'deficiencies' of working-class children[8] and their use of 'non-standard English'[9]; and new debates on curriculum and learning.[10] Some wider political and pedagogical contexts underpinning early education for Māori children are also outlined.

THE 'PROBLEM' WITH EDUCATION FOR MĀORI CHILDREN

The 1944 Ministerial Education Conference identified preschool education as one of the planks for postwar planning.[11] Issues of Māori education were also addressed, but no link was made to preschool education. The focus was on including more Māori children in secondary and vocational education, and increasingly integrating Māori and Pākehā in primary school. In 1944 integration was viewed with caution, with the Minister of Education, H.G.R. Mason, stating:

> I am convinced, however, that, for some years to come, the Maori child will have special needs, which are best catered for in a school system adapted to help him meet his particular problems.[12]

However, by 1949 the government was suggesting that:

> … close association between members of the two races during childhood induces a mutual respect and understanding which is likely to endure. If the Maori child does not learn to associate with the pakeha in childhood his adjustment in later years to the pakeha way of life will be slower and less complete.[13]

Cultural assimilation was clearly the aim.

In urban schools teachers were unprepared for teaching Māori children. The Māori child was deemed a 'problem' and a 'failure', lacking the 'experiences' common to Pākehā children. Previously much of the 'problem' had been secluded in rural and/or Native (Māori) schools.[14] Furthermore, in a postwar social paradigm dominated by a quest for order, Māori visibility in suburbs, services and urban schools signalled potential disorder.[15] The information on 'special home circumstance' collected in 1956 by Auckland kindergarten teachers, for example, indicated not only the attendance of Māori children (and immigrant children) at kindergarten, but also how they were seen to be outside the 'normal':[16]

2 Peruvian children
4 Maoris [my emphasis]
9 children of working mothers, 6 full-time, 3 part-time

1 Chinese girl from an excellent home
1 Maori girl from a good home [my emphasis]
4 broken homes

1 Maori child from a poor home [my emphasis]
1 child of working mother who takes child with her
1 child of broken home – mother works

1 child with father in hospital with TB
3 Dutch children who do not speak English – accommodation not known
1 Indian
4 Maoris [my emphasis]
1 Polish Jew
1 child of working mother

5 working mothers, 3 full-time, 1 part-time and 1 in the family business
1 fatherless child
7 immigrant children (Dutch and Russian on waiting list)
1 spastic child
2 Maori children [my emphasis]

Kindergarten association and Department of Education records otherwise contain no mention of the Māori preschool child until the 1960s when a flurry of interest began. A parallel silence is the fact that several Māori kindergarten teachers were trained in Auckland during the 1950s without raising comment. By the 1960s a similar occurrence might have attracted media attention as Māori children at preschool came under intensive scrutiny.[17]

The few traceable inklings of the idea of preschool education for Māori children came from Pākehā. *The Discovery of Early Childhood* (1997) details a visit by Mrs Parr, from Rātana Pā, to the Wellington Kindergarten Association in 1939. Mrs Parr was visiting on the recommendations of then Prime Minister Peter Fraser and C.E. Beeby. She was interested in the work of the kindergarten, but felt that improving the infant classroom for Māori children was a priority. The possibility of sending two Māori girls to be trained as kindergarten teachers was discussed, but this did not eventuate.[18]

Ernest and Pearl Beaglehole's anthropological study *Some Modern Maoris* (1946) concluded with the suggestion of preschool education for Māori children.[19] The Beagleholes argued for the 'need to bring to bear upon the Maori child a somewhat different technique of infant and child training' in order to 'fit more clearly into the patterns of Pakeha civilisations. By the time the child comes to Pakeha school it is already too late …'[20] Their proposal for a community centre, with resources for adult education, motherhood training and a preschool centre, was modelled on the famed Feilding community centre operated by Gwen and Crawford Somerset from 1937 to 1948.[21]

> The younger, pre-school children should attend a modern, well-equipped, professionally staffed nursery school or kindergarten where they can be trained in habits of discipline, control, and responsibility, and at the same time enjoy as rich an intellectual and emotional life as possible.[22]

A decade later, in the 1950s, the Beagleholes' daughter Jane and son-in law James Ritchie also suggested the idea of preschool education in their research study of Rakau, a rural Māori settlement.[23]

In 1948 Marie Bell completed a Diploma of Education thesis at Victoria University on the idea of Māori nursery schools. This work (now lost) arose from her involvement in the Māori club at Wellington Teachers' College in 1939, learning Māori language, teaching in a Māori school, and her marriage to Pat Metekingi.[24] Influenced by the writings of Susan Isaacs and Margaret McMillan, from Britain, on the benefits of nursery schools,[25] Bell saw possibilities for Māori children, initially in the context of health:

> I wasn't thinking then about them speaking Maori, but more that they would be able to develop their English. McMillan's work with slum children in London was an influence. I mentioned in the thesis, though, that Maori health was not as bad as we were led to believe. There was an arrogance that Maori homes were unhealthy.[26]

Health, rather than education, was the main focus of official interest. Statistics on the mortality and health showed a disparity between Māori and Pākehā preschoolers.[27] A 1954 study indicated a lack of antenatal and post-natal care, inferior diet, less breastfeeding, and poor living circumstances.[28]

Māori families were the responsibility of public health or district nurses. The guiding document was *Ko Nga Tamariki me nga Kai ma Ratao – The Maori Mother and her Child* (1942), originally written by Maui Pomare. The booklet, in Māori with an English translation, was an adaptation of Truby King's Plunket rules, with a particular emphasis on hygiene.[29] Plunket did offer the full implementation of its methods as a solution to Māori child health problems, but there were issues of demarcation with the Health Department, whose district nurses visited Māori families. Few Māori mothers received advice from Plunket. A condition, too, of Plunket's offer was that Māori mothers 'ask for … and be prepared to work for' the Plunket Society in 'the same way as their Pakeha sisters'.[30] There was little interest.[31]

An organisation that had a more direct influence on policies for Māori families was the Maori Women's Welfare League (MWWL). It began operating in 1951 and aimed to 'improve the position of Maori women and children, in the fields of health, education and welfare'.[32] In its first decade the league's work centred on health, housing, employment, education and support for Māori families in the cities.[33] League branches organised activities with the local district nurses concerning the care of babies and children. From its inception the league was an advocate of Māori language, culture and crafts. An agreed policy at the foundation conference was for teaching Māori language,[34] and the idea of a Māori kindergarten was raised.[35] Concern was also being expressed about the survival of the language, and the league urged parents to speak Māori to their children at home. In 1952 two members of the league who were also welfare officers in the Department of Maori Affairs, Rumatiki Wright and Raihi Seargent, established a preschool for Māori children at Frankton in Hamilton.[36] The idea did not spread, but Wright was involved in further Māori preschool initiatives a decade later. In 1958 the league called for the Department of Education to consider an experiment of teaching the Māori language to five-year-olds.

That the rapid migration of Māori had an impact on Māori childrearing experiences is captured in the research of Jane and James Ritchie during the 1950s and 1960s.[37] They suggest that assumptions of Pākehā superiority on all matters caused Māori mothers, particularly in urban settings, to adopt Pākehā ways. 'As we moved from *pa* to rural town to urban families, this data changed towards conformity with Pakeha norms.'[38] This was most evident in the attitudes to the care of infants. The Ritchies noted: 'Western society is virtually alone in its conception that the child may be "spoiled", that demands must be limited from birth, [and] that character must be controlled from the start.'[39] By contrast, Māori rearing of infants, less touched by Pākehā Plunket codes, was more indulgent and attentive. Among urban Māori mothers, the Ritchies found:

> ... trends towards reduced breastfeeding incidence and duration, less maternal contact, a greater readiness to leave children to cry, and so on ... the sensitivity of the urban Maori mothers to Pakeha judgements of their behaviour [was] a not unexpected attitude amongst a minority who are trying to find acceptance in what is essentially an alien environment.[40]

The impact of urban living and cultural assimilation caused a downturn in the use of Māori language. That this might be a concern was predicted by Māori MP Apirana Ngata in 1943. Ngata had spent a lifetime seeking political, economic and education solutions for his people. He noted:

> When the Maori homes and villages were the nurseries of the Maori language, history and tradition, custom and culture, it was assumed that Maori children entering schools were sufficiently equipped in those respects, and their school career was a one way effort to assimilate ...[41]

By the 1950s more of the traditional 'nurseries' were speaking English, and there were increasing efforts to have Māori language taught in school, teachers' colleges and universities. This quest often met with resistance. By the 1960s there was a significant decline in knowledge of te reo Māori among younger Māori who had never learnt the language, and among many older Māori who were not using it. However, the statistics vary widely.[42]

An important political milestone concerning postwar Māori was the publication of the Hunn report in 1960. This contained the government's responses to Māori urbanisation.[43] The new frame for race relations was 'integration, in which Maori and Pakeha would form one nation wherein Maori culture remains distinct'.[44] In 1962 the Department of Maori Affairs provided further clarification, describing integration as:

> A dynamic process by which Maori and pakeha are being drawn closer together, in the physical sense of mingling of the two populations as well as in the mental and cultural senses where differences are gradually diminishing.[45]

Not all shared this view. One response was published as *A Maori View of the 'Hunn Report'* (1962). The authors expressed concern that 'there is a dangerous risk in the present assumption of many Pakeha that all the "adjusting" must be done by Maori'.[46]

The Hunn report gave emphasis to education, noting that:

The state of Maori education – not its quality but the demand for it – leaves much to be desired … Better education promotes better employment, which promotes better housing which promotes better health and social standing, which promotes better education and thus closes the circle.[47]

The assumption was that existing mainstream schools should serve as the 'nursery of integration'. One of the recommendations was to establish a Maori Education Foundation (MEF). In 1963 the foundation appointed a preschool officer. By this time 'preschool education' had also 'discovered' Māori preschool children and many Māori communities were establishing centres.

A backdrop to the interest in preschool was fuelled by research on the language difficulties of Māori children at school. The chairman's address to the board of the MEF in 1962 referred to the 'problem' of Māori children learning English from 'Maori parents whose own command of English is poor [and who] find it difficult to understand the need for their children to acquire a greater facility in its use than they have'. In turn, this meant Māori children did not have, 'sufficient verbal facility in English or depth of conceptual experience'.[48] Studies by Richard Benton in 1963–64 for the MEF, and Ian Barham for the New Zealand Council for Educational Research (NZCER) in 1965, drew on Bernstein's theory of elaborated and restricted codes of speech according to social class. They indicated that the Māori child demonstrated 'a number of widespread structural and vocabulary deviations'[49] and, secondly, that the Māori child 'may be up to two years behind the Pakeha children from the same [parental] occupational group at the beginning of his school career'.[50] Benton saw the issue as an educational opportunity and suggested the consideration of bilingual schooling for young Māori children.[51] Nonetheless, views on linguistic disadvantage held currency. The Māori preschooler and his or her mother consequently came under scrutiny.

SYLVIA ASHTON-WARNER: 'THE LITTLE ONES'
In the 1960s anthropologist Erik Schwimmer sought an explanation for the supposed 'failure' of Māori children at school in the new theories of Erik Erikson (see Chapter One). He suggested that the Māori child felt no 'identity' or 'sense of belonging' in Pākehā primary schools and was caught between two cultures. Following the Eriksonian line of psychology, Schwimmer argued that the Māori child 'runs the danger of developing "a sense of inadequacy and inferiority"'.[52] Schwimmer referred to the work of infant-school teacher Sylvia Ashton-Warner, whose books *Spinster* (1958) and *Teacher* (1963) detailed her

dream and frustrations of working with young Māori children in the 1940s and 1950s in remote rural communities. Schwimmer wrote:

> In the first five years of life, the Maori child has gathered a wealth of experiences that lay the foundation for his socialisation in a modern Maori society. On the other hand, the complaint of the primary schools is that the Maori child lacks experience when he comes to school ... Sylvia Ashton-Warner ... shows that the Maori in the infant school, while by no means poor in experiences, tends to have experiences of a kind that do not readily fit into a standard classroom and school curriculum.[53]

Ashton-Warner rejected the *Janet and John* readers, imported into New Zealand schools in 1950, as sterile and inappropriate for her Māori 'little ones'. She argued that:

> First words must have an intensive meaning.
> First words must be already part of the dynamic life.
> First books must be made of the stuff of the child
> Himself, whatever and wherever the child.[54]

Ashton-Warner's 'little ones' chose their own words:

> ... ghost, bomb, kiss, brothers, butcher knife, gaol, love, dance, cry, fight, hat, bulldog, wild piggy ... If you were a child which vocabulary would you prefer? Your own or the one at present in New Zealand infant rooms? 'Come John come. Look John look. Come and look. See the boats' ... I can't believe that Janet and John never fall down and scratch a knee and run crying to mummy. I don't know why their mother never kisses them or calls them 'darling'. Doesn't John ever disobey?[55]

Ashton-Warner wanted to see Māori children reading and writing at the same pace as Pākehā children. Her 'Key Vocabulary' acknowledged the children's experiences as relevant to school and learning, and a 'plank in a bridge from one culture to another'.[56] She also emphasised the creative in reading, writing, dance and art. Ashton-Warner saw the elements of sex and fear in young children needing to be unlocked. This thinking was at the core of progressive education and the new psychology.

Ashton-Warner is better remembered as a writer than as an educator, but her writing brought her international acclaim as an educator, mainly outside New Zealand. In the US there emerged Sylvia Ashton-Warner societies and students, and 'Sylvian' followers have been able to study courses on her teaching.[57] Eminent educator Lilian Katz writes how 'Sylvia Ashton-Warner seemed to heed Rousseau's injunction to transform our sensations into ideas.'[58]

Lynley Hood's biography, *Sylvia!* (1988), portrays Ashton-Warner as a teacher whose written life in the classroom does not tally with her real-life experience. Ashton-Warner portrays herself as persecuted and ignored by the education authorities, but Hood suggests that Ashton-Warner exaggerated her plight and was an erratic teacher. However, American Sydney Clemens describes Ashton-Warner as 'one of the mothers of early childhood education'.[59] She wrote a rejoinder to Hood's biography, portraying Ashton-Warner as the classroom genius of creativity who was misunderstood in New Zealand. Part of the ambivalence was that Ashton-Warner's life was outside the norm for Pākehā women of the 1950s. Hood writes:

> Conventional people were deeply offended – not only was Sylvia shocking and pretentious, the role reversal in the Henderson household [where Sylvia's husband did hands-on childcare] was a terrible threat to the status quo …[60]

As for the children, Ashton-Warner 'awed them, she frightened them, she excited them, she entranced them'.[61] Student teacher Iritana Tawhiwhirangi, a later leader of Te Kōhanga Reo (Māori immersion language centres), spent a term with Ashton-Warner. Like others, Tawhiwhirangi noted that Ashton-Warner was not in the classroom most of the time, but she nevertheless acknowledges how the 'learning environment' of kōhanga reo was influenced by Ashton-Warner, in that it was 'not just a teaching environment'.[62]

Ashton-Warner's teaching methods did attract attention. In *Teacher* she describes a succession of visitors, one of whom was 'Professor Baille'[63] [Bailey], from the Department of Education at Victoria University, Wellington, accompanied by his colleague Arthur Fieldhouse, who recalled their visit to Fernhill School in 1951:

> Professor Colin Bailey and I used to go up to Hawkes Bay for the Inspector Rollo [Rowland] Lewis every year to do a week's course for teachers. One year he said he was very concerned about a scheme for the teaching of reading that seemed to be having wonderful results, but there were some aspects that he was worried about and would we mind going out to the school to have a look. We asked what the problems were, but he said he didn't want to prejudice us. 'I just want you to see and make up your own minds …' We went to the two-teacher school which was 99% Maori. There was a great buzz of activity going on but it was a meaningful buzz. The children were involved in reading and they came up and wanted to read to you, but my 'hat', what they were reading would rock you. It was all the gossip of the pa. Rollo was frightened that *Truth* magazine or a newspaper would get hold of it. But they could read like mad … It was incredible. It was in fact very heartening. It was hard and fast proof that the theory works.[64]

Both Bailey and Fieldhouse were interested in progressive teaching ideas. Fieldhouse had studied with progressive educator Susan Isaacs in the 1930s. Bailey had chaired the committee that wrote the 1947 government report on preschool education. He advised that 'the basic principles of [Ashton-Warner's] work were sound, that she was tapping into the most dynamic source of teaching – the child's own life – and that it was worth taking the risk to encourage her'.[65] Lewis did so, but efforts to publish Ashton-Warner's Māori readers eventually floundered in a mix of caution, confusion and carelessness. By the late 1950s the Department of Education was developing its own Ready to Read scheme, and a separate Māori reading scheme was viewed as unnecessary.

The international acclaim for Ashton-Warner's novel *Spinster* (1958), which became a Hollywood movie in 1960, generated more New Zealand interest. The line between fact and fiction caused debate. *Teacher* (1963) went to the top of the New York bestseller list, but many education officials and teaching colleagues from New Zealand felt maligned by her portrayal of them, though most said nothing publicly.

Academic interest was more articulate. In 1968 Jack Richards from Victoria University was challenging assumptions concerning 'language problems of Maori children':

> Too often, identification of the language problem with the child or home frees the teacher and the school from further responsibility. 'Cultural deprivation' becomes a convenient escape clause … the Maori children of Miss Ashton-Warner's experience were not culturally deprived. On the contrary, she used their experience, accepting and affirming it as the basis of reading and writing. The psychology and methodology of her approach has received worldwide substantiation and support. It is almost totally ignored in this country.[66]

Some other teachers working with Māori new entrants were also trying new approaches. Alan Simpson in 1957 described for the readers of *Education* magazine a programme that used the medium of creative dance, drama and art as a stimulus for the mind.[67] Simpson also criticised *Janet and John*, which he deemed:

> … not the most suitable books for young Maoris learning to read. Why, the children have yellow hair, and in one picture they have more toys than these children have ever seen in their whole lives … And why are Janet and John wearing shoes and socks when they are presumably playing in the garden?[68]

Simpson, like Ashton-Warner, created his own transitional reading books, although his approaches were possibly more acceptable to the authorities than Ashton-Warner wanted to be. Both, however, tried to break away from a model of early education for young Māori children that placed toothbrush drill and order to the fore, and drew a line between their home and their school experience. The international rationales underpinning the 'psychological benefits of play' that were influencing many early-years teachers in New Zealand were also undergoing some home-grown transformation into creative approaches for teaching with Māori children. Yet these ideas were slow to catch on.

MĀORI CHILDREN AT PRESCHOOL

There are many strands concerning the development of early childhood institutions for Māori children, determined by such things as tribal location, who is telling the story – Māori or Pākehā, and the attitudes and initiatives of individuals and organisations involved. There is a parallel story concerning attendance by Māori children in mainstream kindergartens and Playcentres, and the role and views of the Department of Education.

Everyone wanted to be 'doing something'. There were reservations within the Department of Education and the mainstream early childhood groups about the separate (i.e. segregated) initiatives by Māori groups. Those groups that did not officially affiliate with Playcentre or kindergarten organisations could not get funding. A fuller history deserves to be written, but this section untangles a few of the strands.

In 1959 Rakata Parata wrote to the Department of Education on behalf of the Maori University Students' Association, which was to hold its annual conference in Wellington. One of the discussion groups was to address the 'Need for pre-school education for Maori children in Maori Education'. Parata wondered whether there had ever been any experimental kindergartens and nursery play centres established for Māori children.[69] I have been unable to find the reply in departmental records but it seems unlikely that any such preschool existed. James Ritchie, who spoke at the conference, suggested that:

> … experimental projects be set up to determine the best techniques for Maori preschool education … [which] would go far to overcome the difficulties Maori children faced in their first year at school … If the Maori child was retarded it was because he did not begin schooling as well prepared as his European neighbour.[70]

A flurry of Pākehā scrutiny of Māori preschoolers and do-it-yourself activism from Māori communities was about to create the first wave of early childhood centres for Māori children.

The Hunn report, released in August 1960, recommended that kindergartens and Playcentres be established in Māori areas. Subsequent Māori conferences called to discuss the Hunn report supported the idea of preschool education for Māori as a collective group.[71] In October 1960 two centres were established in predominantly Māori communities on the Whanganui River at Kaiwhaika and at Putiki.[72] Women from the Palmerston North Playcentre Association, who visited with a van full of play equipment, gave support to these early initiatives.[73] In May 1961 the Department of Education opened a file on Māori preschool education and began to survey the issues.[74] A more proactive organisation was the MWWL, which was raising money for the MEF (Maori Education Foundation). Preschool education was considered at the league's 1961 conference in Hamilton, and members began to promote the establishment of centres. While Pākehā agendas were a backdrop to the preschool initiatives, Māori community activism was at the forefront. McDonald wrote later:

> Just as there were persons and groups anxious to promote preschool education, there were also Maori communities anxious to establish their own. One of the striking things about the early 1960s is the number of school committees, parent–teacher associations and Maori Women's Welfare League branches that were making plans for preschool groups.[75]

In July 1961 Iriaka Ratana, MP for Western Maori, reported to parliament that there were now four preschools established in the Whanganui area. She noted that:

> Maori welfare policy stresses the importance of education. It emphasises the need for fostering pre-school services in the Maori community … a child who has had pre-school training makes the necessary adjustment to school training much more readily and easily.[76]

Similar initiatives were under way in Northland. In 1960 a meeting was held in Te Whaka Rongotai Marae at Omapere in the Hokianga. This included members of the MWWL; Mate Toia, a welfare officer; representatives of the Department of Maori Affairs; and Lex Grey from the Auckland Playcentre Association. In 1961 the first Māori women received their Playcentre Supervisor's Certificate.[77] By 1964 Northland Playcentre Association had 19 centres, in which more than 50% of the families were Māori.

In December 1961, at its inaugural meeting, the MEF extended its activities to include a national drive on preschool, subsequently resolving 'to use every endeavour to encourage Māori mothers to provide a more ordered and stimulating home life for the children'.[78] Lex Grey began his appointment as preschool officer with the MEF in 1963. He was ideally suited to forge associations with Playcentre, the preschool preferred by the MEF.[79] The voluntary nature of Playcentre enabled centres to operate successfully in rural areas, often with a small group of families. There were many constraints on opening a kindergarten, in terms of roll numbers needed, building regulations and trained staff requirements. By 1962 Jane and James Ritchie realised that it was too late for experimental projects, instead supporting

> [an] adaptation of the play centre idea … The play centre theory, its basic idea being that children learn with parents, ideally suits the present situation in Maori communities.

The Ritchies warned, however, that:

> A pre-school service is not, and should not be seen as, a bridgehead for assault on the essential values of Maori culture … Pakeha standards about cleanliness and dress, being panted or pantless, about punctuality or regular attendance should not be expected.[80]

Grey worked as the preschool officer for the MEF from 1963 to 1967. He is remembered as an 'inspirational' person in his support of Māori communities keen to establish some preschool experience for their children. Laurel Cleave recalled that, after the visits of Grey to the mid-Northland centres: 'We who were at our wits' end would leave these meetings refreshed and confident in ourselves and our Playcentres.'[81] In 1966 Betty Brown, from Northland, recorded that 'Where Mr Grey has been he has left valuable, refreshing ideas, new approaches and enthusiasm. His help is invaluable.'[82]

Grey was a skilful publicist for the cause, and numerous photographs and articles record the occasion of his visits. These have tended to become the 'remembered' history. Much was also happening spontaneously. By 1962 there were 10 East Coast centres linked to Playcentre (although not fully affiliated).[83] Rona Haig described 'Our Tikitiki Play Centre' in *Te Ao Hou* (no. 41, 1962). The idea originated in 1961 from the MWWL, which invited a Playcentre representative to a meeting. The district nurse then arranged evenings where films were shown on preschool children and play. 'People were able to discuss the idea and mull it over in their minds. Eventually, it was decided to start.'

In 1967 Miria Pewhairangi was employed by the MEF. She described the 1960s as a time of 'Maori self-assertion':

> By and large, Lex Grey's skills masked the contribution made by Maori individuals, communities and organisations. In particular, Maori Women's Welfare League groups throughout the country and Maori Affairs welfare officers … spent many hours beyond the normal call of duty on 'paving the way' for Lex Grey and providing groups with continuous follow-up support.[84]

Many centres, however, had no funding. They did not fit the criteria for kindergarten funding, and even those that became fully affiliated Playcentres were still reliant on local fund-raising. Playcentre in the 1960s received minimal government assistance. The MEF eventually provided some small grants and some MWWL branches raised money. Grey was walking a tightrope of expectations and sometimes found himself in strife. Playcentre associations were unable to respond adequately to the demand. They were voluntary organisations whose members were already busy wives and mothers. Alison Stephenson's study of the Palmerston North Playcentre Association's support of new Māori centres in the Whanganui area suggests that the task became unsustainable in terms of time and resources.[85]

Terse Department of Education and Playcentre correspondence reveals concerns that Grey was raising expectations that the emerging groups could become affiliated Playcentres.[86] The reality was, however, that these isolated centres needed ongoing support, but there was no clear government policy for provision or support outside the mainstream organisations. The success of the campaign on the ground had overstepped the political will. In 1960 there were 141 Playcentres. By 1967 there were 385, with most of the growth in the rural North Island. The Department of Education acknowledged that Grey's work through the foundation had contributed to this growth.[87] Grey, however, was becoming more reluctant to follow departmental and MEF policy:

> I was expected to fit all these people into the playcentre style or into the kindergarten style pre-school and again I said, 'No, if Maori want that, OK that's fine, that's their business, that's their choice.' But there are those who say, 'No. We want to do it our way in the community with our children.' I encouraged them to do that. You should have heard the flak … What happened in the first year using this kind of approach? Eighty-eight Maori communities dotted around from about Kaitaia in the north to Gisborne in the east and Taumarunui in the south began their own kind of pre-school … The government panicked. The Maori Education Fellowship was set up because Maori were supposed to be

failing. Maori were not failing. They were showing good judgement … I was ordered to stop this business of opening centres … By the second year we had one hundred and twenty-two.[88]

The Playcentre model of preschool was not always wanted. A Playcentre delegation that visited Rātana Pā in 1961 reported to the Department of Education: 'We felt that the teachers [at the school] were not really sympathetic to Play Centre ideas. The teachers said that they wanted children to be disciplined before they come to school, and some of our equipment did not meet with their approval.'[89] Mene Murray, from Northland, recalled arguments about the free-play dictum of Playcentre:

> Well … because we knew through our training that we put out all of the play [equipment], and the child could pick whatever he wants to … Free play. That's what I always said, 'Free play'. They couldn't see that because the children [were] running from one place to the other – you know. They thought it was bad …[90]

Māori parents recalled the formality of their own school days and sometimes wanted to replicate the toothbrush and handkerchief drills, roll calls and discipline.

Language was sometimes an issue. Preschool was expected to be in English. Geraldine McDonald reported that many Māori mothers were frightened that 'time spent on Maori would decrease the ability to speak English'.[91] Toia recalled an exchange of views probably common at the time:

> I remember at Ti Tii I told the Kaumatua he should speak Pakeha and he wasn't very pleased with me. 'Oh yes, Mate, you are going to make Pakeha out of my mokopuna!' I said it was to help them develop their English. But it was lovely to hear him speaking in Maori. He said, 'You come back in a few weeks and I'll think about it.' And he did – he agreed. So Playcentre started at Ti Tii.[92]

Most groups did not take a purist stand on English, and while 'preparation for school' was a key motive, it was not uncommon for Māori language to be used. Nevertheless, Benton reported that informants in his linguistic survey in one Northland community claimed that they were persuaded by Playcentre enthusiasts to stop speaking Māori.[93]

By 1970, 52 Māori mothers had completed the Playcentre Supervisors' training course, but there was no groundswell of Māori mothers interested in training. Jane Ritchie later wrote: 'To be a trained play centre person is to be decidedly Pakeha.'[94] The Māori women who became involved in Playcentre acknowledged both benefits and difficulties. Maureen Locke was introduced to Playcentre at Koutu near Rotorua in 1967:

> In those days, in the early sixties, they were looking at pre-school for the Maori children – 'They're eighteen months behind Pakeha children when they go to school. They're disadvantaged!!!'... So there was this big recruitment drive among the Maori communities ... With all this recruitment to train Maori mothers and children I decided that I was going to be a liaison officer and go out and train Maori mothers. I worked extremely hard in the playcentre movement to acquire those skills. I owe an awful lot in terms of my knowledge of early childhood to my early days in the playcentre movement.

Working with Pākehā was not always easy, and Locke recalled how the Pākehā mothers of the Playcentre two miles up the road decided to come and join the Koutu Playcentre:

> We all looked aghast. Within three months they had taken over the committee: they were the secretary, the treasurer, the president ... Within next to no time they'd actually taken over the centre and some of the Maori mothers had disappeared. So we set up our own Maori group and promptly got labelled as racist ... those days were extremely hard ... You had to work your way through everything ... Pakeha expectations for their children were completely different. The Pakehas would all be strung up on toilet training which really didn't appear to be a problem for a lot of Maori people.[95]

In the suburb of Te Atatu in Auckland, which was home to a growing Māori urban community, Māori women had a similar experience. The *Auckland Star* (17 August 1965) reported that the Auckland Playcentre Association had 'reluctantly' given support to Māori women who had decided to form a Playcentre for their own children. The Māori women had tried 'togetherness', but it had failed. They professed to feeling uncomfortable with Pākehā women, who were financially better off and better educated. The reporter suggested that rather than cry 'segregation' Pākehā should look at the situation:

> Deep down they like to identify as Maoris because they have pride in their identity. It seems to me that there is a sub-conscious resistance to the very concept of joint activity because of the fear that they will be submerged.

In 1970 McDonald was doing the field work for the *Maori Mothers and Preschool Education* (1973) project with NZCER. She found that Māori women wanted 'self-determination'. She also found that difficulties arose whenever enrolment included both Māori and Pākehā.[96] There was increasing resentment from Māori families at 'overtones of Pakeha condescension' and suggestions of deprivation and disadvantage.[97]

The story is not all negative. Miria Pewhairangi believed that the early Māori centres were successful because they were organised around Māori values and often used Māori language. She claimed that the late 1960s were 'marked by the emergence of many Maori women with considerable expertise in pre-school education'.[98] In 1967 a group of Māori women from Playcentre forged links with Australian Aboriginal groups in association with the Aboriginal Family Education Centre project. The women worked as voluntary field officers in Australia, alongside Aboriginal women, to support early childhood education and training. This work later spearheaded Te Roopu Awhina Tamariki, which established itself as a Māori early childhood organisation separate from Playcentre. Hine Potaka and Betty Brown claimed that, 'by combining the experience and knowledge of the group, almost largely unused, Te Roopu could help in the community'.[99]

Te Roopu was not the first Māori preschool organisation. Family Play Groups were established in the Waikato. Rumatiki Wright was a key instigator and long-term supporter. In 1964 Lex Grey visited to give support. The motto from the Family Play Groups was 'no fees, no charges, no grants'.[100] They wanted to be independent:

> Our mothers want small scale personal groups with a friendly atmosphere where they will all feel at home ... Some feel the organisation of kindergarten does not involve them enough, or directly enough in their children's learning. Some find Play Centre organisations rather daunting, perhaps a little formidable ... and its training far beyond so many mothers at this time ... But the main reason for our little groups is that we want to keep **all** our preschoolers together ...[101]

In 1967, 11 groups formed the first Māori preschool organisation and constituted themselves as the Maori Family Preschool Groups, which in 1972 became the Maori Family Education Association. In 1968 there were 36 known Family Preschools, involving 575 children and 301 mothers in the Waikato–Maniopoto area. There were other such preschools in Hawke's Bay, Poverty Bay and the East Coast districts, altogether totalling about 80 by 1970.[102]

In 1968 Leone Shaw succeeded Grey in the MEF (after various policy disagreements he had left to work in Australia). Shaw worked in the Waikato and to the south, alongside Pewhairangi in the north. Upon taking up the position she found:

There was an uproar about separatism. There was a very good reason. This was quite different from Maoridom everywhere else because of the confiscation of the land in the Waikato which was only yesterday really … I had had a real battering from the Auckland Playcentre Association, who said, 'They're organising the kids, they are separate. We are going to go down and train them.' I thought … over my dead body you are![103]

The Waikato groups did indeed have

a formality about them. The reasoning was that this was preparation either for kindergarten or playcentre or … school. Ruth [Rumatiki Wright] taught the parents what a proper lunch was. The children were taught to come with a handkerchief, pinned usually … They were interested in play activities for the children but they had a very formal programme with roll call, formal story times, times for going to the toilet, inspection of handkerchiefs and prayers. Food was the central part of the day so that everybody sat and had food together … There were a lot of babies around and a lot of grand-mothers. You had the whole community involved. The interesting thing was that the learning by the parents tended to outweigh what the kids were learning.[104]

McDonald described three distinct groups in the Māori world of early childhood education:

A lot of Maori Family Preschool groups in the Waikato … didn't have enough financial support. It was just hopeless trying to keep them going, but people were trying to keep them alive … There were also Maori children in kinder-garten and Maori children in playcentre … You could say that the Maori Family Preschool groups were an example of Maori doing it for themselves.[105]

Kindergartens made little response to Māori preschool initiatives, although some teachers' colleges moved to recruit Māori women for kindergarten training. Georgina Kerr was Ngāti Porou and from Gisborne. Her arrival at college in Auckland in 1966 illustrates some of the gaps in expectation:

I was nineteen at that time. I found my first day at college horrific because I turned up in jeans. I was virtually told to go around to the back door. They thought I was the cleaner. Everyone else had pearls. I met Auckland society: ex St Cuthbert's, ex Dio [Dioscesan] and Woodford House girls. It was the most extraordinary experience. In fact I nearly walked out, but I bumped into another Maori woman who was also ready to walk out as well. She had trousers on too. We crashed into each other in the toilets and we just cracked up laughing … It was such an alien environment. Everybody else looked so nice in stockings. We had a little lecture within two hours of arriving.

> We were beckoned into the principal's office and asked if we owned any skirts or stockings ... There were 120 students and there were only four of us who were Māori ... They saw us as very good keen role models [but] they were very cautious about us ... Anything Māori was a lost cause there ...[106]

Some individual kindergarten teachers were trying new ways to work with Māori children and families arriving at kindergarten, but this was not widespread.[107] The preschool section of the Department of Education was ill equipped, in terms of staff and resources, to respond to the demand created for preschool for Māori children. The 1962 Currie Commission noted: 'It is a task of some urgency to find a way to do for the Maori child in remoter areas what the home, the kindergarten and the play centre do for the European child.' Specific policy recommendations were not forthcoming.[108] Since 1959 the department had permitted Māori children to attend school from age four and a half where there was no local preschool provision. This totalled hundreds rather than thousands of children at any one time. They were limited to six per class, and there was no extra staffing or funding. Examples of daily timetables understandably indicate a school-based focus to the activities.[109]

One task was to create a database to respond to the political questions about how many Māori children attended preschool. This was not fully operative until 1965. By then there were 1541 Māori children at Playcentre and 660 in kindergartens, making a total of 2201 out of a national figure of 27,482 children at recognised preschools. Māori children attending were mainly in rural and small-town Māori communities. In Auckland, where there were established early childhood organisations and a large Māori urban community, there were only 130 Māori children attending Playcentre and 220 Māori children attending kindergarten,[110] indicating caution and/or lack of opportunity by Māori families.

In 1963 to 1964 the department surveyed a number of schools regarding the impact of preschool experiences on Māori new entrants. The responses were enthusiastic and gave moving accounts of the huge, unfunded effort poor Māori communities were making to operate preschools. An inspector's comment on Ahipara School was typical:

> In spite of what appeared to be insurmountable difficulties we are pleased to report that ... The social habits of this year's new entrants are a great improvement ... The willingness to work and to express themselves is a matter of great credit to the enthusiasts who have voluntarily worked for and carried out this work ...

The new entrant teacher paid tribute to the mothers, noting that 'this type of preschool where the mother helper is actually organising and running a class of children, is in my mind the most progressive step made in our Maori education'. This centre was not affiliated to Playcentre and was therefore ineligible for any grant from the MEF. The teacher noted the hardship.

In 1964 the government increased its grant to Playcentre in recognition of its work in Māori communities. As the first flush of activism passed, however, speeches to parliament from the Māori MPs regularly called for more direct support. Whetu Tirikatene-Sullivan wanted

> a more systematised pre-school scheme … Pre-school experience provided by voluntary bodies with parental co-operation could not meet the urgent needs … What had the Department done in that direction?[111]

The answer was very little, although cases were made by both Māori and Pakeha.[112] The department preferred to link Māori preschool initiatives with the existing organisations. Submissions from Māori groups wanting new policy initiatives were not successful.[113] A 'confidential' memo, attached to a 1967 submission from the Pre-school Committee of the National Committee on Maori Education, stated: 'The whole plan envisages segregated preschool services for Maori children, which I would oppose.' The submission to the department had, however, explicitly stated: ' … we stress we do not desire segregated preschool'.[114]

The New Zealand Maori Council and the MWWL sponsored the first Maori Pre-School Planning Conference in 1968. Māori delegates pointed out that Playcentre standards were beyond the reach of many Māori mothers, 'educationally, socially and financially'. There were

> Maori values that were more important, and easier to impart in the informal atmosphere of family pre-school groups. They did not want to compete with pakeha mothers who knew 'what was best' without consulting them.[115]

An offshoot was to suggest research to look at Māori needs in relation to preschool. McDonald subsequently undertook this work, but the downturn in political interest had begun and Māori initiatives, once flourishing, were flagging. The department's 1971 (Hill) *Report of the Consultative Committee on Preschool Education* (see Chapter Four) paid scant attention to Māori issues, subsuming Māori needs within the generalist phrase of 'children with special needs'. The view by then was that special provision for Māori children was unnecessary and could be covered within general proposals for addressing all special needs, Māori or Pākehā.[116] Furthermore, the report recommended that having separate MEF advisory officers was wasteful. They were disestablished in 1972.

McDonald was concerned that 'the achievements of the Maori groups were ignored just as their problems were'. She wrote: 'There are no suggestions in the [Hill] report as to how to sustain, encourage and develop pre-school education in ways acceptable to those of Maori background.'[117] In 1975 McDonald co-ordinated a research project for a training scheme based on 'a Maori way of running pre-school groups' with the Waikato Maori Family Education Association.[118] Anne Smith and David Swain, reflecting in hindsight on this period, write:

> There was little or no questioning of whether Pakeha institutions were appropriate and positive for Maori families. The mute evidence of the decline in Maori involvement in the early 1970s suggests that many Maori families did experience such inappropriateness.[119]

By the late 1970s there were few Māori-only Playcentres or separate preschools surviving, due mainly to the lack of funding and support.[120] Ranginui Walker later wrote in the *NZ Listener* (11 June 1990):

> Maori parents, contrary to Pakeha theory, were not apathetic. They raised most of the money for the MEF … But by the [19]60s disenchantment began to set in. Some parents seceded from playcentres to establish their own informal play-groups because they did not want their children to become brown Pakeha.[121]

The question 'Who gets to preschool?' eventually became more political. Issues of integration and separate development continued to simmer for another decade; so too, did ideals of Māori self-determination. Jane and James Ritchie, who had been advocates for Māori preschools, seemed to express reservations concerning the consequences of the 1960s campaign:

> It is not only the Maori mother who must be careful not to swap her tradition and heritage for a mess of pseudo-scientific pottage. Many voices now direct the Maori mother where she should now go, and how she should act: the district nurse, the local doctor, the Play Centre, not to mention radio talk, other mass media and, we understand, the Maori Education Foundation.[122]

The balance towards separate development began to tip. In 1982 Te Kōhanga Reo, a Māori and totally separate early childhood venture, began.

The increasing scrutiny of young Māori children during the 1960s was fuelled by contexts specific to New Zealand, but it also gained momentum from international influences. A political campaign in the US to make 'war on poverty' called for an investment in early-years education for the poor. Research was demonstrating the importance of environmental, as opposed to hereditary, factors in child development, and was defining class background as the key variable in school success.[123] Nikolas Rose writes that:

> The cycle of poverty, disadvantage, and deprivation provided a narrative formula that gave meaning to a whole variety of research, reflection, and programmes to do with children, families, and social problems for the next twenty years.[124]

Within this narrative the children were now 'martyrs' whose chances had been maligned by the cultural and economic environment of their birth and poor parenting. In a recurring pattern of early childhood history, there was again optimism that such ills could be cured by early educational intervention. The difference between the US and New Zealand was the political will to invest money.

In the summer of 1965, in what was described as a 'military strategy', half a million disadvantaged four- and five-year-old US children were to be gathered into summer camps in an experiment called Project Head Start. The announcement came from the executive office of the president of the Office of Economic Opportunity.[125] Mrs Lyndon Johnson, the president's wife, was to be the honorary chair of the national committee for the project. The president hailed Project Head Start as a 'landmark – not just in education but in the maturity of our democracy' and claimed that Head Start would 'strike at the basic cause of poverty'.[126] Within a year 10,000 Head Start centres were receiving the first ever federal government funds for early childhood education, catering for 350,000 children. Some 30,000 teachers needed to be trained.

Logistically, the project was overly optimistic. Pedagogically, Head Start was overly ambitious. It became a public testing ground for the theories and ideas of American educational psychologists. Would the theories work in practice?

Urie Bronfenbrenner's book *The Two Worlds of Childhood* (1970) contrasted the upbringing and education of children in the US and the USSR at a time when the Soviets appeared to be winning the space race. President Kennedy had appointed Bronfenbrenner as adviser on issues of public policy and the well-being of children. Bronfenbrenner recalled:

While flattered by the invitation, I felt some misgivings. Like most developmental psychologists of that time, trained as we were primarily in the techniques of the laboratory and the testing room, I had not thought of myself as one who either had or should be engaged in delineating directions for science, let alone policy affecting the nation's children.[127]

Bronfenbrenner became one of 13 scientists given the task of planning a foolproof programme for children that could deliver the political objectives of Head Start. To the frustration of policy makers, this was not possible. The programme developed provided some broad components and aims, with the view that the detail should be determined locally, but not by schools, which had been seen to fail so many American children. Instead, there was a broad community approach, with a focus on health, education, nutrition, parent participation, social and psychological help, and employment and career development for the staff, most of whom were to be recruited from the local community.[128]

The programmes were based on assumptions that economically disadvantaged children were deprived through poor parenting and home environments, and were thus less effective as learners in school. There was the belief that a rich early childhood environment could provide the necessary compensatory experiences as a catch-up for deprivation.[129] Cognitive goals were emphasised, although some programmes maintained a strong emphasis on learning through play, while others attempted a more formal teaching of cognitive skills.

The early years of Head Start were fuelled by much community and political enthusiasm, but complicated by the lack of trained staff and appropriate accommodation. In 1967 the Office of Economic Opportunity developed booklets providing more guidance on programmes, equipment, staffing, social services, health issues etc.[130] A few excerpts illustrate the mood and attitudes at the time:

> Child development centers are for the small children of deprived families. These young children have special needs. Their time is short. They need understanding, sensitive guidance, skilled enrichment **now**, before they pay a needless price in school failure.[131]

> There can be no doubt, however, that an environment meagre in stimulation, and often damaging in terms of emotional well-being, can slow or twist a child's development.[132]

The booklets provided step-by-step instructions from the time the staff arrived at the centre through to the time when 'the children leave like a theatrical cast that has just completed a fine performance: satisfied, exhilarated, ready for a second rejoicing … The child goes to his eager parents who hear no finer music than the account of a good day at school.'[133]

There were high political stakes with the Head Start project. Everyone wanted early evidence of the effectiveness of the programmes. In 1969 the Westinghouse report published an evaluation of the school achievements of the first Head Start children.[134] The 'revolution' promised by Head Start had not happened, although children who were enrolled in the one-year programme showed small gains. Opponents saw the report as proof of failure and the project as a waste of public money. Arthur Jensen, who believed that IQ and scholastic achievement were primarily determined by heredity, published a famous article in 1969 stating: 'Compensatory education has been tried and it has publicly failed.'[135] He believed that the environmentalist assumptions of Head Start were misguided.

Other studies followed. They indicated some immediate benefits and gains for children in their early years of schooling,[136] but not sufficient to enable Head Start to be seen as the magic weapon in the 'war on poverty'. Bronfenbrenner also conceded that the original results were 'disappointing'.[137] Yet he remained a key defender, arguing that the grandiose aims needed to be lowered; that the measures of success needed to be broader; and that interventions must be longer. He subsequently launched the idea of 'ecological interventions' and his theory of the 'ecology of human development'.[138] Mothers and families were pleased with the programmes, but policy makers had hoped for a more foolproof recipe.

In hindsight, Head Start is not regarded as a failure. Despite some lean times, the programme survived. Some of the research projects originally associated with Head Start have since shown that early intervention programmes have long-term benefits lasting into adulthood.[139] Robert E. Cooke chaired the original planning committee. He later recalled:

> In retrospect, Head Start still stands out as one of the major social experiments of the second half of the twentieth century. It was a creative, innovative effort to interrupt the cycle of poverty, the nearly inevitable sequence of *poor parenting* which leads to children with social and intellectual deficits, which in turn lead to poor school performance, joblessness, and poverty, leading again to high-risk births, *inappropriate parenting* and so continues the cycle.[140] [My emphasis.]

The experiment, and its many offshoots, launched early childhood issues onto the political platform of many countries in which 1960s liberal political ideology sought to cure social and economic inequality. But too often the broader structural issues underlying economic inequality were downplayed. Instead, poor parenting, meaning bad mothering, became the focus. That mothers must take the blame was at the core of postwar developmental psychology, to the extent that some researchers concluded that the 'infant–mother relationship … is the single most important factor alleviating socio-economic disadvantage'.[141] In the US this meant black mothers, and in New Zealand it meant Māori mothers, who were told to shoulder the responsibility of being both the root cause of the problem, and also the means of a cure.

REVOLUTION IN LEARNING

The concept of educational disadvantage, as a postwar construction, resulted from applying the philosophy of 'equality of opportunity' to economic and social planning. Not all children were seen to be benefiting from the 'opportunities' provided. The notion of compensatory education arose from views that 'culturally deprived' home environments and 'linguistically deprived' children were a cause of educational inequality. Such was the faith in environmental remedies that programmes such as Head Start were optimistic that developmental psychology could provide a cure. By the late 1960s the psychological 'gaze' was becoming less robust. A sharpening sociological 'gaze' critiqued the ability of early education to bring about economic and social change. Debates on the causes and cures of disadvantage, the relevance and kinds of early childhood education, the nature of children's learning, and the most appropriate curriculum for the early years, were prolific and entangled. With reference to New Zealand, Māori educator Kathie Irwin claimed:

> Compensatory education is not about equity or any sense of fairness or justice. It is about maintaining inequality in society, through education, by ranking cultures and making arbitrary decisions about which cultures will be ranked best … Head Start programmes aimed to take Maori, black and working class children in their pre-school years and give them the middle class white culture necessary to prepare them for school success … Compensatory education denied the reality or the validity of minority cultures.[142]

Earlier chapters have shown how theoretical understandings of child development in the early postwar years were dominated by an emphasis on emotional well-being and psychological adjustment. Maya Pines' popular book *Revolution in Learning* (1966) appraises a new generation of cognitive psychologists. In a chapter on 'The New Mind-builders' Pine explains:

According to the cognitive psychologists, an individual's achievement in life depends very largely on what he has been helped to learn before the age of four. If this startling theory is correct, it requires a radical change in society's approach to the years before a child enters school.[143]

Pines hails the hero of the cognitive psychologists, Jean Piaget, claiming: 'What Freud had done for the emotions, Piaget did for the intellect.'[144] Piaget's pioneering work towards understanding children's thinking and cognitive development shaped the curriculum for teaching and learning in early childhood institutions and schools in many ways. Piaget had begun his work in the 1920s, but it was not until the 1960s that his thinking became standard fare in mainstream education.

Piaget proposed that children construct and reconstruct their understandings of the world through a process he called equilibrium. He defined a universal sequence of stages for intellectual growth, from childhood prerational thinking to scientific rational adult logic. The child's progress from one stage to the next was determined by a combination of maturation and experience.[145] Piaget's infant was an active initiator in constructing knowledge during the sensory-motor stage, when a shift took place from the vulnerable and passive images of the past. As Evelyn Weber notes: 'Now under the impetus of new conceptions of cognitive growth, programs for infants became a reality. Education had reached down to the earliest days of life.'[146]

Piaget depicted the developing child not as vulnerable, but as a 'little scientist' who constructs logical sense out of the chaos of the material world. The new terminology had a powerful impact on early childhood curriculum. The preschool play environment advocated by earlier theorists now needed to provide the appropriate experiences for the trial and error play of the 'little scientist'. Because maturation was also a key to the staged sequence, self-directed experience by the child was the driver, rather than intervention from the teacher, although Piaget said:

> It's not a matter of just allowing children to do anything. It is important that teachers present children with materials that allow them to move forward. It is a matter of presenting to the children situations that offer new problems, problems that follow on from one another. You need a mixture of direction and freedom.[147]

Piagetian students were trained to see the child as a natural experimenter.[148] Millie Almy positioned the Piagetian teacher as an observer, but a thinking one:

To put Piagetian concepts into action requires, above all else, a thinking teacher. He or she looks beyond the child's verbalizations and manipulating and tries to understand what they might mean for the child. This way of looking at and thinking about children was far from easy.[149]

Piaget's faith in the learning environment gave a powerful boost to concerns with educational failure. His theories explained why environments that restricted children's opportunity to explore, to test, to question, might retard their development. The sequences of intellectual development needed a stimulating environment and a 'thinking teacher'.

American optimism in education was fuelled by cognitive psychologists claiming that the preschool years were the optimal time for 'mind building'. In *The Process of Education* (1960) Jerome S. Bruner from Harvard University was concerned that children 'learn how to learn' and that 'precious years' were wasted by the postponement of important subjects. He made his now famous statement that 'any subject can be taught effectively in some intellectually honest form to any child at any stage of development'.[150] Benjamin S. Bloom, from the University of Chicago, argued that the environmental impact on intelligence was greatest prior to school entry at six years.[151]

There was also increasing interest in linguistics. British sociologist Basil Bernstein developed his theory of social class and language development and introduced the view that children learn language from either 'restricted' or 'elaborated' speech codes, depending on whether their families were working class or middle class.[152] Children who used elaborated codes were better prepared for the demands of school. Bernstein, however, was less optimistic concerning intervention; on an American tour he claimed: 'There is nothing I can do to change the effects of social class on education.'[153] Bernstein's work impacted on New Zealand. In the Department of Education booklet for schools *Maori Children and the Teacher* (1972) his theories were explained to teachers,[154] despite criticism concerning the idea of 'non-standard', 'Maori English' as a 'restricted code'.[155] Bernstein did not profess to have a solution to his findings, but was opposed to the psychological notion of deficit and the idea of compensatory education:[156]

> You see the child in terms of something he hasn't got! This loses track of the child's vital experience. It is only one way of looking at the situation, and while it is a valid way, it is dangerous when it is the only way.[157]

Bernstein was concerned that this perspective directed attention away from the broader educational context of schools and society. Nevertheless, the deficit model underpinned New Zealand initiatives in Māori education for several decades. Kathie Irwin claims that:

> New Zealand was a fertile seed for compensatory education. It reinforced the racist and ethnocentric policy of assimilation ... The ideas ... flourished. Indeed they have become something of a weed in the 'garden of godzone', not easily dislodged to this day.[158]

Pines portrays the American debates on the early years curriculum as the raging of a 'fierce though largely undeclared war'. She positions one camp as the 'establishment group'. These were people primarily trained in early childhood education and child development, who believed in educating the whole child and who resisted the teaching of specific academic skills, instead providing a range of free-play 'enriching' experiences for learning with teacher guidance. The other camp, the 'cognitive group', advocated more direct teaching and stimulation, with the view that not taking advantage of the early years might condemn some to a downward spiral of failure. While the 'establishment group' talked of 'fun', the 'cognitive group' talked of 'achievement'.[159] Such distinctions can be dangerously arbitrary, but the debates on goals and methods were real. In New Zealand, for example, 1960s Playcentre play was not always valued in Māori communities, and groups such as the Waikato Family Preschools operated a more formal programme.

Carl Bereiter and Siegfried Engelmann established the most newsworthy programme, at the University of Illinois, by breaking away from the orthodoxy of learning through play. Their view was that preschool must complement the home environment of a disadvantaged child. If the programme was to provide a real possibility of catching up to the middle class child, it must be more academically structured.[160] Their two-hour daily programme for four-year-olds comprised verbal language practice, mathematical skills and cognitive instruction. They claimed: 'Culturally deprived children do not just think at an immature level, they do not think at all.'[161] Bereiter states:

> We have virtually no free play – just the first ten minutes, and the singing, which is pretty structured. Free play is too time consuming and it is superfluous. 'Group experience' and 'playing with peers' are the least of these kids' needs.[162]

Their ideas were too extreme for some, but they represent one end of a spectrum of many positions on a genuine quest to 'do something' about disadvantage through the vehicle of early childhood education. The next section describes a New Zealand project that was influenced by Bereiter and Engelmann.

By the 1970s, however, more voices were challenging the notions of deficit, particularly in relation to culture. Sociological explanations were replacing the psychological and linguistic understandings of disadvantage. In the US William Labov was studying expressions of non-standard English 'as something to be studied and understood in its own way' rather than as something 'negative' to be 'overcome' by education.[163] Views of 'cultural difference' rather than 'cultural deficit' provided for the possibility that Māori children, for example, had their own 'cultural capital' that must be valued as an advantage, not a disadvantage.[164] This would require substantive change from within educational and political institutions.[165] These ideas surface more strongly in Part Two of this book.

TE KŌHANGA: A CHANCE TO BE EQUAL

Commenting on the 1970s Geraldine McDonald wrote:

> Most of the programmes offered in New Zealand are of the free play enrichment type. This type of programme has been widely criticised for being unable to solve the problems of the disadvantaged … Play programmes may in fact be particularly suitable for culturally different children. But it would be socially irresponsible simply to assume this …[166]

From 1974 to 1976 Jane Ritchie led a research project, supported by the Department of Education and the University of Waikato Centre for Maori Studies, which established Te Kōhanga as a preschool experiment for Māori children. The story of this venture is told fully in the books *Tamariki Maori* (1977) and *A Chance to be Equal* (1978). Ritchie called for 'programmes designed to provide what Maori children need and their parents request: a good preparation for school'.[167] This was a specific aim of Te Kōhanga, with a view to 'accelerating development' with a 'language-rich' programme. Ritchie had reservations about the effectiveness of the existing Playcentre and kindergarten programmes for many Māori children. She supported the idea of more direct instruction, claiming: 'It is not enough to provide a room full of attractive equipment and let the children find their own way …'[168] However, there were reservations. Ritchie recalls:

> The programme had attracted a lot of criticism, often based on misunderstanding. In some Wellington circles we were known as the Bereiter and Engelmann programme, even though direct language teaching of the type used by Bereiter and Engelmann for their entire preschool session formed only fifteen minutes of our three-hour session. Visitors to the centre would exclaim, in tones of astonishment, that the children looked so happy! Obviously, they

were expecting a group of sad looking children, sitting in regimented rows for three hours, speaking only when spoken to. Instead they met lively, dynamic spontaneous language speakers, busy and engaged in whatever they were doing, whether it was free play or a structured activity.[169]

Te Kōhanga was named by Robert Mahuta, Tainui elder and the director of the Centre for Maori Studies, and translated as 'The Nest', a ritual place where the rites were performed to ensure a good life. 'Our fledglings were to have few problems as they winged their way to school.'[170] The programme was English based, but included Māori language and culture. Jane Ritchie had had first-hand experience of Head Start programmes in Hawai`i. Te Kōhanga included similar elements, such as support services for families, daily transport for the children, meals, and an ordered daily programme.

Ritchie worked with Nancy Gerrand, a teacher of junior school classes, to devise a programme that provided language skills and concepts judged important for success in the new entrant schoolroom. They used two American resources, the Peabody Language Development Kit and the Distar language programme, both designed to speed the language development of disadvantaged children. About a third of the morning was devoted to organised teaching, and two thirds to the traditional free-play developmental activities. Ritchie felt that the systematic instruction of the language kits was of 'great value', although 'no guarantee of miracles.'[171] This was complemented by a programme devised by Gerrand, where selected books were used as a stimulus to teaching particular concepts and skills, such as asking questions.[172] Supported by Engelmann's book, *Conceptual Learning* (1969), they also sought to identify a range of concepts (such as colour, shape and texture) that children needed to know, and explored how they could be taught.[173] They agreed with Engelmann's view that these things were too important to be left to incidental teaching.

Comprehensive records were kept of children's progress, and compared with two control groups, one made up of Māori children with no preschool experience, and the other a similar group who attended kindergarten. Ritchie was adamant that 'the children learned', and that their gains were in advance of both control groups. It was not possible to keep tracking the children:

> We cannot claim that a year at Te Kohanga would have made a significant difference to each and every child, but it is clear from this study that their preschool experience did make a difference to the Te Kohanga children.[174]

Ritchie admitted to feeling 'bruised and battered' when she left the project.[175] She had resisted what had become the orthodoxy in the mainstream early childhood groups of learning through play, and instead sought to directly 'prepare for school'. However, she claimed that:

> Those educationalists who decry the idea of preschooling as a preparation for school are clearly not on the same wavelength [as] our Maori parents. I feel they are speaking from a middle-class vantage point. Our programme of deliberate preparation for schooling certainly found favour in [our parents'] eyes.[176]

Ritchie's experiment was not repeated, although many kindergarten teachers did run formal group times with children. Interestingly, kōhanga reo programmes established in the 1980s also used more formal ways of learning and instruction. Kara Puketapu, Secretary of Maori Affairs during the 1980s, claimed to have been influenced by reading *Chance to be Equal* in considering the idea of special preschool programmes for Māori children.[177] There are, however, many claimants to the origin and approach of Te Kōhanga Reo within the Māori preschool initiatives of the 1960s–70s.

A few other 'trial' preschools for Māori children emerged, such as Atawhai in Palmerston North. This was run by Joan Kennett, a Pākehā with both Playcentre and childcare background (see Chapter Two), who had spent some years living in a Māori community and had a number of adopted Māori children.[178] Kennett recalls its beginnings:

> At the time Maori children were quite deprived and didn't fit into schools and the Pakeha system. This was the early 1970s. There were no Maori children in preschools in Palmerston. I asked these parents why their children were not in preschool. Mostly I tried to sell playcentre and found that the parents thought they weren't dressed well enough. They found they had to help and felt inadequate and [thought they] wouldn't be acceptable to a lot of the mothers in playcentre who were middle class.[179]

Kennett therefore began her 'preschool' in the corners of jumble sale halls. 'I first took books and then I took puzzles and then I bought an old pram. After a while I asked if I could take the children home. I started with ten kids.'[180] Atawhai grew, strengthened by its associations with the YWCA, Department of Maori Affairs and education staff from Massey University.

To conclude both this chapter and this section it is appropriate to quote Jane Ritchie's final words in *Chance to be Equal*. They illustrate the shift in thinking from the 1940s view that 'social standing in this country has no relation to colour':

New Zealanders say they believe in equality – equality of opportunity, equality in education, in health care, in equal pay. What is happening in the education of deprived minorities is less than equal … The spectrum of changes required in our society to promote equality and make it a reality is very wide; so wide that some would say that only a total revolution could achieve the goal.[181]

This was the 1970s. The tools of psychology had been overlaid by more radical political and sociological critiques. The gaze was shifting away from the individual to reappraise the impact of the structure of society itself on the early education of the young.

PART TWO

Challenge and Constraint
1960s–1980s

CHAPTER FOUR

Politics of Early Childhood

By the late 1960s stirrings of discontent with family life and politics in Western society were generating radical critiques of many things previously deemed 'normal'. 'New Left' writers and activists moved beyond psychological explanations for the causes and cures of social ills, to argue that society itself was sick and the causes were embedded in its own structural fabric.[1] The orderly ideal for postwar society was no longer sustainable, and the boundaries between normal and abnormal were cracking.[2] Issues such as the rights of ethnic minorities, colonialism, apartheid, the Vietnam War and women's liberation fuelled critiques of the power and powerlessness of individuals and groups in society. This social upheaval, with its creativity and chaos, was a far cry from earlier postwar conformity. The language of 'order' and 'adjustment' was overlaid by the language of 'rights' and 'liberation'.

The spirit of this 'counter-culture' was evident in Tim Shadbolt's *Bullshit and Jellybeans* (1971), which documented aspects of the New Zealand protest movement in the late 1960s. Sue Kedgley and Sharon Cederman's book *Sexist Society* (1972) portrayed the roles of wife and mother as unsafe and unhealthy. Arriving in New Zealand were books such as *Down Under the Plum Trees* (1976), which introduced children to the possibilities of the so-called sexual revolution. Likewise, *The Little Red School Book* (1972) brought the language of liberation and protest into the arena of schools, suggesting that children address their own oppression in the education system.[3] Educationist Jack Shallcrass wrote:

> The 15,000 copies around the country may be time bombs of confrontation or a source of co-operative energy and some teachers and principals will feel threatened by the prospect of shared rather than imposed authority.[4]

Radical critique deemed education to be a site of oppression whose institutions reproduced inequity and powerlessness. Jonathan Kozol's *Death at an Early* Age (1968), Ivan Illich's *Deschooling Society* (1971), Everett Reimer's *School is Dead* (1971) and John Holt's *How Children Fail* (1974) presented compelling cases for the failure of education institutions. At the same time there was optimism that new sociological understandings of society could transform education into a tool of liberation rather than oppression. For instance, books such as Herbert Kohl's *The Open Classroom* (1969), Neil Postman and Eric Weingartner's *Teaching as a Subversive Activity* (1971) and Paulo Freire's *Pedagogy of the Oppressed* (1972) focused on how education could be empowering for children, their families, communities and culture. These radical education texts became mainstream reading in New Zealand university education courses previously dominated by the discourses of developmental psychology. Even the *Playcentre Journal* (no. 29, 1974) was once captioned 'Mao, Ivan, Paulo, Julius – and us'. Editor Llewelyn Richards' article was sparked by the visit to New Zealand of socialist President Julius Nyerere of Tanzania – 'another exciting thinker in education'. Richards supported the anti-institution views of the new radical thinkers, claiming that 'the most exciting happenings are Playcentres and all the new movements like them that have sprung up all over the world. In them people help themselves and the children become better educated.' Anne Else wrote in 1983:

> Our society is questioning many of its basic assumptions, and education is integral to the way society works. Early childhood services are included in this trend to politicisation … Politics is about power and power is about the allocation of resources and the definition of values.[5]

The four chapters in Part Two cover the period from the late 1960s to the 1980s, during which demands arose for early childhood institutions to broaden their functions. Campaigns concerning Māori grievances, women's rights, and the status of early childhood teachers and workers introduced a new militancy to the politics of early childhood. This first chapter highlights how concepts of childhood and the role of early childhood institutions become increasingly sociological in rationale. The new 'gaze' was upon rights and liberation in relation to mothers, children and early childhood; new understandings of young children emerged. A consequence of the more political environment was a broad national constituency for early childhood that transcended individual organisations.

The women's liberation movement of the late 1960s and early 1970s challenged the role of women as wives and mothers. In demanding political and economic equality with men, women's liberation groups labelled 'wifedom' as slavery and claimed that the unrelieved tasks of motherhood prevented participation by women in public life. The responsibilities and blame that mothers had shouldered for the mental adjustment or maladjustment of the nation's children was no longer accepted as fair. It was claimed that such intensive attention on childrearing had not been good for mothers or their children. In 1971 psychiatrist Fraser McDonald caused a stir when he pointed to the 'battlefield in the kitchen' and the 'alarming plight' of New Zealand married women who were suffering from the new 'disease' of 'suburban neurosis'. Change was needed, but McDonald told women to 'accept that hoping or wishing or nagging won't do it'. Instead, women should start 'manipulating the environment – send your youngsters to kindergarten ... get a job'.[6]

Women's disquiet and resistance had been growing during the 1960s, but had mainly been contained within the private world of the home. A few women, such as Margot Roth, had dared to speak out. Her angry article in the *NZ Listener* (20 November 1959), 'Housewives or Human Beings', drew a heated response. She wrote:

> So they go in hordes to learn about flower arranging, or cooking, or sewing, or child development ... Such studies too quickly become an end in themselves ... There are several women's organisations catering for mothers and children, but generally they are slaving so hard to organise a ball ... or arranging lectures to tell us where we are going wrong in bringing up our children, that they've overlooked the basic need of many mothers and babies ... [for] relief from the social isolation and the physical strain caused by a 24 hour day.

Betty Friedan's book *The Feminine Mystique* (1963) was a landmark in New Zealand, as in other countries. Friedan rejected the assumptions of 'Freudian psychology', which deemed motherhood to be naturally fulfilling for women, and talked about the 'problem with no name'. A review in the *Playcentre Journal* (December 1964) called Friedan's book 'dangerous', 'stimulating', and 'provocative'. Beverley Morris, a Playcentre activist and mother of four, recalls her own disquiet:

> I had this gnawing feeling inside that something was missing for me. Is this what life is about? ... When Betty Friedan's book came out, it grabbed me

tremendously. When I read it I realised that I had been lucky by filling my life with playcentre work.[7]

Playcentre, however, was not an option or an attraction for all mothers.

The politics of liberation of the late 1960s provided the spark to make the private anger of many women public. Some found outlets in organisations such as the Society for Research on Women (SROW), formed in 1966 when its founders realised that there was no New Zealand research on women. 'The Changing Role of Women' became the popular topic at seminars and lectures. Germaine Greer's *The Female Eunuch* (1972) sold 8000 copies in New Zealand in six weeks, and her visit to New Zealand caused a media storm. The message by Greer and other feminist writers and activists was that marriage and childrearing should not preclude a woman's right to sexual and economic independence.

A narrative of childhood was emerging which differentiated the interests of women and children, in contrast to earlier years, when they had been viewed as synonymous.

CHILDREN HAVE RIGHTS TOO

The growing consciousness of political rights for women led to new insights concerning the rights of children. In 1978 Dugald McDonald wrote of a 'children's liberation' movement in New Zealand, which 'may be explained simply as an outcome of the "decade of protest" or global questioning of social values which characterised the 1960s'.[8] In the 1940s and 1950s parents had been expected to 'control' their children in the interests of an ordered society. By the 1970s permissive ideas, deemed radical in the 1950s, were moving into the mainstream. Parents were expected to be tolerant towards their children, but not necessarily to blame themselves when things went wrong. Child management was now, in the words of Kate Birch, 'to help children become "their own people"; it is not for controlling children ... but for developing potential in both parents and child'.[9] Childrearing literature shifted from viewing the child as a delicate emotional object, who needed the total attention of the mother, to someone whose erratic behaviour was to be survived. Psychological insight was insufficient; mothers also needed survival skills, a view expressed in Trish Gribben's new Plunket-sponsored childrearing manual *Pyjamas Don't Matter* (1979).[10]

Postwar support for families had been intended to ensure a generation of well-adjusted children. By the 1970s there was a reappraisal of the quality of children's lives and challenges to assumptions that all was well. Karl du Fresne wrote:

> The children's rights movement springs from a belief that children born in God's Own Country are a deprived minority. Its supporters are out to challenge the reassuring old myth that New Zealand is a paradise for the young.[11]

The acknowledgement that children's interests should be a matter of public policy did not necessarily cure problems. Nikolas Rose later argued that the Western 'civil libertarian' advocacy for children and the increased 'surveillance' of families and institutions often exacerbated problems for children.[12] Rose also claimed that the liberalising pedagogy of the 1960s and 1970s, which created a child freer than at any time in history, also regulated childhood more intensely than at any previous time.[13]

In 1972 the Minister of Social Welfare, Lance Adams-Schneider, reported 150 cases of child abuse in the previous year and stated: 'It is pleasing to note that … child abuse is not a problem of major social importance in New Zealand.'[14] He was mistaken. Western society was discovering the 'battered baby'. New lenses were seeing new ills, and the case-load of abused and battered children grew dramatically. Bronwyn Dalley suggests that by the late 1970s there was an openness to the existence of child abuse, and social workers became attuned to detecting it: 'Internationally, child abuse was of growing concern, and New Zealand was influenced by overseas trends, particularly the new emphasis on the rights of children as individuals.'[15] During the 1980s the professional 'gaze' came to include sexual abuse. By 1987 the Department of Social Welfare conceded that 80% of children in its care had been sexually abused. Media and public interest increased. By the 1990s this 'gaze' widened to include early childhood institutions, some of which stood accused of harbouring abusers.[16]

The quality of children's lives was also addressed through research. Jane and James Ritchie's book *Child Rearing Patterns in New Zealand* (1970) showed that, despite the growth of permissive views on childrearing, many mothers were harsh disciplinarians. They were fearful of spoiling or losing control of their children. Daily 'spankings' were occurring in 23% of the sample families. 'Control by smacking is its chief characteristic and for many mothers virtually the only control consistently employed.'[17] The Ritchies concluded that:

> New Zealand children are not free spirits following the direction of inner control. They listen not to the still small voice of conscience but the echoes of a loud shrill voice of parental correction.[18]

In a later book, *Spare the Rod* (1981), the Ritchies detailed more explicitly their concern about any kind of violence as a punishment for children. This was not a view shared by the majority of parents.

Dugald McDonald recorded a move away from notions of 'psychological mastery and therapeutic intervention as the principal means of adjusting the behaviour of children towards a *social justice* model'.[19] This was linked with new considerations of the rights of the 'child as a citizen'. New legislation reflected this thinking. In 1969 the Status of Children Amendment Act removed all legal liabilities of children born out of wedlock, and the term 'illegitimacy' was removed from the statute books. The 1974 Children and Young Persons Act deemed that 'the interest of the child shall be paramount' in any care arrangements, and gave children legal protection in court. In 1976 a steering committee, set up by the Christchurch City Council, considered a Bill of Rights for Children. The subsequent Sutherland report addressed issues of children in institutions: their lack of voice, advocacy or legal redress. The tenor of the report revealed conflicts between the rights of children and women. The committee took the view that many parents were neglectful and/or incompetent, and advocated that, where possible, mothers of young children should not join the paid workforce, but stay at home. This view was out of step with the economic realities of family life, and with the aspirations of many women.

The Labour government's introduction in 1973 of the Domestic Purposes Benefit (DPB) was significant for single or separated women rearing children. It brought together issues concerning the rights of both women and children. (See Chapter Two for an outline of the emerging support for single mothers during the 1960s.) In 1970 Major Thelma Smith of the Salvation Army's Social Services had drawn the international comparison:

> In no other country was the single mother who kept her baby left without financial support … In no other country was the housing of the unwed mother left so completely to chance as it was in New Zealand.[20]

By 1973, when the *NZ Woman's Weekly* set up a 'Solo Parent Forum', the tide had clearly begun to shift from condemnation to advocacy, both for the rights of mothers to keep their babies, and for the rights of babies to be reared by their birth mothers.

The DPB was controversial from its inception, particularly as its use rapidly increased. The government had originally argued that the benefit was to prevent children being reared in poverty,[21] but the DPB was soon accused of encouraging the birth of children out of wedlock and causing marriage break-ups. In an early attempt to stem the tide a new National government reduced the benefit during the first six months after separation,[22] but this had little effect. In 1976 the Minister of Social Welfare, Bert Walker, launched his infamous campaign to ascertain whether solo mothers on the DPB were having sexual relationships. The official argument was that if a woman was in a sexual relationship, then her partner should be providing full financial support. A test case concerning Beth Furmage was taken to the Supreme Court and the government lost. In 'Solo Parent Forum' Valerie Davies tuned into the prevailing mood:

> Solo parents are under fire this year. 1977 will go down as the year when they were under constant attack from the community after having gained a measure of acceptance and understanding from it … it is probably the children who will suffer from this unkind attack.[23]

The DPB campaign highlighted the tensions resulting from the new debates on rights. The broader context of this debate, however, caused the government to shift its policy on funding for childcare. This story is told in the next chapter.

WHO GETS TO PRESCHOOL?

In 1970 the government began its first Committee of Inquiry into preschool education since the 1947 Bailey report. The committee had a wide brief: it was to examine the range and availability of services, their educational aims, training needs, administration and degree of state assistance; and indicate principles and priorities for further development. The *Report of the Committee of Inquiry into Pre-school Education* (1971), known as the Hill report after its chair, Clement Hill, suggests little awareness of the impact of the changes in society on early childhood institutions. Issues of rights, however, did cause the question of 'Who gets to preschool?' to become increasingly political. At the time, two out of six children were attending an early childhood institution.[24] It was also the politics of 'Who gets government funding?'

Sonja Davies was deeply disappointed by the Hill report's lack of foresight concerning childcare issues. Economist William B. Sutch, a friend of Davies', was concerned that the committee was 'not given a more imaginative order of reference',[25] and labelled the findings 'the sad little report' that was 'resigned to accepting the slow pace of evolution'.[26] In 1970 there were 300 childcare centres catering for over 6000 children; this included all centres not deemed to be a free kindergarten or a Playcentre. The report noted the growth in centres for 'care rather than pre-school education';[27] it acknowledged a 'growing and already pressing community need',[28] and recommended that industry, the community, kindergartens and Playcentres 'should be encouraged' to initiate the provision of childcare. The means of such encouragement were not given, nor did it materialise.

Recommendations in the report did, however, address the issue of early childhood services for children with special needs. These had been emerging in an ad hoc fashion. In 1960 the Intellectually Handicapped Children (IHC) Parents' Association opened its first preschool, and by 1964 the Department of Education was providing subsidies to the IHC for its centres. The first preschool provision for hearing-impaired children in a regular kindergarten was established in 1960 and the integration of partially sighted children began in Christchurch around the same time. The Education Act of 1964 allowed children with special needs to be enrolled in special schools and classes as under-age placements.[29] At the time, however, only 2.2% of children with special needs were receiving any preschool education.[30]

Following the Hill report, government assistance provided staffing support to enable children with special needs to attend kindergartens and Playcentres. In 1973, 10 groups were set up in selected kindergartens.[31] The emphasis of this policy was to allow for some integration of children with special needs with mainstream groups. David Barney, education lecturer from the University of Auckland, noted a gradual shift in focus:

> [Kindergartens and playcentres] have too frequently admitted atypical children on compassionate grounds and permitted them to stay as long as they do not create a nuisance – that is, they have been willing to provide custodial care. Recent demonstrated concern for the well-being of these children, in terms of calls for help, suggests that the two preschool organisations have decided that they have some kind of educational, in contrast to custodial, role to play.[32]

In a recent review of disability paradigms, Celeste Littek suggests that, in the aftermath of the Hill report: 'The concept of early childhood centres being responsible for the educational well-being of atypical children was emerging – the right of education for all, regardless of disability, was surfacing.'[33]

The Hill Committee took a broad approach to defining special needs. Childcare advocates might have felt sidelined but were quick to grasp the tenor of the focus. Supporting the context of childcare for children with special needs was acceptable. These needs might range from actual physical or mental disability to coming from 'dysfunctional families' or families in economic need or, in a few cases, Māori families. This perception was reinforced by the government's new childcare fee subsidies for parents.

The main focus of the Hill report was to rationalise and strengthen Playcentre and kindergarten.[34] The absence of any forum focusing on social change in relation to early childhood served to institutionalise the two services further. In 1970 there were an estimated 17,109 children attending 592 Playcentres, and 24,389 children attending 311 kindergartens. Additional government funding was needed to meet the continuing demand for places. Kindergartens were seeking to improve their status alongside schools and the teaching profession; they generally accepted that more money meant more government intervention. Not so for Playcentre, however, which saw itself as a radical venture outside the education system. An editorial in the *Playcentre Journal* (no. 21, 1972) stated its position:

> We can be expected to shout if the committee of inquiry findings are not to our liking. **No they are not** … it is inaccurate, ill-informed, shallow, evasive, unhelpful, and recommending disastrous changes …
>
> Firstly, the committee would have New Zealand tie administrative chains around vitality and enthusiasm … You can bet that the officer for [the] Pre-school Federation has already ordered an extra bale of red tape in anticipation … Secondly, the Department of Education doesn't trust us. In this sense we are not alone. They don't trust the Kindergarten Union either. They would bind us hand and foot … In return for cash they would have us agree to uniform training, uniform standards, uniform buildings, uniform supervision, and uniform orders posing as advice.
>
> … The report without saying so in so many words recommends the gradual take-over of pre-school services by the Department of Education … God forbid that we should sell our inheritance of real democracy, parent self-education, family enrichment, vitality, stimulating diversity, cross-cultural success …

The government rationalised, conversely, that increased state intervention was due to a need for better co-ordination, and that higher funding recognised the benefits of early education. This conformed with the governmental ideals of achieving equality of opportunity.[35] There was a growing realisation that relying on community initiative to drive provision was creating good coverage only in middle-class localities. David Barney's book *Who Gets to Pre-school?* (1975) provided some hard data previously missing.[36] Responding to parliamentary questions about the book, the Minister of Education, Phil Amos, stated that the government had given the area of preschool a high priority: 'My aim is to overcome as quickly as possible the situation which Dr Barney has noted.'[37] Barney's study identified 'wastelands' where there were no preschool services. His statistics indicated the impact of geography, socio-economic class and ethnicity in relation to preschool attendance. Nonetheless, by 1973, 46% of all New Zealand's three- and four-year-olds were getting some form of preschool education. This was high by international standards. Yet Barney concluded:

> It is not until this figure is broken down that the uneven nature of provisions on a number of variables can be identified. Perhaps by bringing the grey areas out into the daylight, where they can be seen as inadequate, or even discrimina-tory, the removal of the greyness may be hastened.[38]

Barney called for a 'rethink of traditional beliefs and practices'. He suggested that kindergartens and Playcentres needed to adapt their structures and philosophy towards meeting new needs. He also cited the increased demand for childcare, which had grown in a 'typical New Zealand self-help topsy fashion', stating that:

> … It could be that these traditional pre-school groups are the most appropriate ones to run full-day facilities. It would represent a major change in thinking for the majority of adherents of both groups.[39]

This was not the pattern of innovation in New Zealand. New needs continued to be met by new services rather than the adaptation of existing services.

The Labour government promised increased attention to early childhood policy. The government's best-remembered educational endeavour was the 1975 Educational Development Conference, which aimed to generate nationwide community debate on education. Some 60,000 people from around the country took part in 3000 meetings, and 8000 submissions were received. Marie Bell was appointed the convenor of the early childhood section of the Department of Education, and later recalled, 'I met stirrers all round the country!'[40] The key early childhood recommendation was: 'That provision be made for early childhood education to be available to all children.'[41] When kindergarten waiting lists did not retreat,[42] Amos 'blamed' the conference for 'increasing the expectation of education from the ordinary New Zealander'.[43]

Labour's term of government was fortuitously timed to implement the first wave of policies stemming from the Hill report, such as doubling the kinder-garten building subsidy and opening it up to Playcentres, providing free building sites to both Playcentre and kindergarten, increasing kindergarten training, and improving salaries. What emerged was an increasing focus on preschool provision in working-class suburbs, such as Porirua near Wellington and Mangere and Otara in Auckland. The compensatory model of Head Start (see Chapter Three) was clearly to the fore. These suburbs were home to working-class Pākehā, many urban Māori migrants, and new immigrants from the Pacific Islands. These were issues of concern to Amos; as an opposition MP, he had earlier made the first mention (that I have found) of preschool for Pacific Islands children. In an address in parliament (4 June 1965) Amos noted problems for Pacific Islands children in the ghetto-like areas of Auckland. He called for better preschool provision in these areas, as families were unlikely to be able to afford the establishment costs.[44] As well as a lack of facilities, there was reluctance and/or lack of awareness of early childhood education among families in these areas. While in opposition, Labour had also claimed that the 24% preschool participation rate that the government claimed for Māori children aged three and four was a nonsense, and that the true rate in the urban areas was less than 12%.[45] Barney's research showed that in Auckland, which had the highest Māori population concentration, preschool participation for Māori children was the lowest in the country.[46]

Some attempts at different styles of provision were made to address the issue, such as setting up mobile kindergartens that went mainly into urban areas without preschool centres. Another venture was the Bairds Road Kindergarten in Otara, which operated on a full-day basis. Kindergarten officials assured the public that although Bairds Road was a full-day service for children whose parents might be at work, like others in Otara it would 'emphasise language teaching' for its 50 mainly so-called 'Polynesian children'. A Meals on Wheels service was also provided by Save the Children Fund.[47] The venture was not extended.

The Community Preschool Workers' Scheme, established in 1974, appointed local women to work with their 'neighbours' to promote and encourage preschool attendance. The first appointments were in the suburb of Otara. Preschool officer Miria Pewhairangi worked with the scheme. She tells how:

> Three Community Preschool Workers were appointed – Maori, Pacific Island and Pakeha to represent the main cultures. The concept was that they would be leaders of groups, that they would set up home-based groups and lead them to self determination. It was also felt that through the groups they would build up the kindergartens.[48]

By 1979 there were 28 full-time equivalent positions around the country. A parallel scheme, which employed mainly trained teachers, was the Itinerant Preschool Teacher Scheme for rural and isolated areas, set up after political lobbying by Federated Farmers. A different venture for rural children was the establishment of a preschool section in the Correspondence School. This was started in 1976 with two teachers and 50 children. Within a year there were five teachers for 150 children. From 1977 the Correspondence School also accepted enrolments from children who had disabilities. A decade later there were 17 teachers and 510 children.[49]

In 1968 the establishment of special preschool classes attached to primary schools was approved for areas with no Playcentre or kindergarten. During the 1970s this service expanded, particularly in small Māori communities, although the term 'special classes' reflected the view that this was not a preferred model of preschool provision and that early childhood education was more than a preparation for school.[50] All such establishment and/or growth was encouraged by the Hill report, and the question 'Who gets to preschool?' was reconstructed into a political issue of 'Who doesn't get to preschool?' There was increasing attention to the non-attendance of 'Polynesian' children.[51] Also emerging was some diverse packaging of the idea of 'preschool'.

During the 1970s a few children from the Pacific Islands started attending early childhood centres, but in the public perception, as in government statistics and administration, they were classed together with Māori as 'Polynesian', as if the issues might be the same. In 1972 the Auckland Polynesian Pre-school Pool was formed, and affiliated to the Auckland Playcentre Association. It was composed of Māori and Pacific Islands people concerned with the need for a voice in preschool issues in Auckland.[52] An early reference to children from the Pacific Islands at Logan Campbell Kindergarten, in Freeman's Bay, Auckland, was made in an article written by kindergarten teacher Rose Hanak. She described a programme for 'Polynesian children' where '[English] language is our main concern. To use it is to learn it. We talk all the time, everywhere about everything.' She also wrote:

> Maori and Islanders move to Auckland for two main reasons. Better employment for themselves and better education for their children. Many dreams are shattered. Many disappointments and hardships are experienced. Their welcome is very often cold, [with] over-crowded, draughty accommodations, unsuitable clothing, strange food, and language difficulties.[53]

Both Māori and Pacific Islands families were trying to establish new lives and communities in the cities, but the issues were different. The migrants from the Pacific Islands came from different island groups and brought different languages. Schools were at the forefront of their early assimilation into New Zealand. However, Pacific islands visibility in early childhood issues did not emerge until the 1980s, when populations were large enough to establish centres for the different Island groups. Before them, there were several approaches. An early appointee to the Community Preschool Workers' Scheme was Lucia Aiavao, who worked with newly arriving families to Otara:

> I took one family per day, and worked with the children while Mum did the washing. She could see us. Many families slammed the door in my face and weren't interested … After a while I had playgroups in the open where everyone could see. Street by street, then two or maybe three forming a group. I was building confidence and trust … I was getting letters from teachers, not to speak Samoan, but I was encouraged to work in Samoan and leave the English to the teachers.[54]

A less official venture occurred at Dunedin Teachers' College, where staff and students sponsored a family playgroup for newly arriving families. This operated during 1975–76 (at least). The objective was to 'give English language experiences for Pacific Island children in a setting designed to prepare them for preschool and primary school'.[55] The college also saw the opportunity as a beneficial experience for their students 'in understanding the teaching of English as a second language'.[56] Staff and students judged the programme a success, and the mothers were encouraged to enrol their children at Playcentre or kindergarten. Photographs show a relaxed setting with mothers, babies, food and toys.[57]

The origin of one venture was about cultural and language maintenance, not assimilation. In 1972 a group of Samoan and Cook Islands mothers established a preschool, Lemali Temaita a Samoa, in the North Island town of Tokoroa. Poko Morgan writes:

> Disenchanted with the lack of Pacific Islands perspectives in the town's pre-schools, the mothers of the St Luke's Pacific Islands church organised their own pre-school under the leadership of the minister's wife. The women's own skills in their cultural background, particularly linguistic skills and abilities as natural organisers, made that task easier … Mothers, grandmothers, and aunts willingly became the tutors with a supervisor for overall supervision and planning.[58]

There was no funding from government, because the preschool fitted none of the accepted criteria. Nevertheless, it survived, and this 'do it yourself' venture became a model for the later Pacific Islands early childhood centres (see Chapter Seven).

These centres also had links with initiatives in the Pacific. During the 1970s preschools were being established in several Pacific Island nations. A few individuals were making contact with New Zealand institutions, people and programmes. A decade later, in the 1980s, the impetus and energy of this work came to New Zealand via the emigration of some of these women. Telesia McDonald and Iole Tagoilelagi recalled the beginnings:

> It was Fiji and Samoa who first started the preschools in the Pacific. At the same time, too, the word started to travel around Tonga, the Cook Islands … And that was the time also that we took early childhood correspondence courses from the Department of Education in Wellington.[59]

Both women were involved in the work of the University of the South Pacific to establish a Pacific Islands early childhood training programme for teachers. Contact was made with Jane Ritchie (see Chapter Three), who became an adviser to the programme. The model, developed under the leadership of Tagoilelagi prior to her migration to New Zealand, was innovative and influential in later thinking about early childhood in New Zealand. It successfully incorporated diverse languages and cultures within a shared vision for the early education of children in the Pacific Islands.

By the late 1970s and early 1980s there was an assumption that all children should have the opportunity for early childhood education. Non-attendance was an equity issue to do with culture and class, which might need new kinds of political solutions. Beyond questions of access, there were again questions concerning the programme for early childhood education. The next section outlines some new directions.

An inkling that some parents might want a different kind of programme for preschoolers, other than the current kindergarten or Playcentre, became evident when the first Montessori centre (licensed as childcare) was opened in New Plymouth in 1975. The venture was assisted by an American author of books on Montessori, Elizabeth Hainstock.[60] Earlier in the century a number of schools and kindergartens had been influenced by the work and ideas of Maria Montessori. Interest had waned by the 1920s, but from the 1970s there was an international 'second wave' of interest in a programme that emphasised the sensory experiences of children, and work rather than play. Nicola Chisnall's historical analysis of this 'second wave', still in progress, identifies the key role in New Zealand of Binda Goldsborough, a teacher trained by Montessori herself. During the early years she came up against the wary and sometimes negative attitudes of Playcentre, kindergarten, the Education Department and the education community in general.[61] This renewal of interest in Montessori by a few during the 1970s in fact generated little comment from any of these organisations. The two main preschool organisations were preoccupied with their own changes.

LIBERATING PRESCHOOLERS[62]

Radical education writers and the various liberation movements of the 1960s and early 1970s stimulated a reappraisal by some teachers of programmes for preschool-aged children. By the mid-1960s there was a generation of kindergarten teachers who had been born after the war. Some of these women recall that the boundaries of what had been defined as free play were beginning to be pushed:

> The music had changed. There was Peter, Paul and Mary being sung in the kindergartens. The kindergarten used to get into a mess ... there was lots of creativity.[63]

> In the 1960s there was this explosion of free play that became chaos. In some areas – where both kindergartens and playcentres were hit by the virus – they became chaotic.[64]

Ann Dickason had trained as a kindergarten teacher in the late 1950s. In the late 1960s she was trying to redefine what a child-centred programme might mean:

> While the children [used to have] a choice, the children didn't actually have an influence in the programme, so if the children had any sort of experience the day before, and came into the kindergarten full of excitement, the teachers at that time did not pick up on it and structure the programme to build around children's interests.[65]

As some teachers in kindergartens became more 'laid back' and prepared to let children chart their own path and pace of learning, others were seeing the time at kindergarten as a preparation for school during which much needed to be accomplished for some children if they were not to be disadvantaged later. This became the crux of the debate: where was the appropriate boundary between teacher-determined and child-initiated activity?

The debate emerged from the grassroots experiences in both kindergartens and Playcentres, but was fuelled by wider social and political events of the time. Free play was now being conceived in more political terms as having to do with the rights and autonomy of children. Some teachers were testing the limits of necessary order and questioning old assumptions, often over things that were quite small, such as the limited colours of paint allowed, and sizes of brushes and paper. Cumulatively, this dissatisfaction became an explosion, as teachers began to dismantle the unwritten rules of the kindergarten of the time. Dickason recalls:

> We set up the shelves in the storeroom where children could move in and out and decide what sort of junk they wanted. I guess I was empowering children at that time and allowing children to make choices. We used to make up the mixture of cornflour and gave children the dyes and they could decide the colours they wanted. That's when I first introduced being called by my Christian name and that was quite radical in those days.[66]

Kindergarten teacher Wendy Lee recalls the reaction in 1972 when she too decided that the children should call her by her first name. 'I had my employer regularly on my doorstep. Did I not realise that I was a professional and that children and parents must respect me?'[67]

Georgina Kerr was also attempting to give children real choices. She provides some clues as to why some kindergartens were described as chaotic. 'I just knew that things had to be more accessible; that children, in theory, needed to be able to choose. They needed time to start things and to finish things. Even if it took a week, so what!' It was from this premise she began:

> We had this brain wave where somebody said, 'Let's look at the physical layout of the place. Maybe that will help us initiate some change.' We wanted the whole curriculum area to just transform and to be a place where kids can learn in a way that they want to learn; not where kids learn to behave. We looked at furniture and that was the revolution. We looked at the layout, we looked at where things were, and it just went from there, and then the theories started to come out. But of course it all fell flat because it became uncontrollable. Everything was too accessible. There were too many choices.[68]

The extremes of this situation were righted and out of the seeming chaos teachers such as Kerr began constructing their environment and programmes to foster the autonomy and independence of children, and offer a much greater degree of choice.

Breaking down the separateness of the traditional play areas, such as family corner, block corner, water play and carpentry table, was one aspect of this change. These areas had become the 'subjects' of preschool. Some teachers began exploring the possibilities of a more holistic approach, in which it was all right for blocks to be in the family corner, or sand to be in the water. In some kindergartens there was an explosion in creative artwork. Many kindergartens lost their traditional neat and tidy look: the junk piled higher, the weavings hung lower, and every surface became a possibility for paint. However, innovation and change were not necessarily widespread, as Heather Turner observed:

> Some of the places were still way back in the dark ages in the way that they were controlling children through the formalisation of holding back, to the point where one place was planning to have kites next Wednesday and today was a beautiful blustery day. The kids asked if they could use the kites and they were told, 'No, you can't because we're doing it next Wednesday.'[69]

Just as there was concern with kindergartens that remained in the 'dark ages', there was also concern that chaos had gone overboard. Preschool officer Leone Shaw explains:

> You had these awful situations arising where children had no limits, yet the idea was great. It was sad, because there were wonderful people wanting to do their best, but not knowing when to intervene and when not to … They felt that if they interfered too much, or stopped children or said no to them, they would stop their curiosity from coming to the fore and they would stop their learning in some way.[70]

Lecturer Joan Brockett was a strong supporter of creativity and freedom, but she began to feel concerned that some children were getting lost amidst it all:

> Some teachers did not quite know where they were going … They were standing back and letting things happen … It can't all come from the child. With children in disadvantaged areas you may be widening the gap.[71]

That 'standing back' was the role of teachers was the clear message from the kindergarten training colleges, but, as Margaret Carr explains, there was a mismatch between the theory and the practice:

> The teacher training curriculum was mostly stage-bound, and Lex Grey's book [*Learning Through Play*, 1974] was the Bible. Lex Grey took it by areas, like dough play, carpentry, block play. The stages were totally arbitrary and the implication was that you worked at one stage and then you pushed the children on to the next stage. I never ever saw that in practice.

Carr explains that there were dilemmas in packaging a programme that combined skill-based learning and free creativity:

Once again there were parallel beliefs that were often contradictory … Nobody knew how to put those two things together so what you did was, instead of trying to interweave them, you alternated them in terms of the timetable. You had a mat time when you did the structured skill teaching. But then there was outdoor play which was play.

There was a lot of debate about outside and inside. Inside was seen as much more the skills and educational things … Quite a lot of the three Rs were going on as well. There were debates on whether you allowed children outside immediately, or whether you kept them inside for a while … I inherited a programme that kept children in till ten o'clock, but one of the difficulties was that from quarter-to-ten till ten there was this line-up of anxious children. [72]

Most kindergartens were not on the edge of creative chaos or practising the politics of child liberation. Teachers had clear perceptions about the knowledge and skills that children should acquire at kindergarten. Mat times, themes and often compulsory activities all served to bring order to seeming disorder, and to reassure both parents and teachers that real learning as a preparation for school was occurring. Complex timetables provided some reassurance. 'The programme was determined by the teachers and those were the days of the endless charts … we would have things like art, science, maths, water, sand, singing, games and filling in these blocks would take hours.'[73]

The debate over the balance between child-initiated and teacher-determined curriculum was played out between kindergarten teachers themselves, between teachers and children, teachers and parents, and often between parents and children, as parents wanted evidence that some 'work' had been done that day. School teachers, however, came to expect that children arriving from kindergarten could sit on the mat, know their numbers, shapes and colours, paint and draw, and express their views in front of others. While some kindergarten teachers saw this as a function of their role, there were others determined to view the kindergarten experience for children in its own context, in which the wider aims of autonomy, rights, creativity and happiness were to the fore.

Similar debates were operative in Playcentre. Helen Bernstone claimed to be a 'strong believer in the principle of the child knowing what they wanted and I was prepared to set up a broad structure for the child to get as many experiences as possible'. This was sometimes perceived as radical. Bernstone recalled an occasion in Dargaville after the children had been experimenting with body painting. A man said, 'Oh, you're the new teacher's wife. You're the one who lets the children run around with no clothes on.'[74]

Playcentres were continually concerned about parents who took their children to kindergarten at age four, for reasons of 'school preparation'. Jill Wesselink remembers the stern attitude from Playcentre parents, who were worried about falling rolls:

> At my introductory talk in the Waikato Playcentre Association I got the very clear message that if I was to come to playcentre I had to take my child's name off the kindergarten waiting list. I was very, very angry. I nearly didn't go back, because I felt why should anyone have that power over me to limit my options for the future?[75]

In an attempt to keep the four-year-olds at Wilton Playcentre in the 1970s the committee introduced a fourth weekly session exclusively for them. The issue was political: 'We got letters from the Association ... It was as if we were almost behaving in an heretical sort of manner because we were going beyond the three sessions.'[76] Playcentre had established three sessions in the early postwar years as the optimum experience for children. Free play was also sacrosanct. Supervisor Tony Holmes recalls:

> Playcentre in the 1970s was very socially anarchic ... The naive view [was] that structure isn't really required at all. The idea is that the material and the environment is provided and the kids just go for it as long as they don't actually interfere [with] or destroy each other in the process. We just let them go for it ... The role of the adult was to provide for the child's free exploration as a Piagetian 'little scientist' ... As long as the session flowed and children enjoyed themselves and enjoyed exploring the environment then they weren't to be touched unless they came to you.[77]

This was not necessarily the pattern at all Playcentres: it is difficult to generalise about programmes. In both kindergarten and Playcentre there was considerable diversity. But within both organisations there were attempts to challenge older orthodoxies that had once been radical. As with many of the challenges in other education sectors, the underlying issues were often to do with the rights, freedom and autonomy of both children and adults.[78]

NATIONAL CONSTITUENCY FOR EARLY CHILDHOOD

The 1970s was a decade in which early childhood issues, coupled with the broader concerns of equality for women, became more prominent on the political agenda. Change was slow and substantive policy shifts for early childhood services did not eventuate until the late 1980s. During the 1970s, however, a series of conferences created forums for an early childhood voice distinct from the advocacy of organisations. The decade was dominated by strong demands for childcare provision and funding, but the backdrop was the emergence of a national constituency for early childhood. Anne Meade recalls 'a whole set of events and occasions [in the 1970s] where it was possible to develop the discourse, advance it, and keep it moving in a variety of places. There was [an evolving] network of people.'[79] A blueprint for early childhood policies that encompassed all groups slowly emerged. Similarly, an advocacy of early childhood issues by women's organisations, political groups, trade unions and other education sector groups slowly began. The politics of early childhood became a reality. The new discourses that were gaining acceptance can be summarised as follows:

- A broader concept of early childhood care and education replaced the notion of preschool education.
- Quality childcare was an acceptable form of early education for children and support for families.
- Quality care and education were the right of all children, irrespective of the service they attended.
- Childrearing responsibilities were understood to be a barrier to women's equal participation in society.
- The status of work in early childhood was equal to that of the other education sectors.

The government initiated the first inclusive forum for an early childhood voice after the Hill report recommended the establishment of a National Advisory Council on Pre-school Education (NACPSE), which was to include regional preschool committees. NACPSE was advisory, not political. Policy advocacy was still driven by the respective organisations.[80] Nevertheless, NACPSE and its committees provided a meeting place where leaders from childcare, Playcentre and kindergarten organisations met, talked and tried to find a frame for common opinions. A retrospective view is that this was the only useful role NACPSE played.[81]

The United Nations International Women's Year (IWY) in 1975 provided a stage for linking early childhood education with issues of equality of women. A select committee had been established by parliament in 1973 to 'receive submissions and evidence of the extent of discrimination of women in New Zealand'.[82] Interestingly, none of the early childhood organisations presented oral or written submissions. Yet the committee's report paid considerable attention to childcare, 'accept[ing] the principle that for women to achieve genuine choice in their lives some of the responsibility for the care of the young must be borne by the wider community'.[83] By mid-decade many organisations and individuals supporting equal opportunity for women saw early childhood institutions as a solution to part of the problem. Advocacy was couched in terms of the benefits for both women and children. Each of the early childhood services, to varying extents, aligned their own political advocacy similarly.

For IWY the government funded a Committee on Women, and Rosslyn Noonan was appointed IWY national co-ordinator. A key player in the politics of early childhood over the next 15 years, Noonan recalls:

> 1975 is the crucial year because it brought together early childhood education and the women's movement which had overlapping issues … Early childhood education people … were beginning to analyse their inability to deliver what they saw as incredibly important – equality for all children … A number of us who were in that first wave of feminists also had young children. We knew about suburban neurosis … The issues I was involved with [during 1975] were … focusing not so much on women working full time, but [rather] on gaining a healthier community which supported families with young children. I don't think we succeeded.[84]

The big event of the year was the United Women's Convention, held in Wellington, which brought together 2000 delegates from a broad range of women's groups. Issues to do with childrearing were pervasive throughout the deliberations. There were groups for and against abortion and childcare, and groups separately supporting women in the workforce and homemakers. Divergent beliefs could still be subsumed within a general premise that childrearing women needed more support from society, governments and men. Anthropologist Margaret Mead was the keynote speaker. Her address on the contribution of women in the world was laced with anthropological insights on childrearing.[85] The three commentators on Mead's address all had interesting links to early childhood: anthropology student Cathy Wylie later became a researcher on early childhood policy issues; Ephra Garrett, a psychologist, had a long involvement in Playcentre; and Sonja Davies was a longstanding trade unionist and campaigner for childcare.[86]

Two government-sponsored conferences followed: one on Education and the Equality of the Sexes in 1975, and the Conference on Women in Social and Economic Development in 1976. These again provided a forum for widening the network of women who saw early childhood education as a site for feminist activism. It was during the planning for the former that Noonan recalled her first meeting with Geraldine McDonald, Beverley Morris and Marie Bell: 'They told me what they had been involved in, what they were up against and what the real issues were. They were wonderful, amazing women.' All four women convened working groups at the conference. Not surprisingly, issues relating to early childhood surfaced across a number of the groups. Anne Smith, recently appointed lecturer in education at the University of Otago and an advocate for childcare, was also present. The headline in the conference proceedings stated: 'Early Childhood Education: An Angry Group'. Their report addressed the status of early childhood in the education sector. Noonan wrote:

> An analysis of the staffing structure of early childhood educational services revealed a disproportionate number of women at the bottom and an equally disproportionate number of men at the top. The workers are almost exclusively female, the consumers are children and their families, and [the] decision-makers [are] men. The present structure and status of women in education is simply a reflection of the status and role of women in New Zealand.[87]

The wide-ranging recommendations indicated a new level of thinking about early childhood policy that transcended organisations. This was the first of a series of conference calls to transfer responsibility for childcare from the Department of Social Welfare back to Education (see Chapter Two). There was also explicit recognition that the Hill report had been 'constrictive' in its terms of reference, representing 'a male, white, middle-class view'.[88] At a Twenty Years On conference in 1995 Meade summed up the mood of the 1975 conference, where 'being bold' did eventually pay off.[89] At the time, however a confidential departmental response to the recommendations on early childhood indicated that much needed to be done: the policy frameworks were inadequate, and more political will would be required than government officials possessed.[90] Moreover, a conservative National government had returned to power with a landslide victory in late 1975.

The new prime minister, Robert Muldoon, found himself opening the Prime Minister's Conference on Women in Social and Economic Development in Wellington in March 1976. Muldoon's address indicated a cautious government response to demands for equality of opportunity for women. He emphasised a preference for attitudinal rather than legislative change, and reiterated his government's belief in the institutions of marriage and the family unit.[91] This conference was nevertheless significant for early childhood. One of the three syndicates was on Women and the Care of Children and Other

Dependants, convened by McDonald and Noonan, with Morris preparing resources and Bell ever present: Iritana Tawhiwhirangi from the Department of Maori Affairs, a leader on Māori preschool education issues, was also present, as was Sonja Davies. Two basic premises regarding the care of children were agreed. The first was that the raising of children is the equal responsibility of fathers and mothers, and that there is an overall community responsibility. The second was that it is in the interests of the child and society as a whole for both women and men to participate equally at all levels in the field of early childhood care and education.[92] The conference also addressed the need for a national childcare policy (the detail and the aftermath are discussed in the next chapter). What was emerging was a group of women who were now orchestrating a campaign that positioned early childhood issues in relation to the role of women on the political agenda. Anne Smith sums up the mood:

> It brought together, for the first time, a diverse group of women from all over the country. The fact that we were able to get close to a consensus by 1980 was very influential. This link of feminism with early childhood was very important, because I didn't see it happening overseas where early childhood people had this very nice image, and they wouldn't be too loud. Yet in New Zealand these people were deciding to speak with a clear voice. They began saying that this is important work women are doing that isn't valued, and it isn't getting nearly as much funding as other levels in the education system. We began to get what Anne Meade has talked about, 'a cumulative discourse'. I know the origin of the movement went back to Sonja Davies in 1960, but I think the mid-1970s brought it together.[93]

In the aftermath of this conference the Department of Education advertised a senior position for a Director of Early Childhood. Geraldine McDonald was invited to apply, but in an unpleasant backtracking by the department, ostensibly due to the possibility of an internal appeal, she withdrew her application. A campaign orchestrated by the NZFKU and a senior department official was behind this about-turn. Ultimately a male departmental appointee (but not the early childhood candidate who might have appealed) was appointed. He had no early childhood experience. Early childhood groups all round felt aggrieved.

A series of early childhood conferences and seminars then built up cross-organisational understandings. The first early childhood convention, held in 1975, attracted 50 speakers and 1000 delegates, and brought together people from a range of services, organisations, and government agencies, as well as university academics, researchers and teacher education groups. International guests also broadened the perspective. An address by William L. Renwick, Director General of Education, 'Early Childhood Education: A Moving Frontier', highlighted the changing dynamics of the field since the 1971 Hill report (whose 'verbal banner' was 'preschool education') to the 1972 Labour Party Manifesto (which talked of 'early childhood education'), and the recent 1975 Report of the Parliamentary Select Committee on Women's Rights, which addressed 'childcare'.[94] The governmental response to the 'moving frontier' was slow; nevertheless, Renwick's address signified that change was under way, and that new understandings and directions would be needed. Renwick also noted the emergence of a 'national constituency' for early childhood. Members of the constituency, however, found the translation of changing attitudes into new policies and practices frustratingly slow.

In 1978 New Zealand hosted an Organisation for Economic Co-operation and Development (OECD) governmental conference on early childhood. This was an opportunity to showcase and critically appraise New Zealand endeavours in early childhood care and education. McDonald was determined that early childhood provision should be linked to issues for women:

> I was on the planning committee, which included kindergarten and departmental administrators. The conference was suppose to be about planning. I pointed out that if you wanted to plan you needed to understand changes in women's role. There was a disapproving silence and someone said that she didn't think we needed anything like that. Anyway I was later asked to talk on the topic. Even at the conference there was clearly a fear that to talk about the role of women meant a rabble rousing call for women's liberation.[95]

Anne Meade was on the organising committee, and also a researcher for the conference. Along with Anne Smith, Maris O'Rourke and Rosslyn Noonan she was determined to link issues for women with early childhood provision. Smith recalls the OECD conference as the time when childcare workers started having a voice.[96] Meade remembers

> the final sessions [where] there were discussions about how to take further steps to get a better policy framework. One of the things that emerged was that there wasn't an overall country strategy or framework. Another point was the weakness of the state sector role in early childhood policy and provisions.[97]

During the conference the concept of diversity with co-operation between services was to the fore, and the idea of integrated services for young children, incorporating care, education and health, was seriously addressed. Renwick again provided a frame for the shifting discourse, noting the 'quickening' interest in early childhood that had begun during the 1960s as a response to issues of inequality. Ten years on Renwick acknowledged new 'questions' for early childhood education in relation to 'the institutions of the family ... being reformulated'.[98] In a summing-up address he listed the elements underpinning the 'changing model' of early childhood for a society that included acknowledgement of, for example, cultural diversity, the equality of the sexes, the rights of children, the strains of motherhood, employed mothers, and diverse family arrangements.[99]

The so-called disorder of the 1950s and the challenges of the 1960s were clearly infiltrating mainstream thinking. For example, the negative attitudes of those within Playcentre and kindergarten to childcare showed signs of softening, due in part to the advocacy of people such as Noonan with kindergarten teachers, and Morris with Playcentre.[100] Change on the political front was slower.

THE YEAR OF THE CHILD – THE WORLD OF THE CHILD

1979 was the International Year of the Child (IYC). A National Commission was established and a Committee for Children was appointed to orchestrate events arranged around monthly themes relating to the well-being of children. Early childhood groups and organisations were involved in a range of endeavours. New Zealand buzzed with activity and a Telethon raised $2.7 million for child-related projects. The New Zealand Association of Childcare Centres was successful in getting a grant to support a training programme for childcare staff.

IYC reports from the United Nations provided insight into events and issues worldwide, while in New Zealand *Impact* magazine gave monthly updates on activities. Issues to do with the rights of children were to the fore, and in December a short-lived National Children's Council 'invaded parliament' for a day.[101] The final IYC report presented recommendations on a broad range of issues for children. There was nothing surprising in the strong endorsement of more inclusive early childhood policies. The committee adopted a statement of principles already agreed at the 1978 OECD conference.[102] The 'cumulative discourse', which began the decade with 'stirrers', had gained both momentum and acceptance.

The highlight of the early childhood calendar that year was the second early childhood convention in Christchurch. Urie Bronfenbrenner's visit to New

Zealand was a great success. His bestselling book, *Two Worlds of Childhood: USSR and USA* (1970), had provided fascinating insights into the cultural context of childhood, and the political contexts of childrearing and development. Bronfenbrenner introduced New Zealand educators to his now famous (but in 1979 recently published) theory of *The Ecology of Human Development* (1978), which pushed thinking about child development beyond its older psychological frame of mother–child relationships. Bronfenbrenner used the context of IYC to illustrate an ecological view of development set within a broader social and cultural context. He argued:

> If the Year of the Child in your society or mine is not the year of the parent … the year of the pre-school, the year of the school, the year of the neighbour-hood … if it is only the Year of the Child alone – then it will be a year of loneliness for children and an ill one for their future and ours.[103]

Bronfenbrenner called for a society that cared for its carers. He argued that the carers of children needed supportive institutions to care for them. For Bronfenbrenner, the child and child development were not conceived in a series of ages and stages, but in terms of transitions and connections between the various settings of a child's expanding world.

Bronfenbrenner's visit was timely. He was suggesting a theoretical framework that encompassed diverse family styles of childrearing (the microsystem), existing within an increasingly wider social and cultural network of relation-ships (the mesosystem) and political and economic structures (the exosystem). This allowed different early childhood groups to see a place and a role for themselves, whereas earlier developmental theories had judged particular early childhood institutions as acceptable or unacceptable according to the time spent by children in the daily presence of their mothers. The 'changing model' for early childhood services was moving beyond the provision of preschool education for the benefit of the child alone. A range of services should provide 'caring support' to children, families and communities.

CHAPTER FIVE

Demanding Childcare

It is 1971. The placard around the toddler's neck reads: FREE MUM, FREE DAD, FREE ME, FREE CHILDCARE. Crouched beside the toddler and holding a baby is Pam Croxford, a future president (1985–89) of the New Zealand Childcare Association (as it is to be renamed in 1981). The family was photographed on a women's liberation protest march in Auckland demanding childcare.[1] By the 1970s the issue of childcare was undergoing a transformation, from a service for mothers who 'unfortunately' had to be employed out of the home, to an institution enabling liberation for women from full-time childrearing. The transformation was not so neat and never complete. Nevertheless, the image of assertive motherhood was a shift from the earlier imagery of contented domestic motherhood, and the flipside of the recently discovered 'suburban cabbage'.[2]

In 1971 Sonja Davies wrote from Eastern Siberia describing the childcare she had seen in a five-month tour across Britain, Scandinavia and the Soviet Union:

> The bandwagons of the world are now crowded with people preaching what we have been crying in the wilderness for a long time. I am so hopeful about 1972 and Childcare and I know that we will continue to fight for the goals which are so important to us all.[3]

While women such as Croxford were campaigning for childcare on the streets, Davies was manoeuvring political institutions towards change. She had her hopes pinned on the Committee of Inquiry into Pre-School Education. The disillusionment that Davies felt when the subsequent Hill report side-stepped childcare issues has been described. This pattern of expectation and disappointment was to characterise the many years of activism prior to the 1989 Before Five reforms, which were finally inclusive of childcare. Nevertheless, small gains en route were significant and cumulative towards convincing society in general, and politicians in particular, that childcare was integral to both family life and the early education of children. Davies' activism continued though the 1970s and 1980s, as her increasing trade union presence was combined with championing issues for women.[4] She was also a member of parliament in the Labour government that was to develop the Before Five policies.

This chapter backgrounds the politics of childcare demands and opposition to them during the 1970s and early 1980s. The visits to New Zealand of John Bowlby in 1973, James and Joyce Robertson in 1974 and Bettye Caldwell in 1977 illustrate differing positions in the debate. The broader backdrop of the emergence of a national constituency for early childhood has been outlined. Part of that constituency was a public voice for childcare. Creating an acceptable voice, inclusive of feminist demands alongside older rationales and concerns, was not easy. There had to be a reappraisal of what was good for women and what was good for children. If childcare was to be accepted, the two had to be seen as 'hand in glove' rather than opposed. The 1970s became a decade in which the arguments were polemic, but there was a cautious assessment that all views could be meshed together under a rationale concerning the 'needs of the child'. Not until 1984 would government policy address childcare issues in relation to the 'needs of women'.

CAMPAIGN TACTICS

Geraldine McDonald listed the interested parties in the 'politics of childcare' as including:

> The established pre-school movement, the childcare movement, the Government Departments of Health, Education and Welfare, women's groups of differing persuasions, employers, employee organisations, 'experts' in child development and care, men, political parties and 'society at large'.[5]

Childcare became political in terms of campaign tactics for public and political support. It also challenged the entrenched values that had always constrained its growth. This new visibility won friends, created opponents, and heralded the first cautious acknowledgement that 'something had to be done'. William Renwick's address to the 1975 Early Childhood Convention (see Chapter Four) summed up the 'moving frontier' in early childhood education policy to a mainly kindergarten and Playcentre audience:

> Most of us who have thought about early childhood education find the circumstances of these parents so foreign to our experiences, and the situation of their

children so fraught with the possibilities of damage, that we are ill-equipped to find satisfactory educational answers to the problems they pose.

Renwick went on to pose a much-quoted challenge:

> We have to break the mould of our own convictions and attitudes before we can begin to think constructively about finding solutions to situations as they are, not as we would like them to be.[6]

In 1971 the trade union organisation the Federation of Labour (FOL) adopted a policy on childcare – just one example of new groups entering the debate. Similarly the Labour Party, in opposition, attacked the government, claiming: 'Many solo parents are forced to go out to work, and totally inadequate facilities are available for their pre-school children ... no community can ignore this responsibility.'[7] In October 1972 a petition 'praying that immediate steps be taken to provide financial assistance to childcare centres' was tabled in parliament.[8] Sonja Davies, an organiser of the petition, worked hard inside the Labour Party. She recalls the 1972 campaign trail:

> I opened the morning paper to see on the main page a long and detailed article on childcare. My views on the subject were featured prominently. In a small box in the corner of the page was a short report of a meeting ... addressed by the Leader of the Opposition, Mr Norman Kirk. Oh, I thought, Norm won't like that in election year ... he was not pleased.[9]

Nevertheless, the party announced its intentions 'to provide adequate and supervised childcare centres throughout the country ... [with] consideration being given to the importance of the educational and developmental environment'.[10]

Opinion was divided, although not neatly aligned. The Federation of New Zealand Parents' Centres (FNZPC), which had been at the forefront of radicalism in the 1950s (see Chapter One), leaned towards a conservative stance on childcare. At its 1972 conference delegates 'expressed concern over the current drive toward all-day child-care centres'. A unanimous resolution expressed 'grave concern [about] the uninformed public pressure to establish a network of childcare centres without adequate safeguard'.[11] Delegates were concerned about the emotional risks for children separated from their mothers, and the poor quality of many centres. There was a range of opinion within Parents' Centre itself, from those wanting to stem the tide against childcare, towards an acceptance that it was necessary for some families, and that the Parents' Centre must be an advocate for better-quality provision.

Eminent University of Auckland educationist Marie Clay wrote two key papers informing the FNZPC conference debate. The titles indicate the shifts in thinking. In the first, 'Day-care Centres: Their Psychological Hazards', Clay acknowledged the conflict between the rights of women as individuals and the needs of children. She then outlined the negative consequences for children in full-day childcare, and summed up: ' … no group care ever reaches the heights of interaction that can occur in mother–child interactions'.[12] However, she called for a national training scheme, model nurseries and a government subsidy for solo parents. In the second paper, 'Therapeutic Daycare Centres of the Future', Clay described a venture into childcare in Mangere, Auckland, by the British charity Barnardos, to support families in crisis, and solo mothers in particular:

> There is an important function in this to set against the argument of critics of day-care centres who believe that establishing new centres would encourage mothers to work when their children need them at home.[13]

The 'therapeutic' framework was an acceptable political solution.

Meanwhile, the NZACCC continued to lobby as it waited for the new Labour government to act on its promises. The government, and particularly the Minister of Social Welfare Norman King, were reported to be taking a 'conservative line'. This, it was claimed, had the backing of Prime Minister Norman Kirk, 'a firm believer in the value of the family unit and the worth of the mother's role in raising children'.[14] King was concerned that assistance to childcare should not be construed as 'an encouragement for women to go out and work'. The Minister of Education, Phil Amos, however, was reported to be a 'firm believer in day care', stating: 'Easily available day care facilities would be a great release for frustrated mothers, particularly solo parents, and go a long way towards beating the problem of suburban neurosis.'[15] Consideration of the promised policy for childcare rested jointly with the Ministers of Social Welfare and Education.

In October 1973 the wait was over. The government announced 'the first venture of a New Zealand Government into daycare',[16] and introduced a capital works subsidy for non-profit-making centres that could demonstrate a considerable welfare component.[17] It also introduced a means-tested fee subsidy, via approved voluntary organisations, of $4.50 per week to parents in cases where 'the child would benefit from care'. In an explanation to the Family Life Education Council which had urged caution, the Minister of Social Welfare acknowledged that the policy might cause 'healthy debate'.[18]

He claimed that the policy was based on Clay's idea of 'therapeutic day care', and assured the council: 'This scheme ... will apply only to those children ... in need of day care for their own sake, and not just for the convenience of the parents.'[19] In a parallel policy, as part of a broad welfare package, the minister introduced the DPB as an entitlement for solo parents.[20]

The fee subsidy to parents 'in need' gave sustenance to centres, allowing them to raise their fees to realistic levels. It also encased childcare funding within a welfare framework, separate from education. Sonja Davies felt aggrieved that childcare should be 'regarded as a charitable function for the deprived rather than a positive support for family life ... We cannot see this first step being the real beginning of a sound policy for the future.'[21]

The minister told the 1974 NZACCC conference:

> Normal family life should remain the paramount unit for childcare in the community ... we have not and will not design a scheme which will encourage mothers to place their children in care unnecessarily.[22]

This view remained the basis of government policy until 1984. However, despite government timidity, childcare at last had a 'toe-hold', and the scheme enabled growth in full-day provision, particularly in the community sector. In 1971 there were 2807 full-day places and 6141 part-day places. A decade later, in 1981, there were 5300 full-day places and 6778 part-day places.[23] The subsidy scheme was, however, fraught with injustice. It was dependent on voluntary organisations' ability to administer the approvals for eligibility and the delivery of the subsidy to centres. Even into the 1980s there were regions and individuals unable to access the subsidy.[24] Parents whose children were in privately-owned centres missed out unless there was a voluntary organisation willing to act as an agent.

In 1974 Crispin Gardiner established the Hamilton Daycare Centres Trust, which managed the subsidy throughout the Waikato. He recalls:

> It was a crazy and chaotic way to set up a childcare funding scheme. Administratively the Department [of Social Welfare] derelicted any responsibility towards assisting an orderly development of childcare.[25]

The trust was one organisation that did benefit from the policy. Two centres were established with the new capital works subsidies, and a family daycare scheme was begun. The trust was successful in arranging fee subsidies for a high percentage of its parents across both community and private centres.[26] There was a wide interpretation of the needs of families and children, which embraced financial, welfare and educational rationales. This depended on the advocacy of the voluntary organisation, and the viewpoint of the local Social Welfare official approving the subsidies. There were disagreements and changing departmental edicts; nevertheless, increasing numbers of children and families were judged as 'in need'.

ATTACHMENT AND SEPARATION

In the heat of the debates for and against childcare John Bowlby visited New Zealand, presenting seminars and appearing on television to explain his theory of attachment and loss.[27] Bowlby had distanced himself from the rhetoric of love–hate emotions felt by the child for the mother espoused in his earlier work on maternal deprivation (see Chapter Two). Attachment theory presupposed an innate tendency for babies to want attachment, but also to explore the world. Insecure attachment resulted from situations where mothers were absent or non-sensitive. Such infants demonstrated both 'anxious' and 'avoidant' behaviour, lacked self-confidence and were potentially damaged in their development. Mothers were still central. Elly Singer explains:

> The reason for mental disturbance is no longer the mother [figure] who has been inadequate in helping her child to regulate emotional conflicts, but is now the mother [figure] to whom the child is insecurely attached.[28]

The collaboration of Bowlby and Mary Salter Ainsworth from the US in exploring issues of separation anxiety in young children was significant in informing policy and practice.[29] Ainsworth's famous *Stranger Situation Test* created a laboratory scenario in which the infant was exposed to a variety of situations in which the mother left, a stranger entered, and the mother returned. The scores of the infant's reactions were classified in accordance with symptoms of being securely or anxiously attached.

Bowlby advocated a range of policy measures to facilitate early attachment, including access by mothers to their babies in hospital after birth. While in New Zealand he was frequently asked his views on childcare. He said: 'I look on daycare centres as I look on smoking and its links with cancer.'[30] Bowlby was particularly opposed to childcare for children under three. Bowlby's view of the ideal mother as a psychiatrist or therapist, forever available, responsive and sensitive, was difficult enough for mothers to live up to on a 24-hour basis, but impossible to organise in a group-care setting. And, as Bowlby reasoned: 'If you try to run a daycare centre where each child – every child –

has the opportunity of having a substitute mother, it is very expensive. You price yourself out of the market straight away.'[31]

The broader context of the debate was one of competing paradigms of family life and childrearing, in terms of the role of men and women in relation to children, and the respective needs of women and children in terms of emotional well-being. Singer claims that attachment theory was promoted into a 'philosophy of child raising' as a modern variation of the nineteenth-century 'maternal love pedagogy' of Froebel and Pestalozzi. The child's needs were conceived totally in terms of attachment to a full-time mother figure; conversely, the needs of women were conceived only in relation to their children. The consequence, says Singer, was that 'questions about shared parenthood and child-care outside of the home cannot be answered from within this theory'.[32]

In one New Zealand interview Bowlby was unmoved by women's groups that were looking to increase the role of fathers in childrearing. Bowlby conceded that a father could act as a 'substitute mother' but argued that 'his primary role was looking after his wife'.[33] Advocates for childcare agreed with Bowlby's concern for children's emotional well-being in childcare settings, but they were adamant that the issue was one of quality care. They knew, from their own experience, of young children who were thriving in childcare centres with no apparent ill-effects. They knew that quality was possible, given good staff ratios and trained staff. They knew that children under three could become attached to their caregivers and did not need one-to-one mother substitutes all the time. They knew, too, that attending childcare did not lessen the child's attachment to his or her parents. The research evidence was starting to emerge, and the research questions were starting to shift from: 'Is daycare good or bad for children?' to 'How can we organise quality childcare for children outside of the home?'[34]

Helen Brew was then Dominion Adviser to Parents' Centre. Lines between advocates and opponents of childcare were not always clear-cut, but Brew placed herself firmly in the anti-childcare camp and lobbied hard against government support. In 1973 Brew had been in England, Israel and the US looking at hospital services for children, maternity services and child-care centres. At a Parents' Centre executive meeting in November 1973 she reported on a daycare seminar run by Women's Liberation at Victoria University, also attended by Sonja Davies. Brew described a 'most intelligent group of articulate women, [who were] very angry about many issues that we also should be angry about'.[35] Brew was also angry, but at the seeming collusion between the childcare movement and women's liberation and 'its potential damage for mental health':

> If we don't stand up and scream – we don't catch the media [like the daycare people] who, with a highly educationally unsound basis, are now in a position of directing major government policies ... what we have stood for would be wiped away in a very short time.[36]

Brew was critical of the lack of educational background among the 'daycare people' compared with the 'educationally and psychologically sound foundations' of Parents' Centre. She proposed an 'organised' campaign to lobby politicians about the dangers of childcare. The drawcard was the visit to New Zealand in 1974, sponsored by Parents' Centre, of James and Joyce Robertson, colleagues of Bowlby. Brew urged intensive lobbying at a national level to coincide with their visit.

The Robertsons' visit was successful in attracting media attention, which heralded them as 'champions of the child away from its mother'. Ruth Kirk, the prime minister's wife, expressed interest in meeting the Robertons, whose work at the Tavistock Institute in London on children and separation was well known, and both she and Norman Kirk attended the Wellington seminar.[37] The emphasis was on the broader issues of separation, including mother–child separations in hospital and foster-care situations, but there was again a strong interest in the implications for children attending childcare. The Robertsons saw potential harm in both daycare and residential care, claiming that 'parents often put their children in daycare without knowing the damage they are doing':[38]

> The young child under three, going into day care, will be spending most of his waking life under these conditions and will not have the memory structure or the maturity to be able to remember the parents that are going to be there in the morning and evening.[39]

During the visit, Parents' Centre promoted the Robertsons' film *John*, which tells the story of a toddler who is placed in residential care while his mother is in hospital having a baby. The advance advertising proclaimed him 'John – little boy lost, who may cause a revolution in childcare'.[40] The film displays the immediate grief and longer-term effects on a child placed in an unfamiliar setting with too many changes of staff and no emotional connection. John rejects his mother at their reunion. The Robertsons' views were not always applauded. Duilia Rendall attended the Wellington seminar. Rendall was a single mother and user of childcare, attending teachers' college at the time. There, she claimed, 'John Bowlby was still being touted as the Bible':

> ... part of my political awakening was the arrival of the 'Bowlby people', James Robertson and his wife ... I perceived their arguments as a personal attack on me in that I was using childcare, therefore I was a bad mother. I was angry that day.[41]

Helen Brew had already screened *John* (especially flown over for the occasion) to the members of the IWY Parliamentary Select Committee on Women's Rights.[42] The committee was told that 'Today's young mothers are increasingly ... demanding freedom away from children ...' Brew claimed that these mothers were not 'bonding' with their children, suggesting that 'the vociferous women who speak of the "myth of motherhood"' were likely to have experienced a deprivation of love in their own lives, and 'deprived children grow up to be depriving adults'.[43] The opposite view was expressed to the committee by psychiatrist Dr Muriel Blackburn, who argued that good daycare is 'good medicine' and 'can break down the mother–child isolation ... The tendency to isolate mother and pre-schooler in the suburbs is not conducive to mental health.'[44] *John* was screened throughout the Robertsons' visit, and on television. Parents' Centre members then embarked on a campaign to show the film in schools. At that point NZACCC wrote to the Minister of Education expressing its concern at the way *John* was being used, because of its negative connotations about childcare. They were assured by the minister that *John* would not be distributed to schools (although there is extensive evidence that it was shown).[45] The minister suggested that NZACCC identify some films on quality childcare for circulation.

Following the visit of the Robertsons, Parents' Centre established a Working Party for Children in Separation. This was convened by Elsa Wood, who had just returned from a 'whistlestop tour' to Denmark to 'take a closer look at maternal deprivation'. She noted that the older children seemed well adjusted, but was 'distressed and disturbed' after viewing nurseries for babies and toddlers.[46] The working party was active for several years, lobbying over a range of issues relating to children and separation. A childcare subgroup was formed, which consulted a range of early childhood groups prior to developing a childcare policy statement. There were various drafts, with comments by the Robertsons sent back to New Zealand to toughen up the final version.[47] The group was mindful of 'misunderstanding by the daycare people' of Parents' Centre views on childcare. Nonetheless, the assumptions underlying the policy voiced considerable caution about children in childcare, and opposition to under-threes being cared for by anyone other than their parents or a permanent substitute.[48]

In the *Report of the Select Committee on Women's Rights* (1975) considerable attention was given to the need for the government and the community to accept responsibility for quality childcare, if women were to have 'genuine choice' in their lives. There were seven recommendations relating to responsibilities for quality and provision. Anne Smith points out that the committee still took 'the contradictory and definitely questionable position, based on the old Bowlby view, that up until the age of two-and-a-half or three … the best environment for a child is a one-to-one basis or [with] a mother substitute'.[49] This was the compromise.

ACTIVISM AND ADVOCACY

Much of the activism concerning childcare in the 1970s came from middle-class women, who returned to the workplace, sought further education, maintained or established careers, and tentatively explored the idea of childcare being a good place for children, and a support to family life. Twenty-five childcare centres were established at tertiary institutions during the 1970s; each was the result of fraught activism with the various tertiary authorities. New community-owned or parent co-operative centres opened in larger towns and cities. The impetus often came from women who needed childcare but found there was nothing suitable. Some women became involved in ventures as a just cause for furthering women's rights. Others saw a career opportunity and opened their own centre. Several city councils were persuaded to support childcare ventures; church and charity groups also extended their provision.[50]

By the early 1980s there was a broad range of provision; but, in the absence of any direct government funding or direction, apart from regulation (unchanged since its inception in 1960), most of the centres had a precarious financial existence. They relied on the fee subsidy to parents, huge voluntary effort, and staff who were poorly paid and often unqualified. Economy of scale did help, and charitable organisations such as Barnardos were able to extend their provision. In the private sector several small chains of centres emerged, with cute names such as Tiny Town, Mother Goose and Peter Pan. These were modelled on the American childcare chains such as Kindercare, which also established itself, on a small scale, in New Zealand. The overall picture was of piecemeal provision. Everyone was waiting for government action. In the meantime, those involved worked extraordinarily hard.

Helen Orr could not find the kind of childcare she wanted for her child, so she opened a centre in Auckland in 1971:

> I did it with passion, I suppose. I have been told by people that they've never forgotten the time I told them, 'You never call it daycare. I don't care for "days" – I care for children' ... You also got tired sometimes when people in our field called themselves just minders and carers.[51]

There was a growing acceptance of the idea of childcare as an enriching experience, but one different from Playcentre or kindergarten. Heather Lintott opened her own centre in Hamilton in 1970. She wanted to provide educational experiences for children and saw her work as a social service in the community:

> We felt it was needed and we didn't expect to make money – we didn't expect to lose money either! We were really naive about that. We didn't ever charge enough for the service we provided. I wanted children to have the best. We only ever advertised twice ... the word went around that there was this childcare centre providing things like a kindergarten.[52]

Such centres were able to demonstrate that childcare experience could be beneficial for children, albeit at a huge personal cost to owners and workers. Joan Kennett was for many years owner of a centre in Palmerston North:

> There was no government funding for private centres and we actually charged a lower fee than most ... I've always run the centre as a whanau. I never handled the money and have never taken a wage. To me that is my gift to children. It's a personal thing.[53]

Duilia Rendall had a long involvement at Te Kainganui, an inner-city Wellington parent co-operative centre:

> We were amazingly lucky to get any money out of [the Wellington City] Council at all and it was a tightrope ... year after year preparing those bloody submissions and justifying it always ... always justifying ... A tremendous amount of voluntary labour went into that place. There was the washing of the bed linen ... Finally I got a washing machine. It was a wonderful day. We didn't have a fridge either, but finally one of them came too. A family who had a car would go to the warehouse for us. Every single parent had duties.[54]

Rendall was also active on the political front within NZACCC:

We knew that you just had to keep on battering and it felt like battering. There was the sub-layer at which you knew it wasn't going to work, but if you had thought about it too much you would have stopped, and there was something about small returns boosting you up.[55]

In the mid-1970s Cathy Lythe (president of NZCA 1981–85) was involved in establishing the Adelaide community centre in Wellington at a time when she needed childcare for her children. With Rendall, she was part of a group which set up the Wellington Community Childcare Association.[56] Lythe also recalls the barriers on the broader front:

You suddenly realised that you are up against something that is bigger than just childcare. Childcare was just the manifestation of it. As long as you did nothing for childcare you could keep women in their place.

Lythe did not view feminist activism as the important thrust:

There were no structural links with the women's movement. They were not the doers … The theoretical jargon was fine but the people who were really going to sell it were people already doing it … the belief that children in childcare deserve the same treatment, the same housing, the same conditions as any other children. [57]

This was the key argument that galvanised a broad range of support for childcare. It was successfully used by Margaret Lamb, who recalls that during her term as president of NZACCC (1978–81):

I used to trot along to National Party meetings. [It was Tamaki] and Muldoon was the MP. I would talk to some of these people with their beautiful clothes and beautiful homes about people who were not so lucky as them … I was acceptable because I was from a private kindergarten although I always supported full daycare … They could see I wasn't bra-burning and way out. I still had a husband, I loved my two children (which was the right number to have) and the house was reasonably clean! … You just had to keep on dripping away at the topic … the barriers were being broken down ever so slowly.[58]

The negative academic opinion of childcare changed towards cautious acceptance as the 1970s progressed. Anne Smith had earlier experienced excellent childcare for her two children in Canada. Subsequently, Smith became a tireless activist, researcher, writer and film-maker on childcare issues:

One of the first things I did was give a paper at the first Early Childhood Convention in Christchurch in 1975. It was called 'The Case for Quality Day

Care – Liberation of Children and Parents'…There wasn't a single other thing about childcare at the conference. It was very kindergarten dominated – the kindergarten Mafia![59]

Smith assured delegates that 'The development of quality daycare programmes is not a challenge to the family … Daycare is … an additional means of support [and] may actually improve or enhance the quality of family life.'[60] It was the year following the Robertsons' visit. To support her argument against their stance, Smith used the results of American research indicating that childcare could be beneficial and need not be harmful for children.[61] She also quoted from British psychiatrist Michael Rutter's book *Maternal Deprivation Reassessed* (1972):

> Day care need not necessarily interfere with the normal mother–child attachment and the available evidence gives no reason to suppose that the use of day nurseries has any long-term psychological or physical ill-effects.[62]

Smith's favoured model was community-based childcare with parent involvement and professional support from trained staff, 'which should be provided regardless of the family's ability to pay for it' and for which parents 'must therefore expect a greatly increased level of government support'.[63]

On the local front Smith worked with a group to form the Dunedin Community Childcare Association, which gained a grant from IWY to set up a childcare centre. In contrast to Lythe, Smith saw evident links with feminism:

> We wanted it to be for everyone, but it was more of a feminist thing for women who wanted or had to work. But we also had quality principles that we wanted too. We had some ideals about it being for children too … We talked about parent involvement. We would use psychology to plan an environment that we felt was good for kids.[64]

Also involved was Pat Hubbard, who had seen good childcare overseas.[65] Hubbard became a co-director at the centre and, like Smith, acknowledged the strong element of feminism. One aspect of this was that the parents and management at this centre chose not to fund-raise. 'We were really committed against it. We didn't run raffles or run cake stalls or any of those sorts of things. We just appealed for money. We discovered all the politicians.'[66]

In 1977 the NZACCC sponsored American Bettye Caldwell's visit to New Zealand. Caldwell was a high-profile advocate of the benefits of quality childcare.[67] She had established the first federally funded infant daycare programme at the University of Syracuse, New York, as a research project funded under Head Start.[68] The programme operated for economically deprived infants and their mothers, and successfully demonstrated benefits for the children and their families.[69] It also demonstrated what a quality daycare programme for infants and toddlers might mean in terms of a curriculum for children and a training programme for adults.[70] Caldwell's visit was a boost for childcare advocates and activists. A lasting record was a film produced by Anne Smith, *You Can't Afford to be Casual about Childcare*, in which Caldwell tells prospective parents what to look for in selecting a childcare centre, and assures them that a quality centre will be beneficial for their children.

Caldwell had recently returned from visiting childcare centres in China and the Soviet Union. She worked hard on her two-week tour throughout New Zealand, visiting the Ministers of Education and Social Welfare, appearing on television and radio and addressing many meetings.[71] University academics were also keen to arrange meetings. Caldwell's visit demonstrated that opinion had shifted during the 1970s, even if the political will for change was slow. The NZACCC paid tribute to her for the support she gave it in dispelling the myths of childcare. As Caldwell herself stated:

> In any field of endeavour a set of myths and beliefs can develop, which, in time, are reacted to as though they are hard core facts. How can we in early childhood protect children and ourselves from the effects of premature and over-zealous espousal in inadequately tested ideas?[72]

Urie Bronfenbrenner, too, was questioning the role of the early childhood research profession, suggesting that: 'Much of developmental psychology, as it now exists, is the science of the strange behaviour of children in strange situations with strange adults for the briefest possible periods of time.'[73] In an interview with the *New Zealand Listener* during his visit to New Zealand in 1979 for the Second Early Childhood Convention (see Chapter Four) Bronfenbrenner argued that it was important to invest in families, and that:

> Mothers should be able to work ... and rear children. Ironically we have pitted them against each other instead of allowing them to complement each other. I think one is a better parent if one has an active life of one's own.[74]

By 1980 most academic opinion in New Zealand was supportive of childcare policy that espoused quality care for children and substitute care for women.

Issues of childcare were closely linked to changing patterns in the employment of women with young children. At the end of 1975 the National Party came to power. The prime minister's conference on *Women in Social and Economic Development* was held several months later, as a follow-on from IWY. Childcare was a major issue. A position paper, *Child-care: Facts, Principles and Problems*, was prepared by the government-appointed Committee on Women. The key statement was:

> Whether or not a mother should go out to work or remain at home to care for her children is a decision to be made by the woman concerned … She should ideally be able to make a free choice between the two … the lack of adequate childcare centres means that a mother does not really have a free choice between working in the home and in paid employment.[75]

The Committee on Women presented the view that it was in the interests of New Zealand society as a whole that all preschoolers have access to early childhood educational services. Furthermore, the type of service, full-day or part-day, was a matter of parental choice. But who should pay?

The new government stated its position:

> Only in special circumstances is financial support from the community warranted to pay for daycare … it is not anticipated that the daycare services to the families of preschool children should become universally available as of right to all those families who would like to avail themselves of it at the tax payers' expense.[76]

This position hardened in a 1977 statement prepared by the government for the International Labour Organisation:

> Successive governments have been very reluctant to see any policy change that would tend to encourage mothers in general towards believing that mothers are 'workers' in that they are the 'key operation' in the most important 'industry' in New Zealand's future … In 'normal circumstances' the Government has been no more interested in creating conditions suitable for 'working mothers' than it has for creating conditions which would enable others to hold down two jobs simultaneously.[77]

The statement had to be hastily rewritten, amidst voluble criticism of its 'archaic attitude towards women'. It was to be more 'diplomatically phrased': was a bit too 'hard-lined', admitted the director general of Social Welfare.[78] Subsequent policy statements were more diplomatic, but there was no shift in the basic assumptions. The family, not government, was to shoulder responsibilities for care of the children of employed women.

However, the government did at last acknowledge the need to improve the quality of childcare.[79] In 1978, after another election, an Advisory Committee for Childcare Centres was established, chaired by Anne Smith. Its major job was to compile the *Report of the Review of Childcare Regulations 1960* (1981). It was 1985 before improved regulations were gazetted.

Throughout the 1970s numerous research surveys on the childcare needs of working mothers were compiled. The Society for Research on Women played a key role in revealing the issues.[80] The overall percentage of women in the workforce went from 29.8% in 1971 to 39.1% in 1980. This increase was mainly caused by greater employment of married women. Women sought employment for financial reasons and reasons of personal fulfilment, but there was acknowledgement that women, even with dependent children, should be entitled to seek their own economic security.[81] The impetus of the women's movement also generated a critical scrutiny of discrimination against women in employment, as well as revealing the extent of unpaid and undervalued work by women in the home and society.[82]

The 1976 census reported 45,030 women in employment with children under the age of five; 26,250 of these had full-time jobs. This had risen from the previous census and continued to rise. Between 1976 and 1986 the percentage of mothers in both part-time and full-time employment rose from 11% to 20%. For mothers whose children were between the ages of one and four the percentage rose from 21% to 32%. Childcare centres provided for only a small proportion of these children, with the rest being cared for by friends, relatives or privately arranged 'minders'.

A 1981 study by Claire Hadfield showed that 68% of women in the Wellington suburb of Newtown had taken on paid work at some time while they had a preschooler, but only 10% had used childcare services. Hadfield noted the 'makeshift' nature of many of the childcare arrangements, as well as the 'makeshift' jobs women often took to fit in with family responsibilities. There was also a disparity between the actual arrangements women made and what they would have preferred.[83] A number of employers had opened childcare centres. In 1970 there were 11, and by 1981 there were 41, although suggestions that childcare was an employer's responsibility were not generally accepted by employer groups.[84] Everyone was waiting for the government.

A 1975 headline in the *Dominion Sunday Times* read: 'Childcare Unites Women'. The article named many organisations that agreed that a united front was called for:

The National Council of Women has been trying for over a year to talk with Government about childcare ... We get nice answers from them about what they've done and what they're doing, but their overall commitment seems lacking.[85]

This was confirmed when National MP Marilyn Waring compiled *What's Been Done* (1978), a review of the actions undertaken since the recommendations of the *Report of the Select Committee on Women's Rights*. She concluded: 'The prize for total non-implementation goes to ... childcare ... there is no progress.' She cited the Minister of Social Welfare's response that:

Present Government policy does not accept that central government has a responsibility to initiate and promote the establishment of childcare centres ... the family has and should retain the primary responsibility of childcare.[86]

Just as many groups were lining up in support of childcare, the debate became embroiled in other issues revealing deeper chasms. The increasing legislative accommodation by the state to alternative family arrangements and equal rights for women was interpreted by some groups as destroying the fabric of traditional family life and leading to moral decay. Issues such as childcare, and more specifically abortion, became the focus of polarised campaigns. Both childcare and abortion were perceived to mean abnegation by women of their responsibilities towards motherhood, and evidence of women's potential economic and sexual independence from men. In 1978 the Contraception, Sterilisation and Abortion Act was passed, which pleased neither pro-choice nor anti-abortion groups. A *Working Women's Charter* (1978), promoted by the Working Women's Council, added fuel to the fire. Sonja Davies was a public advocate for the charter, which listed 16 areas needing affirmative action in order for women to have equality in the workplace.[87]

The FOL and the Labour Party endorsed the charter, but there was controversy over the clause calling for 'wide availability of quality childcare with government, employer, and community support for all those who need it, including industrial creches, afterschool care and holiday care'. This was interpreted as meaning 24-hour childcare and the National Council of Women would not give its approval to this clause. Nor would it endorse the clause on freely available birth control, because of its reference to abortion. The resulting backlash was to damage the earlier goodwill towards childcare from the National Council of Women. A much-publicised statement in parliament by a leading anti-abortion campaigner, Labour MP Gerald Wall, referred to childcare centres as 'dumping grounds for parents who off-load their children'.[88] Furthermore, he claimed that 'radical feminists resented children because they were seen as a handicap and only radical feminists supported the Working Women's Charter'. Labour MP Ann Hercus replied:

> I resent any male member of this House referring to childcare centres as dumping grounds. I also resent any implication that the Working Women's Charter is supported only by rabid feminists. I support the Charter and I am only a moderate feminist.[89]

Across political party lines, MP George Gair praised Hercus for her 'spirited defence of daycare centres' and termed Wall's observations 'extravagant nonsense'. Nevertheless, Wall's claim became a catchphrase, despite many letters and articles countering his outburst.[90] A well-orchestrated campaign by Christian fundamentalists circulated pamphlets such as: 'Why the Working Women's Charter is a Dangerous Document' and 'Say NO to the Working Women's Charter'. The argument was that:

> The Working Women's Charter promotes the Marxist vision of the family … it's fine political and economic theory to rear infants in daycare centres but it flies in the face of Mother Nature and common sense … The Working Women's Charter calls for the state to become the principal custodian of children. It denigrates the role of housewife in society.[91]

Connie Purdue, a trade unionist but a leading opponent of the charter, was to state: 'The tinsel wrapping of the charter suggested better working conditions for women … but [these] were just the sugar around the pill.'[92]

It was becoming apparent that increased government support for childcare would be successful only if it was couched primarily in an educational context, with children as the centre of the argument. This was the lesson learnt from the 1970s.

'STORY OF A RECOMMENDATION'

In late 1981 the government released the State Services Commission (SSC) report on *Early Childhood Care and Education* (1980).[93] Its gestation had taken six years and its release was delayed for nine months. During this time the government stalled any action on childcare issues because the report was 'in progress'. Then, in 1982, the government announced that it was shelving further consideration of the report for two years. The story of this report is a useful way to sum up the politics of childcare during the later 1970s and early 1980s. Geraldine McDonald, who was a key player, later documented the report's progress in an essay called 'The Story of a Recommendation About Early Childhood Care and Education'.[94] She likened it to the story of the penny that had many adventures, including a tram thundering over it, which bent it out of recognition. 'Finally a little child saw it in the roadway. The child picked it up, and found it was bent and useless, and threw it down a culvert where it was washed away to a mighty ocean. Centuries passed …'[95] McDonald's later view was that the report

> … got sunk because it began under a Labour government. It was inherited by a National government and Rob Muldoon was totally uninterested in the whole thing. When the report came out he was responsible for putting it on the back burner.[96]

Trying to use government machinery to forge a new policy framework for childcare was, in the end, unsuccessful. However, the experience of remaining on the outer generated new kinds of activism, for example from childcare workers, who began to unionise. The SSC report itself became an icon for advocacy. It outlined views acknowledging the benefits of childcare for family and society, and proposed a policy framework for including childcare as part of the education sector, with direct government funding.

The beginning was Recommendation 7 from the 1975 Select Committee on Women's Rights, which asked that 'the responsibility for pre-school childcare ultimately be vested in the Department of Education'. The Conference on Education and the Equality of the Sexes (1975) passed a similar recommendation. It was, however, Recommendation 32 (passed by the Childcare Syndicate of the 1976 Conference on Women in Social and Economic Development) that formally asked that

> … the Minister of State Services … arrange as a matter of priority for the State Services Commission to take all necessary steps in consulting [a list of Government Departments] … to devise an effective administration for policies relating to early childhood care and education. That in doing this there be full consultation with women's organisations, municipal authorities and interested voluntary organisations with a view to rationalising local provision of early childhood care and education within a national framework.[97]

This recommendation took a broad approach to the issue, although there were specific underlying expectations, which McDonald summed up as meaning: 'on behalf of women, consult us and bring childcare into the range of funded services'.[98] The SSC was selected as 'the agent' because of the possible reallocation of responsibilities between government departments.

The tortuous route of the recommendation cannot be fully related here, but it was buffeted by inter-departmental rivalries and a government with little interest in it. The first 'guardians', as McDonald describes them, were a working group of government officials (all male except one) with no knowledge of early childhood. Their draft report, released in 1978, brought a strong reaction from the early childhood organisations. A rare but united delegation including Playcentre, childcare, kindergarten, employers and teachers, led by Rosslyn Noonan, went to the Minister of State Services to express their concern at the complete lack of consultation.[99] The report was withdrawn. A reconstituted working group was established, with a new chair and Geraldine McDonald as a member. 'Eighteen months after the reconstituted group had been set up members were still asking what a "childcare centre" was,' recalls McDonald.[100] It is a tribute to her tenacious guardianship that the *SSC Report on Early Childhood Care and Education* emerged in its final form. The major recommendations were:

- That there be three early childhood services (Playcentre, kindergarten and childcare) with administrative responsibility in the Department of Education.
- That there be 'equitable' funding for childcare and that this be based not on the 'welfare' principle but on the principle of a contribution to a recognised service.
- That the government eventually subsidise up to 50% of the cost to parents.

The recommendations caused both disquiet and optimism in early childhood circles. Some of the earlier unity dissipated, and groups started to reflect on the impact on their own organisations. Nevertheless, 52 out of 54 submissions supported the transfer of childcare to education.[101] The most vocal were those against. The recently formed Private Childcare Federation (PCCF) represented the owners of some private childcare centres that saw their centres as profit-making businesses.[102] They had a cosy relationship with the National government, which they lobbied hard against a transfer. They feared that private centres might be disadvantaged under the Department of Education, although the report had not ruled out funding to private centres. A backdrop to their disquiet was the review of childcare regulations, which was recommending improved staffing ratios, space and qualifications. The costs of these might lower profits.

Also opposed was one of the larger childcare providers, Barnardos, which feared an erosion of the funding base it had established as a voluntary organisation managing childcare subsidies. They argued that their model of childcare was more aligned with welfare.

Playcentre was more generally concerned that government funding of childcare signified a denigration of parenting, and a lack of protection for the single-income family.[103] In a memorable article, 'Report from the Night Kitchen' (*Playcentre Journal*, no. 52, 1981), president Pam Kennedy restated Playcentre's criticism of the Hill report a decade earlier, and argued that the '[SSC] report is a clear reflection of the hobbyhorses of the committee members. At worst it is inaccurate, ill informed, contradictory ... illogical, prejudiced, condescending and unhelpful ...' The National Council of Women was sympathetic to the Playcentre position: 'While the needs of women in the workforce should be well and fairly catered for, the position of those who choose to remain at home to care for their children should never be threatened.'[104] The more extreme anti-abortion group Feminists for Life claimed:

> The real needs of babies and young children are never mentioned in this report, nor any hint of the harm to the parent and child by regular full-day separation. 'Goody' words like 'quality care' (by experts) or 'early education' – which means take-over from birth to extend to all of childhood – disguise this take-over plan.[105]

This apparent lack of consensus was the justification used by government for shelving the report. The outcry of frustration is summed up by Anne Smith:

> ... it is hard to accept that all the patient, restrained work since the early 1970s is to be set aside; that all the 'expert' and grassroots support, reports and recommendations are to be ignored.[106]

There were debates in parliament.[107] Marilyn Waring reported her 'anger' at the decision taken by her 'all-male Cabinet' colleagues:

> If women had been making the decisions they would have been made years ago ... Men have nothing to do with children under five ... And [the report] goes to a Cabinet who are still stuck with Bowlby and maternal deprivation – the sorts of things that were around in the late '40s about women and childcare. We haven't got a chance.[108]

Maris O'Rourke, a lecturer at Auckland Teachers' College, accused some private operators of being a 'tool of government' and expressed 'concern' that:

> As a developmental psychologist I worry about the long-term effects of not funding and policing day-care ... The future policy it put forward would have overcome many problems.[109]

The Minister of Social Welfare tried to counter the outrage with the argument that:

> Putting the centres under the control of the Education Department would commit the Government to greater expenditure because the centres would have to meet educational rather than childcare standards.[110]

This was not convincing to childcare advocates, who had worked hard to convince the decision-makers that breaking the dichotomy between care and education was in the interests of children.

The SSC report was an important watershed in the politics of childcare. The Labour Party adopted the recommendations into policy, but it was not in power. In the meantime, and in the shadow of the backlash of the SSC report, the National government announced a childcare funding package in the 1983 budget. It was skilfully wrapped in a welfare ideology, with the minister still warning that 'the Government does not regard it as its responsibility to provide childcare services direct to the community'.[111] Nevertheless, there were political shifts. Grants were to be paid directly to centres with trained staff and the eligibility for the childcare subsidies was to be trimmed. There was to be direct funding to NZCA, and teachers' colleges were to provide childcare training. Childcare groups were generally pleased, although the level of funding was small. The losers were parents. The policy capped the dramatically rising cost of subsidies to parents. The loudest protests came from childcare workers, who asked:

> More for child-care but who gets it? Is it for workers or management? Centres are only eligible for the subsidy if they have the right staff. The subsidy depends on the workers but there is NO safeguard that any of this money will pass on to improve the wages and conditions of the childcare workers.[112]

The outcome of this first National venture was well below expectations. The moves were a reaction to a potential crisis and were designed only to keep childcare services afloat a little longer.

In 1984 the Labour Party came to power with an affirmative action policy for women and childcare.[113] Ann Hercus, Minister of Social Welfare (and of the new Ministry of Women's Affairs), announced that childcare would be transferring to the Department of Education, and set up another working party.[114] Beverley Morris, Anne Smith and Geraldine McDonald were members. Their report, in contrast to the SSC report, was ready in seven months. In releasing *Childcare Services: Impact and Opportunities* (March 1985), the minister stated: 'The report lays a lot of bogies to rest.'[115]

Childcare services have changed from being ad hoc services used only by families in need, to become an integral part of everyday life for many families. The time has come for a concerted programme of action to ensure their optimum development for the wellbeing of children, parents and society.[116]

The 1985 budget included a $2.7 million increase in funding for childcare. The wheels were beginning to turn, but the pot of gold that idealists had hoped was just around the corner continued to retreat into the distance. The subsequent story is told in Part Three.

CHAPTER SIX

Working with Children

The postwar growth of early childhood services created new opportunities, beyond motherhood, for women to work with children, for example, as professionally trained and salaried kindergarten teachers, volunteer Playcentre mothers, home-based carers or waged childcare workers. This chapter explores some changing perceptions and politics concerning the work of rearing young children during the 1970s–80s.

Despite the increased attention and investment in young children's well-being, working with them remained (and continues to be) undervalued. Motherhood has lower status as an occupation than men's work as breadwinners. This, together with women's lack of access to income of their own, meant that women's work with children in early childhood was underpaid and the services were under-funded by comparison with the other education sectors. Nonetheless, by the 1970s the previously all-women early childhood employment sector was attracting men to its ranks. However, they were likely to be found in the higher echelons of decision-making: in the Department of Education, in teachers' colleges, on district preschool committees, or as Playcentre association presidents. In 1975 Geraldine McDonald claimed: 'Women have lost ground. Imagine the Boilermakers' Union with women in all the top jobs.'[1] McDonald was concerned at the infiltration of men looking for fast-track career opportunities in early childhood, and more particularly at the women who were allowing it. She suggested: 'Men would, in fact, be welcome but so far there have been no signs of hordes demanding entry [to training] – three swallows do not make a summer.'[2]

Feminist analysis provided new frameworks for understanding the political and economic inequality of women. The childrearing role of women was deemed a root cause.[3] Two immediate solutions were to persuade men to do more childcare, and for early childhood services to expand their functions. A growing split between the domain of working with children at home as a mother, and working with children in an early childhood setting as a paid teacher, worker, carer or supervisor, caused stirrings of activism by women employed to work with young children. The labour of these women released mothers from childrearing to benefit from the economic opportunities of the workplace; their professional expertise was necessary for the well-being of children being cared for en masse. But kindergarten teachers and childcare workers alike were also seeking to increase their own value in the workplace. Assumptions that aligned the unpaid work of mothers and the low-paid work of those employed in early childhood services began to come under strain. Challenges by mothers who wanted more social recognition for their role, and by teachers and workers who wanted more financial and professional recognition for theirs, caused the 'gaze' on childhood to be more inclusive of the interests of women who worked with children. This revealed a tangle of contradictions and conflicts about the work of childrearing: in relation to fathers and mothers, teachers and parents, professionals and volunteers, kindergarten teachers and childcare workers, employers and employees.

ROCKING THE CRADLE

Although issues of women's rights and childrearing had simmered throughout the century, they became key planks of the 1970s women's movement, with the maxim that 'the personal is political'. Feminist analysis challenged the myths of motherhood fulfilment, and generally constructed the work of motherhood as an unfair burden.[4] Writers such as Ann Oakley and Simone de Beauvoir argued the non-existence of maternal instinct.[5] Juliet Mitchell listed the reproduction and socialisation of children as elements enforcing the oppression of women.[6]

Shulamith Firestone challenged the myths of 'child emancipation' and 'child happiness', arguing that the growth of the professional and business industry for managing modern childhood was also oppressive to both women and children. Moreover, there was a conflict between the rights of children and those of women; they oppressed each other. On her 1972 New Zealand tour Germaine Greer argued: 'Locking up children in a brick veneer house in eye to eye contact with one parent all day is a recent and extremely unhealthy perversion for children as well as mothers.'[7] Firestone claimed that opting for the solution of daycare centres 'buys women off. They ease the immediate pressure without asking why the pressure is on women.'[8] Unlike Firestone, Greer did not rule out childcare, telling an Auckland audience: 'Mothers as well as children needed daycare centres for their sanity.'⁹ The radical analyses of these writers were challenging but their suggested solutions were unhelpful to most women.

New Zealander Kay Goodger argued that women were slaves within the family unit and should opt out of motherhood. She called for childrearing to be the responsibility of society, and for 24-hour childcare to be provided.[10] An anti-motherhood bias was a strong theme. Conversely, Adrienne Rich argued that women's ability to bear and rear children was a source of power. She emphasised that the unique strength of the motherhood experience could be transformed into a reassertion of female values and solidarity. This radical feminist view found some sympathy from women. However, realising the dream would require a revolutionary transformation in power relationships. For both Rich and Firestone, this began with the personal. As Firestone claimed: 'A revolution in the bedroom cannot but shake up the status quo.'[11]

New Zealander Jenny Phillips gave some balance to the arguments in *Mothers Matter Too* (1983). She suggested pragmatic solutions to mediate motherhood myths of maternal fulfilment, full-time availability and self-sacrifice. The juggler on the book cover was a mother balancing too many responsibilities – childcare, husband, house and job – but 'self' had been dropped. Robin McKinlay linked the postwar growth of permissive child-rearing with a view of 'motherhood as a service', in which the mother's priority role was to service the needs of the child.[12] McKinlay identified a new style of mothering, in which mothers tried to service their own work and leisure needs alongside those of their children. These women sought to share the role of mothering with others. Follow-on research by James and Jane Ritchie from their 1960s study of New Zealand childrearing, conducted in 1977, also showed a 'loosening of the close mother–child ties'. Mothers were found to be happier with their role than a decade before, particularly when they were working outside the home.[13]

Some women were unprepared to countenance any arguments or changes that threatened the values of traditional childrearing arrangements. Campaigns such as 'Save Our Homes' and the 'Mothers' Petition' were intended to create a 'counter-revolution'. Nancy Campbell, editor of *Above Rubies*, a magazine circulated among conservative and religious women's groups, expressed her concern:

> It is sad today so many women are not really enjoying motherhood. They feel that children are a deterrent and a nuisance to stop them doing the things they want to do. But God never intended that our children should be a curse or a

bondage to us. No, they are given to us as REWARDS … When you accept motherhood with all your heart, you will begin to enjoy it.[14]

Questions of 'who will rock the cradle?' were not so easily resolved. Sue Kedgley argued that 'motherhood hit rock bottom long before the women's movement came along', and cited, among others, Sandra Coney, who claimed: 'All the women's movement did was take the lid off and expose the situation as it really was.'[15]

Some men were taking a more active role in rearing children. During the 1970s fathers were admitted to maternity labour wards, and from there it was a more natural transition to helping with early infant care. Graeme Higgs reported in *Parents' Centre Bulletin*:

A quiet revolution is under way [which] is changing our values … More women are now insisting that their partners share greater responsibility for child minding and rearing. As if these changes are not enough women are now pressing for changes in the traditional values by wanting us to express our feelings and become more sensitive! Worse – they want to raise our children as if there was no difference in the sexes.[16]

The 'quiet revolution' was slow to take off and constrained by the workplace, where there was little acknowledgement that male employees had any responsibilities for their children. Employed women with children often found themselves carrying a double load. A 1976 Federation of University Women survey found that only 42% of women had help with housework from men.[17] A 1986 National Council of Women study revealed little change in men's involvement over the decade.[18] My own study of childrearing women suggested that feminist ideas on childrearing and work during the 1970s–80s provided women with the impetus for change and for resisting the traditional ideologies of motherhood, but real choice remained an illusion. Economic and ideological constraints were powerful limits. Most women made financial, career or personal compromises to maintain relationships with partners, or provide adequate care for children.[19] There were insufficient supports within the home or society for mothers to be sufficiently relieved of childrearing to make the maxims of equality come true.

CAREER AT PLAYCENTRE

During the 1970s the Playcentre movement, now three decades old, demonstrated its resilience as an organisation by aligning itself as pro-feminist, in much the same way as it had aligned itself as pro-child in the 1950s. There was no rejection of the older dictum that children needed full-time mothers, but rather a careful, although sometimes contradictory, overlay of positions supporting both the priority needs of children and the rights of women. In 1978 Playcentre was describing itself as

> largely a women's organisation [that] encourages members to move out of the traditional stereotype to become more independent. Many opportunities have been afforded many women to grow and develop in their own way. Individual differences – eccentricities even – have been appreciated and valued adding strength to the movement.[20]

Playcentre promoted the role of men as active fathers and welcomed the few men who undertook Playcentre training. Russell Bernstone described his experience of 'Fathers' Lib' from the traditional Playcentre role for men of 'breadwinning and muscle-flexing' in the *Playcentre Journal*: 'I had only one chance to learn to play with my children. Playcentre gave me that chance, through the opportunity it gave me to gain my Helper's Certificate.'[21]

In the 1970s Playcentre was broadening its base to include small-town, rural and working-class locations. Nevertheless, the mainstay of Playcentre was an urban, educated constituency of women who were also at the fore-front of the women's movement. Some attributed their political roots to Playcentre, which had provided support, education and advocacy skills. Overall, however, Playcentre families were nuclear, with male breadwinners,[22] and not inclined to rock the boat towards radical feminist ideals. Kerry Bethell explains that the feminist element within Playcentre

> was liberal feminism. It was not a radical model by any means ... playcentre was a very receptive place for feminist ideas ... [but] not those that went against the sanctity of the two parent type. Women had the right to do what they wanted as long as their children came first and that was quite strong.[23]

Within these parameters, Playcentre was empowering. Caryl Hamer described

> a lot of changes. When I first went to conferences [in the 1960s] all the presidents were male ... In a relatively short space of time we started getting female presidents. It was a very powerful time. You saw this as your outlet. This was something where you could have some influence.[24]

In 1974 Geraldine McDonald described Playcentre as successfully effecting a 'compromise between the two roles of mother and worker which in New Zealand are not easily combined'.[25] Playcentre enabled women to be full-time mothers within a professional enterprise which 'employed' its own mothers as supervisors, training directors, liaison and educational officers, standing committee and executive members. Bethell recalls the duality of Playcentre's position in the following statement: 'You didn't leave your children. You didn't send your children to kindergarten. You trained.'

The key was the training. This began with the (usually) compulsory introductory new parent sessions, then the Helper's Certificate, which was the first part of an Association Supervisor's Certificate. Interestingly, in the main cities there were close links with academics (usually male) in local universities and teachers' colleges. On the other hand, the style of learning was not from academia, as Carol Garden recalls. Her experience was

> based on child observation, play workshops and discussions with a tutor, although it was strongly guarded by Otago University people … You had to read Gwen Somerset's 'Work and Play' [1964] and write up observations. There were also weekend workshops in Dunedin. [It was the] first time in my life I had been away from my babies. I loved it. There were lots of women like me from the country who had to make big preparations and arrangements to come.[26]

The quality, style and content of training varied among associations, although increasing national co-ordination and oversight was intended to raise standards. In 1968 a national education committee was established. A new National Supervisor's Certificate and, for a few, the option of a National Diploma provided more rungs on the career ladder. The latter was awarded first to Garden in 1970.

Playcentre philosophy was to empower parents. 'All are experts – all are learners' was the motto.[27] The aim was to encourage parents into leadership positions, but also to ensure that no one became entrenched in their position. In what was described as the 'BDI [beady eye] system', office holders looked for their replacements. The move of Playcentre women into the workplace, and smaller families, made this system imperative for survival. The idea of emergent leadership is attributed to Lex Grey.[28] This meshed with the ideas of the women's movement. Leadership training was incorporated into the advanced Playcentre qualifications and Russell Bernstone ran courses throughout New Zealand. His wife, Helen, later wrote that:

> Empowerment was what it was all about. In fact seeing people take over was as much a thrill for him as his own self-discoveries. He helped people understand that there was always a choice.[29]

These choices often made the personal become political. For instance, Playcentre became a long apprenticeship for Fay Clarke to a career in education:

Once I got into playcentre I did a lot of soul searching about where I was going with my marriage and my children. It was exciting growing. I would come home and tentatively share all the things I was learning at human relationship and leadership courses with V. I think he thought I was mad ... I was scared he couldn't cope with my new self.[30]

Clarke's 'new self' introduced her to the ideas of the women's movement. At the time she was ambivalent. As an education officer for Playcentre she found it equally alarming when women would say to her, 'Oh, gosh, Playcentre's changed my life!'

Playcentre's ladder of qualifications brought self-worth and new knowledge, but not remuneration or the economic independence at the core of feminism. Volunteerism was fundamental to Playcentre, but this sat uncomfortably with the increasing professional rigour and status of Playcentre qualifications and work. Some associations did pay supervisors a small wage but this varied and was often contentious. The volunteer basis of Playcentre was also a contrast to the almost fully professionally salaried kindergarten movement. Yet in 1975 it was reported that Wellington Playcentre Association office holders were working 40–60 hours a week.[31]

Playcentre was aware of change in its midst. A 1976 survey of parent helpers by Geraldine McDonald showed that a third had some paid employment.[32] A 1978 study, *Playcentre in a Changing World*, noted increasing problems in finding volunteers to fill positions. The author stated with irony that 'leisure for mothers' away from children, an original aim of Playcentre, was no longer tenable: 'Most [office holders] deeply committed to Playcentre know little leisure.'[33] Playcentre, however, resisted the idea of too much adaptation, particularly towards meeting the needs of working mothers:

> If we attempt to be all things to all people, Playcentre resources and ideals will stretch so thinly we'll end up standing for nothing. Let others, better equipped for the task, cater more for working mothers.[34]

This did happen as increasing numbers of women who might previously have used Playcentre opted for childcare instead. By the early 1980s the postwar expansion of Playcentre plateaued and began a decline. In a 1980 analysis of economic and demographic trends Llewelyn Richards predicted, first, that 'daycare will gradually grow and other services will shrink' (in which he was correct); and second, that Playcentre would 'die' by the end of the century (about which he was wrong).[35]

The value of Playcentre's 'paper qualifications' became (and still is) a cause for debate. A 1982 survey of supervisors on the effects of national certification concluded that the Playcentre movement provided a springboard for women to continue their education.[36] The dearth of childcare training also meant that Playcentre qualifications provided career opportunities for women in childcare, despite some squeamishness at the idea. In 1981 Carol Nicholson saw the last of her three Playcentre children off to school and applied for a job at a childcare centre. Adapting Playcentre ideas to childcare was not easy:

> I was the only trained person. I used playcentre's idea of putting all the activities out so the children could choose. There were a lot of mumblings about the mess they were making. I also can remember thinking, 'Do these children have to go to the toilet again! Do we have to clean this again!' … The reality was that you had to have routines in childcare but I didn't think that they needed to be so inflexible. It took a lot of sorting out.

There was also a need for 'sorting out' on the home front. This meant ensuring that the family did not notice any change from Nicholson being a mother at home doing volunteer work at Playcentre to being employed in childcare. 'I used to rush around in the morning to get the meal ready. I was very house proud and nobody was going to say I couldn't manage a job and children and everything else – you know the guilt, the emotional blackmail.'[37] There were many variations on this story.

'BROUGHT TO MIND' IN FAMILY DAYCARE

During the 1970s–80s most childcare was provided by women at home minding other people's children.[38] Centre-based provision was scarce and expensive, and its quality was often questionable. Minding children at home provided an income for women at home with their own children. Despite past scandals in the context of 'wet nursing', 'baby farming' and 'backyard care',[39] many women still preferred private arrangements, particularly when the 'minders' were friends and relatives. In many Western countries childminders had to be licensed. In New Zealand childcare regulations were looser, and minders could take up to four children before coming under scrutiny.

Rae Julian's *Brought to Mind* (1977, 1981) provided insight into the approximately 35,000 private childminding arrangements in New Zealand. Julian highlighted the prevalence of informal home arrangements, emphasising that 'any [childcare] policy must start from this reality'.[40] Interviews with parents and minders identified the advantages and disadvantages. The flexibility, convenience, low cost and home atmosphere were advantages to users. These were offset by the instability and the sometimes unsatisfactory nature of such arrangements. For minders, caring for children offered a manageable form of employment. Julian quoted typical responses to being asked why they were doing this:

- company – my husband likes me to stay home;
- don't like the idea of going to work while I have pre-schoolers;
- I like children – have been minding for over ten years.[41]

For the minders, these advantages were offset by low pay, long hours without breaks and, sometimes, conflicts between their own children and those they were minding.

In the mid-1970s a new twist on home minding emerged. Called family daycare, it brought direct oversight to some arrangements. It also brought public scrutiny and comment on the low 'wages' paid to women who mind children. Family daycare appears to have originated in France in 1957, when a 'crèche familiale' was established in a new housing settlement in Paris.[42] It comprised 40 caregivers, each of whom might have up to three children in their home, in addition to their own. The 'familiale' was headed by a nurse and an assistant, who visited the homes and were in charge of the caregivers' education. Parents paid a fee to the agency, which paid the caregivers.[43] In the 1960s similar initiatives began in Denmark and Sweden, both featuring governmental supervision, funding support and training programmes.[44] By the 1970s schemes were established in Canada and the US, although in the latter, concern was expressed that the schemes were 'totally disorganised and under-developed, embodying some of the worst features of out-of-home childcare'.[45] The interest of policy makers in promoting family daycare as a cheap form of childcare was a further concern.

The first family daycare scheme in Australia was established in 1971. With the backing of the Commonwealth government it expanded rapidly over the decade.[46] In New Zealand a prototype operated briefly at the new Eden Epsom childcare centre in Auckland during 1976–77. An early report described the scheme as a response to demands from parents for infant care, which the centre was not licensed to provide.[47] The director matched up 'satellite' minders with the mothers of infants. The scheme foundered over difficulties with collecting fees and finding suitable carers. Nevertheless, some principles were seeded that coloured New Zealand's own version of family daycare, namely a close association between childcare centres and family daycare programmes.

The Auckland City Council began considering the idea of family daycare in 1975. A headline in the *New Zealand Herald* (24 October 1975) stated: 'Family, Not Institution, for Child Who Needs Care'. The article suggested that family-like arrangements were both more 'natural' and cheaper than the 'traditional childcare centres', particularly for under-three-year-olds. A programme began in the suburb of Glen Innes in 1977. In 1978 Barnardos opened a scheme in the suburb of Newtown, in Wellington, in partnership with the Wellington Community Childcare Association (WCCA). Family daycare, originally proposed as a Daily Minders Programme, was to become the cornerstone of the Barnardos venture into childcare in New Zealand. The low capital cost of setting up family daycare schemes was one reason;[48] the demise of the government's capital works scheme for establishing childcare centres in 1979 was a further motivation. In 1978 the Dunedin Community Childcare Association also set up a family daycare scheme, again in co-operation with Barnardos. This became a pattern of Barnardos' expansion.[49] By 1985 there were 33 family daycare schemes operating in New Zealand, and all but two were linked to or run by Barnardos.[50] The exceptions were the Auckland City Council scheme, and the Hamilton Daycare Centres Trust's scheme, which began in 1980.

Underlying these initiatives by Barnardos and the Hamilton Daycare Centres Trust was their role as organisations designated by the government to administer the childcare (capitation) subsidy for families who met the financial and/or welfare criteria (see Chapter Five). Children in the family daycare schemes were also eligible for the subsidy. Government's doubling of the subsidy from $7.80 per week to $13.50 in 1980 made family daycare profitable. Barnardos, in particular, presented family daycare as a preventative welfare service for families and children. This was an acceptable form of childcare at the time.

The structure of New Zealand family daycare schemes was based on the original 'crèche familiale', except that they came under the umbrella of Social Welfare, not Health. The close and at times seamless relationship between childcare centres and family daycare schemes assisted in cementing a view of family daycare as part of the early childhood constituency in a way that has become unique to New Zealand.

The family daycare schemes employed co-ordinators who recruited, vetted and advised the carers (as they came to be called), arranged placements, visited homes with toys and books, administered collecting fees from parents and paying carers, arranged playgroups for carers and children, and acted as troubleshooters. There were variations between the schemes, mainly to do with conditions for carers, fees, the size of the scheme and the frequency of visits. As Barnardos developed into a national provider, there was increasing uniformity.

The idea of family daycare as a form of childcare service was clear but its positioning by some as an early education programme was less easy to project. The levels of supervision and the lack of training for carers were stumbling blocks, as was the perception that preschool education was fostered in institutions, not homes. Barnardos continued to lobby against any shift of responsibility for childcare to the Department of Education until the transfer eventually took place in 1986.[51] Their opposition was fuelled partly by fears about the impact of higher educational requirements.

It was the issue of the status and remuneration of carers, rather than the children's care and education, that became most contentious. Mothers were selected as carers because they could demonstrate that they were, or had been, capable mothers, and that their homes were safe places for children, although such criteria were hard to judge. In 1979 the founding co-ordinator at Glen Innes, Betty Brown, argued: 'To suggest that they undertake a training programme is also suggesting that they are not capable people and denigrates their ability.'[52] The issue of the training of caregivers had been mooted early on, and there were a number of one-off initiatives and informal opportunities; for example, some schemes required mothers to attend induction sessions. But despite discussions, submissions and recommendations, both providers and government backed away from the training of carers until the 1990s.[53]

The remuneration of carers was well below that of employed teachers and workers. To avoid tax and benefit complications they were given an 'allowance' instead of a wage. The rationale was that this reimbursed the mother for the expenses of sharing her home environment. Anne Smith and David Swain later argued that:

> The conflict in many people's minds between childcare as a paid occupation and childcare as the 'natural' outcome of motherhood is clearly demonstrated in family daycare ... [The] collective message is clear. This is not a 'real' job. This work is not really valued ...[54]

When the first schemes began, Sandra Coney warned that:

> Feminists need to oppose the proliferation of Family Day Care because it is not in the interests of women or children ... It is scattered, small-scale and thus

'invisible' ... and [because of this] is not seen as a threat to the nuclear family as publicly provided institutionalised childcare is seen.[55]

Coney also accused the family daycare schemes of 'exploiting' carers by paying them a 'pittance', with 'no workers' rights such as sick pay, holiday pay, tea or lunch breaks'.[56] In 1980 the average allowance paid to carers was $25 a week per child.[57] They earned considerably less than untrained childcare workers, whose own rate of $2–3 per hour was also exploitative.

Family daycare operators were sensitive to such accusations but felt caught between meeting the rights of children, mothers and carers and the realities of government childcare policies of the time. Jill Cameron and Pauline McKinley, co-ordinators of the Dunedin scheme, responded describing their scheme as costing slightly more than centre-based care and therefore not a cheap option for parents.[58] They argued that family daycare was complementary rather than inferior to childcare centres. While they acknowledged that the remuneration was low, their scheme did provide time out for carers, as well as offering sick leave and paid holidays.

Pam Croxford was the co-ordinator of the first family daycare scheme in Christchurch. She recalls:

> I felt ambivalent because it got an extreme reaction from feminists. I saw it in terms of the positive effect it could have on women's self-esteem and the idea that you could get paid for caring for children ... I never pretended [the mothers] were getting paid what they were worth, but there was a radical potential in it. After two years I felt the whole thing slipping away from me. Instead of the women carers going on to demand their rights, the direction [from Barnardos] was to control them and to downplay the caregivers.[59]

Lois Duurloo, the founding co-ordinator of the Wellington scheme, looked to the broader issue:

> Those of us involved in organising it would like to see the care of children recognised by society and the state for the important and consuming task it is, so that those who provide this care, usually women, are paid a realistic wage. This presupposes that parents are earning enough to pay for care in addition to their own basic needs, or that there is state support equal to that of the other pre-school services.[60]

These issues were not resolved. Barnardos, the largest family daycare provider, henceforth became a key player in the politics of childcare. This was an acceptable form of childcare operated by a welfare charity.

TO 'TEACH' IN KINDERGARTEN

During the 1970s the older image of the genteel 'kindy' teacher was shattered. A younger generation of radicalised teachers challenged the ladylike politics of the past. They took control of the Kindergarten Teachers' Association (KTA), took their cause to the streets and made friends with the union movement. Kindergarten teachers became a significant voice in shaping the politics of early childhood. The continuing expansion of and demand for kindergarten places, an overhaul of kindergarten training and conditions of work, and the battles by teachers, won or lost, were all catalysts for campaigns to improve professional status.

Until 1974 kindergarten training, although funded by the government, was under the control of kindergarten associations in small 'genteel' kindergarten colleges in each of the main cities. The shift towards new social codes was slow, although in Wellington principal Joyce Barns moved to widen the selection criteria:

> It used to be the twinset and pearl brigade, [girls] like myself, who were from private schools. Then we started getting girls from public schools, and then women and just before I left [in 1974] the males were coming in.[61]

This college also gained a reputation for trying to broaden the horizons of its students. Former lecturer Cushla Scrivens recalls

> a very open-minded feel about the place. Joyce Barns supported students to the hilt. We had got to the stage that pregnant students were no longer asked to leave … We brought in all sorts of interesting people for the students to hear, like [Maori radical] Dun Mihaka, in a desperate attempt to enlarge their horizons.[62]

The Hill report had recommended the implementation of three-year training for kindergarten teachers, in line with primary teachers, and the integration of kindergarten training into the primary colleges.[63] A step towards parity occurred in 1974, when kindergarten trainees first received the same allowances as primary students and entry qualifications were raised. That year the government announced that kindergarten colleges would be integrated into the primary teachers' colleges for 1975.[64] The suddenness of this announcement, with little consultation, left little time to plan the process effectively.[65] A working party was convened in May to examine the implications and outline the curriculum. The view was that there should be a common core with primary curriculum and separate parts emphasising early childhood.

At this point the participants still thought they were planning a three-year programme.[66] In July it was announced that the training would continue to be a two-year course, which came as a blow to kindergarten supporters.[67]

There were long-term benefits in integration. Kindergarten students gained from the colleges' better resources, specialist expertise and opportunities for university study.[68] However, initially the reality was different. Kindergarten lecturers were told they had no jobs and must apply for the advertised new positions. Those appointed were often split around various primary curriculum departments. At Wellington Teachers' College, just after the change, Val Burns was appointed to a situation where

> the position and status of the kindergarten college principal was lost … We didn't have rooms. It was quite scandalous. We weren't given equipment. We didn't even have a budget. We had to fight all the way.[69]

Kindergarteners were steadfast in their argument that early childhood should retain its distinctiveness, but the colleges' aim was integration. Kindergarten lecturers came from a lower-paid teaching profession. This was reflected in lower college salary scales, and promotion was slow. Kindergarten lecturers initially tended to be treated as if they were the 'preschoolers' of the teachers' colleges. Historian Beryl Hughes describes a situation where:

> [Primary] lecturers already on the staff of one college used to refer to the kindergarten lecturers as 'the little people' and kindergarten staff had to struggle to keep identity and to avoid exclusion from important committees.[70]

In time the kindergarten programmes built a position and identity in the colleges that gained respect, and kindergarten training was brought closer to the mainstream of teacher training, but its minority situation remained.

Meanwhile, kindergarten teachers were also attempting to improve their 'minority situation' in the teaching profession. The vehicle for this was KTA, which began to take a more politically aggressive stand.[71] A key person in this transformation was Wendy Lee:

> The organisation [changed] from being predominantly run by older people. It felt like a coup at the time. We were driven with excitement about moving forward. We had clear goals about the whole salary issue, conditions of service, how appointments were being made, disciplinary processes and the way in which teachers were being treated. Issues of group size and ratios and training issues were appalling. We also wanted some parity with the primary service. All this had to be done yesterday![72]

As president, Lee was immediately embroiled in a skirmish with the Minister of Education, Phil Amos, who attended a 1973 KTA council meeting. Lee presented the issues forthrightly, asking how long kindergarten teaching was to be the 'Cinderella' of the teaching service. She described kindergarten teaching as a 'dead-end job' because of the lack of advancement prospects, and called for a 'career structure which will attract people on the same basis as the other branches of the teaching profession'.[73] The newspaper headlines read: 'Mr Amos Denies Kindergartens are the "Cinderella" of Teaching'. He stated that the 'description did not carry much weight with him or his department [because] all services considered their particular problems as paramount'.[74]

This new combativeness was a shock to some, but Lee was able to unify the membership around the view that sterner measures were needed if, in the first instance, the salaries of kindergarten teachers were to improve. Some teachers were being paid below the minimum wage.[75] A national campaign encouraged local KTA branches to telegraph parliament and lobby MPs. The goal continued to be parity with primary teachers and Lee prepared documentation describing the role of the kindergarten teacher compared with that of the primary teacher.[76] Kindergarten teachers also made their first threat of strike action. The claim was eventually settled in 1974 with a significant boost in salary, although not to a level to achieve parity with the primary sector. (This campaign is still continuing in 2001.)[77]

In 1975 a national office was provided by the New Zealand Educational Institute (NZEI), the primary teachers' union. This positioned kindergarten teachers alongside other lobby groups during the more abrasive politics accompanying the return of the National government in 1975. KTA also gained a new weapon: Rosslyn Noonan was appointed as a part-time (and poorly paid) general secretary, fresh from a high-profile position as the co-ordinator of IWY. Lee recalls:

> It was such an exciting time and we just felt ourselves being physically lifted out of that mire that we were caught in. Ros is not a person who takes over. Her leadership style was incredibly supportive and as a group of young women we learned from her ability to negotiate with people in the department. We felt empowered.[78]

Lynne Bruce attended her first conference in 1976:

> It just blew my mind. I met Wendy Lee, Ros Noonan, Robin Houlker. These were radical people. In the hotel every night they talked politics and early childhood education. I had never met people like them. It was a whole new

world … These women were taking over KTA and were going to change it and make it a political force. In the past it had been run by people too close to the government line and here was a new group of people who had been active in International Women's Year and the Labour Party.[79]

Georgina Kerr recalls:

> … people like Lynne Bruce, Jean Pearson, Robin Houlker, Di Anderson. Ros Noonan was our general secretary. She wasn't a trained kindergarten teacher but was a theorist and an educator. She would throw ideas at us. We used to debate things, and we knew there were better ways of doing things … We had to get strong against organisations like the Kindergarten Union. We had to make political stands against the government of the day because of the appalling wages and our conditions of employment.[80]

Noonan felt she brought the perspective of an 'outsider' and a 'broader sort of political and economic analysis', which helped 'move [KTA] from being quite such polite ladies … I didn't have undue respect for authority … I could contribute by getting beyond that overlay of having to be terribly polite … Knowing it was all right to challenge authority.'[81] Noonan played a pivotal role in linking the kindergarten teachers with the women's movement, and saw the KTA as an agent of change in society:

> In analysing how change could be effected we could better identify what action was necessary by focusing on one specific area rather than trying to change the entire system. As a feminist it's easy to become overwhelmed with despair and frustration.[82]

The focus of the late 1970s and early 1980s was to extend training opportunities, negotiate more professional staffing policies and improve staffing ratios. The 1983 Kindergarten Staffing Scheme started to improve the ratios from two teachers to three in kindergartens with 40 children per session. This was hard fought. In 1979 teachers threatened to close their rolls, leading to the headline: 'Kindy Teachers Sent to Coventry'.[83] Relations between the Minister of Education and the KTA broke down completely. Lynne Bruce, who was then president, recalls:

> I probably hadn't learnt the skills then of knowing where to pick your battlegrounds. I saw Merv[yn] Wellington totally as the enemy. We were sent into the wilderness. We were totally disempowered. We weren't allowed any contact with the Kindergarten Union, with any Department official and no contact with Government. We were completely isolated. If we had teachers in trouble there was nothing we could do about it. It was Robin Houlker who was eventually able to break the deadlock.[84]

In 1982 kindergarten teachers did close their rolls and had their first half-day, nationwide stopwork. Such direct action by women who worked with young children was anathema to the National government. Prime Minister Muldoon accused kindergarten teachers of 'abusing trust' by taking preschoolers (in fact with their parents) on a protest march over staffing levels. Moreover, claimed Muldoon, 'I go further to say it is an abuse of the children themselves.'[85] The Minister of Education called kindergarten teachers 'petulant and childish'[86] and accused KTA of 'shop-floor tactics', becoming 'tainted with the sulphurous smell of pseudo-unionism',[87] and 'stage-managing its approaches to secure the maximum media input and public sympathy for its cause'.[88]

The latter years of the National government's term were a bruising time for all education groups, with funding cuts across a range of services. The Labour government entered parliament in 1984 with a brief to improve both early childhood services and the professional status of those who worked in early childhood.[89] Noonan and other KTA members had played a key role in shaping the policy. Change came swiftly over several areas, and in 1985 the Working Party for Three Year Training for Kindergarten Teachers was set up.[90]

TO 'WORK' IN CHILDCARE

In 1975 the government established the first training programme, of one year only, for childcare workers at Wellington Polytechnic. This set childcare apart from kindergarten teacher training in both placement and length. The message was that to 'work' in childcare required less knowledge than to 'teach' in kindergarten. Regulations allowed childcare centres to operate with no trained staff until 1985. To hold an 'A' licence, centres required one trained staff member, but a range of qualifications was accepted. The main lobbyist for childcare training was the New Zealand Association of Childcare Centres (NZACCC), but there was a vacuum of responsibility. Childcare was under the Department of Social Welfare, which did not see itself as a funder of childcare training. The Department of Education had long been critical of the quality of childcare centres, but the establishment of a national childcare training programme was not a priority. The Wellington programme remained a 'one-off' until the 1980s, when one-year childcare programmes were established in four teachers' colleges.

Despite the chorus of demands for childcare training recurring from conference to conference during the 1970s, years of lobbying yielded little. In 1978 Maris O'Rourke concluded a bleak summary of the situation:

- childcare centres are mainly private commercial enterprises operating on low profit margins, and often unable to pay for alternative staff while others train;
- untrained staff are cheaper. [91]

In the meantime NZACCC decided on a do-it-yourself strategy to train workers on the job. This began on a shoestring budget, with volunteer tutors. In 1979 the Department of Social Welfare gave NZACCC a grant for research into field-based training, and an IYC Telethon grant in 1980 provided operational funding.[92] Thereafter, a $20,000 Lottery Board grant was applied for annually.[93] Under the headline 'Cinderella at the Ball' the *Sunday Times* reported president Margaret Lamb saying in 1980: 'But we're worrying about what's going to happen at midnight because these grants will stop. When the clock strikes twelve, do we go back to the beginning?'[94] Sonja Davies was incensed with the idea that childcare training had to be funded from lottery money, and felt it was indicative of a society not taking the issues of quality for children seriously. 'However we look at it, quality will cost. The question is, are we – as members of society – willing to pay?'[95]

The ad hoc grants kept childcare training afloat, allowing the association to demonstrate the viability of field-based training. This initiative unleashed a demand that could not be withdrawn without political repercussions. As grants ran out in 1980 and new trainees were turned away, local MPs were called on to pressure government. Yet in 1982 the government shelved any action on the SSC *Report on Early Care and Education* (see Chapter Five). The government gave the now renamed New Zealand Childcare Association (NZCA) a direct sum of $25,000 for training, said by some to be compensation. In 1983 the first trained staff subsidies began, accompanied by a substantive training package for NZCA. International research on the importance of trained staff working with children in childcare was starting to be heeded.[96]

Some children gained the benefits from trained staff, but many did not. Key problems were the low wages and poor conditions of work in most childcare centres. Some centres made efforts to provide lunch breaks, sick pay and wage rates that recognised the expertise of trained staff, but a lack of any industrial award for childcare centres meant that most did not. A high turnover of staff was a problem in achieving quality.[97] Centres mainly depended on the fees paid by parents. Few parents could afford higher fees, nor did they generally consider that the childcare workers deserved better remuneration and conditions. Moreover, these women were not teachers; they were workers, who merely 'cared' for children. These workers, however, began to realise that the expansion in childcare services and the low fees for parents, some of whom were carving out well-paid careers, were made possible by the poorly paid and unrecognised work of childcare staff.

Rumblings about unionism for childcare workers began during the late 1970s. However, it was not until March 1982 that the Early Childhood Workers' Union (ECWU) was eventually registered as an industrial union for approximately 2000 waged childcare workers. The story of its beginnings, told elsewhere, is illustrative of the increasing militancy of the politics of early childhood, through its links with feminism and unionism.[98]

The idea of a union for childcare workers came from Sonja Davies. Her work in the trade union movement convinced her that an industrial union was needed to exercise a different style of politics. Through improving the situation for workers, Davies believed that the quality of care for children would also improve. Her first attempt in 1976 did not succeed; neither workers nor employers seemed ready to face the issues that an industrial union would create. Davies set out her views to the NZACCC, in the context of some antagonism from its employer members:

> The association believes that the task of caring for and educating other people's pre-schoolers in childcare centres is so important that thousands of voluntary hours have been spent in trying to upgrade the status of childcare and to provide more and better quality care. Why then should those who carry out this very important work be paid less than people on an assembly line, or low-paid shop assistants or clothing workers?
>
> Will decent wages and conditions close most of our private centres? I don't believe so. In fact, not until professional wages are paid will the low image of childcare alter one iota, and public attitudes to funding change.
>
> The final question we must ask ourselves is – can we as an organisation continue to turn a blind eye to the exploitation of women working in childcare? Some are quite well paid – many are not. I firmly believe that what will emerge is a better deal all round.[99]

Many people in childcare hoped that the idea of a union would go away, thus avoiding such an unseemly and divisive act. In the meantime, Davies was elected to the national executive of the Federation of Labour (FOL). In 1979, with the support of the FOL and the KTA, she made another attempt to unionise childcare. The alliance between Davies and Rosslyn Noonan was crucial. Noonan's broad view of feminist politics played a vital role in KTA sponsorship of a union for childcare workers. She positioned feminist solidarity with other women who worked with children ahead of any kindergarten squeamishness over childcare.[100] Noonan and Davies also had an ideal of forging a unified early childhood union for all early childhood teachers, believing that both kindergarten and childcare were in the business of educating and caring for young children. This far-sighted approach, long before legislation allowed any unity, was crucial for the successful establishment of the ECWU. It also laid the groundwork for the eventual 1990 merger of KTA and ECWU to form the Combined Early Childhood Union of Aotearoa (CECUA).

Davies launched her plan in a whirlwind of enthusiasm and determination at the NZACCC annual conference in Christchurch in 1979. In an earlier history of the ECWU, I wrote:

> I was a newly appointed supervisor of the Victoria University Creche and had started to understand the issues. Sonja announced a meeting of all childcare workers, and employers were not to come. This was seen by some as a scandalous thing to do at an Association meeting of which many members were employers! Sonja told us that a union was going to be formed, how it would happen and that we would have an award within the year. It sounded exciting and straight forward. We put our names and signatures to a piece of paper which gave authorisation to start the formal processes. I had no idea I would become the first president of the ECWU. Also present was Jeannie Truell who was attending the conference as a trainee childcare worker from the one-year course at the Wellington Polytechnic, whose students and graduates were activists in the formation and early years of the union. Jeannie became the second president in 1984.[101]

The task of establishing an industrial union was more complex than Davies anticipated. It took three years, and then another three years before the first award with wages and conditions was negotiated in 1985 – and that covered only 35 employers! Davies was there all the time, leading and supporting. The process of establishing a new union under the Industrial Relations Act was complex. Government employment schemes of the time (with some bending of the rules) enabled ECWU to employ staff in the Wellington KTA office and in Auckland and Christchurch.[102]

From the beginning there was the realisation that if the union was to survive, support had to be galvanised from within the trade union movement. A parallel development to the union support of ECWU was a move by the FOL and the Public Service Association (PSA) to develop more comprehensive childcare policies and to educate their members on childcare issues.[103] In 1981 the PSA set up its first childcare centre for members in downtown Wellington. During the early 1980s the FOL and the Combined State Unions (CSU) sponsored appeals that bankrolled ECWU for several years.

Reaction among childcare workers to ECWU varied. In some areas there was a burst of activism, meetings and discussion of common issues. Other childcare workers felt threatened; they did not want any trouble. Many saw the union as remote and not relevant to them. The reaction among employers was more predictable. Although many acknowledged that childcare workers were underpaid, employers felt financially threatened and/or did not like the idea of political childcare workers. Some employers began setting up an employers' organisation and, with the assistance of the Employers' Federation, campaigned to frustrate moves towards a national award.

Not all employers backed away from the issues, however, and the union began negotiating single-site agreements to test the waters. The first was with the newly established PSA childcare centre. Although the PSA was a sister union, the voluntary agreement was tough to negotiate. ECWU wanted a pay scale that paid more to trained staff and staff in training, a concept that the PSA negotiators found hard to accept. They too were imbued with images of the motherly childcare worker, to whom working with children just came naturally.

Things came to an early crisis in July 1982 when the Auckland Employers' Association interrupted negotiations between the ECWU and the Hamilton Daycare Centres Trust. *National Business Review* reported:

> The country's youngest union was knocked back at the post when the Employers' Association upset conciliation proceedings in Hamilton by forcing the issue to go to the Arbitration Court. The ECWU and the Hamilton Daycare Centres Trust which has thirty employees were willing parties to a conciliation council ... The Employers' Association are concerned that an award settled, say in Hamilton, would act as leverage for the settlement of a national or other awards.[104]

The union and the trust were to win a case in the Arbitration Court against the Employers' Association for the right to negotiate. In the meantime the union became embroiled in the wage–price freeze (1982–84) imposed by the National government, which prevented any industrial negotiations that had monetary implications. Under the regulations imposed, the ECWU was not allowed to negotiate or to register any agreements so far negotiated. The *Otago Daily Times* reported:

It has hit members particularly bad. They have no conditions of work set down – no rights – other unions have existing conditions of work. Applications for an exemption to the Minister of Labour, the Hon J. Bolger, have been unsuccessful.[105]

In a *Listener* interview I stated:

These early battles have meant the union's public profile has been higher than anticipated. Our image has been strident and radical, probably more than the members feel comfortable with. But we've got to shout loudly to be heard.[106]

This stridency was also occurring in childcare centres as childcare workers began bringing grievances to the union. The most difficult area was Auckland, where there were many private employers opposed to the union. ECWU was fortunate to have some tenacious organisers in Auckland, who realised that without an award, the only recourse was the media. The *Auckland Star* reported:

A woman was dismissed without notice of dismissal or wages in lieu of notice. The woman dismissed, who gave three weeks notice as she was pregnant, was sacked five minutes before leaving work in the second week. The owner of the centre at Mt Wellington and three other day care centres refused to comment.[107]

This centre belonged to one of the growing number of privately owned, commercially driven 'chains' of centres. Staff picketed the Tinytown centre and the employer eventually agreed to pay one week's wages in lieu of notice. However, the union could not cope with the number of grievances, and for most there was nothing the union could do without an award.

The ECWU became active in a range of early childhood issues to ensure that the voice of childcare workers was heard. This involved submission writing, public speaking and committee work. Such work was difficult to resource for a union that in its first year had only 159 paid-up members (233 by 1983). With no possibility of an award there was little incentive for workers to join, but the ECWU was determined to survive. My president's report for 1982–83 stated:

We have indeed been victims of unfortunate political and economic circumstances that have continually worsened beyond our expectations. Theoretically and logically we should have crumbled and disintegrated amidst such constraints. But we haven't; we are here. We are hardened, tougher, more politicised, less naive, a lot more knowledgeable, and ironically popular media material. So surely the strength we have gained puts us in a stronger position than we [were in] when we began. This strength, courage, energy and collective spirit is what we will need during this next year.[108]

Such spirit and political lobbying enabled the union to get one of the few exemptions to the wage–price freeze through parliament, in order to negotiate a limited award without wage rates.

Meanwhile, the employers had formed their own group, which was prepared to approach government jointly with ECWU for the right to negotiate. Crispin Gardiner, from the Hamilton Daycare Centres Trust, and Kathy Baxter, a parent at Te Kainganui childcare centre in Wellington, were active in the NZCA. Both were angered at the role that the Employers' Federation had played and they decided to set up an employers' group as a branch of the NZCA.

The *Evening Post* headline on 9 March 1984 read: 'Decision Breaks Award-talk Ban'. This had been a gruelling battle, involving a massive letter-writing campaign by workers and parents. In June 1984, over two years after registration, the union began its first multi-employer negotiation on conditions of work. It was not an easy negotiation, but by 1 July 1984, ECWU had achieved a major breakthrough, with an award giving workers four weeks' paid holiday a year, as well as maternity, domestic and sick leave provisions. Clothing and petrol allowances, paid study leave and five days' infectious disease leave were included too. Limits were also set on the length of the day for working with children. Seventeen employers signed the agreement in the first instance. Less than a year later, with the end of the wage–price freeze, 36 employers joined to negotiate the first award with wages.

Shifting political attitudes towards childcare also contributed to the success of ECWU, helped by a growing awareness of childcare issues in the union movement. In 1982 the PSA booklet *Childcare: A Step Towards Equality*[109] supported the shelved recommendations of the SSC's *Report on Care and Education*. In 1984 the Federation of Labour adopted a new policy on childcare, stating: 'Childcare should be an integral part of unified early childhood service provision supplied by Government to flexibly meet the requirements of parents and communities.'[110] In 1984 the *Labour Party Manifesto* stated: 'Women's opportunities for full and equal participation are too often limited; employment and childcare policies are particularly important in recognising the needs of women.'[111] The impact of these policies will be examined in Part Three.

By 1984 the work of women with children was more visible, and some workers had learnt that street tactics could be effective. However, any radical transformation in the status of those who worked with children was not going to happen quickly. ECWU found that the realities of negotiating better wages and conditions for childcare workers during the remainder of the 1980s were gruelling, and the gains small, although all employers eventually came to the negotiating table. ECWU was not to know that these would be the 'dream years', compared with the break-up of national awards by the National government in the 1990s. Childcare workers and kindergarten teachers alike were to be cruelly affected.

CHAPTER SEVEN

Indigenous Rights and Minority Issues

Liberation politics of the late 1960s–70s created the climate for a more radical analysis of the experiences of Māori as an almost landless minority people, whose language and culture were besieged. The challenges to older cultural policies of assimilation and integration were driven initially by young Māori radicals comfortable with the strategies of protest, and conscious of their connected plight with other indigenous peoples. The challenge was pervasive across the economic, political, social and educational institutions of New Zealand.

During the 1980s early childhood institutions for Māori children became a flagship of resistance by Māori to educational integration, and a demonstration that self-determination was the only way. The script was written according to the principles underlying the 1840 Treaty of Waitangi. How that script was to be read and implemented a century and a half later was still contestable between Māori and the (Pākehā) Crown.

This chapter outlines the political and cultural backdrop to the emergence of the Māori language immersion movement, Te Kōhanga Reo, whose rationale was much broader (to Māori) than the early childhood institution it was officially defined as by Pākehā. The story is well documented by Māori writers and my analysis is guided by their insight. The impact of more radical Māori politics and, more particularly, their expression in Te Kōhanga Reo, rippled through the education sector. A parallel story, making the cultural diversity of New Zealand more visible, is the establishment of early childhood centres by Pacific Islands communities seeking more educational success for their children, as well as promoting the languages and cultures of their Pacific Island nations.

During the 1970s young, urban, educated Māori established a new wave of political groups such as Nga Tamatoa and, in Wellington, the Maori Organisation on Human Rights. Resistance to the 1967 Maori Affairs Amendment Act, which allowed further break-up of Māori land ownership, was one incentive for action. Both groups promoted a range of issues to do with land, severance of ties with South Africa, the teaching of the Māori language in schools, and the honouring of the Treaty of Waitangi. The invisibility of Māori language and literature in the media was a particular concern of Te Reo Maori, a group centred on Victoria University.[1] The later *Government Review of Te Kohanga Reo* (1988) highlighted the importance of these initiatives:

> The tactics and location of their struggles may have been new, but the causes they fought for were the same as those of their tipuna before them: the retention and restoration of land and language, and the right to control their own affairs and resources.[2]

The media paid attention to the Maori Land March of 1975, whose participants walked the length of the North Island. They sought a promise from government that not one more acre of Māori land would be alienated. No such promise was made. The sequel was a series of land protests, such as the long occupation at Bastion Point in Auckland, and an eventual showdown with police.

The cumulative effect of this activism was a cautious shift in government policies. Multiculturalism became one approach for dealing with cultural differences, but this placed the special interests of Māori alongside, and in competition with, those of immigrant groups. In 1974 the Department of Education introduced Taha Maori programmes for schools, initially in the form of resources to provide a Māori dimension.[3] Taha Maori acknowledged the legitimacy of things Māori, but it satisfied few.[4] Nevertheless, during the 1970s a number of schools and early childhood programmes piloted a variety of initiatives to make education more relevant and successful for Māori. An experimental bilingual unit at Ruatoki School was established in 1977, as an attempt to keep the language alive in an area where families were still speaking Māori.[5] During the 1980s more schools opened bilingual classrooms, but success was often hampered by the lack of resources and teachers. Sometimes these classrooms became a 'dumping ground' for 'difficult' Māori children.[6]

On the political front, in 1975 the government established the Waitangi Tribunal to consider alleged breaches of the Treaty by the Crown. In 1985 the tribunal's powers were made retrospective to 1840, and calls were made for government institutions to 'Honour the Treaty'. This was a catalyst for reappraisals by both Māori and Pākehā concerning what this might mean in the late twentieth century. There were differing interpretations of tino rangatiratanga, as cited in Article Two of the Treaty. The general Māori view was that Māori had not, as Pākehā supposed, surrendered their sovereignty under the Treaty.[7]

In 1977 the Department of Maori Affairs launched its Tu Tangata (stand tall) programme. The intention was to utilise the whanau style of working, derived from traditional Māori culture.[8] In the broader sense Tu Tangata was described by Kara Puketapu, Secretary of the Department of Maori Affairs, as 'harnessing "Maori power" to positive new directions … [and] empowering … Maori people to become economically self-sufficient'.[9]

During the 1970s Iritana Tawhiwhirangi, also from the Department of Maori Affairs, became a Māori voice at various government working groups and conferences on early childhood issues. Barriers to finding solutions for Māori children in mainstream institutions and lessons learned from the 1960s Māori preschool movement (see Chapter Three) suggested that new approaches were needed. Tawhiwhirangi believed that Tu Tangata's philosophy forged 'organic policies – policies that actually come from the people [and] out of all that dynamic was born Te Kohanga Reo'.[10]

Some facts about the Māori language were also a catalyst. During the 1970s Richard Benton surveyed the usage of Māori language. His report, published in 1979, warned of the imminent death of the language as the older speakers of Māori died.[11] Very few children were learning Māori as a first language. The birth of the idea of Te Kōhanga Reo is credited to a Kaumātua Hui sponsored by the Department of Maori Affairs at Waiwhetu Marae, Wellington, in 1979.[12] The hui's agenda was wide-ranging, and James Henare made a case concerning the legacy left to the young by kaumātua, concluding that 'the number one priority should be the Maori language'.[13] At a subsequent Wananga Whakatauira in 1980 elders proposed that Māori take more direct control over maintaining the language. The maxim, translated into English, was: 'When the child is born, take it, put it to the breast and begin speaking Maori to it at that point.'[14]

A resolution was passed for the Department of Maori Affairs to implement the idea of a 'bilingual-style preschool'.[15] They presented a case to Treasury for a 'Maori-Style Preschool Project'. Negotiations yielded the modest sum of $45,000. This was sufficient to begin, but rather than being bilingual, an experiment based on total Māori language immersion was begun.[16] Key influences in shaping the total immersion approach were Tamati Reedy, linguist and assistant secretary in the department, together with educationist Tilly Reedy. Tawhiwhirangi recalled how Tamati Reedy 'approached it from a Maori perspective. Nobody taught *us*, you see. I was never taught Maori: it was spoken to me and it was the language spoken in my home.'[17] This was to be the approach for learning Māori at kōhanga reo.

Te Kōhanga Reo was to successfully demonstrate the vision for Māori self-determination. By the 1980s multiculturalism and Taha Maori were being rejected. Kuni Jenkins' view was that 'In promoting multiculturalism the state hoped that it would quieten Māori demands for their language and culture to be taught in schools.' Instead, citing Ranginui Walker, she observed that multiculturalism had become a mechanism 'for doing nothing – it plays off the interests and aspirations of the ethnic minorities against each other, while maintaining the status quo of the dominant group'.[18]

The year 1984 was declared the start of the Maori Development Decade, and was launched with a series of conferences. At the 1984 Maori Educational Development Conference – Nga Tumanako – 300 Māori educators voted to opt out of Pākehā schools and seek their own solutions.[19] Judith Simon reported on research indicating that racist attitudes and cultural deficit beliefs by teachers, as well as the trivialising of Taha Maori in schools, ensured Māori interests would never be met within the mainstream.[20] Donna Awatere's treatise *Maori Sovereignty* (1982) had made a similarly sharp critique:

> The education system is the major gate which keeps Maori out [of participating in white society]. There is an invisible sign over every kindergarten, playcentre, school and university. That sign reads 'Maoris Keep Out. For White Use Only'. White people can't see this sign … Kindergartens are the first of the educational gates. A bastion of white power. Kindergartens have frightened Maori people off pre-school education … Maori parents won't take their children there, not because they don't want to, but because kindergartens, in particular, and playcentres to a lesser extent, don't meet their needs.[21]

Awatere saw the emergence of Te Kōhanga Reo as the first step towards 'decolonisation', predicting a similar withdrawal by Māori at all levels of society. For Hilda Halkyard, this was the only strategy left:

> Maori people have been the scapegoats of the Pakeha education system too long. Enough is enough. What can we do? We have several options: We can accept IT, spit at IT, join in and change IT or make our own alternatives … Te Kohanga Reo is an alternative …[22]

An impetus for political change underpinned Māori support for Te Kōhanga Reo. Pākehā political support had agendas of political and social order. Prime Minister Muldoon's reaction to Te Kōhanga Reo was reminiscent of Premier Robert Stout, a century earlier, who had envisaged that the new kindergartens would mean an end to 'larrikinism' and 'pauperism'.[23] Muldoon told the 1982 Tu Tangata Wananga Whakatauira at parliament that Te Kōhanga Reo would 'mean the end of such things as Maori gangs, which we have heard so much about'.[24] The dream for Te Kōhanga Reo was cultural and political revolution. The contradiction between the dream and the political reality continued, albeit mediated in the process of gaining acceptance and funding, and in the dynamics of gaining control (by government) and/or retaining autonomy (by Te Kōhanga Reo).

In the 1980s the idea of biculturalism (reflecting the two Treaty partners) began to replace multiculturalism as a suggested framework for race relations. Donna Awatere stated, however, that 'Maori sovereignty once offered this country biculturalism. The Maori struggled to be included in the colonial settlers' institutions of the state. The Pakeha refused.'[25] Mason Durie later described a bicultural continuum, ranging from primarily monocultural Pākehā institutions whose goals may be to gain cultural skills and knowledge, to independent but parallel Māori institutions based on the principle of tino rangatiratanga.[26] Durie cited Te Kōhanga Reo as a successful example of the latter. Few Pākehā, however, were prepared to engage in the bicultural sharing of institutions they felt they had created.

TE KŌHANGA REO: OUTSIDE THE MAINSTREAM

In April 1982 a pilot kōhanga reo was opened at the Pukeatua Kokiri Centre in Wainuiomata, Wellington. Three months later the first Te Kōhanga Reo Wānanga was launched at parliament by Dame Te Atairangikaahu, the Māori Queen. 'No Compromise' was the theme.[27] The pilot was followed by three more in Wellington and one in Auckland, all supported by the Department of Maori Affairs from its allotted $45,000 seeding grant. Within 12 months Māori communities had established an additional 107 kōhanga reo. The government provided further funding of $535,000, and each kōhanga reo received a seeding grant of $5000.[28] In 1982–83 Te Kohanga Reo National Trust was set up, with Iritana Tawhiwhirangi at the helm.

The rapid growth demonstrated by Te Kōhanga Reo was something not seen before in the history of early childhood provision in New Zealand. By 1985 there were 377 kōhanga reo catering for approximately 5800 children.[29]

That they were mainly local do-it-yourself ventures was not unusual for new early childhood endeavours. Tawhiwhirangi said it was the 'cultural ownership of the initiative that generated the energy, the drive and the commitment behind its rapid growth'.[30] The fait accompli tactics were the political trump card. She recalls:

> ... it was also important to note that the mushrooming of the movement was greatest when there was marginal government involvement. From 1982 to 1989 the growth rate was approximately 100 new centres annually. Talk about success! This was phenomenal given that government funding was minimal, given that also Maori people occupied the bottom rung of the economic ladder of the country. But this mushrooming, this whole movement just took off like a prairie fire.[31]

Kaumātua John Rangihau also proclaimed success for Te Kōhanga Reo 'under the banner of Tu Tangata':

> It is evident to me that we are no longer bowed down but we are upstanding, taking our destinies into our own hands, actively challenging the world and saying to our people: 'Let us stand and meet these problems head-on and change the face of Aotearoa.'[32]

Te Kōhanga Reo was not easy for Pākehā to define in early childhood terms. An early report in the *Listener* asked: 'How does one describe kohanga reo? Emphatically not as a kindergarten, creche, school or day-care centre – although it embodies all of these.'[33] Tawhiwhirangi told *Māori*, 'It is not a preschool. It is not a preparation for school. It is a preparation for life. It is not just about language ...'[34] Kōhanga reo parent Arapera Royal Tangaere agreed: 'To me kohanga reo was more than a language nest. It was more than a childcare centre. Today it has become a social, political and cultural renaissance for Maori.'[35] Those kōhanga reo that met the regulatory requirements of childcare centres (144 in 1985) became eligible for subsidies from the Department of Social Welfare for parents and trained staff.

The chairman of the national trust, John Bennett, outlined the basic beliefs underpinning Te Kōhanga Reo to early childhood leaders at parliament in 1985:

- It is possible to transmit Maori language in its 'indigenous' state to generations of infants ...
- The best age to do this is as early as possible.
- The residual pool of 70,000 speakers of Maori must be utilised to pass on the language ...

- The Maori people are motivated, aware and care enough about the survival of their language to make a commitment to that goal.[36]

Māori cultural values would be to the fore, such as aroha, manaaki and wairua, Bennett told his audience; 'the Maori people no longer subscribe to assimilation policies but believe that the nation of New Zealand will be culturally wealthier with diversity and mutual respect'.[37] Tania Ka`ai summed up the kaupapa of Te Kōhanga Reo.[38] First was an 'uncompromising' and 'total commitment' to 'he korero Maori'; second, a view of 'whanau principles as the bedrock of the kohanga operation'; and third, Māori self-determination and control of Māori resources, described in terms of 'mana motuhake'. These interrelated objectives, according to Ka`ai, 'revolve around the desire of the Maori people to "stand tall" and to overcome adversity, by producing an era of bilingual and bicultural children'.[39]

The philosophy of whanau development and learning required community participation at all levels of the operation: administration, catering and erecting buildings, as well as teaching the children. The Department of Maori Affairs set out some guiding principles:

> It is envisaged that Te Kohanga Reo programmes will operate using the same principles for childcare and growth at present adopted by the best preschools … The difference will be the use of Maori language as the only means of communication in the centre, and the fact that it is a whanau operation in a true Maori way.[40]

In reality there was considerable debate and uncertainty concerning what the 'true Māori way' and the 'best preschool principles' might mean in practice. The *Listener* reported that the kaiako 'speak with scorn of Pakeha institutions for preschoolers with their structured programmes, masses of equipment and a secular atmosphere – that's not natural'.[41] Many of those involved in the work of Te Kōhanga Reo, however, were ill equipped in terms of Māori language and knowledge of Māori tikanga. This was an issue raised by the *Government Review of Te Kohanga Reo* in 1998:

> … many of the kohanga reo whanau needed to be re-educated … the bilingualism and biculturalism of the kaumatua, koroua and kuia were not initially shared by all whanau members … The process of deprogramming that is re-educating from a Maori perspective and subsequent development has not been without conflict or problems.[42]

Individual stories of the transformation, activism, discovery and debate caused by Te Kōhanga Reo provide insight into the historical story. Rita Walker was living at the Burnham Army Camp:

It was 1982. It was on the news. That was my first exposure to the whole idea that things Maori needed to happen. I remember asking myself, 'Why?' I thought about my girls. 'Do I really want them to be in a totally Maori environment?' It ended up right on my doorstep. The lady over the road came over and she said, 'I think we ought to call a meeting, about this kohanga.' We didn't know what this meant so we decided to bring a lady [from the Te Kōhanga National Trust] to talk to us. It was pretty radical at that time. It took us three months of talking about it and we decided to start one. The good thing about kohanga was that we could control what happened.[43]

This changed Walker's life, as it did for many other Māori mothers and grand-mothers:

We started with the politics of getting the kohanga going. They introduced a training package, the Blue Book Syllabus [1984].[44] We enrolled in training because we thought we could do this with our children. We had a very good kaumatua who took two days leave every month [from his job]. He flared my interest in things Maori. The most important thing at that time was what was happening in the kohanga with the children and me.

The issue of training was crucial for the national trust. At a national wānanga held at parliament in 1983 workshops considered the themes and content that might define a Māori view of child development.[45] These became the basis of a proposed training programme.[46] In 1984 a flurry of political activity provided funding through Department of Labour employment schemes and training branches were set up around the country. A Te Kōhanga Reo Trust Certificate of five modules and work experience was detailed in the *Blue Book Syllabus*. This pattern of establishment, followed by the need and demand for training, was common to all the other early childhood services. Each vested their own philosophy in their training. The stop-gap funding was also similar, but again essential in creating momentum for more secure funding. For Te Kōhanga Reo, this was to come in the 1990s.

Mere Mitchell heard about Te Kōhanga Reo in 1984, when she had a two-year-old:

We had a kindergarten in the area. My child was too young at two and there was a long waiting list. At that time I didn't like the kindergarten. I didn't see any Maori faces. I heard there was a kohanga. I didn't have any transport but I bussed over [to the other side of town] and they took me on.[47]

She found a very different style of learning and teaching from her previous experience in a Playcentre:

The kaiako was an older lady. She was quite strict. She used to have a stick as a disciplinary measure. It was in a small room and there was a lot of rote learning. It was amazing how these three- and four-year-olds would sit there … There was hardly any opportunity for play and I did find that quite hard. They had a few cheap plastic blocks. I knew from my own experience at playcentre that they were not good toys, but that wasn't a priority for the kids to be playing … The programme wasn't totally in Maori. It was what I would now call bilingual but back then I thought, 'Wow, this is neat, these kids are talking Maori.'

Questions of how to operate a kōhanga reo and what equipment to use caused much discussion where Rita Walker worked. What Māori early childhood education might mean in practice was developed through trial and error:

We wanted our children to know their whakapapa. We wanted our children to acknowledge karakia as part of their day. We wanted waiata. We wanted story telling. We began with a mihi. There was an awareness that play was an automatic part of a child's life but we didn't know to what extent. We knew blocks were really important but there were lots of toys I wouldn't consider developmentally appropriate for children now … We decided we needed to find out for ourselves first before we began implementing what we perceived as things Maori. The reo was very important and there was the realisation that language development was really important. As we learnt more about Maori things, like Ranginui and Papa, we began implementing them. We had done this when we were children but we never knew it as the ideas were conceptual to our parents … We were doing wonderful things with our children such as writing our own songs. We were playing a lot outside in the dirt and planting gardens, and when we spoke about Tangaroa we'd have fish nets all over the place. It was a developmental thing we had to go through ourselves. No one could tell us. We had to figure it out.

Kōhanga reo programmes challenged the emphasis on spontaneous play regarded as almost sacrosanct by the other early childhood programmes, and, like the earlier Māori preschools, promoted a more direct teaching role for adults.

The first kōhanga reo national hui was held at Tūrangawaewae marae, Ngaruawahia, in January 1984. One thousand delegates arrived. The hui provided a forum to reaffirm the stated kaupapa, as well as deliberate on what this might mean in terms of the programme for children, the training for kaiako and involvement of whanau.[48] On the political front, the Maori Educational Development Conference – Nga Tumanako, held at

Tūrangawaewae marae in March 1984, was an occasion to position Te Kōhanga Reo in the wider spectrum of education for Māori. Concern was expressed at the 'meagre resources' so far provided by the state and the burden being carried by Māori communities.[49] James Henare opened the conference, affirming his support for Te Kōhanga Reo. He recalled his own upbringing in Māori, where speaking English met with disapproval, and his education at school, where the reverse happened and he was forbidden to speak Māori.[50] In an address entitled 'Picking up the Challenge', William Renwick outlined the past and present policy of the Department of Education. He concluded that 'discussions and arguments' on cultural issues had become

> painful and confusing. Concern for cultural diversity and cultural respect … [are issues] to be faced up to in every aspect of our lives as New Zealanders. [Teachers are] being confronted [with] questions on the way they should act in our emerging multicultural society.[51]

In 1985 the findings of the Waitangi Tribunal Report relating to te reo Māori condemned the policies of the state education system as a failure.[52] The Department of Education was to rethink its older priorities of multiculturalism and Taha Maori.[53]

The government's responses to the rapid expansion of kōhanga reo were cautious. It became necessary, in the (differing) interests of both Te Kōhanga Reo and the government, to clarify the place of Te Kōhanga Reo within the framework of education and early childhood services, as well as within the wider goals of Māori development. There were inevitable tensions: state interest and investment meant increasing state control. The placement of Te Kōhanga Reo outside the existing educational frameworks and state controls had been the kernel of its success, yet financial viability demanded some accommodation. Funding through the Department of Maori Affairs had been mainly untagged, the decisions resting with the Te Kohanga Reo National Trust.[54] Tawhiwhirangi recalls that the attitude was: 'There it is. You manage it. You run it. You decide the policies and how you are going to do it.'[55] It was the 1989 education reforms that finally caused, in the words of Patricia Maringi Gina Johnston, 'the prodigal child [to] come home'.[56]

During late 1984 discussions were under way between the Cabinet Social Equity Committee, Treasury, and the offices of the Minister of Finance (Roger Douglas) and the Minister of Education (Russell Marshall) with a view to developing a long-term funding policy. In the event the solutions were always short term. Proposals that there be a review of Te Kōhanga Reo also moved slowly. Establishing acceptable terms of reference and appropriate consultation processes was a complex process. A $2.5 million grant was given to Te Kōhanga Reo for 1985–86. A further funding allocation to cover the years 1987–89 totalled $11.1 million, but with the proviso that no further allocation be approved until a review had been undertaken.[57] The terms of reference for the review were finalised in 1987, and the report was completed the following year, by which time the government was releasing its blueprints for a wider reform of educational administration. This was to shift Te Kōhanga Reo from the Department of Maori Affairs into a new Ministry of Education.

The findings of the review were not surprising. Most important was the acknowledgement of Te Kōhanga Reo as a 'vigorous lively movement, [which] arrested the fragmentation of the traditional cultural base … revitalised the uses of the marae, and [helped] preserve the Maori language'.[58] Te Kōhanga Reo was increasing the participation rates of Māori children in early childhood education; but more than that, it was involving families and whanau, as envisaged under the original kaupapa.

The review also reported that Te Kōhanga Reo faced substantive problems, to do with stress caused by the lack of skilled people and insufficient money. Fund-raising was a burden on communities. Some key recommendations were: that there be a bulk grant of $20 million provided directly to Te Kohanga Reo National Trust; that the trust assume responsibility for licensing each kōhanga reo; and that the trust and the Department of Education develop basic minimum standards specifically for kōhanga reo. The recommendations vested substantive autonomy in the national trust.

In the event, as the next chapter will outline, the spirit of these recommendations became lost amidst the administrative reforms to bring all early childhood services under a unified regulatory and funding framework, and, by the early 1990s, a national curriculum framework. This was not the dream of autonomy outside the mainstream. Nonetheless, by 1989 Te Kōhanga Reo was the fourth-largest provider of early childhood care, catering for 11% of under-five-year-olds attending an early childhood service. There were 500 kōhanga reo with approximately 8000 children. Te Kōhanga Reo had become the cornerstone of the government's Māori education policy.

KURA KAUPAPA: TRANSITION TO SCHOOL

From the inception of Te Kōhanga Reo there was pressure on schools, as Jean Puketapu told the *Listener* in 1982:

The crunch point will come when the bilingual youngsters start school. 54,000 of them if kohanga reo lives up to its early promise. 'Already our parents are starting to ask what's going to happen when these children turn five,' says Puketapu. 'We tell them they should be starting to demand bilingual schools. We'll certainly have the numbers to fill them. These children will have been speaking Maori since birth. They'll be living in two universes.'[59]

As early as August 1982 the Department of Maori Affairs informed the Minister of Education of the need to plan for graduates from an estimated 332 kōhanga reo by 1985. The minister, Merv Wellington, assured parliament that 'the Department is conducting many schemes to ensure that the expectations of parents are met'.[60] A flurry of activity began in the Department of Education to estimate numbers, compile available resources, and initiate liaison between the local schools and ngā kōhanga reo. Schools reported to the department that they were 'managing'. Some established bilingual classrooms, or enlisted the support of Māori speakers in the community. Within a year, budget estimates were compiled to create extra teaching resources, appoint more itinerant teachers of Māori and employ Māori language assistants in classrooms.[61]

In November 1984 Roger Douglas, Minister of Finance in the new Labour government, called for a report from the Department of Education to 'indicate what policy changes in education are likely to be required to provide for children emerging from kohanga reo, together with an estimate of the costs of such measures'. Douglas noted: 'I consider this to be an important matter as it could have quite large effects on the shape of Vote: Education over the coming years.'[62] The 1984 annual report of the Department of Education stated that a Māori language syllabus for primary schools had been prepared for trial at selected schools. Programmes to train and appoint kaiarahi reo to work in primary schools began. *Te Kohanga Reo Review* reported, however, that:

> The Department of Education resources and policies did not keep pace. Dissatisfaction emerged within Maoridom for a number of reasons. The most cogent was that many of the children lost the language within a term at school. Some schools were unable to provide the teachers with the necessary skills and knowledge; others said they could only provide for the children if the parents paid for the salaries of fluent speakers required.[63]

Kōhanga reo whanau reported a host of grievances about the experiences faced by their children on arrival at school:

Tikanga Maori takes second place to tikanga Pakeha. This represents a major re-orientation … the children become a Maori minority in their learning environment … learning no longer takes place in a whanau context.[64]

Dissatisfaction led to the establishment of the first independent Māori immersion primary school – kura kaupapa Māori – at the Hoani Waititi marae in Auckland. At the opening in September 1985 Prime Minister David Lange acknowledged that: 'The school has been established because efforts within the state system to incorporate Maori elements into general education have been too slow for many.'[65] By 1989 there were six kura kaupapa operating 'privately' outside the mainstream, extending the principles of Te Kōhanga Reo into school-aged programmes with full Māori immersion. Linda and Graham Smith later wrote that:

> Te Kohanga Reo and Kura Kaupapa Maori, by their very existence outside of the state structures, provide a manifest critique of existing state schooling. In a sense Maori parents have moved to respond to the crisis within the state education by a resistance strategy of withdrawal.[66]

However, withdrawal was not a financial or logistic option for many parents. Two years earlier the Department of Education had published *A Guide to Bilingual Education for New Zealand Schools*. It stated that '… a plural society [bilingual and bicultural education] provides a mechanism whereby cultures are able to be integrated whilst still retaining distinctive cultural identities'.[67] By 1991 the primary school sector had 154 bilingual classes and 21 bilingual schools, but the kaupapa underlying these bilingual initiatives in the mainstream remained contentious. Kuni Jenkins criticised the approach:

> Bilingual education has two specific foci: developing fluency in te reo Maori, and fully maintaining the standard school curriculum at every level … bilingual programmes, in order to be judged successful, must have an element of enrichment for the mainstream … These policies … have little commitment to Maori language and culture itself.[68]

The politics of establishing a bilingual classroom were not easy. The experiences described by Rita Walker provide some glimpses of the determination and frustration involved. As a kōhanga reo parent she found herself embroiled in the politics of what was going to happen to their Māori-speaking children:

> We decided we would keep an eye on the newspapers and have a look at all the local school AGMs where some of our parents had children. When they had their AGM we decided to go and stack the committees … I had become quite political … The principal at the first school thought all his birthdays had come

at once when he saw all these Maori people. We nominated five mothers who had children there already. We were really happy because that constituted about 60% of his committee. Then we got to put the agenda on the table and we said we wanted discussion on a bilingual unit … He just jumped at me, 'I'll have none of that nonsense at my school, thank you. I'll have no separatism.' So we all just stood up and left and the five mothers put in their resignation. He had to have another election. We kept our eye on the paper and then went to the next school. The same lot of people [went]. There were thirteen of us.[69]

This pattern was repeated until, forewarned, the principal of Fifth Avenue School in Hamilton pre-empted a wrangle at his own AGM. He visited the women at their kōhanga reo and said: 'You don't have to stack my committee because I'm prepared to talk.' As Walker recalled, 'He was happy to give us a room. He was happy to give us a teacher but we had to give him one of our parents who had te reo … Our children started school in September 1986. It was the first bilingual unit in Hamilton.' Within a year parents were again unhappy because their children were speaking too much English; with the support of the principal they began a total immersion programme.

These kinds of political issues were being addressed by Māori parents in different ways in different places, but it was from these beginnings that many kura kaupapa began. This was rarely easy, as Walker recalls:

We saw white flight, we saw brown flight … We ended up Maori fighting Maori. It was very painful … It split families and friendships. We had to do it to give our children a choice, to give Maori people a choice … the fights we had with the Ministry [of Education] were awesome. It took six years from our first bilingual unit until the whole school was total immersion … Lots of times when you're involved in Maori education you feel like opting out because it's too hard.[70]

This was 1992, and under the new education policies of *Tomorrow's Schools* (1988) a kura kaupapa inside the state system was possible – if the school community could be persuaded.

EARLY CHILDHOOD RESPONSES

Initiatives during the 1960s to persuade Māori parents to send their children to preschool increased the participation of Māori children from 15% of three- to four-year-olds in 1965 to 38% in 1973.[71] During the 1970s, however, there was a decline in the uptake of Maori Education Foundation (MEF) support for Māori preschool initiatives.[72] Renewed efforts by the MEF in the Waiariki district during the late 1970s to early 1980s indicated a range of initiatives in rural, city, mainstream and Māori settings. The MEF preschool officer, Hine Potaka, was running the bilingual Awhina Whanau programme based at Maketu, a development from the earlier Te Roopu Awhina Tamariki (see Chapter Three).[73] Potaka had become prominent in developing Māori early childhood programmes based on Māori family values, language and the use of natural materials. She worked across Māori and Pākehā groups. Her reflections on the emergence of kōhanga reo in the area are insightful:

> While the philosophy of Kohanga Reo was readily accepted there was a certain amount of apprehension, as once again the community was seeking some positive direction on how to implement the programme. The community groups turned to the MEF for this direction, which unfortunately caused conflict with the programme organisers in the district. If Kohanga Reo is to be successful there will have to be greater liaison between these two naturally complementary programmes.[74]

One was total immersion and one was bilingual. In the event, the former (with the backing of the Department of Maori Affairs) eclipsed the earlier MEF approaches. Nevertheless, Potaka's Awhina Whanau programme continued, and its pioneering approaches were a resource for some kōhanga reo. The earlier Māori preschools, or those Playcentres with mainly Māori children, tended in time to become kōhanga reo.

The popularity of Te Kōhanga Reo dramatically increased the participation level of Māori children, and by 1991 it accounted for 46% of all Māori enrolments in early childhood programmes.[75] The others were attending mainstream programmes, many of whose staff were ill-prepared to provide a programme inclusive of even Taha Maori. In 1980 the Department of Education produced *Nga Tamariki Iti o Aotearoa – The First Steps in the Introduction of Maori Studies for Preschool Children*. William Renwick stated in the foreword that it was 'designed to help teachers and pupils understand Maori culture … This is the first effort at developing resource material for preschool groups.'[76] 'Dawn Ellis', a Māori Playcentre parent, recalls the debates in the early 1980s between the Taha Maori approach from the department and those parents who 'were wanting to integrate Maori in a more in-depth way'. 'Ellis' could see both sides: 'I guess I was in a bit of a privileged situation where I could move between both worlds … Even though I don't speak Maori I do switch between the two within my family environment.' The Taha Maori focus was on:

Waiata, words, numbers, colours … [One woman] from our playcentre wanted to take it further than that … There was a lot of resistance. One time correct pronunciation came up and people got upset. I remember a friend saying that she wanted her children to have the opportunity to learn about their Maori culture and she wasn't prepared to put the energy into convincing and bringing a whole centre on board when it was just as easy to drive down the road.[77]

The emergence of Te Kōhanga Reo heightened debates, but also spurred endeavours by mainstream services to be more responsive to Māori issues, not only in relation to Māori children. The *Playcentre Journal* (no. 55, 1982) told its readers:

Maybe your centre has no Maori children. It is very easy to ignore culture altogether in that situation. But we all need to learn about other cultures around us, and it is up to the majority culture to make sure our children don't miss out on the enriching experiences of another language and other values.

This upsurge of Pākehā interest in Taha Maori could not be sustained by Māori. In a challenging address in 1987 Kathie Irwin analysed 'the Pakeha response to kohanga reo'.[78] There was the issue of the resourcing, which 'is being funded off the backs of Maori community. A community that is already under-resourced and under tremendous stress.' There were issues for Māori children not at kōhanga reo. Irwin wondered:

What bicultural education programmes will they receive in our kindergartens, in our playcentres and in our creches? What will they learn about cross-cultural interaction and understanding? What will they learn about our culture?[79]

Participating in the Department of Education course 'Taha Maori in Early Childhood Education', held at the Lopdell Centre in 1988, Royal Tangaere said:

The challenge was put by the Maori women to their Tauiwi sisters to stand beside them, and not only [to] support Kohanga Reo but also to acknowledge the Maori people as Tangata Whenua. In order to do this it was necessary for Tauiwi to acknowledge the true intentions of the Treaty of Waitangi.[80]

The participants, representative of the main early childhood organisations, proclaimed that:

To honour the Treaty of Waitangi we require that all early childhood policies and provision be consistent with the principles of partnership, power and participation which are embedded in the Treaty.[81]

An eight-point 'statement of intent' was published to hasten considerations by early childhood organisations of Treaty issues. Five months later the statement was considered by the 1989 Lopdell Centre course 'Racism and Anti-Racist Strategies for Early Childhood Education'. Participants analysed the 'web of racism' threaded though education and early childhood institutions. They urged that the statement be adopted by the Department of Education working groups being set up to plan the implementation of the 1989 education reform policies for early childhood.[82]

In the early 1980s Jenny Ritchie was a young kindergarten teacher at Huntly West, keen to redress the racist attitudes she saw in the kindergarten setting, and concerned that the programme was primarily designed 'to keep the middle-class white parents happy'. The kindergarten had about 60% Māori families, 'but it should have been 90%'. The starting of a kōhanga at the nearby marae had little impact. The kindergarten and kōhanga reo 'worlds' were distant even in a small town. Māori were also divided:

> We didn't have liaison with kohanga reo at all. I just knew about it. They didn't invite us to visit and we didn't approach them. A lot of Maori families still came to the kindergarten because I guess Te Kohanga Reo was new and hadn't got a lot of credibility outside of the Maori community … A lot of Maori families still wanted their children to be ready for school and they wouldn't have articulated that in any other way.[83]

Ritchie subsequently became involved in Project Waitangi, which sponsored courses for Pākehā on anti-racism and Treaty issues, and undertook a lot of work with early childhood groups. Nevertheless, trying to implement ideas related to the Treaty in the kindergarten was a challenge, as head teacher 'Lesley Howes' recalls:

> It was a very difficult transition for parents and teachers and therefore children. I experienced a lot of bias and a lot of mixed feelings. We have had to work very hard with Maori and Pakeha parents to get where we want to go …
>
> *What were the issues for parents?*
> It was the language to begin with. There was just no way they wanted their kid to be taught Maori … There was no way they wanted Maori words on the front door. It gradually became less threatening and … the community slowly accepted the idea.
>
> *What were the issues for Maori parents?*
> I remember a Maori parent coming to see me in the early stages and saying, 'If you can't speak the language properly then you shouldn't be doing it at all.' … That was important.[84]

Initiatives within mainstream childhood groups and organisations to address Treaty issues, as well as issues of biculturalism and racism, were contentious and often uncomfortable for both Māori and Pākehā. Kindergarten teacher Georgina Kerr recalls the occasion she wrote an article in the *KTA News* inviting Māori teachers to form a Māori group within KTA:

> The flak I got was just amazing. I was told I was setting up an apartheid nation. I went through all the difficulties and upsets of people. In the end because of the feedback and the flak from kindergarten teachers, only six of us registered.[85]

The first informal hui of Māori early childhood teachers was held in 1982 at St Joseph's School, Napier. In 1986 the KTA and ECWU sponsored a first official hui of Māori teachers. Kerr recalls the impact on KTA (and later CECUA):

> Conference came to be a minefield. We just battled it out and had confrontations … I was determined we are going to get those remits [on Treaty issues] through even if it takes four years, five years we are going to do it properly … Teachers were not coping with the lesbian faction of kindergarten teachers. They were not coping very well with the fact that the untrained [childcare workers] were coming into the system, let alone the Maori thing. In the end it was a matter of just fronting up to them. The last straw was when we had a remit over the nuclear free thing. It was too much at one Hamilton conference. I can remember one older kindergarten teacher saying, 'Oh, what next, what is the world coming to?' It was all those issues. They were exciting times, but gosh, it was political.[86]

Changing dynamics were positioning and revealing early childhood education as a much more explicitly political arena.

Early childhood training programmes were gradually addressing cultural issues in both practical and political ways. Val Ford was working in a childcare centre and training with NZCA:

> Acknowledging that there was another language spoken by some people in this country caused enormous strife. To sing a Maori song was quite major. For some staff it was, 'Well, why should we bother, we don't have any Maori children.' There was a lot of discomfort and it took some courage to be different. I can remember a Maori person coming in to visit the centre. She spoke to the babies in Maori. One young staff member was quite put out. 'Why should she come in here and speak to the babies in Maori when we have no Maori babies and they don't understand her anyway?'

NZCA had been fortunate to have Maureen Locke as training director. After many years' involvement in Playcentre and childcare she was committed to improving the situation for Māori children in mainstream settings.[87] She persistently nudged NZCA towards adopting more bicultural approaches in its operations and training delivery. In 1988 a grant from the Roy McKenzie Foundation helped with the implementation of 'bicultural perspectives' into the training materials. That same year the association stated a commitment to examining its responsibilities in line with the principles of the Treaty of Waitangi. Māori tutors were employed to work alongside Pākehā tutors, and funding was set aside for in-service training on Treaty issues.[88] The intentions of the NZCA leaders, however, were not easy to realise in practice, nor were member centres always interested.

For Playcentre groups, despite their long involvement in Māori education, the issues were similarly contentious. The 1980s saw a similar transformation from thinking multiculturally to biculturally. The author of a lead story in the *Playcentre Journal* (no. 44, 1978) had rejected the suggested idea of 'separate programmes' for Māori and Pākehā mothers at Playcentre, but acknowledged that 'Playcentre training is under fire from all quarters … We impose the values of the dominant group upon the minority.' Ten years later Rahera Barrett-Douglas reminded Playcentres about Pākehā responsibilities towards reversing the low status of Māori in New Zealand society. 'These goals cannot be achieved by kohanga reo alone.'[89] The 1989 Playcentre conference passed the remit: 'That Playcentre publicly endorse the Treaty of Waitangi.' Jenny Ritchie was the guest speaker and organised workshops addressing issues of racism. Jill Wesselink was an organiser at that Hamilton conference:

> The intention was to set up a working party to look at what that might mean [for playcentre][90] … There were driving forces from the outside. All of the country and all organisations were needing to look at what the Treaty might mean to their organisation.[91]

The year 1989 was a watershed for early childhood education. and the aftermath is the focus of Part Three of this book. For a brief period, education reforms required all education institutions to address Treaty issues within the operation of their service.

PACIFIC ISLANDS EARLY CHILDHOOD CENTRES

By the 1980s there were large Pacific Islands communities in New Zealand. In the aftermath of the success of Te Kōhanga Reo, new early childhood ventures for Pacific Islands children were poised to begin. Concerns for immigrant Pacific Islands children had already spurred some attempts to encourage their attendance at preschool.[92] A 1984 study showed that 47.5% of Pacific Islands four-year-olds had attended an early childhood centre, compared with 85% of European children.[93] More likely was the attendance of Pacific Islands children at Sunday schools.[94]

In 1972–73 Cook Islands and Samoan mothers had established Lemali Tamaita a Samoa, in Tokoroa (see Chapter Four). This is believed to be the first Pacific Islands early childhood centre in New Zealand, demonstrating a programme in which the respective Islands' languages and culture were to the fore. One account describes 'chants, songs, ditties, stories, picture books and stories written by the mothers. Dance and drama play an important part, using Pacific Islands instruments to explore rhythm patterns for dance accompaniments.'[95] Another programme, Te Punanga o te Reo Kuki Airani, was set up by community officer Tepaeru Terora at the Wellington Multicultural Resource Centre around 1982–83. This catered mainly for Cook Islands children and their families; it operated weekly and was staffed by volunteers. A playgroup was a later development. When Iole Tagoilelagi arrived in Auckland in 1982 from Samoa, several Pacific Islands centres were operating. She described them as not particularly 'Pacific'. There was no focus on indigenous Islands culture and language, but a concentration on English as a preparation for school.[96]

Various threads underpinned the establishment of Pacific Islands centres in the mid-1980s. The impetus of Te Kōhanga Reo was a model, and accounts for the borrowing of the term 'language nest' for some of the early centres. The issues of cultural and language maintenance were centred mainly within the burgeoning immigrant Pacific Islands churches. This connection was a distinctive feature underlying the emergence and support of Pacific Islands early childhood centres.[97] During the 1980s the Pacific Island Polynesian Education Foundation (PIPEF) and the Pacific Women's Council (PACIFICA) were providing a representative voice for Pacific Islands interests, particularly in relation to education. PACIFICA had been aware of the growth of Te Kōhanga Reo and was supportive of its aims.[98] PACIFICA was also committed to promoting the Islands languages of children now being born in New Zealand, as a means of retaining links with the cultures left behind.

Plans to establish a Pacific Islands centre in Wellington began in 1974, but did not come to fruition until 1985, when Fereni Ete, the wife of a church minister, established the first Samoan A`oga Amata in Newtown.[99] This was 'blessed with the support of the whole congregation. Grandmothers and young mothers who did not work were all there to support the centre.'[100] This was the first of a network of A'oga Amata, particularly around Wellington, but also in Dunedin, Christchurch, Palmerston North and Auckland. Most were under the auspices of the Samoan Congregational Christian Church. Ete wrote:

> I strongly argue that without the church, many Pacific Island people, especially Samoans, the largest migrant population in New Zealand, would have had no access to early childhood education in their own language and culture ... When the government did not offer venues and facilities ... the church offered halls. They offered the good leadership of ministers and wives. They offered the care and concern of church members. Ministers and wives worked voluntarily.[101]

Another catalyst was the immigration of several trained preschool teachers from the Pacific Islands. Their qualifications were not recognised in New Zealand but they arrived with a vision of establishing early childhood centres for children from the Pacific Islands. Tagoilelagi, a teacher and the wife of a church minister, established an A'oga Faataitai in 1986, through the auspices of the Women's Fellowship at her Mangere church. Tagoilelagi's previous work training preschool teachers from different Islands nations at the University of the South Pacific was a key resource:

> We brought those ideas [to New Zealand] and established our own preschools. But looking at it we sensed there was a difference in the children ... Although these children have Pacific Island connections they are New Zealand born and they are growing up different. Which is their land? This is their land. They belong here ... So what we are trying to do is to make our children aware of their roots, their cultures, because that is their family tie ... then make them confident to travel to the future ... We called other Pacific Island women in the area. The Cook Islanders came and observed in our centre. They started their centre. The Niuean women came and later established their own centres.

The centres were varied and culturally specific, but there were some common patterns. A description by Feaua'i Burgess of the Newtown A'oga Amata provides some insight to the mix:

> A typical day of the A'oga Amata starts with children arriving with their parents and together choosing a developmental activity ranging from imaginative play through to craft activities and block play. The difference from other preschools is that the Samoan language is being used, members of the extended family are taking part, and Samoan cultural values are being emphasised. An example is the practice of saying lotu (a special prayer at appropriate times).

This is a feature of Samoan home, church activities and children experience it again at the Aʻoga Amata.[102]

There were elements of formality in the programmes. Diane Mara noted that

in some groups the methodology was initially identical to some Sunday school programmes – children sitting in rows, chanting the alphabet, copying the supervisor/adults, singing – all for long periods of time.[103]

In 1986 the best estimate of the total number of Pacific Islands children attending early childhood centres was 2101, comprising 20% of the under-five Pacific Islands population.[104] This figure was to increase. Within two years 14 Pacific Islands language groups (as they were then officially called) were operating. In 1990 the number had increased almost elevenfold to 151, and catered for Islands groups from Niue, Samoa, Tokelau, Tonga, Fiji and the Cook Islands.[105] By 1992 there were 6893 Pacific Islands children enrolled in early childhood education, half of whom attended one of the Pacific Islands language groups. The growth of centres and participation levels continued. As with Te Kōhanga Reo, the way this was achieved was through voluntary work. 'Our journey is one of pain, struggles and hardships. You know, whenever we overcome a milestone we laugh and cry amongst ourselves, shed tears, then laugh,' says Telesia McDonald.[106]

Unlike Te Kōhanga Reo, there was no national co-ordination or any political impetus from government to fund Pacific Island language groups until 1988–89 when the government allocated $463,000, rising to $1,197,000 in 1990–91. This contributed to the increasing rates of participation, and was in line with funding for part-time community playgroups. Many of the Pacific Islands language groups, which started as informal playgroups, wanted to expand to provide full-time care and education, as well as parent education. Initially, only one Pacific Islands centre met the criteria for licensing and funding as a childcare centre. Unsuitable buildings and the lack of trained staff were the issues.[107] The 1989 education reforms created more barriers and marginalised the Pacific Islands centres. By 1992, only three groups were chartered for funding. McDonald, along with many others, continued to be unhappy with government policy. In 1995 she told Maris O'Rourke, secretary of the Ministry of Education: 'Pacific Island people do not want to stay as playgroups forever. They want to be licensed. You have to do something about it.' Shortly after this the first targeted money was allocated to help Pacific Islands groups meet requirements for licensing and chartering.[108]

Training had also been a barrier. Existing training programmes were not very useful in terms of their curriculum content, and their academic entry criteria excluded many Pacific Islands women. A noteworthy exception was NZCA, which agreed to fast-track the training of four Pacific Islands women, including Tagoilelagi. She predicted, accurately: 'There will be a day when our Pacific Islands women will write a training programme of our own.'[109] In 1988 the Department of Education offered additional funding to NZCA to support this work,[110] and in 1989 Iole Tagoilelagi in Auckland, Feaua`i Burgess in Wellington and Jean Turae in Tokoroa (soon to be replaced by Mi`i Tangaroa) were appointed area training supervisors responsible for delivering the NZCA training programme to 40 Pacific Islands trainees. Their fees were funded through PACIFICA. The following year there were 70 students.[111]

Separate from these initiatives, Burgess was involved with Fereni Ete in Wellington in the establishment of the A`oga Amata training scheme, initially funded through a Department of Labour Access programme. This provided a 12-week programme in the Samoan language. Between 1987 and 1990, 123 Pacific Islands women graduated from training programmes, 80% of them from the A`oga Amata programme, although this was not recognised as a sufficient qualification for licensing and chartering an early childhood centre.[112]

In 1990 the separate Pacific Islands groups established the Pacific Islands Early Childhood Council of Aotearoa (PIECCA) to represent and negotiate their interests with the government. Soon there were separate network groups representing the Cook Islands, Samoa, Tonga, Tokelau and Niue respectively.[113] These groups were affiliated with PIECCA, but also liaised separately on behalf of their own communities.

Parallel to these centre-based developments there was the work of Anau Ako Pasifika. Its origins were different. The Bernard van Leer Foundation from the Netherlands invests in early childhood development projects, particularly for minority groups or in developing countries. The particular situation of Pacific Islands families in New Zealand met its criteria. An idea was seeded prior to the emergence of the Pacific Islands centres. By 1986 the Department of Education, in consultation with PACIFICA and PIPEF, was developing a proposal for a home intervention programme. The following year the Minister of Education announced the Anau Ako Pasifika project in Tokoroa, Auckland and Wellington, co-ordinated by Poko Morgan, a New Zealand-trained primary teacher from the Cook Islands.[114] The work of the project was carried out by home tutors, who visited the homes of families. They provided resources, fostered parent–child interactions, (first) language development and pre-literacy skills, and supported parents in the early rearing of their child. 'We practise the use of natural materials, revitalising our own music and songs, revitalising our language and giving our children confidence and competence to move on …'[115] By 1991 192 families had been involved in the project, which continued to operate after the completion of the research phase.[116] Morgan became a prominent advocate for promoting Pacific Islands early childhood interests, and for improving understandings within the early childhood sector of the particular issues facing Pacific Islands communities. In the same year as the Anau Ako Pasifika project began, Morgan was appointed to a government working party convened by Anne Meade to develop a new blueprint for the funding and administration of early childhood services. There was therefore from 1987 a voice for Pacific Islands centres at the table of the most significant political early childhood forum in New Zealand since the Bailey report of 1947.

By the mid-1980s government policy was promising to address equity issues. Indigenous and cultural issues were now to the fore, as were the politics of childcare and the employment of those who worked with children. The values, codes, populations and politics of 1980s New Zealand had shifted. Early childhood education, which had once consisted solely of kindergarten and Playcentre, now encompassed the diverse childcare sector and included strong voices from Māori and Pacific Islands communities, whose do-it-your-self approach was so revealing of the inequity of existing government policy for early childhood services.

PART THREE

State Interest and Devolution
1980s–1990s

CHAPTER EIGHT

Winds of Reform

The latter half of the 1980s was a time of governmental and economic reform: by the 1990s the effects were rippling through all aspects of life in New Zealand.[1] There were winners and losers. The impetus came from a Labour government returned to power in 1984 after nine years in opposition. Frustrations with the conservatism of the National government, from both the left and the right, created the climate for change. The agenda was guided by an ideological shift to the economic right. The new government questioned the relevance of centralised bureaucracy, and the extent of state involvement in the economy, for both ideological and fiscal reasons. Devolution and deregulation was the aim, based on the view that private-sector approaches and market forces would make the state sector more effective and efficient. Val Burns, director of the early childhood division in the Department of Education, described the 'quiet revolution' to a London audience in 1989:[2]

> New Zealand is in a transition stage and no-one knows whether these reforms will work. Many are bewildered, some feel betrayed, others think it is too dangerous an experiment for a small country … There is no turning back the clock … At the time of my departure the latest government department to enter the Place de la Concorde and face the guillotine is the Department of Education. Madame Defarge has knitted into her scarf the names of many senior departmental officials.[3]

Anne Meade portrayed New Zealand knitters in a less sinister way, telling a Hong Kong audience that same year: 'New Zealand is in the midst of knitting a new early childhood "sweater". In fact, it is in the middle of making a whole new set of clothes.'[4] A National government, re-elected in 1990, further questioned the government's role in social services. Older expectations of universal welfare services crumbled. New codes of provider contestability, user-pays and targeted assistance emerged.[5] Breaking 'dependency' on the state was the goal.

Education was a focus for restructuring by both governments. The language and ideology of private-sector business and management were applied across the board as the state became active in shaping a new construction of childhood, linked to global economic agendas. New Zealand needed to become more competitive. Older educational goals of psychological well-being, equality of opportunity and/or child-centred learning were deemed to have failed to create the necessary skills for an 'enterprise society'.

Labour's restructuring devolved responsibility for the operation of the education system to the 'self-managing school' or institution. 'Administering for excellence' was the catchphrase used by the 1988 Picot Taskforce, which spearheaded the first wave of reforms.[6] Critics, however, were not convinced that a market approach would solve the problems of inequity and disadvantage, as later reformers promised.[7]

The chapters in Part Three place the institutions of early childhood in the context of the reforms by both Labour and National governments. Labour was persuaded that there was a crisis in early childhood, and that an increased investment would bring benefits to children, women, families, communities and the nation. Early childhood education moved to centre stage on the government's agenda. The subsequent reforms were part of the wider educational and governmental restructuring but, more particularly, the result of orchestrated campaigns by early childhood groups. From 1989, a new era seemed about to begin for early childhood, with the services entering a more equitable, if sometimes fraught, partnership with the state.

Early childhood services were the first rung in a seamless education system, which positioned the Labour government's gaze on the 'before fives' within its broader economic goals for education.[8] Despite devolution, this meant more centralised control over the curriculum content. Children's learning became a focus for governmental audit. New government agencies required evidence that measurable learning outcomes, useful for school success and workplace employability, resulted from the play of children. Chapter Eight appraises the reform process and its aftermath for early childhood. This was a dynamic engagement of 'accommodation and resistance' by early childhood groups to rapidly changing state agendas.[9]

It was a welcome change when the Labour Minister of Education, Russell Marshall, announced in 1985 that 'kindergarten teachers should probably be paid professors' salaries and professors should get kindergarten teachers' salaries ... [to] give a truer reflection of the educational impact of each group'.[10] But turning rhetoric into action was not easy, as Val Burns recalled:

> Russell Marshall was making supportive noises about early childhood but nothing seemed to change in the department. It was still the outside groups pushing for childcare and early childhood. The men in the department didn't want to hear it ... There was a block. You have to remember that as director of early childhood I was not at the top of decision-making. I was fourth down.[11]

Expectations from the early childhood sector for change were high. The 1985 government report *Childcare Services, Impact and Opportunities* positioned childcare as a key issue for families, with the view that the financial responsibility should be shared with the state. This shift in attitude was the result of 20 years of lobbying by some, and a decade of strategic planning. The Ministers of Education and Social Welfare announced that discussions would start on bringing all early childhood services under the Department of Education.[12] Another report, *Childcare in Transition* (1985), was produced.[13] Equity issues to do with access, funding and the poor quality of some centres also needed to be addressed.

The showcase of the government's early childhood policy was a parliamentary forum in 1985. Anne Meade was the organiser:

> Government needed to reassure people who were a bit nervous about what had been recommended in the Social Advisory Council report ... The other important thing was that for the first time Kohanga Reo publicly worked in partnership with the rest of early childhood. Politicians were watching this. It was important for Kohanga too because it gave them an occasion to couch their position in ways that Pakeha understood.[14]

Kaumātua John Bennett outlined the directions for Māori preschoolers at kōhanga reo.[15] More bluntly, Donna Awatere told the audience: 'Integration and assimilation have suffocated us. To survive we have to leave you.'[16] Nevertheless, all groups shared similar concerns over funding, and the principle of equitable funding for diverse provision was further cemented.

Prime Minister Lange opened the forum, acknowledging that 'It has taken far too long for early childhood care and education to begin to be taken seriously.' He promised government support in this process. Delegates were told that their brief was 'to come up with strategies to make improvements in the area'.[17] The feeling of most delegates was that the strategies already existed and the delay was government tardiness. Maris O'Rourke recalled 10 years of conference-going:

> We made many fine recommendations … We wanted to change the world. I still do because in some ways nothing has changed. I have seen many of the same women, saying many of the same things, on many occasions since then, and again here over the last two days.[18]

Rosslyn Noonan paid homage to

> all the wonderful cheeky, impudent and, above all, disagreeable women in the early childhood sector, particularly those who over the last 20 years have brought us to the position where a political party elected as government has, as a major policy priority, a commitment to the development of early childhood care and education … Unfortunately, the challenges we have to face today are exactly the same as the ones we've had to face in the last 10–12–20 years.[19]

Noonan was angry at government delays in the transfer of childcare services to the Department of Education. Summing up, Geraldine McDonald told ministers and politicians that the conference was in fact about 'cake! … about wanting a share of the cake, needing a larger cake, but actually getting crumbs and leftovers'.[20]

The transfer of childcare services finally took place in 1986. Few other countries had managed to combine the components of the care and education of young children within one administrative agency. The historical and pedagogical divisions were too deep, and the advocates were less united than in New Zealand. However, there were some harsh realities to deal with. One education officer recalls her induction into her new role of checking childcare centres for regulatory compliance:

> [The other officer] took me to this centre and she said, 'While I am talking to the owner, you have a look in the cupboard under the stairwell.' I wondered why. I found three children in there. The owner had seen us coming and put three children in the cupboard. The owner was over number.[21]

The funding imbalances between the services remained. Pam Croxford, president of NZCA, told the media: 'The real issue is that childcare needs substantive funding increases, not just top-ups from government.'[22] The working party on the transfer had agreed that substantive funding was needed immediately. A matter they could not agree on was whether the privately owned centres should get new funding.[23]

The issue of private centres was contentious. Increasing government subsidies encouraged business ventures in childcare. Some private centres set up their own advocacy organisations – the Licensed Childcare Centres Federation (LCCF) and the Associated Childcare Council (ACC) – to ensure that demands for increased wages, improved regulations and higher qualifications did not erode profit margins. Some of these centres were threatened by the strengthening industrial demands of ECWU, which in 1985 negotiated its first collective award for wages with mainly community employers. The next year a breakthrough was made (with help in the Arbitration Court): the establishment of a national award and unionisation for all childcare workers. In 1987 industrial action raised salary levels again, although they were still well below those of kindergarten teachers. Continual pressure by ECWU ensured that the issue of childcare funding remained to the fore with both employers and workers, who, in turn, kept up pressure on the government.[24]

A significant achievement during Labour's first term was three-year early childhood teacher training. This gave parity at last with primary teachers and allowed for university degree options. The longstanding quest for three-year kindergarten training had been continually shelved. In 1985 a working party had been established,[25] but events overtook this group. The one-year childcare courses in four colleges of education had only reinforced the old divisions between kindergarten and childcare. In 1986 a childcare working party had recommended three-year integrated training.[26] Treasury was against the idea, arguing that 'it is inadequately justified, [and] it has potentially large downstream costs' due to demands by early childhood teachers for higher wages.[27] However, the department's early childhood division strenuously argued the importance of better qualified teachers, and Minister Russell Marshall was a keen supporter, so the policy was passed.[28] The first programmes began in 1988. This policy was lucky to slip through the political process just before the minister lost his job, and there was an upsurge of Treasury's power in government.

Kindergarteners were somewhat taken aback by the sudden disappearance of their specialised training. Colleges of education were directed that the new programmes must be inclusive of care and education, cover programmes for care of babies, and have more emphasis on education studies and the cultural and family context of children's lives.[29] New Zealand again became an international leader in breaking down the historical divisions between preschool and childcare training.

Pieces of the mosaic were coming together for change: uniting care and education, raising the status of teachers, and addressing quality issues. At the Fourth Early Childhood Convention in 1987 it was timely to reflect on the Labour government's first term. I told the audience:

> The politics are confusing ... The government has listened to the early childhood constituency. We are on first-name terms, we talk of co-operation, we don't have to wear our pearls! But does it work? ... 1986 was the year when everything was going well for us. The machinery was put in place. It's been jobs for the girls and the occasional boy ... But there are limits to what you can do with beautiful policy if you don't get the funding. In the childcare centre where I come from, fees to parents continue to rise. It costs $120 per week to keep my one-year-old infant in childcare. The irony is that I can probably afford it now because I got one of the jobs for the girls [at Hamilton Teachers' College].[30]

Government interest in increasing its investment in early childhood attracted the scrutiny of economists, who wanted hard measures of the costs and claimed benefits to children, women, families and society.[31] The convention visit by David Weikart, founder of the High/Scope Preschool Project in the US, was opportune. His longitudinal study demonstrated lasting social and educational gains to the participants where the early childhood programme was a quality one. Weikart told the audience: 'You are more effective crime fighters than anyone in the country. You are the most effective people in the nation for reducing teen pregnancy.'[32] Weikart was taken on a whirlwind series of ministerial, media and departmental visits, including Treasury and the renowned financier, Bob Jones. The hard data of Weikart's research revealed that at age 19, those who had participated in the preschool programme in the US had significantly lower rates of crime and teenage pregnancy, and were more likely to have attended college and have a job, than those who had not. Weikart's message was that the long-term savings to society were a profitable return on the investment.[33]

The media were interested. The *Dominion* reported:

> Mr Marshall urged early childhood workers to help him battle Treasury for more education dollars and convince the Minister of Finance, Roger Douglas, of the value of early childhood education; [but noted that there might be] political dangers in Mr Marshall's very public battle with his Cabinet colleagues.[34]

This showed an inkling of the divisions ahead, although Douglas claimed that he, too, saw expenditure on early childhood education as beneficial:

Only 2% of New Zealand's huge total spending on education has been going to early childhood. This Government has already begun to put that right. So I am not arguing that early childhood should get no new money. But I am arguing that early childhood has much more to gain, if it can persuade the rest of the education system to get its priorities right.[35]

In March 1987 the government released the Roper report on violence. Marshall told many audiences that the 'seeds of violence were sown in the early years', and that increased support for early childhood provision and parent education could be part of the cure.[36] The political scrutiny on early childhood was both intense and contentious.

AGAINST THE ODDS

The Treasury briefing papers for the second term of the Labour government, beginning in 1987, have been regarded as marking the ascendancy of 'New Right' thinking on the role of government in education.[37] Treasury argued that:

> In the technical sense used by economics, education is not in fact a 'public good' … education shares the main characteristics of other commodities traded in the market place[38] … State intervention is liable to quash or discourage the development of new or experimental forms of education provision but which cannot readily be accommodated with existing institutional forms.[39]

Prime Minister Lange assumed the education portfolio, arguably to highlight the importance the government placed on education, but also to hold the line against Treasury's agenda. Education became a contestable 'battleground'.[40] The 43-page 'Treasury case' against early childhood sought to limit the state's role in early childhood by assuming that parents (meaning women) 'universally' have the primary responsibility for the care and development of young children. It asked 'Why intervene?', 'Who benefits?' and 'Who pays?', particularly in relation to childcare, where Treasury identified individual mothers and the workplace as the main beneficiaries. The papers conceded the possibility of societal benefits from early childhood education, but only for children of low socio-economic status. Treasury asked the government to consider a greater emphasis on targeted funding assistance (i.e. means testing) and the possibility of attaching funding entitlement (i.e. vouchers) to the 'consumer' (i.e. children) rather than the 'provider' (i.e. centres). In the event, and 'against the odds', Treasury's view did not prevail.[41] Lange held to a position of universal provision, even though the 1987 sharemarket crash tipped opinion towards a monetarist viewpoint. A Royal Commission on Social Policy had been deliberating since 1986.[42] Its task was to reposition the welfare state in the late twentieth century and Rosslyn Noonan was one of the commissioners. However, by the time the report was released, social policy had been sidelined for economic and education reform. It appeared that early childhood education, too, might be pushed from its central position.

Despite the storm clouds, several factors were in place to support early childhood. Women were rising in the ranks of the union movement, which still exerted an influence on the Labour Party. More women MPs had been elected to parliament, including Sonja Davies. Margaret Shields was the Minister of Women's Affairs, and KTA activist Lynne Bruce was appointed to her office. Anne Meade's appointment in 1988 to a position as social policy adviser on education in the prime minister's office was crucial. She was also asked to convene another working group on early childhood care and education, part of the Cabinet Social Equity Committee programme of education reform. The linking of early childhood concerns with the broader reforms detailed in *Tomorrow's Schools* (1988) and *Learning for Life* (1987) was crucial for keeping their place on the government agenda – even if the ride was rocky.[43]

The subsequent report, *Education to be More* (1988), known as the Meade report, is seen nationally and internationally as a significant philosophical statement on the benefits of early childhood education for children, their families, their communities and society.[44] Myths that had long constrained early childhood policy development were finally buried. The report acknowledged the holistic nature of early childhood care and education and its benefits for both the present and the future. Essential elements of the proposed model were features addressing the interests of children, the interests of women as caregivers and workers, and the interests of cultural survival.[45] The authors argued that a substantive injection of funding would ensure affordability, access and quality.

The idea of charters, as a contract between government and the providers of education services, was useful, as Meade recalls:

> We were all pretty much of the view that we needed more funding and we needed more equitable funding. But we could see considerable reluctance on behalf of government to substantially increase the funding if it didn't have the accountability with it.[46]

The Meade report proposed a 'universal' funding formula per child per hour above the equivalent kindergarten rate, recognising that kindergartens were also underfunded.

Most of the rest of the committee other than Treasury were in agreement with substantial increases, but there was a reluctance with Treasury to go with the rest of us. Because of Treasury's position in the Cabinet process they exercised their right and put in their own report.[47]

This restated Treasury's 1987 view that 'Most benefits would seem to accrue to the children themselves and their families and thus the case for higher general subsidies seems rather weak.'[48] Treasury wanted to contain and delay anything substantive or universal.

The agenda for restructuring education moved fast. As Meade recalls: 'Early childhood would have been left out and left floundering if I hadn't had those dual roles.'[49] The issue of timing was a concern, but the working group's decision to fit the new pattern as much as possible kept early childhood on the rollercoaster. The Meade report recommended that each centre or organisation be governed by a board of trustees similar to that proposed for schools. This was strenuously rejected by private centres, and eventually abandoned. One difference from schools was an Early Childhood Development Unit (ECDU) to co-ordinate advisory and support services for centres. The proposed Review and Audit Agency (later the Education Review Office – ERO) was intended as a place of 'last resort'. This balance also changed.

A FOOT IN THE DOOR

Meade described *Education to be More* as a 'foot in the door', particularly for the childcare groups that had been excluded for so long.[50] The working group had refrained from making recommendations on Te Kōhanga Reo, because their own review was still under way (see Chapter Seven). A submission from two kōhanga reo, however, endorsed the way the working party had created

> a system where Maori have the opportunity to develop according to their own choice, and to realise their aspirations. To this end the Treaty of Waitangi principles can be suitably transferred to a contemporary model of implementation … Other Government working parties could benefit from this approach.[51]

There was fairly united support for the broad principles of *Education to be More*, although centres and organisations wondered how they would fit into the unified blueprint.[52] Private centres had concerns with a proposed increase in parental rights, and there were legal problems with the notion of boards of trustees. Early childhood organisations seemed to be sidelined in the proposal for bulk funding per child going direct to centres. Maris O'Rourke told the

New Zealand Sunday Times that the bulk funding model for equitable funding was 'one of those simple, elegant solutions to an incredibly difficult problem'.[53] Not all agreed. Amidst the general relief and praise that *Education to be More* had shaped an acceptable way forward, there were concerns by some that the Treasury view also had a 'foot in the door' and there were fundamental flaws in the proposed model.[54] Noonan recalls her dismay at the 'economic theory' of bulk funding. It 'reduced the provision of early childhood to individual needs that would become isolated and competitive … [whereas] what had produced quality for children in the early childhood sector had come from the organisations'.[55] Bulk funding was a particularly contentious industrial issue for the school and kindergarten sector, whose teachers were employed by the state. In the event, bulk funding was not initially applied to these groups, and for early childhood organisations that managed centres, including Te Kōhanga Reo, the bulk grant would be made en masse rather than direct to individual centres.

Lange announced that the government was likely to adopt the principles of *Education to be More*, but was unlikely to come up with the '$150 million' funding boost recommended. (The optimum figure suggested was actually $236 million. The lesser figure gave no increase to kindergartens.) Funding was central to all the early childhood demands, but there was opposition. Meade wrote:

> The interests of capital and male power-holders joined together and came to the fore. The Business Round Table and other key proponents of the New Right economic discourse were spelling out the political advantages of the Government decreasing its expenditure.[56]

I commented:

> Although the struggle was one of economic philosophy, to women activists in the early childhood movement it had all the appearance of the patriarchy in a newly purchased cloak. Over the past twenty years many arguments had been used by governments to justify their unwillingness to increase early childhood funding. We had heard and fought against all of them.[57]

The government's report, *Before Five* (1988), retained the substantive recommendations of *Education to be More* although for pragmatic reasons the existing management structures would remain. Lange's introduction to *Before Five* indicated that he had ignored the Treasury view:

> Research shows that resources put into early childhood care and education have proven results. Not only do they enhance the individual child's learning, [but]

the advantages gained create success in adult life. Improvements in the sector are an investment for the future. Our children are our future. They need a good start in life. I believe Before Five will help give them that.[58]

How much this would cost was the issue. *Before Five* laid some ground rules, stating firmly that 'the early childhood sector will have equal status with other education sectors'. The *Auckland Star* (7 February 1989) saw the funding issue as Lange's 'personal dilemma' from which he 'pledged [not to] back-slide ... Thousands of parents ... will not allow a back-slide.' But the *New Zealand Herald* (8 February 1989) took the opposite view: 'The economy is in no position to afford every social bauble ... The latest example of the syndrome is pre-school education.'

In 1989 the restructuring began. An Implementation Unit established a raft of working groups. The Before Five implementation process was managed by Maris O'Rourke, after which she was appointed Secretary for the Ministry of Education. The implementation exercise was a consultative process involving early childhood groups and advocates, many of whom had worked for many years to see these reforms. The mood was deceptively jubilant.

Monitoring the process in relation to Treaty issues was a runanga. Maureen Locke was belatedly appointed as an early childhood representative.[59] She arrived with guidelines for all the Before Five working parties, which included the 1988 early childhood Statement of Intent on Treaty issues (see Chapter Seven). The qualifications working group recommended that the new three-year diploma of teaching be phased in as the benchmark requirement for a trained person in early childhood.[60] The funding working group detailed an hourly formula per child according to age, applicable across the early childhood services, which they hoped would be acceptable to a government.[61] The national guidelines working group drafted the content of an early childhood charter, and minimum regulatory standards to apply across all services.[62] The political process watered down the recommendations of all groups, but the basic tenor of the Before Five principles survived. That the funding recommendations would survive the political process was more doubtful.

Internal divisions within the government were becoming harder to contain and eventually ruptured with the resignation of Lange as prime minister. Anne Meade summed up the struggle:

> The funding proposal became a focus of the struggles between David Lange and the 'wets' arguing for benefits for small children, and the 'dry' supporters of Roger Douglas. What occurred in 1988/89 was that a temporary wedge was

driven through the hegemonic barriers constructed by the male power-holders and the so-called captains of industry.[63]

Lange remained an advocate, but was now outside the power loop. He stated that:

> It is tedious to hear talk of seamless education when what happens before school is so appallingly different from what happens when you turn five … After three years' training a kindergarten teacher gets less than half the pay of a new constable with a fraction of the training …[64] Like Cinderella, early childhood education has had three sisters – primary, secondary and tertiary, not necessarily ugly, but who have in various ways bullied, ignored and exploited her … yet early childhood was the sister with potential.[65]

The government was conscious that its days might be numbered. Early childhood was now a lesser priority. In a final effort to achieve a funding package, unions, women's groups and early childhood services mounted the Campaign for Quality Early Childhood Education. Forty-two petitions were separately tabled in parliament. There were rallies at the Beehive in Wellington and in Auckland's Aotea Square, as well as intense lobbying inside parliament, co-ordinated by the parliamentary women's caucus.[66] Politicians realised that women's votes were at stake. The compromise was a five-year staged funding package. Kindergartens would not benefit until year four, but the other services would get a substantive boost to their funding, particularly if they had children under the age of two. This finally made 'New Zealand's integrated early childhood policy … the focus of much envy and admiration', claimed Anne Smith:[67]

> I still find that when I go overseas childcare is considered totally different from preschool education. We'd thought that through a long time back. We were small enough and had enough contact with people in power to be able to do something about it … people who knew each other and [who] shared a vision for the future … [and] an early childhood division in the department that had a core of really well informed people who were attending to those policy issues.[68]

Victory was sweet but short-lived. The 1990s were spent trying to hold on to the Before Five gains.[69]

IMPLEMENTING BEFORE FIVE

The Ministry of Education, replacing the old department, opened for business in October 1989. Responsibilities for early childhood were fragmented around the new ministry. The early childhood expertise was scattered around the new education agencies, which, with the exception of ECDU, took a generalist approach to business. The new processes caused turmoil for a while across the whole education sector. In the longer term the holistic approach to early childhood policy was lost. ERO and the Qualifications Authority (NZQA) were independent of the Ministry of Education, and the co-ordination of early childhood policy and operations became fraught. In 1990 I presented a paper to an education policy conference entitled 'From a Floor to a Drawer – A Story of Administrative Upheaval' and recounted a discussion with a senior ministry official who (possibly tongue-in-cheek) explained: 'We now have a drawer labelled Early Childhood and once a fortnight a few of us, who used to be in early childhood, put on our old hats, pull out the drawer and deal with any issues.'[70] This perception of devolution was not far wrong. The lack of any early childhood 'voice' in government became a problem.

A 'Purple' Management Handbook (1989), delivered to all early childhood centres, laid out new guidelines that organisations, owners, management and/ or parents needed to address.[71] Each centre was to have a charter, setting out quality standards for staffing ratios and trained staff above the minimum regulations, as well as requirements on equity issues, the Treaty of Waitangi, parent involvement, curriculum and staff development. Each organisation and/or centre, in consultation with parents, needed to develop policies for delivering the charter requirements, which were to be negotiated with the Ministry of Education. Treaty of Waitangi clauses in the charter required centres and organisations to reflect on consultation with Māori parents and the appropriateness of the programme for Māori children, as well as providing Pākehā children with some understanding of Māori language and culture. This was a challenge. The process was slow and sometimes painful, but over the decade, more early childhood centres came to reflect upon their bicultural and multicultural obligations.[72]

The new funding began in 1990. For most centres, apart from kindergartens, funding was increased by approximately 50%. For childcare centres with infants, the increase was sometimes several hundred percent. The intention of the funding was to improve the quality. For playcentre and kōhanga reo, in particular, this meant first meeting requirements for safe buildings. Parents were also hoping for affordable fees: balancing expectations and demands was not easy. Each organisation or centre made some hard decisions. In 1989 ECWU filed a claim against the employers arguing: 'High Time for a Fair Deal',[73] and asking workers: 'Are You Ready for the Most Important Award

Round Ever?'[74] The Consenting Parties Award with 150 employers settled wage increases up to 38%. The National Award with mainly private employers was contentious and ended in the Arbitration Court, before settling increases of between 17% and 27%. Meantime, 130 employers were persuaded to leave the National Award to sign up to the Consenting Parties Award, which was more generous to staff.

After the award round KTA and ECWU, now amalgamated into the Combined Early Childhood Union of Aotearoa (CECUA), reported: 'It is glaringly obvious that accountability measures currently in place for employers in receipt of government funding are totally inadequate.'[75] The question of accountability, particularly in the childcare sector, had been a hot issue in the Before Five implementation working groups. Recommended measures to ensure that new monies were spent on improving quality for children and staff, and affordability for parents, were ignored by the government. There were no formal directives as to how the money ought to be spent, and the funding began before any charters had been negotiated.[76] The ethos of deregulation and devolution won the day. Even a submission by the Audit Commission on the matter was ignored.[77]

Within six months the scandals began to surface. 'Misuse Feared of Childcare Funding Bonus' read a headline in the *New Zealand Sunday Times* (19 August 1990). Crispin Gardiner, a member of the funding working group, stated that 'the majority of childcare operators have used the money responsibly'. But he was concerned that the funding scandals were 'bringing childcare into disrepute [and] could jeopardise a funding package which was hard fought for'.[78] In one newsworthy case a parent claimed: 'What really bugs us parents is that taxpayers' money was targeted to benefit our daughter and she didn't get one cent of benefit from it.'[79] The owner of this particular centre, Paul Wilson, justified his business interests in childcare:

> It is inappropriate for others to direct us how to operate and run our company, particularly as to how it should spend its money and what it does with the money received. This is our business. It is not run as a community facility but as a business facility and the ability of the operation to make a profit must not be a matter of public accountability.[80]

Lockwood Smith, Minister of Education in the new National government, intervened. Centres would have to provide evidence that government funding was spent on supporting the indicators of quality, such as wage levels, staffing ratios and training, as well as balancing affordability in relation to fees.[81] The guidelines were issued in November 1990.[82] The July 1991 budget, however, removed the accountability guidelines linked to quality standards. In October 1991 new guidelines were gazetted concerning, primarily, financial auditing practices rather than quality for children.[83]

The other early loss was the demise of the charter. Within a month of centres completing their first charter, the 'Purple' Management Handbook guidelines were superseded by a document (known as DOPs) called the *Statement of Desirable Objectives and Practices* (1990).[84] This removed the quality guidelines set out in the handbook, as well as the references to the Treaty of Waitangi. The process of signing an agreement to implement the objectives became easier to administer, but the experiment of a dynamic engagement among parents, communities, staff, management and the government was lost.[85]

For the next decade a group of academics, researchers and activists vigilantly documented the early childhood policy story, creating a fuller historical picture than we have for any other period. That writing on early childhood became part of mainstream academia was just one sign of the changing status of early childhood, even if the politics were still fragile. The selective and summarised account in Part Three draws on this work.

NATIONAL DIRECTIONS

Upon assuming office in 1990 the National government announced 17 reviews of social and educational services as a lead-up to the 1991 budget. There was a wider agenda, linked partly to fiscal concerns, as well as a wish to redefine the role of government in its support of individuals. The process was orchestrated, under the cloak of budget secrecy, by a Prime Ministerial Committee on the Reform of Social Assistance, called the Change Team, which explored a number of scenarios for targeting social services.[86] The four early childhood reviews were out of proportion to the relatively small government contribution to early childhood services ($179,098,900 in 1990), compared with the other social and education services. Early childhood appeared to have been placed on the agenda not so much for possible fiscal savings, as Lockwood Smith claimed, but for ideological reasons.[87] Meade told the worried early childhood community at the Fifth Early Childhood Convention in Dunedin:

> What seems to be happening in 1991 is a re-run of the same ideological battle, with early childhood education again the meat in the sandwich. Early childhood education was, and is again, an arena where ideological conflict is being worked out.[88]

The radical potential of early childhood services, in the view of the dominant power-brokers, needed to be restrained.

The early childhood review groups, composed of government officials, received 853 submissions in three weeks. Most people had only a vague idea of the terms of reference of the review, because these were not made public. Consultation with early childhood organisations was curtailed to meet a budget deadline. The submissions reflected the strong anxiety in the early childhood communities about any cuts in funding, with 96.1% in support of keeping the existing funding provisions.[89] Early childhood expertise, which had been valued in the Before Five policy development, was now deemed ideologically suspect. One independent early childhood representative, Crispin Gardiner from the Hamilton Daycare Centres Trust, who was also a professor of physics, was contracted to the funding working group. He later dissociated himself from the review and wrote an independent report.[90] The Ministry of Education convenor and early childhood expert Rosemary Renwick also left (or, according to the media, was 'ousted from') the working group, to be replaced by a State Services Commission official.[91] Gardiner's independent report differed markedly from the official report released after the July 1991 budget.[92] He used mathematical modelling to assess the impact of targeting funding for early childhood services, and strongly recommended against any policy of targeting, except in a minimal form.

The funding review acknowledged the conflict between the goal of promoting equal opportunities and improving women's labour market participation, and the government's priority goal of reducing 'dependency' on the state. Gardiner's report showed the potential success of the Before Five policy, and in particular noted the overall growth of 6.7% in provision in 10 months and the improvements in quality made by many centres. However, he warned that a targeted funding regime would jeopardise the voluntary contribution to early childhood, which was approximately 31% of total costs. In all scenarios of targeting, from heavy to mild, the effect was to improve funding for Te Kōhanga Reo, Pacific Islands language centres and Playcentres. The other services, such as kindergarten, home-based schemes and childcare, would suffer a considerable reduction in funding. Such a scenario, even in its mildest form, was probably too radical for National's constituency.

The 1991 budget is remembered for its cuts in social services spending and the introduction of some tight targeting. Fortunately for early childhood education this was of a weaker kind than originally discussed by the Change Team, and early childhood funding still retained a considerable measure of

universality. There were, however, cuts to regulatory requirements on qualifications, staffing ratios and accountability, on the grounds that they 'made it
unnecessarily difficult to providers to offer early childhood education at a
reasonable cost'.[93]

The cuts were met with outrage, but the voice of early childhood had little
political clout. The government's staged plan for funding was dropped, with
centres left at step one. Centres with children under the age of two took a drop
in funding, saving $18 million from the early childhood budget, which amounted
to 11% of total funding -- the highest level of cuts to any education or social
service. This was a selective attack on the fastest-growing early childhood
services, leaving Playcentres and kindergarten (whose rolls were static)
unaffected. The funding cut to childcare centres with infants caused hardship.[94]
Kindergartens were dealt a different kind of blow by being bulk funded on a
formula that might force fees to be charged, worsen ratios, or force the
employment of untrained staff. The impact of this is to be examined separately.

After 50 years of slow improvement in the quality and funding of early
childhood services, the downturn started before the equity policies implicit in
Before Five could be achieved.[95] In an analysis of the review reports, Cathie
Bell of the *New Zealand Sunday Times* (11 August 1991) concluded that there
had been a stand-off between Treasury and the State Services Commission
and other members of the working groups – usually the Ministry of Education
and the Ministry of Women's Affairs. The Treasury view was invariably the
one accepted. Treasury, however, did not feel that the substantive issues had
been grappled with in the early childhood funding review. The Cabinet agreed
to a further review to 'examine the overall strategic framework for government
investment in early childhood education and care, and the appropriate share of
the costs that should be met by the state and the individual'.[96] It was as if the
decade of debates and consensus in the 1980s had not happened. The
government was placing early childhood services in the continuum of the
education sector, but at the same time was realigning the funding of early
childhood as a social service to be targeted according to need. The rationale for
all social services was to 'encourage people to move from state dependence to
personal and self-reliance'.[97]

In the midst of the 1993 election the National government embarked on
another series of reviews, labelled the 'Hidden Agenda' by the opposition. The
promised review of early childhood funding began, by officials only, and again
in secret. No early childhood expertise was included and consultation was
cursory. The objective was 'to evaluate the Government's investment

in the early childhood sector' and measure the 'costs and benefits'.[98] The review covered all aspects of Before Five, with targeted funding again to the fore. A summary of submissions to the review was later made public.[99] They gave overwhelming support to the notion of universal funding. There was much evidence on the continuing hardship caused by funding shortfalls, and a strong view that the government was backing away from quality.

In early 1994, in the midst of the review, and with the early childhood sector feeling under attack, the Ministry of Education convened the Speaking Directly conference. There were similarities to the 1985 Parliamentary Forum. The ministry hoped that a new consensus could be forged to encourage early childhood groups to look forward within the government's new parameters, rather than back to Before Five. Maris O'Rourke was the convenor; in her role as Secretary of the Ministry she had possibly protected early childhood from even larger raids. The delegates were angry, not least with the consultants who organised a merry-go-round of workshops designed to deliver some agreed statements. In the end the delegates were able to provide an almost cohesive statement to politicians that diverged little from the principles of Before Five.[100] This was the blueprint that delegates wanted implemented. That the blueprint had been undermined and distorted was, according to academic Carmen Dalli, 'a major contributor to the problems which now face[d] the sector'.[101]

The funding review did not surface until the 1995 budget. It showed that the government's position had shifted towards the idea of targeting quality rather than disadvantage. 'Quality funding' provided a higher tier to the bulk grant for all centres, apart from kindergartens, and was linked to staff qualifications. A working group, including organisational representatives and Anne Meade, developed an acceptable formula in consultation with the early childhood organisations.[102] This allowed for different services, such as Playcentre and Te Kōhanga Reo, to meet the qualification criteria in different ways, an enlightened approach that went beyond the 'one formula fits all' principle of the earlier reforms. 'Quality funding' began in 1996, but by 1998 the uptake was still less than half of what was available, because centres found that the cost of meeting the criteria was not worth the extra funding. The working group approach was a signal that perhaps the tide was turning and that it might be possible for a more consultative partnership with the government on issues to do with funding and quality.

In 1994 CECUA merged with the New Zealand Educational Institute and Te Riu Roa (NZEI–TRR) to form a united industrial union with primary teachers. Rosslyn Noonan was the general secretary. The 1991 Employment Contracts Act had fragmented national awards, with a detrimental effect on workplace conditions. In 1992 only eight early childhood employers out of 350 chose to remain in the national childcare award.[103] Staff from many childcare centres were employed on individual contracts holding conditions and wages to the minimum. Early childhood officials within NZEI–TRR resolved to take a more proactive stand towards shaping policy directions.[104] In 1995, Linda Mitchell and Clare Wells initiated the Future Directions Early Childhood Education Project, which included all community early childhood groups apart from the private-sector Early Childhood Council (ECC, formed in 1991 from the LCCF and ACC).[105] Chair Geraldine McDonald wrote:

> In the last seven years early childhood education has had its fair share of change … A feature of early childhood policy development has been the carrying out of 'top down' reviews.[106]

The exercise modelled community consultation. *Future Directions* (1996) delivered a number of recommendations towards realising three goals: first, universal funding for early childhood services on an equitable basis with schools; second, a partnership in policy development between government, providers, parents and practitioners; and third, a strategic plan for the early childhood sector.

The organisations involved embarked on a media and political campaign to bring attention to the 'directions' suggested. It was again election year. Opposition parties incorporated the goals of *Future Directions* in their policies. The report was criticised, by both the Ministry of Education and the new Associate Minister of Education, Bill English, for excluding the views of private-sector childcare.[107] In 1997 a series of petitions totalling 14,000 signatures arrived at parliament recommending the adoption of the report and urging consideration of an increase to the bulk funding rate, including a plea for kindergarten funding.[108] The Education and Science Select Committee held hearings and petitioners were invited to present their views, and a small funding increase was subsequently announced in the budget. In 1998 the Select Committee advised that it would not be making recommendations to parliament as it was satisfied that the ministry was already working on a number of issues raised in the report. Wells noted that *Future Directions* had been kept 'in front of politicians and officials for nearly two years'.[109] The Ministry of Education did start engaging in a more consultative style of policy development. There were no more secret reviews, and from around 1996 there was more resolve to address some of the issues and anomalies relating to funding and qualifications that had confounded the implementation of earlier policies. The exception was the kindergarten sector.

Three months before National's term of government ended in 1999 the Minister of Education, Nick Smith, gave an upbeat appraisal of his government's term to the Seventh Early Childhood Convention in Nelson: 'We have so much we can be proud of in our early childhood sector. We have innovation. We have standards. We have diversity. And our children are the winners.'[110] As evidence, Smith cited the growth of funding from $139 million in 1990 to $310 million in 1999, an (inflation-adjusted) increase of 92%, compared with a 42% increase in the primary sector. However, the figure was actually due to 45,000 more children attending early childhood. Participation had certainly increased, but the real increase in the level of funding to early childhood education services was in fact small.

PARENTS AS FIRST TEACHERS

Before the National government came to power in 1990, education spokesperson Lockwood Smith had watched a television show on 'hot-house' programmes in the US that claimed to accelerate the learning of very young children.[111] One of the less radical ventures was the Missouri Parents as Teachers (PAT) programme in which professional educators paid home visits to children from under three years of age in low socio-economic areas. The premise was that deficits were evident by age three, and remedial education would by then be too late.[112] Educators provided an educational programme, toys, diagnostic screening, and advice and support to the parents (usually mothers). The Missouri project claimed 'dramatic results':

> The parents' income, education, occupation or race made little difference – their children were consistently among the top achievers in their age group. You could not tell which children came from disadvantaged backgrounds. There was another benefit – the problem of child abuse was virtually eliminated in the families involved in the programme.[113]

Smith persuaded his party to include a New Zealand spin-off called 'Parents as First Teachers' (PAFT) in its election policies. PAFT became the first of six interconnecting components of government strategy on achievement and lifelong learning.[114] It would focus in particular on health awareness and language development, as a step towards redressing the failure of some children at school.

PAFT provided National with its own 'high ground' on early childhood policy: a focus on the home and the responsibilities of parents, rather than early childhood institutions and teachers. The theme of poor parenting was a concern shared by Lesley Max, whose book *Children: Endangered Species?* (1990) gave a grim picture of the lot of some children in New Zealand. Max also asserted that children might be endangered by the new early childhood policies, which she described as a feminist plot to institutionalise childhood.[115] Max was interested in more directed teaching programmes for disadvantaged children, such as the Home Instruction Programme for Pre-school Youngsters (HIPPY). Smith frequently referred to the success of HIPPY in reducing the achievement differences between African immigrant and European-educated children in Israel. Linking HIPPY with the Missouri PAT programme, Smith told audiences: 'These findings are exciting. They have clear implications for reducing Maori under-achievement at school.'[116]

Cost was another theme underlying Smith's enthusiasm for PAFT. Mindful of Treasury warnings of the 'fiscal risk' of Before Five policies and three-year teacher training, Smith claimed that: 'Trained teachers in the system cost so much, but a trained parent educator costs nothing.'[117] He also highlighted the potential cost saving in the school system of early intervention if PAFT was successful. His comments alarmed early childhood groups, who feared that there could be a shift in focus from institution-based to home-based programmes, particularly in the light of Smith's reported views that '[School] teachers are not responsible for student inadequacy to grasp the 3Rs. Dr Smith blames it on the slow start children get in their first three years.'[118]

Early childhood groups were lukewarm to PAFT, although not to the idea of parent education and support. An imported programme seemed inappropriate. All successful early childhood programmes had grown out of community need, not the dreams of politicians. Moreover, it seemed that Smith was failing to recognise the parent support work that Plunket, Playcentre, Te Kōhanga Reo and family daycare were doing, and could do better if they had the funding. For many women, placing early childhood programmes in the home was not the kind of liberation from childrearing they had so long fought for. Some in the sector were also mindful of the limitations of programmes for parents. From the US, Douglas Powell argued that:

> No amount of ... home visits will take the place of jobs that can provide decent incomes, affordable housing, appropriate health care, optimal family configurations, or [an] integrated neighbourhood where children encounter positive role models.[119]

Early childhood academic experts refuted many of Smith's claims for the PAFT policy. Carmen Dalli took exception to the focus on parental responsibility:

> The rationale used is that if schools do not help prevent reading problems … then [parents] must be deficient in some way and we must 'help them' train them up. We must intervene to put them on the right track. This rationale suggests an overly simplistic conception of how we can cure our educational ills.[120]

Feaua`i Burgess and Pepe Robertson provided Lockwood Smith with a list of parent support programmes, including their own Pacific Islands centres, urging him to consider them as a better investment than PAFT.[121] Leonie Pihama argued that 'PAFT is clearly not an emancipatory programme for Maori people. The theoretical underpinnings are located within the "deprivation" theories …'[122] From Otago University, Bruce McMillan was also concerned about a programme based on the notion of deficit, which was placing both the responsibility and the blame on parents of young children:

> With the best intention, those who look for deficits rather than strengths will find them … My greatest concerns are not with the programme implementation itself, but with the social and political context which has authorised and endorsed the principles believed to be essential for its purpose. The most significant one is that through this programme, parents will ensure that their children become suitable employees for a business-oriented society.[123]

McMillan expressed his concern to Smith about a national policy being based on a programme that lacked any evidence for its claimed benefits.[124]

The beginnings of PAFT were rocky. Not only was the criticism vocal, but its launch was part of the 1991 budget announcements, which cut funding for infants in childcare centers and slashed benefits for sole parents. Despite assurances from the minister that PAFT's money came from elsewhere, the centres and parents affected did not believe him. PAFT began in 1992 with four pilot trials contracted through Plunket, whose nurses were skilled in infant health and development matters, but had no training in early childhood education. Copyright restrictions initially prevented much adaptation of PAFT from the Missouri model. Trainers were sent to New Zealand and parent educators were required to use the US manual as a curriculum for the programme.[125] Preliminary research evaluations from the universities of Otago and Auckland (published in 1994 and 1995) offered only cautious support for the benefits of PAFT, although parents and families were positive.[126]

In 1993 PAFT was extended to eight more sites, three of which would be catering for Māori and Pacific Islands families. In 1994 the minister indicated that ongoing expansion would allow places to be available to all families who wanted them by 1998.[127] In a significant move the new projects were managed by ECDU. This forged a link between PAFT and the broader early childhood community. Some experienced early childhood teachers were employed, and voiced growing concern with the Missouri manual. In 1994 Mere Mitchell was cautiously optimistic:

> I actually came into my PAFT work thinking that I didn't like the programme. I supported the philosophy but not the delivery. I now believe the philosophy can be implemented if you have the right people. We're lucky here in Hamilton because we all come from an early childhood education background. In other areas there are people coming from a health or community background and they operate a bit differently. It has at times been frustrating getting a shared understanding of the child development.

Mitchell had previously worked in a kōhanga reo. She saw the worlds as separate, but without conflict:

> That parents are first teachers goes with whanau philosophy of whanau being first teachers. I've made it my business to try and pick up Maori families. I'm doing a lot of adapting but I have learnt over the years as a Maori worker you do that anyway … The three [co-ordinators] have found we have to do a lot of adapting. You can't go into different homes and deliver the same programme. We have lots of paper fights with our national office …[128]

Negotiations by ECDU with Missouri gave more autonomy for New Zealand to determine the changes it needed. This began with semantics:

> The American terms 'crib', 'pacifier' and 'yarn' [were] replaced by the words 'cot', 'dummy' and 'wool', more commonly used in New Zealand. Suggested children's book titles were replaced with books familiar to New Zealand families.[129]

By 1997 the manual had been significantly revised and ECDU was ensuring that the project, the staffing and the message were culturally sensitive to the settings in which PAFT operated. PAFT administrator Sharyn Devereux Blum claimed that 'PAFT empowers parents and supports them in positive, non-judgmental ways. Continual feedback from parents involved in the ECDU PAFT programmes certainly supports this.'[130] There was no research, however, to suggest that PAFT was the cure for poor parenting and poor school performance. The ministry's research evaluations had themselves become the focus of controversy. Ian Livingstone later concluded that:

This comprehensive and thorough investigation, using both quantitative and qualitative methodologies, has uncovered very little in the way of positive, measurable results that can be attributed unequivocally to the PAFT programmes … For some parents, particularly sole parents, the basic needs of adequate housing, finance and support need to be catered for more adequately, before they are in any position to be effective first teachers of their children.[131]

This was towards the end of a decade in which the older welfare supports for housing, health, and education had been eroded. There was, however, more peace in the early childhood sector, and an acceptance that PAFT was now one of a raft of programmes to support children and their families. In 1999 PAFT was operating in 64 locations, working with 9000 families and employing 209 parent educators.[132]

THE KINDERGARTEN FLAGSHIP

For many years kindergartens had regarded themselves as the Cinderella of the education sector as a whole, but alongside the other early childhood services, kindergarten was described as the 'flagship'.[133] By the late 1980s kindergarten's partnership with the state was longstanding. Their teachers were in the state sector and creeping towards pay parity with primary teachers; the state owned their land and buildings; and their operations were funded by the government, to the extent that they were still called 'free kindergartens'. Nonetheless, unlike schools, the state did not own the kindergartens. They belonged to, and were operated by, community-based kindergarten associations, and parents undertook considerable voluntary work. The other early childhood sector groups had long aspired to equitable funding with kindergartens, although their diversity dictated different priorities for funding allocation.

The Before Five reforms were designed to advance the quality of provision of all services, including kindergartens. With the halting of the staged funding plan, kindergartens received no financial benefits. Successive governments, and some in the early childhood sector, saw kindergartens as still privileged by comparison. Kindergarteners, however, felt as if their 'flag-ship' was sinking as the government moved to bring kindergartens into line with the rest of the sector.[134] In 1994 the Associate Minister of Education, John Luxton, accused kindergartners of holding on to the 'sacred cows' of sessional provision, trained teachers and no fees. Kindergartens were told to face the realities of New Zealand's economic structure of the 1990s and adopt a more businesslike approach. Luxton argued that the government had two objectives: 'to be fair to all organisations and be financially responsible with the use of taxpayers' funds'.[135]

Throughout the decade kindergartens experienced selected cutbacks. These were designed to force them towards the private or community-based model of childcare provision outside the state, as favoured by a government bent on devolution. At the heart of the matter was the kindergartens' reluctance to charge fees (beyond the established practice of voluntary donations) or to employ untrained teachers. Kindergartens expressed ongoing concerns about funding shortfalls and their less-than-quality staffing ratios of 1:15 (and in some cases 1:20, which contravened early childhood regulations). But these were met by government advice to charge fees. Kindergartens argued that this would restrict access to many low-income families. The government's view was that fees could be balanced through targeted assistance – the childcare subsidy available for low-income families.

The 1995 budget offered a change to the funding formula for kindergartens, but this meant opening for additional sessions and weeks of the year and charging fees. It was unacceptable to the associations, who calculated that there would be few financial gains, or to the teachers themselves, for reasons Claire Davison summarised: 'It would considerably increase the hours of work and workload of kindergarten teachers and reduce their comparability with the working conditions of teachers in the primary sector.'[136] Luxton accused kindergarten associations of 'burying their heads in the sand', and stated that he would not 'marginalise other sector providers who offer similar educational facilities' by increasing kindergarten funding.[137]

At the 1997 Education and Science Select Committee hearing considering petitions on kindergarten funding, the Ministry of Education's submission argued that kindergartens wanted 'preferential funding treatment'. Officials summed up the government's role in managing the 'business' of early childhood, arguing: 'Under current policies the government buys educational hours of a particular quality from early childhood services and overall is neutral in terms of the service type.'[138]

In the saga of the confrontation between kindergarten and the government, offers of improved funding packages would be forthcoming only in return for operational concessions from kindergartens.[139] Each time these were rejected. In 1996, amidst lobbying, strikes by teachers and an election campaign, an increased funding package was altered three times before it was eventually acceptable to kindergartens. Davison recorded how:

The combined strength of a relatively small community consisting of kindergarten teachers, the New Zealand Educational Institute and kindergarten associations had proved to be effective. [140]

The backdrop to kindergarten agitation was bulk funding, introduced in 1992, and the removal of kindergarten teachers from the State Sector Act in 1997. Both were intended by the government to distance kindergartens further from the school sector.

In fact, the National government wanted to bulk fund the entire education sector. This initially applied only to the tertiary and early childhood sectors, excepting kindergartens. In the school sector, bulk grants to boards of trustees covered only operations, while the salaries of teachers remained a government responsibility. Strong teacher unions vigorously opposed full bulk funding, concerned that schools would be pressured to employ lesser qualified and therefore cheaper teachers. In the notorious 1991 budget, the government had announced the bulk funding of kindergartens. This was a weaker sector than schools, and it immediately went into a state of internal dissension, eventually resulting in a complicated series of secessions from the New Zealand Free Kindergarten Association (NZFKA, previously the NZFKU) and the formation of the New Zealand Kindergarten Federation (NZKF). This fragmentation weakened the kindergarten movement in its subsequent negotiations.

Bulk funding began in 1992. The government claimed that it was not reducing the overall amount given to kindergartens, although it acknowledged that it was now up to local associations to find the extra money needed for salary increases previously covered centrally. Ministry of Education spokesperson Lyall Perris told kindergartens that 'shortfalls would be made up in the long term as senior staff left and were replaced by low-grade teachers'. They were also advised that 'it is possible to make up for any loss in funding with wise investment of the bulk grant'.[141] Soon after, the government began offering the bulk funding option to schools.

Several studies were conducted during the early years of kindergarten bulk funding.[142] A 1995 study suggested that 'the quality of services delivered to children had not suffered but that association and kindergarten staff and management had insulated children from potentially negative impacts of bulk funding'.[143] Kindergarten associations experienced deficits. In not charging fees they were dependent on fund-raising, which meant there were winner and loser kindergartens, and on keeping the rolls at the maximum to attract the highest level of bulk grant. This put pressure on teachers, who found managing

80 and then later 90 children (and their families) through their two sessions per day a poor-quality and often stressful experience. A few non-viable kindergartens closed. The main problem, as for the rest of the early childhood sector, was the capping of the bulk grant. All services and organisations made compromises in balancing the impossible equation of affordability for parents, quality for children and wage levels for staff, as well as, for some, a profit share for owners.

Some sectors, such as Playcentre and Te Kōhanga Reo, contained their costs with the use of voluntary labour. The childcare sector could balance salary levels with fee increases. None of these groups had fully trained staff, although some aspired to. In 1995 the Auckland Kindergarten Association (AKA) split from the national collective employment contract for teachers. This was ostensibly to give themselves more flexibility to manage their bulk grant. It was, however, no coincidence that Richard Prebble, later the leader of the right wing ACT Party, had just been co-opted onto the AKA council, which was already determined to become more entrepreneurial. Further fragmentation of contracts followed. That kindergarten teachers' salaries were still in the state sector became an 'anomaly' and an irritant to the government, particularly when salary increases negotiated with the state were used by the associations to leverage increases in the bulk grant – a successful strategy in 1996.[144]

Another agreement gained in the 1996 contract negotiations was a job evaluation to compare the work of kindergarten teachers with that of primary teachers. NZEI–TRR described this victory as a 'lever for further pay increases'.[145] The 1996 election resulted in a coalition government led by National. Briefing papers to the new government indicate the concern with the 'concessions' gained by kindergarten funding campaigns, suggesting instead that 'improved management style of associations was needed'.[146]

On 29 April 1997, under parliamentary 'urgency' procedures, the government introduced a bill to remove kindergarten teachers from the State Sector Act. Neither the associations nor the union knew about the bill until that morning, although the paper preparations had been under way since February. The Treasury, the State Services Commission and the Ministry of Education all supported the move.[147] By taking urgency, it could bypass the select committee process. Cabinet papers noted:

> The Bill is likely to be contentious. Both NZEI and the kindergarten associations are likely to oppose the Bill through the parliamentary process. This is also likely to coincide with a public campaign accompanied by community action. Kindergarten closures are likely.[148]

The bill was passed into law the next day in what Linda Mitchell described as a 'shocking, unjustified, undemocratic act'.[149] On the morning of 30 April, 11 of the 13 national early childhood organisations petitioned the government to refer the bill to a select committee. The private-sector ECC did not sign. Its vice-president Ross Penman welcomed the government's move, on the grounds that it removed 'apparent layers of privilege and superiority that had caused irritation in the sector'.[150] Kindergarten teachers and associations saw the removal as putting further pressure on the bulk grant, and the beginning of a peel-back in conditions they had worked hard for. Jenny Shipley, Minister of State Services, summed up the government view:

> It is true that kindergarten teachers and, in particular, the New Zealand Educational Institute, have been able to use their industrial muscle. The time has come for that to stop … This is an avenue to secure extra funding for wage increases that is simply not available to other early childhood providers. The government is not prepared to allow this inequity to continue in the forthcoming contract negotiations.[151]

There was support and sympathy for kindergarten teachers, but it was too late: the bill was passed. A few weeks later, on 9 June, an across-the-board increase of 5% for all services was announced. This was a bitter sweetener for kindergartens. An immediate consequence was the splintering of the two collective kindergarten contracts into 13 separate contracts (by 2000 there were 16). A further consequence, eventually halted by a change of government, was a move recommended to the associations by their legal advisers, Peat Marwick, to get rid of the union from negotiations.[152]

Throughout National's remaining time in office, kindergarten teachers campaigned against their enforced new status. In late 1999 a Labour–Alliance coalition government came to power. In the characteristic 'swings and roundabouts' of early childhood policy, the new Prime Minister, Helen Clark, promised that the new government would not, unlike recent 'successive governments', be 'downgrading kindergarten':

> I have been a great supporter of the kindergarten movement. Partly because it is the main choice of parents for early childhood education … you know at the kindergarten your children will be taught by a fully educated and trained teacher and you know that you will always be getting a very good standard of education. Long may that be the case.[153]

The government announced that kindergarten teachers would be brought back under the State Sector Act, and bulk funding for schools would be terminated.

Earlier in 1999 the job evaluation study comparing kindergarten and primary teaching had concluded that there was 'sufficient similarity and overlap between the teaching roles in the primary and kindergarten sectors to warrant alignment of their pay'.[154] Labour promised to 'work towards implementing a unified teaching pay scale to include early childhood teachers … a process for phasing in pay parity will occur in the first term of government'.[155]

History has now caught up with the present; how these issues will be managed in relation to the rest of the early childhood sector, many of whose teachers also want pay parity, is still unknown. One can only conclude this chapter of events with the knowledge that 'promises to be phased in' have not boded well for early childhood in the past. On the other hand, early childhood advocates, and particularly NZEI–TRR, are aware that they are likely to achieve such a goal only under a Labour-led government. They also know that early childhood teachers in the Correspondence School have pay parity with primary and secondary teachers. NZEI–TRR quietly negotiated this in 1997, but strategically decided that it should not be fanfared too early.

On the broader industrial front, in 2000 the Employment Contracts Act was replaced by the Employment Relations Bill, designed to restore the viability of collective agreements. Only two small collective childcare agreements remained: the Consenting Parties Award, with 130 employers, and the Otago–Southland Award, with 28. Private childcare employers who had earlier been the main signatories to a national childcare award were not pleased at the prospect of renewed union involvement. Allan Wendelborn told fellow ECC members:

> An undisciplined union official could stir up anti-employer feelings with your staff, pass on confidential information to staff *and competitors* [my emphasis], and you could be powerless to stop it.[156]

Wendelborn's concerns were about the future of childcare as a profitable industry, not as a teaching profession. Nor was there any mention of children.

CHAPTER NINE

Measures of Quality

At the end of century the political 'gaze' on early childhood institutions, staff and children was framed by a discourse on quality. In this chapter several determining aspects of this discourse are examined. At issue were questions about quality experiences for children: what was the recipe, who was responsible, what was the cost, and how could quality be measured?

In the absence of significant increases in early childhood funding, the emphasised role of government was to encourage and/or require centres to establish policies, systems and processes for achieving 'quality outcomes' for children. These too were defined (with a view to possible measurement) in a national early childhood curriculum. Government agencies were proactive in shaping the experiences of children in early childhood programmes, relying less on the profession or provider organisations to take the lead. Publications such as *Quality in Early Childhood* (ECDU, 1996), *Quality in Action* (MOE, 1998), *Quality Journey* (MOE, 1999), and the ERO report series *What Counts as Quality in Childcare* (1996), *Kindergarten* (1997), *Kohanga Reo* (1997) and *Playcentre* (1998), detailed measures for auditing quality.

Outside government, professional groups, organisations, activists and academics launched various campaigns and/or projects, mainly in the belief that government policies were undermining quality. The argument was that early childhood services were insufficiently resourced and that government 'standards of quality' were too low (or for some too high), or not always inclusive of the whole diverse sector. CECUA's 1993 Campaign for Quality Early Childhood Education was a reaction to government cuts to the Before Five policies (see Chapter Eight). Anne Smith's film *The Search for Quality* (1993) was produced for similar reasons:

> In the free market the only mechanism available for fostering the development of good quality is free choice, so a great deal of emphasis is put on parent choice …

The Treasury position is that the care and development of young children is the private concern and responsibility of parents ... Hence one rationale behind the production of this film is to attempt to articulate for parents what we know about good quality early childhood educare so that they might be empowered to choose and demand quality early childhood educare. Yet I strongly believe that governments have a strong responsibility to ensure that good quality services are provided.[1]

Te Kōhanga Reo National Trust developed *Te Korowai* (1995), defining its own measures of quality as a parallel requirement to the Ministry of Education's Desirable Objectives and Practices (DOPs) for early childhood centres.[2] Te Tari Puna Ora o Aotearoa (TTPOoA-NZCA) established a *Quality Register* (1996) for centres prepared to undergo a peer appraisal process.[3]

At the other end of the spectrum, a spate of international court cases on abuse in early childhood centres, including New Zealand's own controversial Christchurch Civic Creche case (1992–93), sparked a raft of policies that increased the surveillance of children in the name of protection and prevention.[4] By 2000, child surveillance (for child safety) and observation (for measuring learning) had become a time-consuming task for staff, an audit trail for managers, and an assurance for parents.[5] Documenting child profiles and daily records represented the tip of a culture in which children were perhaps becoming more real on paper than in person.

QUALITY DISCOURSES

Quality debates in New Zealand originated in the 1970s. Campaigns for quality childcare distinguished between 'poor-quality' centres, which were possibly harmful, and 'good-quality' centres, which were beneficial to children and supportive to their families.[6] Campaigners for 'quality' childcare argued that, with the correct 'measure' of resources, regulations and knowledge, attending a childcare centre was as beneficial for children as any other preschool experience. The issue was one of quality rather than kind, a view eventually underpinned in the Before Five policy. This early discourse on quality was not applied to kindergartens or Playcentres. The assumption was that their particular ideological mix already provided the necessary measures for quality.

From the 1970s American research, such as the National Day Care Study (1979), the National Child Care Staffing Study (1989) and the Costs Quality and Child Outcomes Study (1995), identified optimal mixes of staffing ratios, training levels, staff conditions, group size and costs.[7] The questions were designed, and the results intended, to convince American policy makers to fund and/or regulate childcare programmes. These measures of quality resulted in standards, scales and good-practice guidelines for early childhood services that were exported into many other Western countries.

During the 1980s-1990s quality issues in the early childhood sector were influenced by the language of the marketplace and its quest for efficiently produced 'quality products'.[8] In 1996 Heather Te Huia, president of TTPOoA–NZCA 1993–98, stated:

> There's a political move for childcare centres to become businesses and move out of government dependency. The Minister says to me that it is about time I accepted the reality that government should not be responsible for childcare because childcare should be run like a business, just like they're making schools and education all run like businesses … The Early Childhood Council are major childcare owners. Most of them run chains of childcare centres and are making money out of childcare. Now they are making money by using government funding so they are not really running a business.[9]

Te Huia did not accept that a business model produced quality for children. New Zealand was the only OECD country where private centres received government funding with so little oversight of fees, salaries or quality. Childcare became a business prospect that turned government subsidies and/or parent fees into profit. A 1998 newspaper advertisement in the Business Opportunities column read: 'Childcare. An industry which will return you 20% on your investment. From $300,000–$1.4 million.'[10]

From Europe at the end of the twentieth century Gunilla Dahlberg, Peter Moss and Alan Pence claimed:

> … there is no denying that [the concept of quality] now plays a dominant role in our thinking, our language and our practices. The 'age of quality' is now well and truly upon us, and not just in relation to early childhood institutions, but every conceivable type of product or service … It is what everyone wants to offer, and what everyone wants to have … the concept has achieved such dominance that it is hardly questioned. For the most part it is taken for granted that there is some thing – objective, real, knowable – called quality.[11]

The 'age of quality' framed research with questions from governments and providers such as:

> How do we measure quality? What are the most cost effective programmes? What standards do we need? How can we best achieve desirable outcomes? What works? The common feature of such questions is their technical and managerial

nature. They seek techniques that will ensure standardizaton, predictability and control.[12]

In Britain, Martin Woodhead was concerned at the impact of Western 'minority world' measures of quality on indigenous and/or developing 'majority world' early childhood programmes:

> I challenge the global distribution of any one single framework of quality. Such a framework might inevitably lead to a world of uniformity, a standardised recipe for the quality of childhood.[13]

New Zealand did not avoid the impact of globalised measures. Early childhood advocates had actively used such measures to further campaigns for government funding and regulations, particularly in the childcare sector. Conversely, Anne Smith, Anne Meade and Sarah-Eve Farquhar contributed to international debates, particularly on the multiple perspectives on quality.

International commentators and researchers acknowledged the leading policy position forged by the Meade report (see Chapter Eight).[14] Before Five blueprinted a framework in which diversity, equity and biculturalism became distinctive measures of quality in New Zealand. Charters, too, allowed each centre and/or service to develop its own style of programme within broad national guidelines. Nevertheless, operating within a charter was a measure of standardisation not previously experienced by centres and organisations.

Farquhar's research on the chartering process of centres caused her to claim that no single measure of quality was possible. Different services and cultural contexts, as well as the views of staff, parents and researchers, created multiple perspectives.[15] This was a view pursued by Martin Woodhead, who cited different 'stakeholders' associated with early childhood programmes, including the children, each with a perspective on quality. He suggested a negotiated approach, related to the context and functions of a programme and the shared goals of the stakeholders:

> A prerequisite of quality assessment is recognition that there is no single set of indicators that can prescribe for a quality environment in a once-and-for-all-way ... There are also limits – boundaries of adequacy in any early childhood environment, defined by children's basic needs and rights. But within these boundaries, there are numerous pathways to quality in early childhood.[16]

Anne Smith expressed concerns that moving too far in the direction of value-based definitions would lead to the dangers of 'anything goes'. She challenged the comments of Pence and Moss, who claimed that 'quality child care is, to a large extent, in the eye of the beholder'.[17] Smith argued:

I have a lot of difficulty with this. Does this mean that we can say that hitting children in centres is all right because it fits with someone's idea of what quality is? Is it all right to say that quality involves large group sizes and child/adult ratios because this makes childcare cheaper for parents?[18]

Smith suggested that negotiations towards defining quality should be framed around national values of the best interests and rights of children. She argued that the viewpoints of 'stakeholders' were not based on equal knowledge, acknowledging that 'this may not be a popular view'.[19] Evidence for this position came from research on the indicators of quality in 100 childcare centres with under-two-year-olds.[20] Smith found a zero relationship between parent satisfaction and the research-based measures of quality. Parents with children attending the 'worst' centres had the fewest criticisms concerning quality. These findings were of concern during the 1990s, with Treasury-led views on deregulation. The Treasury assumption was that parents were the key clients on behalf of their children, and the significant determiners of quality. Parents would, in the best interests of children, seek high-quality centres, meaning that poor-quality centres would not survive in the marketplace. Smith's research did not support these assumptions.

Issues of 'whose measure of quality?' periodically became media news, particularly on occasions when the Ministry of Education or ERO recommended the closure of a school or early childhood centre. Many parents stood in defence of the place their child attended, indicating the complexity of defining what quality meant for all concerned. Smith's position was that:

> Parents do of course have an important role to play in defining quality, as do government agencies, and employers. However, I would like to suggest that both researchers and trained people working within early childhood centres also have a role, and indeed a major role, in defining quality because they know it both from the inside and the outside.[21]

This was a view regarded with suspicion by a National government intent on paring back the influence of the profession in the education sector. Echoes of this view were still apparent when Labour MP Trevor Mallard became Minister of Education. He cited parent support as his reason for not closing the Cotton Tails childcare centre in Feilding after a report from ERO cited force-feeding:

> I was extremely concerned by reports from the Education Review Office and had there not been such support from a majority of parents still using the centre, I would have encouraged the Ministry to revoke the licence.[22]

The centre closed its own doors.

The longitudinal Competent Children Project, initiated by Anne Meade and Cathy Wylie in the early 1990s, had been a politically astute move to document the long-term impact of early childhood programmes on the competencies of children in the education system.[23] Children are being assessed every couple of years or so. In the first assessment high-quality centres were linked with higher scores in communication, perseverance and peer social skills. The high-scoring centres shared key structural measures of quality: reasonable salary levels, trained staff, adequate group size and good staffing ratios. Only half the centres reached a good standard, though only a few were either very good or very poor. Even at age 10, the benefits of having attended an early childhood centre were still apparent, particularly if the centre had well-trained and -paid staff, the child had started before the age of two, and there was a good mix of interactions, activities and equipment. Delivering this mix of quality often rested on issues of money, as Helen Orr, the manager of a workplace childcare centre, summed up:

> How can centres put in extra staff or more staff? How can they give their trained staff more in recognition? There is just not enough money to do everything with … It is like saying, 'Yes, there are carrots in the garden next door. You are welcome to them, but you have to climb through the barbed wire and the electric fence to get them.' People can see it, they can glimpse it but it is too difficult to get.[24]

Early childhood services were accountable to their charter, which was inclusive of DOPs. The revised DOPs (1996) set out quality standards for learning and development for children, communication and consultation, and processes of administration.[25] It was ERO's task to check compliance with regulatory standards and monitor the requirements of DOPs. The ERO series of reports *What Counts as Quality?* were critical of the quality of many centres when measured against the objectives of DOPs and, for kōhanga reo, *Te Korowai*. This caused controversy in the sector and was contested.[26] The separate service reports, however, articulated profiles of quality with differing criteria and emphases across the sector. This was positive.

The 1996 'quality funding' package (see Chapter Eight) provided a carefully contained second tier of funding towards balancing the structural costs of quality, but many centres regarded the 'carrot' as increasing the 'barbed wire' barriers. The overall take-up rate by 1999 was 45%; for Playcentre it was only 3.2%, despite alternative criteria for meeting the qualification requirement.[27] Linda Mitchell's view is that: 'A purely financial incentive approach [puts] some centres into a downward spiral: they don't meet the standards so their funding is reduced, so they can't meet the standards because they can't afford to.'[28]

Encouraging quality was the focus of Ministry of Education professional development programmes and new print resources. Most important was the national curriculum (discussed in a later section). The first resource, *Quality in Action – Te Mahi Whai Hua* (1998), provided user-friendly guidance for implementing the DOPs. A third tier to the quality funding 'carrot' was announced in the 1997 budget. The Quality Indicators project, led by Anne Meade, resulted in *The Quality Journey* (1999), which gave guidance on developing quality improvement systems. The Secretary of Education, Howard Fancy, wrote:

> Turning daily experiences [for children] into high quality early childhood education entails good procedures, sound judgement and informed action. Quality improvement systems are centred on such processes.[29]

The Minister of Education, Nick Smith, described *The Quality Journey* as a 'new benchmark of quality' and the 'first step to better rewarding those providers that can deliver high quality'. However, the funding earmarked in 1997 had not materialised by 2000. The new Labour-led government admitted that the structural ingredients might not be right. Further indication of a swing was an announcement that criteria for 'equity funding' for early childhood centres would be developed. 'The state has a role to make up some of that difference in opportunity through the education system … "closing the gaps"' (27 April 2000). The 'age of quality' would still dominate policy initiatives, but the shift in direction suggested that producing the 'quality product' might be less reliant on market forces. Quality systems and assurance processes that became the benchmark of quality during the 1990s might be balanced with some real resources.

WHO GETS TO PRESCHOOL NOW?

Issues of access and participation were major planks of the Before Five reforms. The answer to 'who gets to preschool?', the question posed by David Barney in 1975 (see Chapter Four), was much clearer at the end of the century. There had been a large increase in participation of under-five-year-olds, and changes in the kinds of early childhood service chosen by parents. Issues of access in relation to class, ethnicity and geography remained, although lesser in scale. Affordability had worsened, and 'donations' and fees were the order for all services. The original 1973 childcare subsidy, after various transformations and departmental shifts, still provided fee subsidies to low-income parents. Uptake in 2000 varied regionally from 18% of all childcare users in Auckland to 43% in Hawke's Bay.[30]

It is useful to examine some patterns of the 1990s decade, when general participation rates in New Zealand were high by international standards. The government's own measures of the success of its policies emphasised increasing participation, although it appeared to some critics that quality had been sacrificed for participation.[31] By 1999, 59% of all under-five-year-olds attended a licensed early childhood service, compared to 46% in 1992.[32] The extent and the regularity of attendance were not so clear, but there had been an overall increase of 45% since 1990. Broken down by age, the statistics were more revealing: 99.5% of four-year-olds and 90% of three-year-olds were participating, compared with 56% of two-year-olds and 14% of under-one-year-olds. Māori and Pacific Islands children had lower levels of participation.

The 1999 figures suggest that numbers in the sector may have been levelling after the growth during the decade. A decline in the zero-to-four-year-old population was a cause.[33] The major increases in participation were for children between the ages of one and three years. Lessening rates of participation for younger children were mainly due to parental choice, but constraints of cost and availability were also barriers. The presence of infants and toddlers in early childhood institutions in large numbers caused a change in the appearance of early childhood education during the period covered by this book. That this experience might be beneficial for infants, toddlers and their families demonstrated a turnaround in beliefs, which also caused early childhood services and training institutions to rethink what might be appropriate programmes for the very young.

Between 1990 and 1999 the number of centres increased from 2890 to 4148. This included 758 licence-exempt playgroups, Playcentres and Pacific Islands early childhood groups funded separately by Early Childhood Development (ECD) as it became in 1999. The growth of the informal unlicensed sector was noticeable. Some were groups moving towards licensing and chartering, but others were choosing to remain outside full funding entitlements or, conversely, saw the requirements of licensing as an impossible barrier.

A feature of New Zealand early childhood programmes from the 1970s was the inclusion of children with special or developmental needs. After 1989 most children with special needs were mainstreamed into regular rather than segregated programmes. In 1999 there were 26,279 children (1.5%) with an Individual Developmental Plan (IDP) enrolled in regular services.[34] IDPs are jointly developed by parents and educators to set clear goals for what the child needs to learn and the support and resources the child might need. Inclusion policies were increasingly about rights – to a place in their early childhood centre, to share the same experiences as others and to be with friends and siblings.[35]

Montessori centres were another growth group.[36] The post-1970s revival in the popularity of the Montessori curriculum and its specialist-trained teachers was a trend in Western countries. By 1999 there were 96 centres in New Zealand attracting 5.6% of all children. There were also 22 Rudolf Steiner centres. Like Montessori, their collegial community was international, although both groups had difficulties finding a niche amidst the tightening requirements for New Zealand-based qualifications and curriculum.

Early childhood participation was not evenly spread throughout the community, even by 1999. Participation by rural children was lower than in urban areas. Rural children had always had a smaller range of services, although this had improved since the 1970s.[37] Additionally, nearly 1000 children were enrolled in early childhood programmes with the Correspondence School. Participation by Māori and Pacific Islands children in early childhood programmes remained lower than that of European children, despite their increased enrolments over the decade. Between 1990 and 1999 Pākehā participation rose from around 50% to 65% of all under-five-year-olds, but Māori and Pacific Islands participation rose from approximately 35% to plateau at around 42% in 1992.[38] Māori enrolments increased from 21,705 in 1991 to 32,037 in 1999.[39]

The existence of Te Kōhanga Reo was a factor in the increased participation of Māori children in early childhood services, which reached a peak of 13,543 children attending in 1993. This levelled off at around 12,400 in 1999. By this time there were, in addition to kōhanga reo, 360 centres which operated with some degree of Māori language; these catered for 17,700 children. Eleven of these centres, like kōhanga reo, had full Māori immersion programmes. There has been little public comment so far about the reasons for this growth of Māori language immersion centres outside Te Kōhanga Reo. For Pacific Islands children there was an increase from 6893 enrolments in 1991 to 10,596 in 1999, but there were still barriers. Both Te Kōhanga Reo (which accounted for 43% of all Māori enrolments) and Pacific Islands language centres (with approximately 34% of Pacific Islands enrolments) were reliant on considerable voluntary commitment from communities, often in low socio-economic areas, with high levels of unemployment.

The situation of Pacific Islands centres was of particular concern. In 1997 only 41 out of 191 Pacific Islands centres were able to meet the requirements for licensing and chartering; the others were thus 'fenced off from full funding'.[40] The first targeted Discretionary Grants to redress this began in 1998 (see Chapter Seven), coinciding with the Ministry of Education's Pacific education strategy *Ko e Ako 'a e Kakai Pasifika* (1996). Early childhood was a key plank of the latter, and it was also evident in the 1999 *Pacific Vision* strategy on pathways for achieving Pacific peoples' aspirations.[41] In 2000 there were 67 licensed centres, with 10 more in the pipeline, and a further 138 unlicensed Pacific Islands early childhood groups.

Resolving issues of access and participation across the whole sector has been a multi-faceted exercise. Early Childhood Development has played a key role in managing a raft of programmes encouraging participation and providing parent support. Eligibility for the government's 'equity funding' policy announced in 2000 is not defined, but documents suggest that priority will be given to centres with low-income parents, or those operating in remote areas, or attended by children with special needs, or those incurring the costs of dual or immersion language programmes.[42]

The 1990s were a time of consolidation for Te Kōhanga Reo. The Before Five reforms brought Te Kōhanga Reo under the umbrella of education. Its model theoretically encouraged autonomy and devolution, core principles too for Te Kōhanga National Trust. However, the reality for early childhood services, including Te Kōhanga Reo, was that government control increased over many aspects of operation. The trust negotiated a number of separate arrangements in relation to chartering, funding and training in an effort to ensure that its kaupapa of language immersion and whanau development were compromised as little as possible.[43] In 1999 simmering dissatisfactions became public after an ERO accountability review report was critical of the finances and programmes of some kōhanga reo. Long-serving chief executive Iritana Tawhiwhirangi expressed frustrations at 'fitting a cultural framework into a mainstream framework':

> When the movement came under the wing of the education ministry it meant it could access more funding, but it also meant an overlay of bureaucratic requirements. One pays a price ... I'm not conceding the cultural thrust to satisfy government. We'll go as far as we can. But if it compromises the kaupapa, we won't go. Money's not that important.[44]

Accommodating the diversity of the early childhood sector was a cornerstone of the Before Five policy; accommodating Te Kōhanga Reo was a cornerstone of successive governments' Māori education policy. But governments also wanted statistical evidence that their policies were closing gaps. Accommodating Māori aspirations for self-determination, in the context of Te Kōhanga Reo and the Treaty, was not resolved. Still in press is 'Pono ki te Kaupapa Puna ko te Reo: A study of early kohanga reo and their whanau'. An iwi-focused collaborative project between Te Kōhanga Reo National Trust and the New Zealand Council for Educational Research, it provides insight into the benefits of Te Kōhanga Reo for mokopuna and whanau.[45] It will provide a ground-breaking first research appraisal of kōhanga reo.

The greatest growth in the 1990s was in childcare. This was unsurprising, given that Before Five had its roots in advocacy by childcare workers, women's groups and some unions. By 1999, 42% of all preschool enrolments were in childcare services, including 5% in home-based, mainly family daycare programmes – an average increase of 10% annually since 1990. This was a dramatic shift from the postwar pattern, when kindergarten was the largest provider in preschool care or education. During the 1990s kindergarten's annual enrolment increase levelled off at 1%; Playcentre enrolments decreased on average by 4% annually. In 1999 over half of all childcare centres were private, and the number of private centres had increased from 300 in 1989 to 801 in 1999. One in four (25%) of home-based schemes were also in the private sector. Private enterprise was significant in extending provision, albeit in locations that could yield a profit.

In 1999 there were only 143 workplace childcare centres. Elsewhere, government investment in childcare has sometimes been linked to labour-market initiatives. New Zealand, however, took a distinctive stance, to embrace childcare within the education sector. The Before Five policies were a catalyst in meeting increasing childcare demands. However, the 'ball' that had been dropped from the Before Five policies was affordability. The cost of childcare remained a barrier to many families. Balancing the needs of working parents with the need for quality early childhood for children was an unresolved tension, highlighted by Paul Callister and Val Podmore in *Striking the Balance: Families, work and early childhood education* (1995).[46] One conclusion of their research was that the benefits of a publicly funded childcare system and parental leave provisions might outweigh the costs.

The report of the Prime Ministerial Taskforce on Employment (1994) recommended increasing the childcare subsidy, noting issues of access for low-income families, and in particular for Pacific Islands families. The taskforce highlighted the need for early childhood services to be more responsive to the working patterns of families, but the issue of quality for children was not addressed.[47] The New Zealand Childcare Survey 1998 provided evidence that difficulty in accessing early childhood services was a barrier to workplace participation for 15% of parents, and in particular for low-income parents. Some 20% of all parents surveyed wanted more hours of childcare, at a different time, or in a different service.[48] Expectations that early childhood provision can solve all childcare issues for families are unrealistic. Government policies must protect quality for children, and can address access and affordability of childcare, but other solutions need to be applied to workplace, industrial, economic and family policies.

By 2000 the statistical picture of early childhood provision was encouraging in terms of policy goals and parental support, but statistics indicate that the right mix of policies was not yet in place. There was almost total reliance on community and private endeavour for licensed provision. A discretionary grants scheme to help centres meet regulatory requirements and establishment costs was highly discretionary. Beyond participation, there were issues of rights: the rights of parents to make choices for their children and to access appropriate services, particularly in the context of culture and geography; and the rights of children to a quality environment, particularly as under-fives were spending more hours at a younger age in institutions resembling schools than earlier generations did.

WEAVING TE WHĀRIKI[49]

In 1996 the Prime Minister, Jim Bolger, launched the final version of Te Whāriki, the national early childhood curriculum.[50] This was the first time a prime minister had so explicitly stamped government approval on what children might do on a daily basis in early childhood centres. Thereafter, early childhood services were required to demonstrate that their programmes were operating according to the principles, strands and goals outlined in Te Whāriki. These were incorporated in the revised DOPs.[51] The development and wide acceptance of Te Whāriki as a curriculum within the early childhood sector was a surprising story of careful collaboration between government and the sector. There was both accommodation and resistance to government agendas.

In 1991 Margaret Carr and I were contracted to co-ordinate the development of a curriculum that could embrace a diverse range of early childhood services and cultural perspectives; articulate a philosophy of quality early childhood practice; and make connections with a new national curriculum for schools. The story of this policy development spans the 1990s. Wisely, the government did not rush it.[52] The draft of Te Whāriki was released in late 1993,[53] followed by a process of trialling.[54] Professional development programmes to support staff in understanding and working with the document began the following year.[55] The ministry subsequently funded four research projects towards developing frameworks for evaluation and assessment based on Te Whāriki.[56] In 2000 the Ministry of Education released *The Big Picture*, the first video of a series on Te Whāriki.

The development of a national curriculum framework for both early childhood centres and schools was part of an international trend to strengthen connections between the economic success of the nation and education. So-called progressive approaches to curriculum that relied on child interest and ideals of individual growth and development were under attack. The draft *National Curriculum of New Zealand* (1991) for schools set the new direction and emphasised primarily the need to 'define a range of understandings, skills and knowledge that will enable students to take their full place in society and to succeed in the modern competitive economy'.[57] It set out seven principles, three of which were explicitly to do with the workplace and the economy. These underpinned the later *New Zealand Curriculum Framework* (1993), which defined seven learning areas and eight domains of essential skills. It was amidst these initiatives that the government decided there would be a national early childhood curriculum.[58]

Governments had not previously been concerned with curriculum in the early childhood sector: each of the different early childhood services had its own approach.[59] The term curriculum itself was rarely used, although a 1988 Department of Education working group developed a curriculum statement that was later incorporated into the *'Purple' Management Handbook* for chartered centres.[60] Early childhood organisations were wary of the idea of a national curriculum, concerned that it would constrain their independence and cut across the essence of their diversity. Yet the alternative, of not defining the early childhood curriculum, was dangerous: the national curriculum for schools might start to move downward. Our involvement was a response to these concerns.

The development of Te Whāriki involved a broad consultative process with all the services and organisations. More specifically, the writers wanted the curriculum to reflect the Treaty partnership of Māori and Pākehā as a bicultural document model grounded in the contexts of Aotearoa–New Zealand. This was a challenge. There were no New Zealand or international models for guidance. This became possible due to collaboration with Te Kōhanga Reo National Trust and the foresight of Tamati Reedy and Tilly Reedy, who developed the curriculum for Māori immersion centres.[61] The theme of empowerment was important for Māori, and 'empowering children to learn and grow' became a foundation principle. Tilly Reedy emphasised the maxim for Māori: 'Toko Rangatiratanga na te mana matauranga–knowledge and power set me free'.[62] A set of parallel Aims for Children (later named strands) in Māori and English were developed, not as translations but as equivalent domains of empowerment in both cultures:

Manaatua	Well-being
Mana whenua	Belonging
Mana tangata	Contribution
Mana reo	Communication
Mana ao turoa	Exploration

Each aim was elaborated into Goals for Learning, which were expanded to illustrate what they might mean in a variety of contexts: for infants, toddlers and young children; for Māori immersion programmes (including children with special needs, home-based programmes, and 'Tagata Pasifika' settings); and for management and adults who worked with children. This contextual elaboration was considerably reduced in the 1996 document, with government favouring a more integrated approach. We opposed and regretted this.

The title 'Te Whāriki', suggested by Tamati Reedy, was a central metaphor. The early childhood curriculum was envisaged as a whāriki, translated as a woven mat for all to stand on. The principles, strands and goals provided the framework, which allowed for different programme perspectives to be woven into the fabric. There were many possible 'patterns', depending on the age and interests of the children, the cultural, structural or philosophical context of the particular service, and the interests of parents and staff. This was a curriculum that provided signposts for individuals and centres to develop their own curriculum weaving through a process of talk, reflection, planning, evaluation and assessment.

The conceptualisation of Te Whāriki around aims for children differed from the traditional developmental curriculum approach of physical, intellectual, emotional and social (PIES) skills, which dominated Western curriculum models. Te Whāriki acknowledged a theoretical debt to Piaget and Erikson, whose theories had underpinned earlier curriculum practice of learning through play,[63] but it was also grounded in the theories of Bronfenbrenner and Lev Vygotsky, which placed the learning experiences of children in a broader social and cultural context.[64] It also emphasised the contributions of Vygotsky and Jerome Bruner towards defining a more active role for the teacher, whose task was to 'scaffold' children towards more complex thinking and increasing competency.[65]

Meade used the phrase 'warm demanders' of children to describe staff who were teaching well; she also referred to the lost and 'unreturnable moments' that teachers missed when they were not more actively involved in supporting individual children's learning.[66] Anne Smith emphasised the importance of Vygotskian theories of learning, in which the teacher 'leads instead of follows children's development'.[67] Te Whāriki also made a political statement about children: their uniqueness, ethnicity and rights in New Zealand society. Jenny Ritchie described Te Whāriki as 'about countering racism'.[68] For people from the Pacific nations (and other cultures) Te Whāriki provided a curriculum space where language and cultures could be in the foreground and not an add-on.[69] For Tilly Reedy, Te Whāriki was about self-determination. She told a mainly Pākehā audience in Auckland: 'Our rights are recognised and so are the rights of everyone else … Te Whāriki recognises my right to choose, and your right to choose too.'[70]

Transforming a national curriculum into practice to make a difference for children was a challenge. By 2000 the visual presence of Te Whāriki was apparent in most centres, but implementing the document was complex, partly because it resisted telling staff what to do, by 'forcing' each programme to 'weave' its own curriculum pattern.

Ministry research trials highlighted support for Te Whāriki, but indicated that there would need to be ongoing professional development in a sector that had large numbers of untrained or poorly trained staff.[71] It was apparent, too, that staff turnover and staff–child ratios were significant factors in its success or otherwise. ERO was critical of Te Whāriki. The holistic principles, strands and goals were not easily understood or measured by ERO's mainly school-sector reviewers. Their report on the *Use of Te Whāriki* (1988) referred to its 'complexity', noting the high levels of training and/or guidance expected. ERO's 1997 survey found that 16% of centres reviewed were lacking in confidence to implement Te Whāriki. Another 38% needed to improve.[72] This was only a year after the final document had been released. Centres needed time and support to reflect upon what Te Whāriki might mean in their particular context. This was not a quick process. Diane Mara's study of this process in the different Pacific Islands communities was illustrative of the barriers and possibilities.[73]

Academic interest in Te Whāriki was high and generally supportive.[74] Joy Cullen from Massey University took a more cautious view. She highlighted the tensions between the developmental and socio-cultural perspectives inherent in Te Whāriki, and expressed concern that much of the current professional development and training was conducted by educators unfamiliar with the theoretical underpinnings of the latter. The issue of training was a crucial one to Cullen, who thought that 'for the busy practitioner, implementation of Te Whāriki is likely to be constrained by a superficial understanding of its rationale and implications for practice'.[75] By 2000 Cullen was more 'optimistic that the early childhood field is better equipped to work with such tension'. Professional development programmes for teachers and the increasing number of early childhood professionals studying at the postgraduate level had contributed to the pool of increased understanding and knowledge.[76]

There was international acclaim for the rationale of Te Whāriki as a national curriculum statement.[77] Cathy Nutbrown, from Britain, highlighted its emphasis on children's rights as a source of curriculum and also the respect for children as learners.[78] The framework of multiple curricula was of particular interest. Frode Sobstad co-ordinated the development of a Norwegian curriculum framework, and wrote:

> The most interesting aspect of the New Zealand curriculum is that the name of the curriculum and the profile is taken from the minority culture, the Maori people. We have not given the Sami culture a chance to influence our national program for day care institutions in Norway. Instead they have been given their own chapter. But is this enough?[79]

The Early Childhood Forum in Britain adapted the model of Te Whāriki for its curriculum 'foundation for early learning' (1997, 1999).[80] This project was intended to counter the British government's own national nursery education document, which was prescriptive, content focused and skill based.[81] Tina Bruce urged her British colleagues to speak out and clarify for the politicians 'what we want for our children in early childhood. This has been done in New Zealand … the radicals have been allowed to speak.'[82] This was not always assured!

The redrafting of Te Whāriki into its final version was undertaken by the Ministry of Education, with the intention of retaining the philosophy and framework of the 1993 draft, which had been so well received. Nonetheless, the redrafting was subject to various 'raids', with considerable relocation, removal and a changing emphasis coming from authors who did not originate in early childhood. The early childhood community, however, was relieved and surprised that the principles, strands and goals of Te Whāriki survived such a complex political process intact.

There were ongoing challenges. First, there was an assumption that early childhood centres would have the funding and the trained staff capacity to operate quality programmes. This mismatch undermined the implementation of Te Whāriki. Secondly, the holistic and bicultural approach to curriculum of Te Whāriki, inclusive of children from birth, was a challenge to staff who were more familiar with the traditional focus on play areas and activities for preschool-aged children in mainstream centres. Thirdly, a political climate of accountability made increasing demands on early childhood staff in relation to assessment and evaluation. Much of this was a new language for staff and parents.

Margaret Carr, initially, and later Val Podmore and I undertook research to develop frameworks for assessment and evaluation linked to the strands of Te Whāriki. Mindful that the government wanted evidence that children were learning, and was concerned that inappropriate assessment was filtering into the early childhood sector, particularly under pressure from ERO, Margaret Carr suggested five learning dispositions relating to the five strands as a focus for recognising and describing children's learning. With this knowledge staff could more effectively support and direct its pathway.[83] As with Te Whāriki, Carr was again drawing a 'line in the sand' against the deficit models that dominated school assessment practice, and forging new ground nationally and internationally.

QUALIFIED TO TEACH

The level of qualification needed to work in early childhood and necessary for licensing purposes was contested throughout the 1990s. Research evidence convincingly presented the importance of qualification levels for ensuring quality experiences for children,[84] but the costs of more and/or better-qualified staff was a burden that services could ill afford. Private-sector childcare centres lobbied successfully for the government not to increase regulatory requirements concerning qualifications, arguing that this would erode profits as well as affect fees for parents. Cost was only part of the issue: the unavailability of qualified staff, particularly in some locations, was another problem. Worsening industrial conditions caused recruitment and retention issues. For services such as Playcentre, voluntarism was a core aspect of its philosophy. In 1997 voluntary staff made up over 40% of all staff working in early childhood,[85] keeping the fees affordable in many centres and services.[86] The increasing trend toward a better-qualified and professionalised workforce in the early childhood sector was a threat to the viability and philosophy of some groups. Argument and confusion over qualifications across volunteer and professional divides characterised the decade. The situation was not resolved during the term of the National government. The tangled tale is too complex to unravel fully here.

The three-year Diploma of Teaching (DipTch), taught in the six colleges of education, was at issue. In 1989 there was a consensus view that the DipTch should be the benchmark qualification for licensing purposes. All services would need to employ at least one person with this qualification or its equivalent. This was the crux of the problem. Very few people had the new qualification, although the existing qualification of kindergarten teachers was deemed equivalent. A phase-in period was needed to provide ways in which staff with different, lower-level qualifications could attain the benchmark, and ways in which organisations that had their own training and qualification system, such as Playcentre and Te Kōhanga Reo, could gain equivalence to the benchmark for licensing purposes. Individuals wanted qualifications that were portable across sector groups. The issues were substantive, and compounded by the longstanding lack of funding and training in the sector. The challenge of Before Five was to negotiate a way forward in which the principles of equity and diversity could be accommodated within a unified qualification-regulatory framework.

A phase-in 'blueprint for the future' was approved by the Labour government in 1990.[87] This specified a four-year timeframe for staff to upgrade their qualification to DipTch; the scheme was to run parallel to the Before Five staged funding plan. A system of points was developed and assigned to existing qualifications, with the DipTch set at 120 points. The requirement for licensing would be 80 points; for chartering (and funding purposes) it would be the full 120 points. Individuals could have their qualifications accredited and be told what courses they needed to gain an 'equivalency diploma'. The process was to be managed by the New Zealand Qualifications Authority (NZQA), which would issue the diploma.

The change of government in late 1990 and the education reviews in 1991 (see Chapter Eight) terminated the staged funding plan, and derailed the blueprint and the timeframe. Requirements for chartering were cut back to 100 points. This created a new 'animal' of 100 points for which there was no qualification.[88] The 100 points became an accumulation of low-level qualifications and courses. Meade strongly expressed her concern:

> I reiterate, 100 points built up by a hodge-podge of courses does not equate to a qualification. I have fears for what it might mean for children's education. Will such staff be able to plan, implement and evaluate their centre's curriculum based on Te Whāriki?[89]

In 1994 NZQA ended its 'equivalency diploma', which few had regarded as a 'real' DipTch. After this, some people acquired far more than 100 points, but no qualification (affecting 1198 people in 1999).[90] The aftermath of this complicated saga, only briefly outlined here, continues.

In 1996, as a result of the government 'quality funding' package, a short-term Pathways Programme was developed.[91] This offered another opportunity for staff to upgrade their qualifications to a DipTch. Colleges of education were persuaded to offer their own qualification, with a package of third-year courses built on 80-point qualifications.[92] The programme was only partially successful. The recommended funding to improve access for staff and offset costs to centres did not materialise. The programmes often took longer than the promised one year. Colleges felt that academic quality was compromised when other qualifications assigned 80 points did not equate with the level of their own courses. The scheme was soon phased out.

In 1998 the government sought to tidy up the chaos. Recommendations and options for the DipTch to be the licensing benchmark were presented, accompanied by the weight of research evidence.[93] The minister responsible for early childhood, Brian Donnelly, was supportive, but the timing was wrong. The minister was from New Zealand First, National's coalition partner in government. The coalition suddenly fell apart and the ball was dropped, but an incoming Labour government picked it up. Trevor Mallard's letter to the sector on 9 May 2000 summed up the play:

> My vision for early childhood education is one where all centre-based early childhood educators will have at least a Diploma of Teaching (ECE) and will be registered teachers. I realise that it will be some time before this vision can fully be realised. Issues around qualifications are complex, and the diversity of the sector further contributes to this complexity … Improving the qualifications and quality of early childhood educators will be done in phases …

The timeframe was extended to 2005, the requirement still only one qualified person per centre. However, ECC vice-president Ross Penman claimed that 'hundreds of early childhood teachers could be forced out of the profession' (*Dominion*, 20 May 2000). He was concerned about the minister's resolve not to grant equivalent status to staff who did not have the qualification, but were already in positions of responsibility. The 1999 statistics showed that 35% of the paid staff in the sector held a DipTch or its equivalent, 20% had no qualification, and 50% had lower-level or part qualifications.[94]

Broader changes across the education sector in the delivery and packaging of qualifications affected early childhood in the 1990s. In 1989 NZQA had embarked on establishing a national qualifications framework. This was another complex story. Early childhood qualification issues were caught up in a pedagogical debate on the nature of knowledge and how it should be packaged for training and qualification purposes. NZQA proposed to repackage the knowledge content learnt by anyone, from secondary school upward, into unit standards. These were discrete, sequential, portable and designed to measure competencies or skills that 'successful workers actually perform on the job today'. NZQA described the process:

> The concept of competency focuses on action or outcome rather than on the learning or teaching process; it embodies the ability to transfer and apply skills and knowledge to new situations and environments.[95]

The framework was promoted as an essential base for producing the skills the nation needed.

NZQA decided to apply the unit standards model, developed for the trades, to the field of teacher education, including early childhood. The process was fraught, both pedagogically and politically. NZQA brooked no critique and those who tried to debate or challenge the appropriateness of the philosophy fell by the wayside.[96] Carr, one of the earlier combatants, contrasted the NZQA Competency Model with what she called the Teacher Change Model. The latter was to do with teaching pedagogical understandings that were an essential part of the process of training of staff who would be critical thinkers as they worked with children.[97] Carr assessed the Competency Model as more appropriate for a technician than a teacher.

At issue, too, was the ECC's quest to 'seize' the opportunity to develop a lower-level qualification, so that graduates might cost less to train and pay. Carr and I embarked on a bruising and unsuccessful attempt to 'hold the line', due mainly to concerns that Te Whāriki was in danger of being toppled by unit standards that seemed unable to embrace its holistic approach to knowledge and curriculum.[98] With others in the front line, the turbulent and divisive politics continued, until early childhood unit standards were approved by NZQA in 1997. NZEI-TRR, colleges of education and kindergarten organisations formed a formidable cabal and held the line for a qualification equivalent to the existing DipTch, although several lower-level qualifications were also approved. By then, the political tide was turning against NZQA. The government slowed, and in some cases halted, unit standards development. Universities staked an independent path, and there was no take-up of the unit standards qualification at diploma level by early childhood training institutions. At best, they provided a broad map for those institutions whose qualifications had to be approved by NZQA.

Another backdrop to early childhood training was the practice of contestability, which affected all aspects of government business. There were some gains for the early childhood sector, but the loss of collegiality and co-operation by institutions and organisations forced to compete for contracts was detrimental. Colleges of education and universities became providers of advisory services and professional development that had originally been located with ECD. The alignment of these services with teacher education and research had positive spin-offs in early childhood centres, however.

In 1995 the government made the delivery of teacher education contestable. Polytechnics and private training providers could be accredited by NZQA. This coincided with the early childhood quality funding package and the subsequent pressure for qualifications. Several private providers applied to offer the DipTch. Concerns were raised about the capability of some of these providers, but political pressure for private enterprise in teacher education and a level of desperation in the early childhood sector led to a wide range of courses being approved; some were clearly destined to the bankruptcies and scandals that followed, leaving students with worthless or no qualifications. The increased number of training providers certainly improved access across the country, but created too many poorly resourced programmes. There were 12 training courses in 1992; by 1998 there were 60 providers offering 80 courses.[99] Even colleges of education were under pressure to keep their intakes sustainable, particularly in the light of increasing student fees. From 2000, private and community providers were eligible for the same level of funding as state tertiary providers. The Labour government, however, promised to review the number of training providers engaged in teacher education, because of concerns about quality and after various scandals, particularly in the early childhood sector.

During the 1990s a two-tier system of providers emerged, differentiated by diplomas and degrees. All colleges of education, in partnership with universities, offered degrees, and two colleges actually merged with universities, at Waikato and Massey. Early childhood teachers with degrees started entering the profession in significant numbers. From 1996 colleges of education offered their own degrees. This caused some 'divorces' from university partners, particularly after a three-year teaching degree was approved. Early childhood academics seized the momentum of these changes, some of which were beneficial for early childhood. By the end of the 1990s all colleges of education were offering degrees in early childhood teaching. At the universities of Waikato, Massey and Victoria there was a direct progression through to master's level and doctoral programmes. This academic up-skilling of early childhood was a significant factor in creating a burgeoning early childhood research community, closely linked to the profession and increasingly active in New Zealand and international forums.[100]

The dynamics continue to shift. The two-tier division is possibly dissolving. Several polytechnics have started to offer early childhood degrees, and several colleges have retrieved their diploma. The Montessori Association of New Zealand has negotiated a degree course with the Auckland University of Technology, a former polytechnic that has become a university.

The diversification of training providers has had other spin-offs. Te Kōhanga Reo National Trust registered as a private training provider in 1992. It established parent support and language programmes through to the three-year Whakapakari Tino Rangatiratanga programme for kaiako, equivalent to the DipTch. Pacific Islands training and qualifications were also established, although more often within the mainstream settings of colleges of education and polytechnics. Family daycare qualifications for carers were established in polytechnics. The training of nannies was a growth area in polytechnics and in the private sector. In a new development, some of the nanny agencies became chartered early childhood service providers, similar to family daycare schemes.[101] In some institutions nanny qualifications became a stepping stone to a DipTch – but not in colleges and universities, which were reluctant to compromise academic standards for too much diversity of style and delivery. These issues pose an ongoing dilemma in the early childhood sector.

In the 1990s marketplace of training there were winners and losers. Some people gained degrees, others ended up with qualifications of little value.

Qualifications and training issues in the sector reveal the complexity of defining a benchmark across diverse cultural, philosophical and professional contexts. However, a consensus framework for different but equivalent pathways to the DipTch benchmark seemed possible, and it was functioning in some policy contexts. At issue still was the cost of qualified staff, many of whom now had the same level of qualification as primary and secondary teachers. New political thinking about pay parity across the teaching profession was to later force a major rethink of funding to early childhood services and centres.

AFTER BEFORE FIVE

Successive governments during the 1990s supported the notion of a seamless education system from early childhood through to tertiary level.[102] The reality left a chasm caused by a range of industrial, delivery, funding and philosophical divides. The anticipated occasion of 'going to school' at age five was often not a smooth transition for children and their families.[103] In 1997 the Children's Issues Centre at the University of Otago and the Institute for Early Childhood Studies at Victoria University of Wellington hosted a national seminar called Transition to School. Teachers from both sector groups, preschool and primary, attended, and the atmosphere was strained. One of the organisers, Tony Holmes, reported:

> ... there was little positive reference to the school environment and little understanding about the pressure primary teachers are facing. From the early childhood teachers we heard criticism of the reception new entrants received.[104]

Conversely, primary teachers displayed little knowledge of the work and ethos of early childhood centres. It became apparent that the transition to school experience, for children and their families, was bearing the brunt of policy pressures from the government, and heightened expectations by parents. A clue to the burgeoning interest in the issues was several research projects documenting the transition experience for children, parents, and teachers and, in one study, for boys.[105]

The histories of early childhood education and early school years are separate in New Zealand, although the various pedagogical and political waves described in this book impacted across both sectors.[106] Government investment in early childhood education throughout the half-century was justified as a foundation for learning at school, although the rhetoric and rationale was tuned to the times. In other countries sharing this view, the structural alignment of early childhood (particularly the later years) and early school, moved closer and sometimes merged. Australia's preschools and Britain's nursery schools were examples where the transition was also at age five. Increasing political interest in the connection between early childhood and school was global. In richer countries there was an expectation that children would enter school from an early childhood programme. In developing countries, powerful agencies such as the World Bank were promoting and funding projects to establish early childhood education as a national economic investment.[107]

The tangible expression of the New Zealand government's interest in a seamless connection for education was its curriculum policy. Structural linkage was not on the agenda. Government policy promoted devolution, and the organisations sought to uphold their autonomy. Government also wanted to maintain a clear demarcation between the 'voluntary' (for children) and mainly 'fee-paying' early childhood sector, and the 'compulsory' and mainly 'free' school sector. Curriculum was to be the connection. It was therefore important that the early childhood curriculum articulate its connections with the subject-based learning areas and essential skills of the school curriculum.[108] The early childhood sector, however, was determined that the early childhood curriculum should position learning in the early childhood years as different from learning at school. Te Whāriki outlines these connections, but as the Transition to School seminar revealed and research has documented, in practice there was a mismatch between sectors and disruption for children as a result.

The New Zealand Curriculum for schools and pressure from ERO hugely increased the assessment and documentation of children's learning. Evidence of learning became a requirement from a government seeking to benchmark the performance of New Zealand children on international tables. Schools needed to demonstrate the abilities of their pupils to meet the expected levels and outcomes. Parents, too, were seeking assurances that their children were acquiring the skills of reading, writing and mathematics. A downward pressure of these expectations affected five-year-old children. Upon arrival at school they found themselves in classes timetabled around the new learning areas, and undergoing assessments in relation to literacy and numeracy that were not reflective of the broad-based learning dispositions they brought from preschool.[109]

What happens 'after Before Five' was to become of more political interest to the early childhood sector. The sector had demonstrated that, in the main, it could hold the line against the worst aspects of the downward demands of global education and economic trends, but vigilance and more cross-sector engagement is needed. The establishment of the first degree in early years' education (0–8 years) in 1999 at Massey University and Dunedin College of Education were initiatives driven by early childhood staff, with a view to the long-term benefits of graduates working across sector groups.

The maxim of 'after Before Five' is also political in the broader context of early childhood policy. In an overview of the Before Five decade, entitled 'The Price of Partnership' (1999), I concluded that there had been 'positives and pain', and blamed the pain on poor implementation and a lack of political courage to address the substantive issues.[110] In response, Linda Mitchell argued:

> There are fundamental flaws in the Before Five policy itself because it failed to provide structural underpinnings for its aims. Before Five was couched in partnership and equity terms but these have never been realised.[111]

Mitchell spent most of the decade addressing and documenting the consequences of policy limitations, political timidity and at times sabotage. *Future Directions* (1996) documented the constraints of Before Five (see Chapter Eight) and set a framework for moving forward. This is now happening, but Mitchell argued that the way forward needed a new agenda, and a debate about childhood to reappraise the role of the government in supporting families, children and the institutions of childhood. Mitchell herself embarked on this task.[112]

From a different perspective, so did the government. In 1998 the document *Towards a Social Code of Responsibility* (1998) was circulated to all homes and comments were invited.[113] The role of government in the funding and delivery of early childhood services was again under scrutiny. Government policy was to promote individual and family responsibility and continue devolving its own responsibility, but the demarcation between family and government was not so neat. The lives of many families had few safety nets when buffeted by government economic, social welfare and housing policies.

Mitchell suggested there was a need to reposition the state as 'supportive' of early childhood. The partnership between government, the early childhood profession, providers and users needed to be rebuilt upon values that allowed genuine involvement in policy making. Mitchell's concern was that:

'The Before Five policy was easily dismantled because there were no con-values keeping it safe.'[114] Reconceptualising childhood and the institutions of childhood is an issue challenging other early childhood thinkers, who were trying to move the paradigm beyond the economic rationales that framed its focus and appearances in the latter part of the twentieth century. From the US, Gail Sloan Cannella wrote:

> If early childhood education were reconceptualised as the pursuit of social justice for younger children, new images could emerge as the framework for action. These could include a struggle to learn how to respect others, the recognition of multiple realities, the belief in the inhumanity of creating others as objects, the practice of radical democracy, and the willingness to take revolutionary action.[115]

Some of the values for such a rethink were in place in New Zealand. Te Whāriki was about social justice for communities, families and children. The Early Childhood Code of Ethics for teachers, launched in 1995, was about rights and responsibilities.[116] History's lesson is that the sector can debate new ideas and formulate consensus positions. It was time for a new debate. The government's announcement in May 2000 concerning the development of a strategic plan for the sector, a recommendation in the report Future Directions, offerd one forum for this to occur.

Dahlberg, Moss and Pence suggested in 1999 that early childhood institutions could be understood as 'public forums situated in civil society in which children and adults participate together in projects of social, cultural, political and economic significance'.[117] This is not new to New Zealand. Te Kōhanga Reo and Playcentre, for example, have at different times demonstrated the dynamics described. New early childhood institutions often emerge as radical forums of activism, involving far more than early childhood education for children. Early childhood advocates, too, have a track record of being radical and revolutionary; some, such as Marie Bell, Iritana Tawhiwhirangi, Beverley Morris, Geraldine McDonald and Sonja Davies, have worked in the political arena on behalf of women and children throughout most of the years this book covers. Linda Mitchell's dream for change is that:

> Early childhood [should] be conceptualised as community institutions playing an important role in fostering a democratic society. A new discourse could lead to a reconstruction of the role of the state ...[118]

This is possible. The history documented here shows that early childhood discourses in New Zealand have had success in shaping the political 'gaze'.

In 2000, I concluded the first edition of this book knowing that the lesson learnt was that we had to be active in constructing the discourse. Early childhood education was taken seriously on the political front. This was a potential problem, as politicians, employers, parents and schools saw the institutions of early childhood as the solution for many things. Early childhood had always been the site for experiment. The issue was whose experiment, and which blueprint, would guide future policy? I argued that we needed to ensure that we were active in the blueprint's construction, because history clearly had taught us that in the new century, childhood 'before five' would be different from the childhood we know today.

PART FOUR

Strategic Directions
2000s–2010s

CHAPTER TEN

'Blue Skies' in the 'Playground'

Chapter Nine was written in 2000, the fifth Labour government's first year in office. During 2008, with an election looming, opinion polls were indicating a swing to the right and indeed by the end of the year a National-led government was elected. During the 1990s the politics of early childhood were dominated by National's policies of less government and more individual responsibility while, in the 2000s, they were framed by promises to develop and implement a strategic plan for the sector. The strategic plan was intended to redress structural flaws still impeding access to early childhood services for some children and families, to reduce costs for parents and provide the resources necessary for high quality early childhood care and education. The professional standing of early childhood teachers and their qualifications would again be under scrutiny. Both Labour and National place value on early education participation – the difference between the two being one of emphasis, with Labour taking a more 'hands-on' approach to the task. During the 2005 election, both Labour and National were accused of promoting a 'nanny state', a metaphor signifying differing solutions for early childhood education.[1] Amidst a buoyant economy, Labour campaigned for more spending on social services and promised free early childhood education, while National offered tax rebates for working parents.[2] By 2008, it was evident that a world economic downturn could shift the priorities of government spending.

The first edition of *Politics in the Playground* was launched by the Minister of Education, Trevor Mallard, in July 2001. The event was held at my workplace, the Institute for Early Childhood Studies at Victoria University, and was attended by members of the minister's Strategic Plan Working Group (of which I was one). We had spent the past year developing a ten-year plan for the sector and had recently submitted a report to the government.[3] The launch also provided the occasion venue for the minister to offer Clare

261

Wells a job in his office. As a past union activist, Wells' work with Linda Mitchell within the primary school and early childhood teachers union, NZEI–Te Riu Roa, spearheaded the *Future Directions* (1996) project that first recommended a strategic plan for the sector.[4]

Speaking without notes, the minister graciously acknowledged the contribution of the working group. In a way this congenial event updated the story that concluded in Chapter Nine. An election promise to develop a strategic plan had been delivered. Nevertheless, the question uppermost in the minds of those in the working group was whether or not the government would accept and implement the proposals. The content of the minister's prepared speech for the launch was, however, different from what he said. After recognising members of the working group in the audience, the minister must have decided not to publicise his official reaction to the report, which included the recommendation 'for whānau and families to have a universal entitlement to a reasonable amount of free, high quality early childhood education'.[5] The working group argued that, in addition to positioning New Zealand alongside most of its OECD partners, this was a necessary outcome of the emphasis given within the strategic plan to the Articles of the United Nations Convention on the Rights of the Child, the Treaty of Waitangi and the Principles of Te Whāriki.[6] In the prepared speech, Mallard deemed free early childhood education 'blue skies thinking' and stated that the working group should be more 'fiscally responsible' in its recommendations.[7] The minister subsequently requested that some trimmings be made and a second report was later submitted.[8] Even so, the recommendation remained unchanged, except for the phrase '(or almost) free' being inserted in brackets. Mallard has since said that the 'time was not right' even though he personally supported 'universal quality ECE'.[9]

The development and roll-out of the government's strategic plan, *Pathways to the Future: Ngā Huarahi Arataki 2002–2012*, dominates the story of the 2000s and highlights some dramatic shifts in thinking and political manoeuvring around the policy for free early childhood education.[10] It is useful to examine the developments of the 2000s in light of increasing advocacy for the young citizen child. I have previously argued that the rationale for political interest in early childhood has been framed by 'political gazes' that have shifted as the state has become an increasingly active partner in rearing children. At the same time, however, the state has managed to cloak its gaze in precise ways.[11] The first edition of *Politics in the Playground* outlines the state's shifting political interest for investing in the education of preschool-aged children. In the early postwar years, political interest and policy was influenced by psychological theories of developmental readiness for school and new 'understandings' of mother–child relationships. Later, support for early childhood services was framed around issues of equity for children, women and minority groups. During the 1990s, it was rationalised as a prudent economic investment for the nation. All of these gazes remain operative. By the 2000s the cautiously seeded view that the state should support its preschool-aged child citizens began to gain currency.[12] This consideration is surprisingly tardy when compared to Peter Fraser's oft-quoted statement, crafted by C.E. Beeby, outlining the 1939 Labour government's vision for the education of the school-aged child:

> The government's objective, broadly expressed, is that every child: whatever his level of ability, whether he be rich or poor, whether he live in town or country, *has a right as a citizen, to a free education* of the kind for which he is best fitted and to the fullest extent of his powers (my emphasis).[13]

The intent of this quotation is revisited later in this chapter.

Evidence of the government's new interest in early childhood education is its increased spending, which went from $409 million in the year ended June 2002 to an estimated $771 million in 2007 – double the budget of 1999, when Labour took office. As a consequence of these new streams of funding, together with the implementation of the strategic plan policies, past inequities and divisions in relation to care and education were further eroded. However, at the same time a new distinction emerged between parent-led and teacher-led services. New policies concerning qualifications, funding and free early childhood education were intended only for teacher-led services. This gave rise to funding issues around whanau and parent-led services, such as kōhanga reo and Playcentre, and equity issues for Pasifika centres unable to meet the requirements for a teacher-led service. Divisions also sharpened between community-based and privately owned providers of early childhood education. Even though the Labour government tried to reign in corporate profits and require adherence to new qualification and funding regimes, the private sector continued to expand throughout the 2000s. A number of private early childcare businesses were listed on the stock market. In 2008 Carmen Dalli suggested that some 'unintended consequences of well-intentioned policies' were beginning to emerge.[14]

A political watch has documented the impact of new policies and tracked a steady increase in early childhood participation across all ages. Although factors, such as the unknown extent of dual enrolments, make statistics deceptive, clear trends in the levels of participation remain evident.

- Overall participation rates in early childhood education for children upon starting school increased from 92.3% in 2002 to 94.5% in 2006. For Pākehā children this increased from 96.6% in 2002 to 98% in 2006.
- For Māori and Pasifika children participation rates are lower but with rising percentage increases between 2002 and 2006: from 86.5% to 89.9% for Māori children and 79.4% to 84.2% for Pasifika children.[15]
- Despite this increased participation, a Salvation Army 'State of the Nation' (2008) report described 'a large and lingering inequity of access for poor and generally brown children'. In 2005–2006 the overall enrolment rates for preschoolers was 64.9%, up from 59.7% in 2001. However, there were variations around this national average, with an enrolment rate of only 44% in Manukau City compared to 86% in Tauranga. Similarly, in Otara, Auckland, just 33% of preschoolers had early childhood places compared to 80% in Wellington City.[16]
- Other statistics indicate shifting patterns of provision. In 1998, enrolments in all-day services made up 42% of all enrolments; in 2005 this figure had risen to 60%. The children mainly attended education and care centres, with 58.4% being enrolled in privately owned centres. Overall, 36% of children were enrolled in privately owned services including home-based provision.
- For both home-based services and education and care centres, the average hours of attendance also increased, with significant increases in the participation rates of one-, two- and three-year-olds.[17]
- Attendance at kōhanga reo and Playcentre continued the decrease already evident in the 1990s.[18] The commitment required by whanau and parents was a reason as the trend toward all-day provision increased. Nevertheless, the voice and presence of both kōhanga reo and Playcentre was still strong in policy development.
- Between 2003–07 enrolments in kōhanga reo declined by 10.5%, with an overall decline of 52% since 1995. There were, however, an increasing number of Māori immersion programmes existing outside of kōhanga reo. By 2007, 11 of these centres were providing a Māori language environment of between 80–100%.
- Between 2003–07 the decline for Playcentre steadied at 3.5% but there had been a 30% drop in enrolments since 1995.

innovative approaches to curriculum.[26] Furthermore, if by the early 2000s New Zealand had been included in the first review, its commitment towards implementing policies that supported the integration of care, education and diversity within early childhood services would have been noteworthy. That the provision of quality early childhood education was 'firmly on government agendas' was reaffirmed in the second OECD review, *Starting Strong II. Early childhood education and care* (2006).[27] Again, if New Zealand had participated, its policies for creating a teacher-led profession and implementing a measure of free early childhood education would have been showcased. The decision not to take part in these reviews was made in the late 1990s under a National government. Although it might have been possible for New Zealand to join the second round, the failure to do so was partly due to cost.

New Zealand did participate in the 2002–2005 OECD study of ten countries' policies for reconciling work and family life: *Babies and Bosses*.[28] The study originated from the Directorate of Employment, Labour and Social Affairs which had an explicit economic rationale to invest in early childhood education so as to maximise the participation of women with children in the workplace. The report on New Zealand recommended funding policies directed towards parents and the hours they were employed, rather than early childhood institutions. In comparison with *Babies and Bosses*, the *Starting Strong* reviews originated in the Directorate of Education, under the premise that investing in the wellbeing and education of children was a public benefit. As a result, tensions between these two positions have arisen for the institutions of early childhood care and education, the professionals who work in these institutions, and the government policies that support their provision and quality. In New Zealand the emphasis has been mostly towards the *Starting Strong* position. That said, the strategic plan straddles both, with the intention of improving the quality of care and education, realising benefits for children 'here and now' and in the future, and better accommodating the needs of working parents. Overall, both positions have been framed as an active social policy intent on investing in people to improve the 'social, educational and economic health' of the nation.[29]

The idea of a strategic plan for the sector emerged in the mid-1990s amidst the implementation of the Labour government's 1989 *Before Five* reforms. In 1995, NZEI–Te Riu Roa initiated the Early Childhood Education Project to develop a policy strategy to address the divide between the 'haves' and 'have nots' across the sector.[30] The subsequent report, *Future Directions* (1996), made recommendations for realising the goals of universal funding for children, pay parity for teachers, and a strategic plan for the sector.[31] In 1999 the Labour Party made a strategic plan for early childhood an election promise, linked to the political aspiration of 'closing the [economic] gaps'.[32]

In 2000 the Labour government appointed a working party to develop a 10-year strategic plan.[33] The primary goals were to implement quality provision and improved participation. There was an acknowledgement that the government would be required to play a more supportive role. Although harder to grapple with, the third goal of 'promoting collaborative relationships' recognised the role of early childhood education (beyond the benefits for individual children) in community development.

The Strategic Plan Working Group outlined a range of strategies to improve the infrastructure so as to provide quality participation. A draft report, released in 2001, indicated a high level of support from sector groups, with calls for 'speedy implementation'. Victoria Carter, president of the Auckland Kindergarten Association, however, expressed concern that the report might be 'All talk and no walk'.[34] Later, Carter, and many others, may have preferred that the 'walk' would slow down.

In 2002 Prime Minister Helen Clark launched the strategic plan under the title *Pathways to the Future: Ngā Huarahi Arataki 2002–2012*. The plan made a commitment to:

• New funding and regulatory systems to support diverse services to achieve quality early childhood education
• Better government support for community-based early childhood services
• A teacher-led early childhood profession.[35]

Pathways to the Future signalled the possibility that community and privately owned services, as well as teacher-led and parent-led services, could develop along different lines. In the prepared speech originally intended for the book launch of *Politics in the Playground*, Trevor Mallard made clear his concerns about private centres, outlining the government's 'responsibility … to look at ways in which all children have access to quality early childhood education. Private providers do not have that wider commitment.'[36] Even so, the government subsequently softened its attitude towards privileging community-run services over those provided by the private sector.

The strategic plan outlined a staged schedule whereby all adults in teacher-led centres would be registered teachers or completing qualifications by 2012. Previously, depending on the size of the centre, only one staff member might have been required to hold a teaching qualification. Teacher registration, a two-year period of professional supervision, was to become compulsory for all teachers in early childhood education and care settings. The government's commitment towards establishing a teacher-led profession remained firm throughout the decade, despite opposition from a variety of sectors, including private operators, areas that had difficulty meeting the demand for qualified teachers,[37] those experiencing the political and industrial effects of increased costs, and from parent-led services such as Playcentre and kōhanga reo. Some kōhanga reo did qualify as teacher-led centres, and parents and kaiako in both organisations were recognised as 'teachers' for licensing and funding purposes. There were also issues for the growing number of Pasifika, Montessori and Rudolf Steiner centres, whose distinctive character required staff with qualifications sympathetic to the particular philosophy.[38] Ideals of diversity have been constrained by the teacher-led policy, the early impact of which can be summarised as follows:

- Between 2002 and 2006 the proportion of early childhood teachers with a recognised qualification increased from 49% to 54%.
- In Auckland in 2006, where there is a strong private early childhood sector, only 46% of teachers held recognised qualifications.
- At the same time, 46% of unqualified teachers were enrolled in a tertiary institution to upgrade their qualifications.
- Enrolments in early childhood teacher education programmes increased by 65% between 2001 and 2005.[39]
- By 2007, almost 70% of all teacher-led centres had 50% of their teachers qualified. This statistic also applied to Auckland.[40]

The transformation in the structural landscape of early childhood teaching led to a 're-think' of the role of the professional early childhood teacher.[41] Carmen Dalli and Sue Cherrington suggest that distinctive professional qualities defining early childhood teachers in New Zealand began to emerge.[42] According to Dalli and Cherrington, these included particular 'pedagogical styles and strategies' and a distinctive 'professional knowledge and practice', underpinned by a framework of 'collaborative relationships'.[43] The principles and goals of Te Whāriki, the goals of the strategic plan, and the new Centres of Innovation (COI), a strategic plan policy intended to showcase excellence, are all seen as having helped to shape this uniquely New Zealand early childhood teacher. By 2008, some 16 centres had, after a rigorous selection process, undertaken a three-year action research cycle to extend and showcase to other teachers an area of innovation and excellent practice in their programme. Anne Meade, who led the COI work, has written of the transformative experience in which 'teacher–researchers have become educational leaders, by making their practice-based knowledge both explicit and public'.[44] This has been showcased on both national and international fronts.

Since 2002, the government has invested considerable resources towards realising a teacher-led policy, which is supported by research evidence that the presence of qualified teachers in early childhood centres has long-term positive outcomes for children.[45] In 2005 a new funding model was introduced that differentiated between teacher-led and parent-led services.[46] Linked to the actual costs of employing qualified teachers, funding would increase as centres phased in the requirements for qualified and registered teachers. This favouring of centres that employed qualified staff caused concern amongst private childcare centre owners, who had a legacy of reluctance to employ more teachers than the regulatory requirement. Despite ongoing difficulties with the implementation of the teacher-led scheme, government policy remained firm, demonstrating a significant shift in political opinion from earlier decades, particularly in the context of childcare. The National Party's early childhood election policy released in July 2008 indicated a future softening of political resolve. For children under two years of age the National Party proposed that only 50% of staff needed to be qualified. While relieving pressures on centres to meet the targets, the promise suggested that infants and toddlers are easy work rather than deserving of the best.

Designing the new funding model was not easy and the early advice from government officials and their departments did not support such a universal approach. Linda Mitchell, a member of the Strategic Plan Working Group, became a member of the technical working group charged with developing more specific funding proposals. In her doctoral thesis, Mitchell revealed the mismatch between the advice government received from its officials, the aspirations of *Pathways to the Future* and the government politicians who supported it.[47] The Ministry of Education's initial funding proposal was for a strongly targeted model linked to affordability for parents, combined with a level of base funding to recognise the costs of qualified staff.[48] Mitchell reported that Treasury took an even stronger position on targeted funding, with the view that disadvantaged children would gain the most in terms of long-term achievement and outcomes.[49] Mitchell reported:

In a courageous political decision, Trevor Mallard, the Minister of Education, rejected this proposal. He asked officials to go back to develop and cost alternative options for providing totally free early childhood education by the year 2012.[50]

This seeming turnaround by Mallard, since the launch of *Politics in the Playground* two years earlier, was only known by a few at the time. The behind-the-scenes development of the free early childhood policy is told in a later section.

PAY PARITY RESOLUTIONS

In 1998, the last year of the National government's term in office, primary school teachers won a campaign for pay parity with secondary school teachers.[51] The imagery of 'Susan's Shoe Size' which they successfully employed became the new icon of the long-running kindergarten pay parity campaign. 'Susan's' younger sister 'Sally' protested that neither should her smaller 'shoe size' determine the salary level of her teacher.[52] The NZEI–TRR campaign 'A teacher is a teacher' was launched in 1998 under the slogan of 'One Teaching Profession One Teaching Pay Scale'. In 2000 kindergarten teachers were reinstated as state employees under the State Sector Act (see Chapter Eight). Trevor Mallard noted, 'By taking responsibility for the terms under which they are employed, the Government is taking leadership for setting benchmark standards.'[53] The NZEI–TRR also negotiated a settlement whereby kindergarten teachers would progress towards pay parity, hopefully in 2002. A ministerial working party was established to make recommendations for a phase-in process. NZEI–TRR mounted a separate 'Road map to pay parity' campaign for teachers working in early childhood education and care centres. One poster for the campaign did not disguise the bends and barriers ahead, but drew the finish line with some runners in sight of reaching it.

Pathways to the Future had established the timetable for instituting a registered teacher-led profession for the early childhood sector. NZEI–TRR was determined that pay parity be included in new early childhood funding policy. Linda Mitchell was no longer employed by NZEI–TRR, but represented their interests well through her work with the technical working group.

The Labour government began its second term in July 2002. The day after the election, one of the first statements made by the prime minister was to announce the go-ahead for kindergarten pay parity. Settlement was reached in August 2002, with a phase-in period of four years. While kindergarten teachers were jubilant over the success of their three-decade campaign, the

Dominion Post headline, 'Preschool teachers win 61pc pay rise: A job that's child's play?', captured the still-lingering public perception concerning the nature of their 'work'.[54] Secondary school teachers did not support pay parity, even with primary school teachers, and stepped up a campaign for new qualification differentials. Teachers employed in early childhood education and care centres were unenthusiastic about the success of the kindergarten teachers, as they felt aggrieved that government had expressed no commitment to their campaign. As teachers in the childcare sector were not state employees, the issue of their pay parity was positioned outside of government interest and involvement. The problem for the operators of early childhood education and care centres was that there was insufficient government funding to cover the costs of qualified teachers. Increasing the fees for parents was an unpalatable option.

As outlined in Chapter Six, the Early Childhood Workers Union established and negotiated the 1985 Consenting Parties Award with a group of mainly community childcare employers who, under the umbrella of the New Zealand Childcare Association, were committed to conditions of work that would support quality early childhood education. A fuller account of this Award, which became the Consenting Parties Agreement (CPA), was written in celebration of its twentieth anniversary in 2005.[55]

Prior to any funding decisions, the NZEI–TRR was determined to inch the CPA further towards pay parity. Te Tari Puna Ora o Aotearoa–New Zealand Childcare Association was again the bargaining agent for the employers. The association had also been energetic in both the development and implementation of the strategic plan. In December 2003 settlement was reached with 150 employers to introduce a salary structure comparable to state sector teachers. The NZEI–TRR president Bruce Adlin explained:

> This is a significant step as it will provide further recognition that teaching in early childhood is a profession ... Being paid a salary moves early childhood teachers in these centres a step closer towards gaining pay parity with the teachers at state kindergartens and state schools ... Moving these teachers onto salaries will enable us to quantify the pay gap ... NZEI Te Riu Roa is determined to bridge that gap and achieve pay parity for all registered and qualified teachers working in the early childhood sector.[56]

The government budget of May 2004 included details of the new early childhood funding package. There were two key features, the most newsworthy being the announcement that, by 2007, all three- and four-year-old children in community-based centres would get 20 hours of free early childhood provision a week. The second announcement concerned a new funding formula linked to the costs of teacher-led centres. Trevor Mallard gave a special early childhood budget briefing, telling the sector that, 'Parity is coming, relativities are lifting … we are professionalising the early childhood sector.' After much applause, the minister reckoned on an 'eighteen-month lag between pay for staff with the same qualifications'.[57] This was interpreted to mean that the implementation of pay parity would be finally complete in 2008.[58] However, this was only a verbal statement.

In June 2004 the Ministry of Education released the *Guide to the New Early Childhood Funding System: Implementing Pathways to the Future – Ngā Huarahi Arataki*. The CPA was now positioned as pivotal to the funding process:

> There are likely to be funding bands which match with the proportion of registered fulltime equivalent teachers in a service … This additional funding would need to be passed on to teachers in their salaries so that teachers' salaries are at least at the level of the Consenting Parties Agreement.[59]

Centres that met agreed quality criteria associated with qualifications and salary levels would be funded at a higher rate.

In October 2004 the NZEI–TRR tabled its 'historic' pay parity claim for the Consenting Parties' contract negotiation. Agreement for a phased-in settlement using the minister's earlier reckoning of 2008 was reached, with a contingency clause to be triggered if the funding was not adequate. A teacher with eight years experience and a bachelor degree in early childhood would, over four years, get a salary rise from $37,600 to $56,000.[60] Nancy Bell, the chief executive of TTPOoA–NZCA, who led the employers' negotiating team, stated that the 'employers who have agreed to this historic settlement have done so because they care about the quality of early childhood education in Aotearoa'.[61] TTPOoA–NZCA told its members that pay parity was 'around the corner' and that it believed this would 'significantly improve the sector's ability to attract and retain excellent teachers'.[62]

There was some irony in the turnaround in fortunes of the CPA. Although there had been much difficulty getting it established in the 1980s and it had been undermined by government in the 1990s, it was now the new benchmark, except for the kindergartens, for the new funding policy. Both the union and the association hoped that more employers would join the aAgreement. There were, however, many unknowns concerning the implementation of the new funding regime and its linkage to the CPA.

The *Early Childhood Education Funding Handbook* (2005) provided the specifics for implementing a process referred to as 'attestation'. Centre managers needed to provide information to the Ministry of Education so that their funding rate could be calculated. Each centre had to 'attest that the registered (ECE) teachers employed are paid **at least at the level** of the Consenting Parties Agreement'.[63] With the Consenting Parties' settlement in late 2004, a semi-government-sanctioned mechanism to ensure pay parity for teachers across the early childhood sector seemed to be happening. There was, however, no reference to pay parity in any government documentation.

The new funding regime was to become effective from 1 April 2005. At the 'eleventh hour', in fact on 23 March 2005, the Ministry of Education released Circular 2005/5 – Early Childhood Education Funding – Attestation: Registered Teachers' Salaries. The circular again reiterated, in bold, the previous statement about the CPA, and explained:

> The key objective of this new funding condition is to ensure that registered teachers employed in care and education services are recognised and required for providing quality. This will further strengthen the early childhood education work-force.[64]

This time the government defined the required 'level' of pay but referred only to the first step of the CPA rates. At worst, the low level of the 'requirement' would allow centres to receive additional monies without being required to pay salaries on a path to pay parity by 2008.

On behalf of the employers in the CPA, Nancy Bell complained to Trevor Mallard that the information in the circular 'misrepresents the agreement' and the result would be 'a significant backward step' from pay parity for teachers, thus 'compromising the future ability of the sector to achieve quality'.[65] There was, however, some caution in her criticism of a minister who had shown considerable resolve to implement a teacher-led profession and attempt to curb profit-making by the private sector. Nevertheless, the dream of government-sanctioned pay parity became a political casualty of election-year pragmatics. Bell told association members that, 'Markets create winners and losers. We don't think it's good enough to leave teachers' salaries – or the quality of ECE services – to the whims of the market.'[66] As the flurry of acrimony continued, the Minister of Education did eventually clarify his position:

> [Centres] are also funded on the basis of rewarding experience, as set out in the Consenting Parties Agreement, and I expect that *good centres* [my emphasis] will pay at least that rate.[67]

This clarification of political expectation did not provide a mechanism to ensure that the full salary scale of the CPA would be passed onto the staff concerned. Market forces kept salaries for qualified teachers in the childcare sector high, but the notion of pay parity across all education sectors was fragile and incomplete.[68] Wayne Wright, the founder and chief executive of Kidicorp's 80 education and care centres, expressed the difficulties of getting qualified staff in stating that he 'could place 200 teachers tomorrow if I could find them'.[69] Demand had driven his salary bill up by 25% in the previous 18 months.

In 2008 new Minister of Education Chris Carter deflected questions regarding issues of pay parity from the Ministry of Education's Early Childhood Advisory Committee. Kindergarten associations wanted assurances that funding rates would allow them to match a recent salary settlement for primary teachers, benchmarked against the settlement for secondary teachers. Furthermore, on behalf of the employers in what was now called the Early Childhood Education Collective Agreement (ECECA), Nancy Bell asked whether the funding rates would support their goal for teachers in education and care centres to achieve pay parity with kindergarten teachers in 2008. The minister indicated that his officials were preparing advice on these matters.[70] The ECECA might have been the benchmark salary agreed for funding purposes but the full extent of its scale and conditions still only covered 142 employers. Moreover, some centres face a particularly challenging task in trying to implement pay parity, as they did not receive the level of funding that kindergartens got with their fully qualified teacher workforce.[71]

ABC OF PRIVATE ENTERPRISE

Private ownership of childcare centres has a long tradition in New Zealand, mainly as owner-operated centres in private homes. During the 1980s a few commercial chains grew, the most well known being the Kindercare franchise, established in New Zealand in 1978 by Allan Wendelborn and Glennie Wendelborn [Oborn]. By 2006 Kindercare had 48 centres in Auckland and Christchurch. In 1990 the Early Childhood Council (ECC) was established to represent the interests of private centre owners, although never exclusively. The scope of the ECC's services to its members always attracted a wider grouping of education and care centres. In 2008 62% of centre members were private and 38% community based.

During the 2000s, the dynamic of the private sector of early childhood education changed dramatically, with big business and the sharemarket becoming politically powerful and, some would say, 'dangerous' players.[72] Corporate chains listed on the sharemarket, such as Australia's ABC Learning Centres Limited, Forward Steps operated by Australia's Macquarie Bank and the New Zealand-owned Kidicorp, became significant providers with proactive strategies to buy out operating centres. In 2007 corporate chains operated around 150 of the 1133 privately owned centres in New Zealand. ABC is reputed to have 'made millionaires' of local centre owners since its arrival in 2006.[73] The administrative complexities of meeting the requirements of the strategic plan policies overwhelmed many individual owners and small community management groups. Glennie Wendelborn reported that the plan had created a 'Catch 22 situation' where the 'more you are funded [by government] the more it costs to administer it'.[74] It was not accidental that the flurry of big business and sharemarket jockeying for the private childcare market coincided with the government's intention to increase its investment in early childhood provision. Big business was not only conducted through the trading of shares. Macquarie Bank bought centres in 2005, then on-sold them to ABC as a 'profitable bundled package' in 2007.[75]

The ECC and corporate childcare providers have reshaped the political landscape of early childhood politics, more recently by campaigning against many of the Labour government's policies. These policies have curtailed some of the possibilities for profit-making and have required a more inquisitive government eye on money flows, fee levels, qualifications and curriculum. New requirements, due to start in 2009, for the renewable licensing of services will further increase the role of government in monitoring what many private providers regard as their own business. Despite government efforts, the political environment has continued to foster the growth and power of the private sector. In an international context, the trend towards increased early childhood education has created a market in which, unless governments become providers or their policies exclude private operators, the private sector is needed and often more able to swiftly meet the need for more provision. In the US, Canada, Australia and UK the trend is similar. By floating shares on the stock market big companies have gained access to large amounts of capital to fund a level of expansion that is unobtainable for individual centres or even larger community providers. Sue Thorne, the CEO of the ECC explained the reasons for the trend:

… former owners found it was getting too hard to run a centre in some parts of New Zealand. They were having to cope with a significant staffing shortage, and compliance is arduous. The people who have sold centres have just had a guts full. But corporates are getting involved because daycare is a 'good investment' and a growing part of the infrastructure of the early childhood sector because more women are going back to work.[76]

Wayne Wright believed that, 'Providing a good service to parents, having high quality early childhood education and making a profit can coexist.'[77] Wright delisted Kidicorp from the stock market in 2007. 'I was never going to be able to satisfy the parents who didn't want fee increases, the teachers who wanted wage increases and the shareholders who wanted dividends, out of not enough dollars.'[78]

Wayne Coullat, chief investment manager for Fisher Funds Management, a shareholder of Kidicorp, supported Thorne's view that the strategic plan policies created the market for the corporate growth, claiming that the qualification policy pushed up the costs of childcare and created a scarcity of staff in the market. Property costs to build new centres were also an issue:

> All these factors lead to a corporate structure and sophistication to offer people the opportunities they want. We will gradually see the number of small, local early childcare education providers diminish, just as supermarkets have led to the demise of the corner dairy. It's inevitable.[79]

The absence of any government policy for the planned expansion of early childhood education has meant that provision remained essentially ad hoc and determined by market forces. This has benefited the suburbs and districts that house the more affluent. Not only do such districts resource community endeavours more successfully, they provide a profitable niche for private enterprise. The only funds favouring community provision were the Ministry of Education's – over-subscribed and administratively cumbersome – Discretionary Grants Scheme for capital works, as well as the Equity Funding for community centres that either provided for children from isolated or indexed low socio-economic localities or had a high proportion of children with special needs or from non-English speaking backgrounds.

From Australia, Deborah Brennan described the early childhood policy landscape as a 'bonanza of big business'. She cited one private owner who stated:

> The childcare business is the best business I've had in my life. The government pays subsidies, the parents pay you two weeks in advance and property prices keep going up.[80]

Brennan has been critical of the rise of ABC Learning, which listed on the Australian share market in 2001. By 2006 ABC had grown twenty-fold and had expanded globally through the US, UK and New Zealand as well as acquiring franchises in the burgeoning Asian markets of Hong Kong, Indonesia and the Philippines. In 2006 the chief executive, Eddie Groves, was named Australia's richest individual under 40 years by the *Business Review Weekly*.[81] In September 2007 Australian newspapers reported that ABC was the world's largest childcare provider and that its profits were up 76% on the previous financial year. Share prices rose from 21c to $7.07 (Aus) between 2005 and 2006. According to the *Melbourne Age*, ABC had made 'acquiring new business look like child's play'.[82] Groves' next moves would see him become the largest childcare operator, not only in Australia but also in Britain, while continuing to buy up the small New Zealand and the huge US markets. ABC received around $400 million worth of Australian taxpayer subsidies in 2007. Between 2006 and February 2008, ABC purchased 116 New Zealand centres and transformed them with the ABC branded appearance, play equipment and daily programme, all managed from Groves' Brisbane corporate headquarters through state of the art technology.

In late 2007 ABC announced its intentions to operate across the states of Canada under the trade name '123 Busy Beavers'. For the first time the pendulum swung, as a coalition of community organisations lobbied both the state and federal governments to prevent access.[83] In Canada 80% of childcare was community operated. The questions posed were:

> Is it [childcare] a public service or a business venture? Is there room for profit-making in the care and education of our youngest children? Is it time to reconsider who should own and operate childcare?[84]

These same questions were posed in New Zealand by NZEI–TRR in a position paper, 'Quality Public ECE: A vision for 2020', presented to its 2007 annual meeting. NZEI–TRR was seeking 'a radical change in direction' from 'a system that encourages, and in some instances advantages, private provision'.[85]

Canadian economist Gordon Cleveland supplied evidence concerning the costs and benefits of childcare provided by both private and publicly operated institutions. Cleveland became a regular visitor to New Zealand and Australia and his research was cited by those concerned with the recent corporate expansion in the sector. In 2007 Cleveland released the results from four large

Canadian data sets that confirmed the superiority of public provision by showing that it had a 'quality advantage' of between 7.5% and 15% over private provision.[86] Cleveland stated:

> Although there are good quality non-profits and poor quality non-profits, non-profit centres are over represented at higher levels of quality and under-represented at lower levels of quality.[87]

He concluded:

> For policy makers who are anxious to provide good quality early learning and child care at a reasonable cost, this quality advantage of non-profits is important. However, non-profit status is not, by itself, a magic elixir. Our findings in 'thin' markets suggest that in conditions of inadequate financial support, efforts to encourage quality can fail. Government policies that support and encourage the development of a higher level of quality in early childhood education and care services are also necessary to permit non-profits develop a culture of quality that we call the non-profit advantage.[88]

Cleveland's research confirmed smaller studies carried out in New Zealand.[89] Linda Mitchell's 2001 study, for instance, showed differences in the proportion of staff with qualifications across centres that were community owned (42%), privately owned (35%), or owned by education or workplace institutions (54%).[90] The strategic plan policies have, however, improved these figures across all types of centre. Mitchell was also the co-researcher of a national survey conducted during 2003–2004 to provide base-line data in the early years of the strategic plan. The survey again highlighted differences between community centres and private centres. Teachers in private centres generally had poorer working conditions than teachers in community centres and were less likely to be involved in decision making as a team. There was a higher turnover of staff in private centres.[91] On the other hand, the ECC's Sue Thorne claimed that 'she could take parents into a number of different centres and wouldn't be able to tell which ones were community owned, run by Mum and Dad operators, or by big corporates'.[92]

In the early 2000s the Labour government indicated its intention to rein-in the profit-making possibilities of corporates and private centres. Trevor Mallard, the Minister of Education, expressed little sympathy when private centre owners campaigned against the timelines and deadlines for meeting the targets of qualified staff, stating that they 'need to get it into their heads that this Government is keen on lifting the quality of the service'.[93] Parts of the private childcare sector had, for many years, been tardy in supporting or requiring their staff to get qualifications, despite a range of government schemes to encourage existing staff to upgrade qualifications.

The ECC, however, waged an effective campaign highlighting the problems for their members in implementing the strategic plan policies. The *Sunday Star Times* reported that:

> Education Minister Steve Maharey issued a warning to the main commercial chains, telling them that they cannot expect to continue to make profits on the back of heavy government subsidies for childcare ... with the growing emphasis on quality care there would be little scope for private operators to deliver a return to shareholders ... any surplus should be reinvested to deliver quality care and education.[94]

In this strongly worded statement, Maharey also foresaw that 'the sector will over time become more and more like compulsory schooling and the chances of making a profit ... almost nil'. As a consequence of these statements there was an immediate drop in the share prices of corporate childcare companies and Maharey was subsequently reprimanded by the NZ Commerce Commission. This was deemed to be political interference in the market. Politicians were now walking a fine line between promoting and protecting quality early childhood care for children and the interests of business in childcare provision.

On 25 February 2008 ABC Learning released its half-yearly results as at 31 December 2007. In an upbeat and colourful powerpoint presentation, the company forecasted a positive political climate for increasing government support for early education across the US, UK, New Zealand and Australia.[95] While income was up 66%, however, net profit was down 42%. The report also noted that, on 31 December 2007, ABC had secured three-years' refinancing of its debt facilities. A day after the results were released there was a shudder in the stock market that rippled across many countries and into the world of childcare. Over the next two days ABC's shares dropped 70% and trading was eventually halted. Groves and his ex-wife partner sold 18 million of their own shares after which, on paper, he owned a paltry $4883.42 stake in the company. ABC's rapid expansion, particularly into the US market, compounded by a credit squeeze, was deemed to be the cause of the share crash. Macquarie associate director Julian Cook analysed the tumble for an author unused to the language of the big business of childcare:

> What caused the share price crash was the realisation that they had probably overpaid for the US businesses and taken on too much debt. This was coupled

with the general credit crisis in the markets at the time to make people very bearish. Also the founder had borrowed against the value of his shares and the stock was aggressively shorted by the hedge funds to drive the price down and forced him to shell his shares. In short the company and the founder were geared too highly in an environment where credit was very tight and hard to get.[96]

The boom business of childcare was at least to slow down, if not halt, for a while. Due to its reliance on ABC's 1095 centres for childcare provision, the concern was such in Australia that both state and federal governments were braced to intervene. The Queensland premier announced the possibility of government intervention if the company collapsed.[97] The prime minister expressed his concern for 'every working family' on ABC radio. The federal government subsequently promised to ensure that all childcare places were maintained. The *Brisbane Times* reported that the deputy prime minister, who was ultimately responsible for this issue, would not comment directly because of the potential impact on the stock market.[98] There were rapid reassurances from ABC that it could remain afloat. New Zealand parents using ABC centres were told that 'The children in our centres remain our highest priority.' New Zealand spokesperson Scott Emerson told the *NZ Herald* that 'Nothing's changed – we've taken a hit in the share price but that doesn't affect the centres at all.'[99] Frances Nelson, president of NZEI–Te Riu Roa, issued a media release urging the government to buy up the ABC centres:

> Corporate early childhood services receive public money but much of it ends up offshore. The government should commit to providing a national network of publicly owned early childhood services … The difficulties being experienced by ABC Learning illustrate the risk of leaving early childhood education to the vagaries of the market.[100]

It is hard to assess the impact of the collapse on curtailing or halting the trend towards corporatisation. ABC's lead position was faltering. By 8 March 2008 Groves had negotiated the sale of the company's US assets.[101] Deborah Brennan called for a rethink of Australia's approach to the provision of childcare.[102] A few days earlier she had hosted a symposium on childcare policy at the University of New South Wales. Invited delegates came from Australia, Sweden, the UK and the US, and included the author Linda Mitchell and Nancy Bell from New Zealand, and from Canada Gordon Cleveland and Sue Colley, a leader of the coalition of community childcare advocacy groups. Symposium members analysed the issues and concerns of corporate childcare and ABC in particular. The collapse had not been anticipated. Canadian advocacy groups were hopeful that 123 Busy Beavers, the Canadian ABC subsidiary, would not proceed. There was a fear that 'the collapsing empire – built with public funds – is being sold to other large companies, and a new global childcare company might come to Canada'.[103] Community childcare advocate Martha Friendly stated:

> But whether the corporation is foreign-owned or made-in-Canada, the fundamental issue remains the same: Are preschoolers primarily consumers to be wooed for their profitability, or are they worthy of the same kind of interest and support we devote to their older siblings in the public education and university systems.[104]

At the time of writing, 123 Busy Beavers had bought 11 centres in the state of Alberta and had made offers on facilities in both British Columbia and Ontario.

In New Zealand, the government was silent on ABC's misfortunes. At an Early Childhood Advisory Committee meeting on 5 March 2008, Nancy Bell, CEO of TTPOoA–NZCA, questioned the Minister of Education, Chris Carter, on the issue. He replied that he 'shared the previous Minister's distaste for public funds generating large profits'. However, he 'also recognised that a large number of families were using these centres'.[105] All of ABC's New Zealand centres continued to operate, with the company intending to trade its way out of financial difficulty. In 2008 the Australian ABC company went into receivership, causing the Federal government to guarantee that not all centres closed. In December 2008 all 120 ABC childcare centres were on the market. Expressions of interest were being sought.

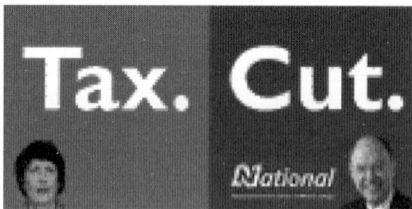

'NANNY STATE' DIVIDES

The 2005 election was a timely gauge for the government's early childhood policies. The election was closely fought and revealed divided views concerning early childhood policy and the role of the state itself. This was the divide between the centre right and centre left politics of the respective National and Labour parties, starkly expressed in the National Party advertisement. National offered the electorate an immediate tax cut, on the presumption it would shift various state responsibilities to individuals and families, whereas Labour offered to shoulder more of the increased costs of living that were causing stress to some electors. Early in the campaign, a *Dominion Post* editorial headline, 'Nanny tax cuts or nanny state', accurately portrayed the different positions between the left and the right concerning the role of the state.[106] The catchphrase became a metaphor for a range of electioneering positions. The origins of the 'nanny' slogan came, not surprisingly, from the early childhood education sector where the policies in *Pathways to the Future* were gathering pace.[107]

The 2005 election gave the National Party the opportunity to offer an alternative pathway for early childhood. Families with preschoolers and others with vested interests in the politics and provision of early childhood education were presented with two options: either three- and four-year-olds in community-based centres receive 20 hours of free early childhood education, as promised by Labour, or working parents receive tax rebates on childcare fees, as proposed by National, which would axe plans underway for free early childhood services. The selective coverage and benefits of each party's policy was strongly critiqued by the other. Labour's Michael Cullen labelled National's policy a 'nanny tax bribe' for well-off parents that excluded beneficiary parents. Labour's policy was labelled as being unfair to parents with children attending privately owned education and care centres.

In an article headlined 'Nanny state', *Listener* columnist Jane Clifton was critical of both policies, warning that 'politicians mess with motherhood at their peril'. She concluded:

> In a nutshell, both schemes are probably thoroughly offensive to most parents, but they'll take the money if they can. In a political campaign climate where every policy round is a push-me-pull-you, parents will be pragmatic and vote for what best suits their circumstances. Will they be socially engineered? Probably not. They'll be too busy working or learning or job hunting, while also trying to raise their children as well.[108]

Clifton saw an overbearing 'nanny state' apparent in both schemes where both parties 'want to encourage us to be different people'. The differences were deeper. The cover story graphic of the 1 October edition of the *Listener*, headlined 'The big divide: How deep are the rifts?', portrayed geographic and political divides between town and country, and the left and the right. Despite the apparent cohesion of the early years of the decade, when there was broad early childhood sector support for the strategic plan, the 2005 election revealed a divided landscape. Early childhood politics were now split between two pathways to the 'nanny state', with supporters on both sides claiming, in the titles of separate policy perspectives, to be *Putting Children First*.[109]

Linda Mitchell, in her version of *Putting Children First* published by the NZ Council for Educational Research, argued that the interests of young children participating in early childhood care and education were best served by a 'well qualified early childhood teaching workforce'.[110] She outlined the links between research on quality provision and the government's 'strategic' policies for improved outcomes for children that favoured a teacher-led sector.[111] Mitchell had been promoting this pathway for many years, both as an early childhood union activist and as a researcher. Mitchell's paper was a reaction to media headlines that, 'Hundreds of preschools across New Zealand face mass closure next year as the sector struggles to cope with the new qualification requirements.'[112] Citing statistics from the Education Review Office, Mitchell showed that most centres would meet the 2005 requirement for the 'person responsible' in each centre to hold a qualification. A Ministry of Education workplace survey of staff qualifications similarly indicated that predictions of 'hundreds of closures' was not substantiated by the evidence.[113] Mitchell was concerned the government might retreat from its scheduled implementation of qualification requirements. Recalling the not too distant 1990s, she wrote:

> The early childhood sector has a history of training requirements being weakened and changed. This is one reason why a long-term strategic plan was sought and why we do not have a fully qualified teaching workforce today.[114]

Conversely, the ECC commissioned the NZ Institute of Economic Research to provide an 'independent' analysis of the sector. The strategies it recommended for 'putting children first' were to ensure that parents could choose across the spectrum of private and community provision. This would first require the removal of funding differentials related to ownership, such as the Discretionary Grants Scheme and Equity Funding. Of most concern to the institute was the proposed 20 hours-a-week free early childhood provision for children attending community-owned centres:

In addition to being unfair and lacking in any policy rationale, the '20 free hours' policy will bias parents towards certain services solely because they are more heavily subsidised, not because they have been shown to be 'better'…[115]

The policy was, however, rejected as being beneficial for children or parents. Second, the report's authors questioned 'the government's reliance on staff qualifications providing an assurance for quality'. They argued that the interests of children would best be served by replacing the current emphasis on qualifications and teacher registration, with a 'broader approach to quality' that recognised 'staff competence and parent opinions'. The authors acknowledged that 'higher qualifications *may* raise quality', but pointed to 'the evidence … that quality education [is] associated with the *quality* of teachers (and management) rather than qualifications'. They recommended giving a more 'dominant role for industry' in setting qualifications standards based on job competency, rather than academic qualifications.[116]

Amidst the diverging pathways and positions of the closely fought 2005 election campaign, private sector dissatisfaction attracted a great deal of media attention. In response, the Prime Minister, Helen Clark, 'out of the blue' announced the extension of the free early childhood policy to private centres. When the ECC welcomed the election turnaround over 'free early childhood' it was accused of 'putting principles aside'.[117] In a letter to the *Listener*, Sue Thorne from the ECC replied that this was 'not correct' and went on to explain that:

> The government, quite rightly, saw problems with its policy and changed it. Despite the fact that its solution was not our solution, the government deserved praise for doing this.[118]

The ECC had spearheaded the National Party's proposal to introduce tax rebates on childcare fees that would immediately benefit working parents.

In this shifting political landscape, Australia's Macquarie Bank timed its decision to 'invest in New Zealand early childhood education'.[119] A bank spokesperson denied that the move was influenced by the increased funding for the sector, claiming instead that Macquarie investments in Australia ranged from preschools to a theme park, and it merely saw an 'opportunity' in New Zealand's 'fragmented' early childhood education sector.[120] The bank carefully chose its 'opportunity' to sell 18 months later. In the aftermath of the election, Kidicorp strategically shifted its business approach from buying up centres to building purpose-built new centres in 'strategic sites likely to earn a profit'.[121]

On her website Sarah Farquhar exclaimed that, 'never before has so much money been offered to parents to fund childcare … yet the policies of Labour and National are very different'.

> Whether it is best for children to deliver assistance directly to their parents or to early childhood services depends on which side of the fence you are standing on.[122]

Siding with the ECC, Farquhar saw 'fewer fish hooks' in National's policy:

> Whereas Labour is setting out to alter the landscape of provision and use of early childhood services, National's intention is to leave it much the way it is but give parents who need childcare support greater flexibility in their ability to purchase what they want.[123]

This was at the heart of the early childhood policy divide and the political divide between the left and the right. In the event, it was Labour's policies, along with coalition party support, that gave it a third term in government. At his first meeting with representatives of TTPOoA–NZCA, the new Minister of Education, Steve Maharey, tried to accommodate both sides. Speaking in a more restrained manner than his admonishments of the private sector would be in 2007, he positively acknowledged the role of privately owned centres that acted in the 'public good' and not for profit:

> It is unreasonable to distinguish between services that invested in providing high quality programmes on the basis of their ownership structure … The focus is on what these institutions contribute to the public good – public value is the uniting factor … However, we are not going to fund you to make large amounts of money.[124]

It was again full steam ahead down the *Pathways to the Future*. However, the promise to provide all three- and four-year-olds '20 hours free' in teacher-led services created the technical challenge of developing funding mechanisms acceptable across both community and private settings. This decision signalled a shift from the government's earlier intention to privilege community-owned services. Not only was the private sector lobby too strong and its provision too essential, its co-operation was needed for meeting the wider goals of the strategic plan. This was particularly so in relation to teaching qualifications, a position the government continued to uphold despite the private sector critique.

In January 2006 the ECC released a second 'independent' report from the NZ Institute of Economic Research: *Early Childhood Participation*.

Is 20 hours free the answer? The authors said 'No' and argued that the policy justification for free early childhood education was weak given the already high participation levels. The institute favoured the introduction of more generous targeted assistance for low- and middle-income families using the existing child care subsidy, combined with tax rebates for working parents. The former would be more like a voucher that 'allows parental choice' because it 'followed the child'. The latter would provide benefits to all parents paying childcare fees. 'Fee control', as the authors likened the free early childhood policy, would be ineffective because centres would then 'dress up fees as voluntary donations. This is already the practice amongst kindergartens.'[125] This did become an issue. It is now timely to consider the political backdrop of the '20 hours free' policy.

FREE EARLY CHILDHOOD EDUCATION

In 1987 a *Frontline* television documentary examined the situation of childcare in the midst of concerted advocacy to persuade the Labour government to make good its promises to redress the inequities for families whose children attended childcare centres (see Chapter Seven). David Lange had just led the Labour government into a second term of office and appointed himself as the Minister of Education. Lange could not be interviewed due to ill health but sent a statement concerning funding for childcare. *Frontline* reported that Lange 'could not see a time when childcare would be fully funded like the school system'. Moreover, he 'was not convinced that full funding is a responsible use of taxpayer money'.[126] Lange lived to see the 2004 Labour government's proposal for free early childhood education inclusive of education and care centres. He died in 2005, two years prior to the policy starting. It is not known whether Lange remembered his earlier prediction, but his statement is a reminder that early childhood policy had undergone some dramatic shifts since the 1980s. The Labour government established the necessary infrastructure for these shifts during 1984–90, in particular during Lange's term as Minister of Education from 1987–90.

In 1939, as previously stated, the Fraser–Beeby school-aged child 'whether they be rich or poor or live in town or country' had 'a right as a citizen, to a free education'.[127] By contrast, the political consideration of the preschool-aged child was subsumed within welfare state policies to provide safety nets for families, and the priorities of infant and maternal health. Sixty years later in 1999, when the Labour government assumed power, political interest in the preschool child had transformed towards a cautious consideration of the young child citizen whose wellbeing would be assured by 'closing the gaps' (or in later terminology by 'removing disparities') between rich and poor.[128]

The intention of the Strategic Plan Working Group was to move the political focus of early childhood education beyond the ongoing concerns of regulating quality, increasing participation and improving access, towards realising the possibilities of the rights of the preschool-aged child. Universal and free early childhood education was a fundamental aspect of this. The working group included members from both private and community groups and the report did not propose how 'free early childhood education' could be applied across the sectors. This was to be the task of a proposed funding task force. As noted earlier, the government release of *Pathways to the Future* did not include free early childhood education. Moreover, government officials embarked on a different model of funding than envisaged by the working group. It was only after the intervention of the Minister of Education, Trevor Mallard, and strategic work by Linda Mitchell, a member of the funding taskforce, that officials were sent back to the drawing board.

The progress of their work can be tracked in the relevant government papers released under the Official Information Act (except for the large sections marked 'information not relevant').[129] The first document, from the Ministry of Education to the Minister of Education on 2 May 2003, reports on a meeting the minister had with 'two representatives from the ECE sector'. The representatives, Linda Mitchell and Raewyn Ramage, both members of the Strategic Plan Working Group, were not named but recorded as '9(2)(6a) (i)'.[130] The officials were instructed to work closely with '9(2)(6a)(i)' to report on the 'cost of providing totally free ECE by the year 2012' and develop scenarios for the amount of free entitlement that could be provided. The document states that '9(2)(6a)(i)' were concerned to ensure that 'the calculations take account of the government funding all costs associated with ECE'. The Ministry of Education noted that 'free ECE' was likely to increase demand and that this could be mitigated by determining 'an entitlement to a certain number of free hours'.[131] In the event, 'an entitlement' did not eventuate, except as a later perception by parents.

On 31 July 2003 officials met with the minister and presented a range of funding scenarios.[132] In addition to one developed on the advice of Linda Mitchell that costed lower teacher–child ratios, the scenarios included the costs of implementing the strategic plan policy for qualified teachers and the flow-on effect of pay parity. During the meeting, the question was raised as to whether 'free entitlement' was a 'guarantee or a best endeavour promise?'[133] On 8 September 2003 two options were presented to the minister: one for '15 or 20 hour free entitlement for all children', the other for '20 or 30 hour free entitlement for 3 and 4 year olds'.[134] Again there was debate about the 'nature of free entitlement'. The officials recommended that the government promise 'near-free entitlements', otherwise 'it would be necessary to regulate for this entitlement'. One of the 'risks' identified was that 'some communities may value continued quality improvement above government in requirements'.[135] The latter 'risk' subsequently became an issue, as the 20 hours free policy was funded at a regulated standard which, for many professionals and parents, was a minimum rather than a quality standard, particularly in relation to staffing ratios. During the latter months of 2003, consultation was undertaken with the ministry of Social Development and Treasury. Neither was supportive of the minister's preferred option for a universal free entitlement of 20 hours. The minister's secondary position was to phase in the free hours for under-three-year-olds between 2007 and 2011.[136]

By January 2004 the policy was fixed at 20 hours free early childhood education for three- and four-year-olds, but only in teacher-led community-based centres, and any notions of 'entitlement' had slipped away. Firm proposals were developed for Cabinet consideration in the lead up to the budget release planned for May 2004.[137] It was argued that the proposal for '20 hours of free ECE' would 'send a strong signal of the importance of ECE and the public benefits that accrue from ECE participation'. It was also argued that 'private ECE services may find their enrolments decrease ... and some private services might exit ECE provision over time'.[138] Mallard held strongly to this view and, throughout this phase, he resisted warnings from a number of others, including the prime minister and Cabinet, that the demand for free early childhood would outstrip demand if limited only to community services.[139]

Outside these negotiations the sector had no inkling of the policy changes until the budget announcement on 27 May 2004. A proposed consultation document was never released. The caricature, printed on the front page of the *Dominion Post* the day after the budget was announced, of Minister of Finance Michael Cullen as the 'nanny state', was a symbolic indicator of the government's new interest in the young child – albeit a very young one, for whom the policy was not intended.[140]

In the *Listener* the following week, the comedian Jon Gadsby wrote new words to the song, 'On the first day of Christmas my true love gave to me … a partridge in a pear tree …' Gadsby's version had the resounding chorus: 'And a little bit of childcare for free':

> *On May the 27th, Dr Cullen gave to me*
> *Another budget surplus*
> *A crust to education*
> *A boost for health-care spending*
> *A nod towards the rental*
> *And a little bit of childcare for free*[141]

The budget announcement was welcomed with surprise by many of the sector, although it was a more targeted policy than earlier demands for a 'child's right to a free education'. The private sector saw this as another attack from the left on their business interests in childcare, but strategically argued against denying 25,000 children the possibility of receiving free placements. The ECC orchestrated the opposition to the policy. Its spokesperson, Ross Penman, was concerned that private centres would be forced to close, claiming that 'Trevor Mallard's socialist finger prints were all over the plan'.[142] Sandy Dodds, a private centre owner from Balclutha, asked:

> Does the Minister plan to buy us out and turn us into community-owned centres so that families can access his funding? Does he plan to provide daily buses to the city for all the families who would like to take advantage of his free funding offer? The plan as it stands discriminates against our parents by taking away their choice and telling them how and where they should educate their children.[143]

The minister acknowledged that the decision to exclude the private sector was 'philosophical', but admitted it was also about 'drawing the line somewhere to keep it affordable'.[144] He was also concerned about the level of concentration of unqualified staff in the private sector.[145]

Instead of the good news story expected, the media headlines were captured by the aggrieved. On 2 June 2004 the Ministry of Education released a memo that provided staff with 'some approaches to answering questions'. The explanation for the private sector was that the 'government wishes to encourage community-based provision because community-based services are governed and "owned" by the community'. A second possible answer was that the budget announcement was 'a first step on the way'. Playcentre parents were upset that the 20 hours free policy did not recognise voluntary work. While they were to be reassured with an offer to meet the minister, Ministry of Education staff were also instructed to emphasise to any aggrieved Playcentre parents that the 'Cabinet paper was explicit about the policy only being in teacher-led services'.[146] Sixteen months later there was a second 'step on the way' and the policy was extended to the private sector. In the heat of this announcement, Trevor Mallard offered Playcentre parents the carrot of a funding review.[147] This did not happen.

Kōhanga reo's initial reaction was described by Arapera Royal Tangaere as 'angry', because the policy 'cut deeply against the grain' by creating a hierarchy amongst those kōhanga reo that qualified and those that did not. The fact that funding policies were linked to qualifications was already an issue for kōhanga reo, which had a broader view of the factors determining quality, such as the inclusion of kaumātua, the participation of parents and the presence of whānau-based learning.[148]

Carmen Dalli subsequently commented that, 'Clearly, there are troubling equity issues involved in not extending the 20 hours free policy to non-teacher-led ECE services.'[149]

'TRAVELLING THE PATHWAYS'

In May 2007, a midway point in the implementation of the strategic plan, the Ministry of Education hosted an early childhood sector symposium, 'Travelling the Pathways to the Future: Ngā Huarahi Arataki'.[150] There was a 'celebration' of the positive effects the strategic plan had on the sector. However, delegates noted that there was still much to 'evaluate', particularly in relation to issues such as a widening divide between teacher-led and parent-led services, the difficulties some locations had in meeting the requirements for having qualified teachers in centres and the balance of the new partnership between government and the sector.[151]

Although the debate surrounding its implementation had become heated, the 20 hours free policy, soon to commence, was hailed by government as a further initiative to encourage access to early childhood education. Peter Moss, from the United Kingdom, told symposium delegates that New Zealand was 'leading the wave' of early childhood innovation. More particularly, New Zealand had 'confronted the wicked issues' with the development of an integrated and coherent national approach to funding, regulation, curriculum and qualifications.[152] Moss identified further challenges towards overcoming constraints to participation. He called for a 'universal entitlement to a free

ECE service from 12 months',[153] a re-echo of the original proposal from the Strategic Plan Working Group in 2001. The actual 20 hours free policy was about to start within two months.

After the policy was implemented on 1 July 2007, it had an immediate impact on the quarterly Consumer Price Index, which recorded a drop of 32.4% in the cost for parents of early childhood education, causing a 5.2% drop in the overall price of education in the country.[154] With the policy only in its first year of operation, it is too soon to fully evaluate its consequences. However, the government has been monitoring the take-up.[155] By February 2008, 76% of centres were participating, including home-based services, benefiting 85,000 children, comprising 83% of the three- and four-year-old children enrolled in early education.[156] Kidicorp joined, but only after the government conceded that, legally, there was nothing to stop centre owners, like schools, charging an 'optional fee'. Strict guidelines were issued to ensure there were no penalties for parents who did not pay a donation, and to stop costs being shifted to the fees of younger children or other hours used outside of the 20-hour scheme. By June 2008, the uptake of services offering free early childhood had risen to 80%.[157] While only half of the privately operated centres had joined, most of the centres owned by the executive members of the ECC were included in the scheme, and in July 2008 there was the announce-ment that all the ABC Learning centres would be joining.

The level of funding for the scheme was always contentious. The Barnardo's childcare organisation claimed that, for the time being, it would carry the costs of the shortfall.[158] The Auckland Kindergarten Association reluctantly joined the scheme, with the intention of charging an 'optional fee' of 50 cents per hour to meet the shortfall. This was considerably less than Kidicorp, who proposed an 'optional' fee of $3.75 per hour. ABC's late joining of the scheme came after the government's announcement of increased funding rates as a follow-on from the settlement of the kindergarten teacher's pay parity collective agreement.

During 2007, in the lead up to the launch, there was extensive and heated media debate. The first big issue was the expectation of entitlement. Parents soon realised that the 20 hours free policy was flawed if the centre their child(ren) attended had not opted into the scheme, or they lived in small towns, rural settings or certain city suburbs where parents had little choice in the kind of service available. The *New Zealand Herald* raised their fears with the headline, 'Thousands face missing out on free pre-school'.[159] Their concern was further fuelled by the ECC recommending to its members not to participate in the scheme. Parents of 50,000 children received a pamphlet entitled, 'Early Childhood Education. Why your child might miss out?'. The reason given was that the level of subsidy providers would receive from the government was too low. The sentiments of rights was to the fore:

> The government promised free ECE for your child. Please act now to make sure you get what you were promised. It is only fair – no ifs, no buts, no maybes.[160]

In Auckland a number of parents formed a lobby group named '20 hours free please', organised a petition to government and maintained a lively website campaign.[161] Like the ECC, these parents saw the problem as insufficient funding for centres to opt into the scheme. Conversely, the Minister of Education, Steve Maharey, saw the reluctance of some providers to join as the 'problem'. Although the policy did not guarantee 'entitlement', Maharey seemed to be supporting the notion when he told the reporter for the *Sunday Star Times* that free early childcare 'is about the principle of 20 hours free and the right of young New Zealanders to that education'.[162] The opposition National Party MP, Katherine Rich, claimed that the '20 hours-a-week-free policy' was a 'fraud'.[163] Although the policy would not have eventuated under a National government, the popularity of the policy amongst parents and the high and rising uptake eventually caused a National Party turnaround. In July 2008 the party announced that, if elected, they would 'maintain' the existing scheme because 'thousands of parents are using it and we do not want to cause uncertainty'; and the policy would be 'enhanced' by including all kōhanga reo and Playcentres. However, the word 'free' would be dropped, 'because we don't think it is', said Paula Bennett, the National Party spokesperson. Instead the policy would be known as '20 Hours ECE'.[164] If elected, the new government may find that parents do not drop the word 'free' even where, in some centres, there are 'optional charges'. Beyond its stormy implementation this is a popular scheme with the parents who can access it that has made a difference to family budgets. The possibly brief experience of free early childhood in name and reality will not be forgotten or undermined so easily.

Other issues to arise in relation to the scheme related to questions of quality and cost. The ECC described the free early childhood policy as 'dangerous' and 'the biggest threat to quality of early childhood in our generation'.[165] There was some justification to the complaint that the policy could undermine quality. A further concern related to the extent to which fees or donations from parents and subsidies from government should fund the actual costs of quality provision or be used in part to enhance profits. It is ironic that the ECC's statement was made on behalf of providers who had resisted any policy that could increase costs and reduce profits.[166] In the heat of the free early childhood debate, the New Zealand Council for Educational Research released data indicating private centres provided a lesser quality service. Linda Mitchell argued:

> If the government remains reliant on the commercial sector to ensure all children can get up to 20 hours free, then it becomes vulnerable to those services' demands for higher government funding, not to spend solely in their centre but also so they can offer private investors – who may not even be New Zealanders – a return on investment. [167]

The strategic plan policies have significantly increased the costs of early childhood education. On the other hand, new regulatory standards with the aim of keeping costs down by shifting the minimum staffing ratios, are to be implemented in 2008.[168] Staffing ratios are at the heart of the issue of cost, as government funding to implement the 20 hours free policy was based on a regulated standard. However, many centres have higher staffing ratios than those set out in the regulated standards. The private owners of the Treehouse centres, for instance, termed their 'optional fee' a 'quality education surcharge', as it was intended to cover the cost of 'good staff ratios, guest speakers, a beautiful and aesthetic learning environment and provision of nutritional and sumptuous morning tea'.[169] The September 2007 Consumer Price Index survey indicated that one in seven providers were charging an optional fee, affecting 34% of children attending participating centres and home-based services.[170] A Ministry of Education survey in February 2008 indicated that 504 services (out of 2300) were requesting optional charges.[171]

This early commentary can only identify the issues and illustrate the polemic of the rhetoric concerning the 20 hours free policy. The divisions within this debate have made apparent the structural tensions underpinning early childhood policy. Balancing the multiple interests in the sector is a difficult task. These interests can be summarised as follows:

- Interests of centre providers in balancing the business of free early childhood education with the costs of quality
- Interests of private business in protecting its profit levels
- Interests of community services being the preferred provider
- Interests of early childhood teachers in achieving full professional status and pay parity
- Interests of parents in gaining access to free early childhood education

- Interests of government in increasing participation in cost-effective quality early childhood education.

The central issue regarding the interests of children, except in the sense of 'your child might be missing out', was almost absent from the media debate. The policy is a result of political, professional and scholarly consensus that participation in quality early childhood education is a significant benefit for children and their families both 'here and now' in their daily life and also in the future at school and beyond. While there is still no right or entitlement for access to free early childhood education, New Zealand is inching towards this in terms of both policy and rhetoric.

It is timely that in this 2008 election year the significance of the Labour government's early childhood policy was noted across the wider spectrum of New Zealand politics. In the view of Colin James, an esteemed political commentator, Labour would lose the election. However, in a headlined obituary on 'Labour's Legacy', written 10 months prior to the election, he stated:

> When it comes time to memorialise Labour's fifth spell in office, it may be remembered most lastingly for early childhood education ... Making early childhood systematic ... takes us deep into a zone of policy debate: on citizens' access to participation in our economy and society. This debate is no longer just about the absence of legal or administrative impediments. It is about what constitutes genuine capacity to participate ... So early childhood education is investing in infrastructure, just like building roads. It is arguably Labour's most important initiative, its biggest idea.[172]

That James understood exactly the breadth of Labour's vision is reassuring even if, in his commentary, he concludes:

> Who thought it up and drove it? Trevor Mallard, back in the 1990s and then as minister. It will be his memorial too.

Certainly the documents detailed in the previous section show that the policy needed New Zealand's 'hard' politician in Cabinet and probably a woman prime minister, Helen Clark, in power. Nonetheless, James overlooked the concerted and cohesive advocacy across the sector that was required to shift the government's interest in early childhood education beyond its selective and cautious gaze of earlier years. Jocelyn Harris reminded James of one campaigner whose 40-year academic career was instrumental in achieving this:

> All praise to Trevor Mallard ... but let us not forget the bold and pioneering contribution of policymakers such as Prof Anne Smith ... who did the research,

presented the data and carried out the lobbying and advising so that this fundamental change in thinking about child care and education in early childhood became a reality.[173]

One must also record the contribution of Linda Mitchell, the insider watchdog '9(2)(6a)(i)', whose presence and pen played an important part in keeping the free early childhood policy on the agenda.

THE PLAYS OF CHILDHOOD

In the 2000s the daytime plays of early childhood are now significantly contained within a range of educational institutions that are supported, organised, regulated, researched and theorised by an army of professionals on behalf of the state that significantly funds the industry. *Politics in the Playground* has told of the quest, over 60 years, to have the state broaden its interest beyond a few preschool children attending kindergarten and Playcentre as a social and playful preparation for school. The policy is now inching towards universal participation, at least for four-year-olds, with high levels of participation for children under four years of age. The gaze of the state now includes diverse institutions providing a range of services, care, education and support, with different cultural and philosophical traditions, for children and their families.

While there is broad approval for the policy directions of the 2000s, there is also some disquiet. Some of the voices engaged in the debates surrounding the government's key policy initiatives have been heard in this chapter. In this final section, some deeper concerns and cautions surrounding the extent, the balance and focus of government interest are identified. The journey has again reached some crossroads and it is timely to consider the possible pathways to take.

In early 2008 Sarah Farquhar hosted a personal forum in a Wellington venue where policy makers, politicians and national organisations could step across the road to participate.[174] Farquhar had her own concerns with the 20 hours free policy:

> The early childhood sector is set to become more like the school sector. Parents are being told that to start their child's learning they must enrol in an early childhood service, for 20 hours and with registered teachers … the policy and associated advertising is sending a strong message to parents that they are not teachers and that their children's education from the age of 3 is now the responsibility of the State.[175]

The forum was intended to demonstrate that a broad constituency of parents were concerned that the government's policy directions appeared to be privileging parents whose children participated in teacher-led services.

> The provision of non-parental childcare/early childhood education is closely linked to economic development and is a big issue in times of a labour shortage. The focus of current early childhood policy is on increasing the supply of childcare services and hours to raise levels of women's labour force participation.[176]

Considering the extent that the care and education of young children should be the responsibility of institutions, Farquhar asked, 'what are the consequences for children?'

> … with changes happening quickly and with early childhood public policy likely to have a significant impact on the kind of people children will become and on the generations to follow.[177]

According to Farquhar's 'rose tinted' view of the past, traditional early childhood services, such as kindergarten and Playcentre, had operated 'in partnership with families' and been 'developed in response to parent and child need'. That partnership, claimed Farquhar, had been replaced by 'government control of the early childhood sector'.[178] This view, however, overlooks the long years of campaigning by parents for quality and affordable childcare provision, and forgets that a key principle of Te Whāriki concerns partnerships with family and whanau. There was lively debate about the directions of the strategic plan policies, with not everyone sharing Farquhar's negative view. Nevertheless, Farquhar's concern with an increasingly institutionalised and regulated childhood industry touched a deeper chord for some. Maureen Woodham's analysis of the free early childhood policy was similarly cautious about its long-term benefits. She suggested that while the policy was intended to remove cost as a barrier for participation in early 'education' in 'approved services', it was also about 'conditioning parents to place their young children in out-of-home care so that they themselves can participate in the workforce'.[179] Woodham, like Farquhar, was concerned that the presumed benefits for the child were at the expense of 'active parenting'.

For others broadly in support of the government's policies, the deeper issue was the nature of participation in early childhood education and what this might mean for the rights of young children. In the foreword to *Pathways to the Future*, Trevor Mallard wrote that, 'The Government's vision is for all New

Zealand children to have the opportunity to participate in quality education, *no matter their circumstances* [my emphasis].'[180] The latter emphasis is reminiscent of Fraser–Beeby's 1939 statement that the school-aged child had a 'right as a citizen' to education. Policy for the preschool child of the 2000s was still framed around 'the opportunity to participate'. Around the time of the release of *Pathways to the Future*, I crafted two reconceptualised versions of the Fraser–Beeby statement. Using a mix of original and recent rhetoric, the first statement is penned in the spirit of current government policy objectives, as was the original statement:

> The government's objective, broadly speaking, is that every child, whatever their family circumstances, whether their parents are solo, separated or married, at work or at home, whether they be rich or poor, whether they live in town or country, are Maori or Pakeha, should have the opportunity to participate in quality early childhood education that meets their family needs, recognises their cultural heritage, and provides a rich learning environment so that each preschool child is empowered to learn and grow to their fullest potential prior to arrival at school.

The second statement is inclusive of advocacy and 'blue skies' aspirations concerning the role of early childhood institutions for young children:

> The government's objective should, broadly speaking, be that every child, whatever their family circumstances, whether their parents are solo, separated or married, at work or at home, whether they be rich or poor, whether they live in town or country, are Maori or Pakeha, should have a right as a citizen to a free early childhood education that meets their family needs, recognises their cultural heritage and provides a rich learning environment in a community of learning that empowers both adults and children to learn and grow as equal participants in a democratic society.[181]

While 'travelling the pathways to the future' it will be necessary to further interrogate the possibilities of what participation as a citizen child might mean in terms of participation, pedagogy and policy. United Kingdom sociologist Alan Prout has argued that:

> Childhood has been turned into a project. In a large part this project has been concerned with children's protection and provision rather than their social participation … that is the tendency to see them as a group to be socially shaped rather than socially included … This was a twentieth century failure that could, given the will and the resources, be remedied in this century.[182]

In an analysis of new discourses shaping the young Australian citizen child, Frances Press acknowledges that 'citizenship for children is highly contested' and its 'expression is often limited', 'silenced' and 'invisible' in an early childhood context where provision is at the behest of corporate interest. Press is seeking to 're-imagine' the space of childhood in which the centre is a site for the practice of democracy for children, parents and teachers.[183]

Commenting on the New Zealand context, Sarah Te One writes that the 'position of children as citizens entitled to an education' must move beyond the issues of 'access (in terms of attendance) and quality (in terms of standard measures)' to also include 'appropriateness'.[184] In addition to being inclusive of Māori as tangata whenua, and Pasifika people, this broader focus must also be cognisant of the rights of the child as a citizen to participate in decisions that affect them, as enshrined in Article 12 of the United Nations Convention on the Rights of the Child.[185]

The aspirational principles of both Te Whāriki and *Pathways to the Future* perceive New Zealand children within early childhood education as both powerful and participating. Realising this in policy and practice has been more challenging. For example, the 20 hours free policy highlighted the complexity of translating visionary ideals into workable policy and allowing multiple pathways and perspectives for the journey. Although it is assumed in principle, the notion of citizenship has not been strongly articulated in curriculum policy documents.

The most tangible pedagogical evidence of children participating in Te Whāriki has been Margaret Carr's development of the Ministry of Education's *Kei Tua o te Pae – Assessment for learning: Early childhood exemplars* (2004). Sandy Farquhar has written that:

> At the heart of curriculum texts such as Te Whāriki and Kei Tua o te Pae are implicit statements of participatory democracy founded on notions of reciprocity, sharing and negotiation between child and adult; mutual reconstruction through community, intergenerational dialogue, project and enquiry.[186]

Carr's learning story framework of children's interests, strengths and dispositions to learn, is a shift from internationally dominant paradigms of assessment for your children based upon checklists and developmental measures of competency, skills and content.[187] Both Te Whāriki and *Kei Tua o te Pae* are premised on principles of reciprocal relationships and power sharing that include children, family and teachers as joint participants in both 'weaving' and documenting the distinctive pattern of each child's education through narratives of learning. Although fully realising these aspirations in practice for all children may be 'blue skies', the political intent to realise the aspirations of Te Whāriki justified the teacher-led qualification policy. As statements, both Te Whāriki and *Kei Tua o te Pae* are aspirational, participatory and non-prescriptive, but as official government tools they are also intended to regulate and audit the learning environment. This has created a tension between education and regulation.

This tension is likely to be apparent in the soon-to-be-released Kaupapa Maori Learning and Assessment Exemplar resource *Te Whatu Pōkeka*, which translates as 'weaving the baby carrier'. Since 2003, Rita Walker and Lesley Rameka have, against the tide of international assessment measures and understandings in relation to indigenous peoples, developed a framework of assessment that 'privileges and empowers Maori children and insists that the concept of a powerful, rich Maori child be at the heart of understandings about learning and assessment'.[188] Beginning from Te Whāriki's principle of empowerment, Walker and Rameka use the transformative power of the ancient Māori knowledge of creation as a foundation for theorising about learning and development for the modern Māori child. The pōkeka provides a 'strong, secure, nurturing and flexible' environment for the child. Like *Kei Tua o te Pae*, *Te Whatu Pōkeka* is an official government resource intended to meet the requirements for assessment in Māori early childhood settings, as well as for Māori children in mainstream settings. The premise of the powerful Māori child is a challenge to dominant discourses within government itself, whose gaze is towards the problematic, 'at risk and unprivileged', Māori child.

In international forums, Te Whāriki is a showcase of a socio-cultural and liberatory curriculum and its language and structure have been adopted and adapted by other countries.[189] During the 1990s, however, most scholars and early childhood professionals refrained from criticising Te Whāriki in an attempt to ensure its political survival. Similarly, the unexpected international acclaim it received proved to be deceptively dangerous. Today, a more critical analysis is emerging from early childhood practitioner doctoral scholars in New Zealand, some of whose work I have either supervised or examined. This analysis gained momentum with the publication of a collection of papers edited by Joce Nuttall, entitled *Weaving Te Whāriki* (2003), which is the first collection of debate and analysis by both New Zealand and international scholars on the Te Whāriki phenomenon.[190] Nuttall was herself a scholar of Te Whāriki. Her doctoral research indicated the gap between rhetoric and reality in how teachers, and children and teachers together, negotiated the curriculum in the everyday world of the childcare centre she observed.[191] Nuttall's research is one of several ethnographic doctoral studies, from Victoria University's Institute for Early Childhood Studies, that drill deep into the minutiae of the everyday practice of Te Whāriki and which constitute what Alison Stephenson calls a 'collective conversation'.[192] These studies include Margaret Brennan's study of the enculturation of children in centre life, Sarah Te One's investigations into children's rights in action (or not) in several early childhood settings, and Alison Stephenson's study of the boundaries of acceptable (or not) curriculum in an early childhood centre.[193] The authors of these studies, like Nuttall, question the possibilities for teachers to fully translate the aspirational principles of Te Whāriki into practice. They have seen much evidence of the surface expression of Te Whāriki. On the other hand, its deeper possibilities of power sharing have seemed too dangerous and difficult for teachers to consider. Deeply held beliefs by teachers, structural inadequacies within early childhood centres in relation to staff/child ratios, group size, management interests, and government requirements, can create a mismatch between the rhetoric of Te Whāriki and the possibilities for its pedagogical practice.

A different academic critique has emerged from the University of Auckland. In three doctoral studies I was privileged to examine, Andrew Gibbons, Iris Duhn and Sandy Farquhar consider the global contexts creating and shaping the New Zealand child of Te Whāriki and the preferred plays of early childhood through the traditional disciplines of education philosophy and sociology. They emphasise the necessity of space and time for the democratic debate that was once at the heart of Te Whāriki.

Gibbons draws upon Heidegger, Foucault and Derrida to problematise the universal theories of play that are being increasingly enshrined in the power and surveillance of government machinery through national curricula. 'The play expert's toys have marginalised what parents, teachers, communities, and children themselves can say and think about play.'[194] Duhn uses the literature of the sociology of childhood to reveal the underside of Te Whāriki's ideal child – the 'child at risk'. In mapping the landscape of the modern global child, Duhn claims that Te Whāriki's child, who is 'empower[ed] to learn and grow', is also a child constrained in global and universal discourses who might easily become endangered.[195] Through the lens of the philosopher Paul Ricoeur, Farquhar re-reads the curriculum texts that premise the competent and capable Te Whāriki child. Like Sarah Farquhar, Sandy Farquhar questions the assumptions of 'de-familiarisation' that use the rhetoric of quality to 'promote the idea that children will thrive outside the home'.[196] Like Gibbons and Duhn, Farquhar acknowledges the potential of Te Whāriki to create the conversations for interrogating the institutions of childhood and negotiating what 'are "good" spaces for children'. She suggests, however, that 'its influence is being ring-fenced by the prevailing policy regime' which is still shaped by a mainly economic narrative.[197] Te Whāriki itself is at risk of 'prescription, closure and finality'.[198]

The various critiques of Gibbons, Duhn and Farquhar surely serve to keep open the debate so vital for the aspirations of Te Whāriki to be realised. The academia of early childhood teacher education in New Zealand has lively scholars, such as those named above, who have opportunities for engaging the hearts and minds of the next generation of teachers. But academia must also continue to engage in policy development despite the seeming distaste towards the intentions of policy makers. Te Whāriki, *Kei Tua o te Pae* and *Te Whatu Pōteka* have their roots in academia and surfaced as pedagogical tools as a consequence of government demands for a defined curriculum and assessment measures. These have not always been easy collaborations and have only been possible due to the strong support they have received from the profession and a certain tolerance by policy makers who believe that early childhood education in New Zealand should have its own specialist pathways.

This may be overly optimistic and an attempt to avoid a troubling end to a book that traverses many of the years and endeavours of my own writing, advocacy and engagement in early childhood matters. I am not sufficiently distant to analyse what this contribution has been. I have found that penning the story is in itself powerful. In the concluding weeks of writing this book, another 'blue skies' venture is being floated.

In April 2008 NZEI–TRR called a meeting of representatives of community organisations representing or providing early childhood education. I was asked to be the chair. Linda Mitchell was also there and chaired the second meeting in June. The intent is to build broader support for the NZEI–TRR fledgling project 'Quality public ECE: A vision for 2020'.[199] The NZEI–TRR is seeking consensus for a partnership across the community providers of early childhood education. The NZEI–TRR argues that publicly funded early childhood education is central to realising the rights of children and their families to participate in early childhood education, and that the commercial interests of wealth accumulation conflict with the education and community values of *Pathways to the Future*.

Commercial operators are able to set up and access public money wherever they see a business opportunity. There is no mechanism to ensure that responsive, community-oriented services are universally available. Low income communities, migrant communities, Maori and Pacific families and rural communities are those most likely to miss out. [200]

Winning this debate will be difficult because neither of the major political parties is inclined towards full public provision of early childhood services. The community sector itself would be wary of ending their current independence by a state takeover and the discourses of sociology and philosophy warn of the motives underlying state interest in the institutions of childhood. Such a campaign may divide a sector that has been successful in forwarding policy by working cohesively when necessary. The task of the community groups will be, in the first instance, to explore the possibilities for shifting the balance of provision back towards government support for community ownership. Convincing successive governments that public ownership of early childhood services is the essential stepping-stone towards realising the full rights of preschool children to a free early childhood education will be a long-term campaign. The New Zealand success story has been about 'travelling the pathways to the future' with a cohesive vision and policy. The risk right now is that divergent 'pathways' might emerge. Engaging in this new 'blue skies' endeavour might enhance the possibilities for democratic and social participation of the preschool citizen child of this country. Linda Mitchell has long been hopeful that:

A new debate could enable different voices to be heard and new possibilities constructed for early childhood services as sites for building a democratic society.[201]

The landscape for this debate, though, is changing. Not only has there been a government change from Labour to National, there has also been a world-wide economic downturn. Prior to the November 2008 election the newspaper headline read, 'Treasury's books sea of red ink – Treasury's news worse than expected'.[202] One of the causes listed for this less-than-favourable situation was the cost to government of the 20 hours free early childhood policy. The new political and economic times are undoubtedly going to need new strategies for politics in the playground.

CHAPTER ELEVEN

Agendas for Young Children

In the aftermath of the 2008 election that ousted the three-term Labour government, its early childhood initiatives languished. Writing Chapter Ten a decade ago I concluded there was a risk that 'divergent pathways' might emerge. They did, and those divergent pathways are the subject of this new final chapter.

The incoming National government was determined to curb Labour's 'blue skies' policies – such as '20 hours free ECE' and '100% qualified teachers'. Early childhood education became consigned to a social investment policy agenda targeted toward 'vulnerable' communities and families 'at risk'.[1] Selected ministers, including Minister of Education Hekia Parata, signed up to deliver 10 targets over a five-year period across areas of economic and social concern. Her target for 98% participation in early childhood education prior to school came close to meeting its goal.

The two chapters in 'Part Four – Strategic Directions 2000s–2010s' of this book present contrasting policy agendas.[2] I first explored the shifting policy emphasis in *The Changing Fortunes of Childcare 2003–2013*, reviewing five years under Labour and five years under National. Chapter headings adopted exemplar quotations from interviewees: '2003-2008 – "sense of excitement"' and '2008–2013 – "loss of momentum"'.[3] These metaphors are aptly extended to this broader analysis. Linda Mitchell summed up the 'divergent pathways' as shifting from 'a child rights to an interventionist approach':

> New Zealand's policy regimes … have highlighted different policy agendas reflective of differing views of the role of the state: a supportive state (Labour-led government) which works in collaboration with early childhood communities and a minimal state (National-led government) where onus is placed on early childhood communities to 'step up' to their responsibilities …

Children are treated as dependants within their families and the government intervenes when it regards families as unable to provide. By contrast, under the supportive state approach, children, family and teacher participants in ECEC are empowered and supported to participate and contribute to the ECEC service.[4]

The narrative shift, however, was never completed because the policy infrastructure and funding mechanisms remained unchanged. Rather, Labour's policies were undermined and market forces left to shape provision.

National's agenda was to increase child participation in high-need areas. Treasury summarised its social investment approach as 'investing up-front to support people most at risk of poor outcomes later on in life … This reduces the number of New Zealanders relying on social services and the overall costs for taxpayers.'[5] Early childhood participation projects had some success but were resourced from cuts elsewhere in the sector. Soon after forming the Labour-led coalition government in 2017, Prime Minister Jacinda Ardern announced that a less targeted approach to welfare would guide social policy that did not conflict with the value of 'universalism'.[6] Minister of Education Chris Hipkins subsequently announced a bold agenda for 'strengthening the [early childhood] sector', 'turning the tide' from profit-focused provision, 'returning to the principle of free public education', and 'limiting the detrimental effects of competition' between services.[7]

This chapter concludes with the release of the new government's *Strategic Plan for Early Learning 2019–29*[8] as a draft for consultation.

Two data sets summarise the changing landscape of early childhood. First, the ECE annual census reports summarise the trends shaping early childhood services over the past 15 or so years. In 2018:[9]

- There were 200,793 children in licensed early childhood services. Attendance had hovered around the 200,000 from 2013 after a growth in enrolments between 2005 and 2012. Of these children, 48% identified as Pākehā-European, 24% identified as Māori, 16% identified as Asian and 8% identified as Pasifika.
- The enrolment rate in relation to the population of under-five-year-olds was 64.4%, an increase from 58% in 2005.[10]
- The proportion of enrolments across services showed 67% of enrolments in education and care services, an increase from 55% in 2008. In decline were the proportion of enrolments in kindergarten (from 23% to 15%), Playcentre (8% to 5%) and kōhanga reo (5% to 4%).

- The percentage of four-year-olds attending an early childhood service six months prior to school reached 96.7% in 2016 – 98.1% for Pākehā-European children, 95% for Māori children and 92.9% for Pasifika children. This was an increase of 5.2% for Māori and 6.2% for Pasifika since 2010.
- The most significant change was the proportion of qualified teachers. Overall, 97% of teacher-led centres had achieved the 80% qualified funding band. Across these centres 68.6% of staff held a teaching qualification, an increase from 54% in 2006. However, the sector faced a teacher shortage and any impetus to increase the proportion of qualified teachers had stagnated due to the lack of financial incentive.
- Mirroring increases in government subsidies, the proportion of private ownership of services continued to grow from 41% in 1992 to 57% in 2007 to 64% in 2016. Neither party in government stifled the growth, although the Labour government 1999–2008 did attempt some measures, and the current government again promises to 'turn the tide'.[11]

Secondly, the 'Growing Up in New Zealand' longitudinal study has a cohort of 7000 children representing the ethnic diversity of New Zealand. The study began in 2009, prior to the birth of the children, and continues in 2019 with the children at school.[12] The findings are rich but lightly mined here to note matters pertinent to early childhood education:

- *Before we are born* (2010) surveys indicated that the children recruited would be born into diverse family structures. One in three children would have at least one parent not born in New Zealand. Issues around child poverty were evident in that the parents of four out of every 10 expected children were living in the most deprived areas of the country and half of the families were living in rental accommodation.
- *Now we are two* (2014) findings showed a high level of mobility, with a third of families moving house since their child was nine months old. Half of the two-year-olds were participating in early childhood education for an average 24 hours a week, primarily due to the work commitments of their parents, but also because parents viewed the experience as being positive for their child's development.
- Two reports on child vulnerability were compiled using 12 risk factors for young children.[13] At two years, 13.3% of the children had a high level of vulnerability with four or more cumulative risk factors. By contrast, 41.2% of the cohort had no risk factors. However, the broader statistic of 58.8% of children falling into a category of medium to high-risk vulnerability was salutary as a snapshot of the well-being of young children and their families.

- *Now we are four* (2017) showed that one in seven children were living in the most deprived decile of the NZDep scale. High mobility was still prevalent, with half of the children experiencing a shift between the age of two and four years. One in five families relied on benefits and were experiencing hardship. Two-thirds of mothers were now in paid employment, and by the age of four 87% of the children were attending an early childhood service with a mainly positive view from parents about their child's forthcoming transition to school.[14]

The study presents a snapshot of the well-being of preschool children and their family circumstances. Early childhood education sits at the nexus of family life both as a support to parents and an educational benefit to children. The findings revealed issues around poverty, housing and vulnerability outside the realms of the early childhood sector to fix but having an impact on families within their services.

In the following pages selected issues and happenings cumulatively illustrate the wider policy framework shaping and shifting the politics of the early childhood over the past decade. In the early childhood 'playground' itself and its supporting institutions these were at times turbulent years, in which older voices and pens remained active, but as well a younger generation of teachers and teacher educators, many of whom had been nurtured on earlier editions of this book, were variously active in protest, petitions and penning the stories.

CUTTING THE COST

The election of a National government in 2008 caused a shift in early childhood policy guided by a determination to curtail the building of 'big picture' infrastructure cited by Colin James earlier in the year (Chapter Ten). It is useful to consider what had been achieved in ECE by 2008. Peter Moss, a British policy commentator, described New Zealand as 'leading the wave', having 'confronted the wicked issues'.[15] His outsider view was that:

> New Zealand has developed a national framework, which brings some coherence to the system around issues of equity and access … Underpinning these structures, and perhaps the most radical change of all, New Zealand has an integrative concept that encompasses all services – 'early childhood education', a broad and holistic concept that covers children, families and communities, a concept of 'education-in-its-broadest-sense' … New Zealand has, in short, understood the need to rethink as well as restructure early childhood education and care.[16]

Under the incoming National government the Ministry of Education immediately removed the strategic plan from its website and, as promised, the word 'free' was dropped from the '20 hours [free] ECE' policy. This allowed 'optional charges' for so-called extras to be actual fees. Notwithstanding, the perception by parents of 'free ECE' remained, and many centres did not drop the description. Early in 2009 Minister of Education Anne Tolley addressed the conference of New Zealand Kindergartens Te Pūtahi Kura Pūhou o Aotearoa (NZK), and gave assurances there would be no major unravelling of the strategic plan policies. Instead, the government wanted to 'increase participation', 'support parent choice', 'reduce unnecessary compliance burdens' and 'find the right balance between regulation and choice'.[17]

Funding retrenchment in the aftermath of a global fiscal crisis justified the immediate culling of the Centres of Innovation programmes, tertiary training grants and professional development. The 2010 budget signalled more changes and removed the 100% qualified teacher subsidy, with 80% being the maximum. Those centres with over 80% qualified staff had their funding cut. New initiatives were announced, firstly to extend '20 hours ECE' funding to parent-led kōhanga reo and Playcentre programmes, and secondly to improve participation in 'high needs' locations. The government justified its moratorium on funding by claiming that Labour's policies had failed to redress low early childhood participation for these children.[18] This judgement turned out to be premature. The government's own evaluation in 2011 showed increased participation in early childhood, including by low-income parents, because of the '20 hours free ECE' policy.[19]

News headlines characterised the budget cuts as a 'Brutal blow to children and families' and a 'Black budget for ECE'.[20] A *New Zealand Herald* editorial (24 May 2010) summed up conservative opinion:

> Plainly National does not regard specialist teaching of pre-school children to be quite as important as Labour did. It is probably right … Did childcare centres ever need to be fully staffed by trained teachers? Or is this a classic case of 'qualification inflation'? … It is easy to insist little children deserve nothing but the best … but 'the best' at that level might not require professional training. The Government is right to direct more of its early education support to areas where children are missing out … Contentious the decision may be but it seems educationally harmless, socially equitable and financially necessary.

Early childhood organisations organised protests, which in Dunedin brought a thousand teachers and parents onto the streets. Kindergartens determined to keep their flagship position of 100% qualified teachers and free ECE. NZK embarked on a round of lobbying, armed with its paper *Quality ECE: Worth the investment* (2010), outlining the benefits for children, their families and society of investment in quality ECE. The budget cuts removed 13% of kindergarten funding. Neither lobbying nor protest was to any avail and the cuts took effect in 2011.[21]

The issue remained contentious, reflecting political divides over universal versus targeting funding. Minister Tolley justified the government's position:

> Taxpayer investment in early childhood services has trebled over the last five years ... Despite this growth in funding, too many children that the evidence tells us would benefit most from ECE are still missing out. They are at a disadvantage before they even start school. The economic reality is that money will be tight for the foreseeable future, so more than ever we must invest in the areas that will make the biggest difference to children and their families.[22]

Of concern to the profession was the trade-off between quality, affordability and participation. In justifying another 'zero budget', Minister Parata stated:

> Budget 2012 continues to target areas of high need ... This will support vulnerable children who are not receiving sufficient support to succeed in education. By targeting resources to these learners we will raise participation to given them a strong platform for their compulsory school years.[23]

To offset this shift the minister announced that the subsidy for 20 hours ECE funding would not be inflation adjusted. Te Tari Puna Ora o Aotearoa New Zealand Childcare Association (NZCA) estimated that two-thirds of centres would experience a reduction in funding:

> Services have already had to reduce the number of qualified teachers, freeze salaries and increase fees to parents. This is likely to be an ongoing scenario ... We understand that there is no new money to spend at this time, but reducing investment to early childhood education is short-sighted. The slow erosion of funding to the early childhood sector is likely to have unintended long-term consequences.[24]

A more sympathetic *New Zealand Herald* (25 May 2012) headlined the 'freeze' as 'Cuts by stealth to strained centres': 'Thousands of families could pay more for their early childhood education after the budget put a funding freeze on subsidies in favour of targeted spending.'

Heated debate around the cost of qualified teachers had escalated to the prime minister, John Key, who declared: 'It is a matter of personal belief as to whether a high proportion of all centre staff should be qualified (*NZ Herald*, 3 May 2010). In response, Linda Mitchell and Margaret Carr argued:

> It is a matter of an informed and evidence-based educational decision. These questions would never be raised about adults who teach 5-6- (or older) year-olds in school … We had hoped that 100% qualified teachers for *all* children in ECE [would] contribute to the government's aim of equitable and quality outcomes for all children.[25]

Minister Tolley had claimed there was no evidence to show 100% qualified teachers were better than 80% qualified teachers. Investigating this premise became the focus of the research project spearheaded by NZCA. Quality indicators in centres with 100% qualified teachers were compared with those from centres with 50–79% qualified teachers. Researchers led by Anne Meade identified the effects of having 100% qualified teachers in a centre:

> Children in these centres benefit from more teachers asking more open-ended questions and posing challenges that lead children to more complex thinking than in centres with 50–79% qualified. Children in these centres with the most qualified teachers have more interactions with qualified teachers, more conversations with these teachers and more episodes of sustained shared thinking and teacher mediation that assist their concept development. The children in these centres have higher scores on indicators to do with independence and concentration …[26]

In launching the research findings, CEO Nancy Bell concluded on behalf of NZCA: 'We'll never give up on our commitment to 100% qualified because we believe that teachers make the difference and that every child deserves a qualified teacher.'[27] The government was not persuaded.

ECE TASKFORCE AND *AN AGENDA FOR AMAZING CHILDREN*

In 2010 National established an ECE Taskforce. The terms of reference emphasised the 'effectiveness and efficiency of the Government's expenditure' and 'cost effective ways to support children's learning in early childhood'.[28] The taskforce with asked to develop a new funding model 'without increasing current government expenditure'.[29] There was concern at the 'lack of consultation' around the taskforce's establishment.[30] NZCA noted the shift in language from 'ECE as an investment' to 'ECE as a cost', urging that the benefits of spending on ECE also be quantified.[31] Unlike previous policy think-tanks that included wide sector representation, the taskforce was small, light on early childhood expertise and tightly controlled by government officials. Chair

Michael Mintrom, a former Treasury official and public policy academic, was an advocate for the government's policy directions. He later wrote:

> Through its social investment approach to working with vulnerable individuals and families the National-led government drove changes that could well signal a paradigm shift in notions of the social functions of public policy. If sustained, the approach promises to deliver higher levels of public value, from which all New Zealanders will benefit.[32]

The ECE sector took heart from the appointment to the taskforce of Anne Smith, who had widely researched children's rights, early childhood quality and qualifications. As the only taskforce member with longevity in the sector, however, Smith found the task challenging and eventually submitted two minority reports – on qualifications and funding.[33] Her dissenting views drew personal attacks. The ECE Taskforce report, *An Agenda for Amazing Children* (2011), proposed targeting funds to 'priority children' and cutting the level of universal funding; and urged a 'stepping up' by the sector, including parents, to take responsibility with less reliance on the state.[34] This was at odds with Labour's strategic plan, in which the government had proposed 'stepping up' to become a more 'supportive state'.[35] Smith countered in her minority report: 'Qualified teachers provide more sensitive and responsive learning opportunities for children … Logically the more qualified teachers … the better outcomes there will be for children's well-being and learning.'[36]

The funding recommendations were equally controversial, resulting in Smith's second minority report:

> I am concerned that the proposed new funding model may have a negative influence on participation rates in ECE for some groups, most particularly middle-income earners … Making these hours free allows families to use these services in a more sustained and regular way, which is a very favourable outcome for children and families. The argument is that the new funding system will be better for low SES [socioeconomic status] and Māori and Pasifika, but there is little information about how the new scheme will be able to accurately seek out and identify targeted groups.[37]

Treasury advice to the taskforce was that middle-income parents would be prepared to pay more.

The dissension that bubbled up in the taskforce was evident in terse email exchanges. In a response to an email from the taskforce chair, objecting strongly to Smith's dissenting views, Smith's reply reveals the tensions in the task:

I am surprised at your reaction to my disagreement with one section of the Taskforce report! You said it would be possible for the report to have minority and majority-supported recommendations, which is apparently not unusual ... I have never in my long career and participation in numerous committees and working groups been labelled as 'self indulgent', 'quarrelsome' or 'uncollegial'. I am known for my rationality and for fighting for what I believe in. I would be very surprised if my concerns about funding aren't shared by a great majority of ECE teachers and parents with children in ECS. It has been a great deal of work and a stressful experience participating in the taskforce. I do not take the action of expressing my disagreement lightly. It would be easier for me to 'let it go'. I cannot agree that my disagreement will undermine the whole document ...[38]

Anne Smith independently asked Gordon Cleveland to model the data. Cleveland, a renowned Canadian economist, had undertaken extensive analysis of the consequences of early childhood funding models.[39] An excerpt from Smith's communication to Cleveland after the publication of ECE Taskforce report is again revealing of the differences:

Your input had a big effect. If it hadn't been for you looking into those figures, it would have been an apple pie report! Colleagues of mine in academia and in the unions and NZCA all came out against the new funding system in the media. I got interviewed on [Radio NZ's] *Nine to Noon* and *Morning Report* – so at least on the radio my concerns got good coverage ...[40]

Smith was concerned too by the difficulty accessing documents held by the ministry that would yield evidence on key policy areas. On one occasion she wrote to the chair:

I have asked [to see] Linda Mitchell's report on the impact of the strategic plan several times at meetings and by emails with secretariat members, but have received no response. Have you seen it, and if not why not? I am sending this email message to you but it is an issue I will be raising at tomorrow's meeting.[41]

Smith later outlined her broader concern to teachers, being the taskforce's focus on economic development as opposed to child well-being or the rights of children, on getting parents into the paid workforce without acknowledgement of the value of unpaid parenting work, and the support for the unfettered childcare market.[42]

Representing kindergartens, NZK commissioned economic strategist Suzanne Snively to develop a case around a report entitled 'The Economics of Early Childhood' (2011), which documented the costs and benefits to government of funding ECE and the costs and returns to the taxpayer. NZK also mounted a forum at their conference to debate the issues, including Minister Tolley, Snively, Mintrom and MPs.[43] But the political mindset was not going to change, and NZK's post-conference paper signalled strategic directions for 'future-proofing' kindergarten in the less favourable policy environment.[44] Meeting with Minister Tolley after the release of the taskforce report, NZK CEO Clare Wells addressed the issue of increasing participation for 'priority children'. She argued that kindergartens were often the only service in a community with high numbers of families in the 'target groups', including Māori and Pasifika children.[45]

The taskforce restated evidence that there was a strong case for investment in high-quality early childhood, especially for the children of low-income families. It also cited evidence of allegedly poorly performing centres, including kōhanga reo, which had a high rate of supplementary reviews by ERO.[46] This assessment sparked Te Kōhanga Reo National Trust's claim to the Waitangi Tribunal, a story told later.

There were recommendations to provide a tighter quality framework around provisions for infants and toddlers and home-based services, and it was acknowledged that 'one of the most important indicators of structural quality of an ECE service is the availability of appropriately qualified staff'.[47] In 2012 two ministerial ECE advisory groups reported with 'cost neutral' advice on implementing the taskforce recommendations on improving quality sector wide, and improving the quality of services for children under two years.[48] Both of the minister's advisory working groups highlighted the costs of quality, and both endorsed regulating for 80% qualified teachers as a step towards 100%.

The minister promised a response during 2012, but this was not forthcoming. This was probably contingent on the findings of a third ECE advisory group tasked with designing a new funding model. The taskforce recommendations subsequently went into political limbo. Work on a new funding model continued but was not concluded.

In 2013 the *Herald on Sunday* (3 March) published its investigation into the impact of the early childhood policy shifts, under the headline 'Kiwi families conned':

> 20 hours' free childcare for 3- and 4-year-olds was hailed as a world-leading initiative to provide happy learning environments for the nation's children and allow mums and dads to return to work. But a *Herald on Sunday* investigation

reveals the government has turned a blind eye as preschools quietly force parents through a variety of hoops, making them pay through the nose.

The *Herald* reported that some centres were requiring parents to 'purchase' up to 30 hours in order to get the 20 hours free, and/or charging various top-ups, so that the 20 hours was not actually free. The article claimed that 'reduced funding had led to redundancies, less training, buttoning down costs, and inevitably an increase in parent fees'. Taskforce member Peter Reynolds, CEO of the Early Childhood Council (ECC), representing mainly private centres, said:

> Government has consistently, through three successive budgets, carved revenue from mainstream ECE centres … The Government will say 'We've actually put money into the sector.' They have, but it's targeted. So mainstream centres have lost money.

Some of government's tardiness with a radical redrawing of the funding blueprint was nervousness at the impact among its own heartland voters.

PARTICIPATION PRIORITIES AND THE VULNERABLE CHILD

Treasury briefings in 2011 for the re-elected National government recommended a better alignment of policy to the government's social and economic objectives and some 'carefully managed trade-offs'.[49] Government ministers and their department heads were charged with delivering '10 challenging results' across areas of social and economic concern, including reducing long-term welfare dependency and supporting vulnerable children.[50] This was the context of Minister Parata's target of 98% participation of four-year-olds in ECE prior to school entry.

The Ministry of Education established a range of intensive community participation project trials in 'vulnerable' communities where up to a quarter of children were starting school without having attended an early childhood service. The process was assisted by surveys and data analysis of designated suburbs, almost street by street, as well as in several rural regions. The trials focused on community development and supporting cultural identity, with the inclusion of all children whose parents wanted the kind of service offered. They included initiatives such as increased support to parent-led playgroups in communities with children not participating in early childhood; the Engaging Priority Families Initiative that worked alongside individual families to facilitate their child's regular attendance in a programme; and a home-based initiative provided for families who might prefer that.[51] These initiatives were, in part, a repackaging of older projects but collectively showcased the government's focus of reaching its 98% participation target.

The Ministry of Education contracted Linda Mitchell to evaluate the programmes.[52] At one level her findings were positive and she later wrote:

> An evaluation of the ECE Participation Programmes found out much about barriers to participation of priority families and whether and how the initiatives are addressing these. Services in the evaluation that were doing well in catering for priority families were developed as an integrated service that housed or brokered support by bringing together interdisciplinary teams for families/whānau to access.[53]

The barriers to participation were around structural features. Mitchell concluded: 'In other words, it is how services are funded, organised and located, and whether they are a "good fit" and responsive to families that matters most.'[54]

The backdrop to the participation policy initiative was wider social concern over 'vulnerable' children, families and communities who were a 'priority' for government policy. In 2011 the government released for consultation its *Green Paper on Vulnerable Children: Every child thrives, belongs, achieves*,[55] followed by a *White Paper* in 2012. This quantified 20,000–30,000 vulnerable children who 'live a life far below the norm' and are 'at significant risk of harm to their well-being now and into the future', caused by a mix of abuse, neglect, and health and poverty issues.[56] Ensuring access to ECE for vulnerable children was one of a range of strategies contained in the *White Paper*'s 'Children's Action Plan'.

Some early childhood providers strategically adopted the political rhetoric, although in reality for most it was business as usual. NZK's publication *Increasing Participation* (2013) outlined how kindergartens could assist the government achieve its goals, noting that 20% of children attracting a high deprivation rating were in kindergarten. This was a reminder that while kindergartens represented only 15% of early childhood services, the percentage of four-year-olds in kindergarten was significant.[57] Reflecting on these years, Amanda Coulston, CEO of the Wellington region Whānau Manaaki Kindergarten Association, wrote:

> We had suffered a 14% loss in funding and we were constantly rearranging ourselves while keeping an eye on the non-negotiables … We shouted and we cried … but we also determined to be proactive in tapping into new funding steams associated with the government focus on vulnerable children and increased participation for Māori and Pasifika children.[58]

Whānau Manaaki won several government contracts and became the first group of services to reach the minister's 98% target for participation prior to school.

Meanwhile the broader government agenda in relation to participation was under critique. In a joint statement, 80 organisations with 'a collective voice for New Zealand ... urged the Government not to cut services for better off children in its drive to target the most "vulnerable" children'.[59] At issue was the stigmatising of children defined as 'vulnerable'. The collective agencies, inclusive of early childhood organisations, asked, 'Who will be categorised as vulnerable, how is it defined, and who decides?' The agencies urged the government to retain universal and free services for children, while also tackling the wider policies contributing to 'vulnerability' such as labour market and welfare policy, adequacy of family income, housing etc. This was 'big picture' infrastructure from which the National government had retreated.

Linda Mitchell had deeper concerns about the government's agenda for ECE, arguing for policy frameworks that enabled and sustained the democratic participation of teachers, families and children.[60] Policies initiated by Labour in the 2000s had, in Mitchell's view, been undermined by National's social investment agendas.[61]

The issue of targeting became particularly contentious in 2012 with the roll-out of 'social obligations' for beneficiaries with children, the first being that children from age three were required to attend 15 hours a week of early childhood education. Non-compliance could lead to a 50% reduction in benefit payments. A small study published in 2015 found that beneficiaries and early childhood service managers were critical of what they saw as an intrusion into the lives of families and the labelling of children.[62] Early childhood organisations raised concern at the practicality and ethics of such compulsion. There is no evidence, however, that the policy was strongly enforced.

In May 2017 the National government announced new Better Public Service targets (BSPs), including the reduction of welfare dependency. However, the name of the new Oranga Tamariki Ministry for Vulnerable Children was short lived. The incoming Labour-led coalition government in December 2017 dropped the word 'vulnerable' to make it Oranga Tamariki Ministry for Children, and abolished the targets. The architect of the social investment policy (and briefly Leader of the Opposition) Bill English objected:

[Abolition of the targets] for no other reason than an ideological dislike for them is disgraceful … Getting rid of them undoes years of work to focus the public service on changing lives by digging into our hardest social problems, rather than just throwing money at them.[63]

Labour's new strategic plan development reflected the shifting policy agenda intended to emphasise universal policies, yet acknowledging the value of proactive participation initiatives.

A TREATY OF WAITANGI CLAIM

On 25 July 2011 a hīkoi of 400 kōhanga reo supporters delivered a claim to the Waitangi Tribunal on behalf of Te Kōhanga Reo National Trust Board seeking an urgent inquiry into the 'acts and omissions of the Crown in relation to kōhanga reo'. The immediate concern was allegations in the ECE Taskforce report of poor quality and declining enrolments in kōhanga reo, and anger at the lack of formal consultation by the taskforce. The claimants considered that the taskforce report, in including adverse comments about the Trust and kōhanga reo, had failed to recognise the nature and purpose of kōhanga reo and their kaupapa. The Ministry of Education, whose officials justified their policy intentions and refuted the Trust's claims, primarily represented the Crown. This judicial event was unprecedented in the history of early childhood, and laid bare grievances the Trust had long held with the Ministry of Education and agencies such as ERO and the Teaching Council of Aotearoa New Zealand | Matatū Aotearoa. The claim was heard over two weeks in March 2012, and the tribunal's findings were released in 2012, with *Matua Rautia: The report on the Kōhanga Reo claim* published in 2013.[64]

Earlier chapters of this book outline the beginnings of the idea of preschool education for Māori children (Chapter Three) and the emergence of kōhanga reo (Chapter Seven), including the story of Te Whāriki undertaken in partnership with Te Kōhanga Reo Trust Board (Chapter Nine). The Treaty of Waitangi claim revealed possibly unintended consequences of policy agendas that the Trust claimed breached the Treaty. In the decade prior to 2011 there had been a decline in the proportion of Māori children enrolled in kōhanga reo – from 33% to 22%. This decline underpinned the Trust's claim that the Crown had breached the Treaty in its management of kōhanga reo. The claims and counter-claims submitted to the tribunal added up to 60,000 pages.

The Trust's claim was based on the view that the Crown did not 'properly understand that the kōhanga reo are not "ECE centres" but are about "strengthening te reo me ngā tikanga Māori through the empowerment of whānau"'. The Crown 'wrongly' treated kōhanga reo as mainstream early childhood centres through regulatory, licensing and funding policies. This had not only 'assimilated' kōhanga reo into the mainstream, but led to the application of 'unfair', 'inconsistent' and 'incorrect' assessments concerning 'capabilities and quality' by ERO. Moreover, the Crown had 'discriminated against' kōhanga reo, for example, through its qualification policy, because the Teaching Council did not recognise the Trust's kaiako training programme as teaching a qualification adequate for funding purposes. Cumulatively this had resulted in 'significantly declining participation which had contributed to the perilous state of te reo Māori'.[65] The Trust blamed the Crown for ignoring recommendations and findings of reviews stretching back to the 1988 *Government Review of Kohanga Reo*, and proposed to the Waitangi Tribunal that kōhanga reo be removed from the legislative framework of the Ministry of Education, to 'allow whānau greater control and responsibility over their taonga, kōhanga reo'.[66]

The Crown responded that it could 'not accept the stark submissions made on behalf of the Trust', but acknowledged: 'There must be a way forward. Kōhanga reo are too important, to their tamariki, to their whānau, to the Crown and to te reo Māori to allow these current disagreements, some of them longstanding, to go unresolved.'[67] The Crown noted the apology in the Ministry of Education's submission for failing to direct the ECE Taskforce to consult with the Trust, and promised better processes.[68] While acknowledging that the relationship had been 'difficult' and 'challenging', with 'widely divergent viewpoints',[69] the Crown also cited examples of partnership, such as the development of Te Whāriki, as well as the Crown's overall $1 billion in funding support, with $2 million annually given in direct support to the Trust and $85 million annually for around 10,000 children and the broader well-being of their whānau. The Crown reiterated concerns about the variability in the capacity of kōhanga reo to meet regulatory standards, stating that regulatory standards for health, safety and staffing ratios were a necessary assurance for parents and accountability for government funding. The ministry described as inaccurate the Trust's view that regulation had led to 'systematic disadvantage' for kōhanga reo, and argued that the regulations allowed for flexibility around changing tables and sleeping arrangements, both cited as concerns by the Trust.[70]

The tribunal heard a large number of submissions on behalf of both the Crown and the Trust. It is useful to canvas a few of the contributions here. For the Crown, Anne Meade outlined to the Waitangi Tribunal the government's early childhood policy trajectory. She had chaired two of the government working groups that produced policy blueprints: *Education to Be More* (1988) and *Pathways to the Future: Ngā Huarahi Arataki 2002–2012* (2002). Both shifted the position of kōhanga reo within the spectrum of early childhood services, blamed by the Trust as assimilating kōhanga reo. The 1989 'Before Five' reforms had introduced integrated administrative, funding and regulatory systems for diverse early childhood services, including kōhanga reo, which were previously within the Department of Māori Affairs. There were significant funding gains under 'Before Five' for kōhanga reo, but with the addition of compliance measures.

Meade told the tribunal that the 1988 *Government Review of Kohanga Reo* had 'sought to place Te Kōhanga Reo in the broader context of Māori development, not education', with funding channelled through Māori Affairs and distributed by the Trust.[71] However, the recommendations from this review did not progress; moreover, as Meade noted, there was further 'erosion in the 1990s of the coherence of the policies of "Before Five"'.[72] A strategic plan working group in 2001 appointed a Māori caucus that included Dame Iritana Tawhiwhirangi, longtime CEO of Te Kōhanga Reo Trust and a founder of the movement. The working group recommended that the sector be split and funded according to whether centres were teacher led or parent led. This would disadvantage kōhanga reo, as few kaiako had a formal teaching qualification. At the same time the working group recommended that 'the Ministry of Education and Te Puni Kōkiri work together with iwi, kōhanga whānau and Te Kōhanga Reo Trust to develop a process by which devolution of kōhanga reo from the Trust to iwi will occur within the next five years'.[73] The government did not adopt this recommendation. At a ministry symposium in 2007, to review progress of the strategic plan, Meade was critical of the lack of progress on support for parent-led services including kōhanga reo.[74]

Submissions were presented to the tribunal from Arapera Royal Tangaere and Iritana Tawhiwhirangi on behalf of the Trust. Tawhiwhirangi stated: 'The Trust spent a lot of time trying to inform the Ministry of Education about the kaupapa of kōhanga reo but more often than not they just didn't understand the kaupapa, or did not accept it.'[75] She accused the ministry of being 'concerned about contractual risks more than our concerns for the survival of te reo, the well-being of our whānau or mokopuna'.[76]

Arapera Royal Tangaere attributed the decline in kōhanga reo enrolments to Crown policies that had 'hindered the movement's progress and have become barriers to the main purpose of kōhanga', causing the 'decline in numbers of mokopuna and whānau attending kōhanga reo during the last 20 years'. Royal Tangaere rejected the Crown's view that the decline was not its fault.[77] In a comparison of ERO evaluation reports, Royal Tangaere rejected the categorisation of the 33% supplementary reviews of kōhanga reo as evidence of poor quality, as 21% contained recommendations, not requirements. This was 'judging kōhanga reo against an ECE framework for which they were not designed'.[78] In summary, Royal Tangaere argued that the Crown's funding regime discriminated against and undermined kōhanga reo:

> The Ministry sends the message that a kōhanga reo without qualified teachers is somehow inferior in quality to ECE services. This value system rewards ECE qualifications which primarily transmit non-Māori educational and social values. It belittles the value of kaumatua and undermines the kaupapa of kōhanga reo. The Crown's continued insistence that, in order for kōhanga reo to access a higher rate of funding, they must have either ECE qualified teachers and/or have Tohu Whakapakari approved as a teacher education course undermines both the Trust's role as kaitiaki and the kaupapa of kōhanga reo.[79]

The Waitangi Tribunal concluded that the claim was valid and that 'many of the issues relating to this claim might have been avoided had an adequate policy framework, based on sound understanding of the Crown's Treaty obligations to actively protect te reo through kōhanga reo in ECE been developed'.[80] Moreover, 'There has been serious prejudice to the kōhanga reo movement as a result of these Crown actions and omissions.' The tribunal made five recommendations intended to redress the 'prejudice', including an apology from the Crown.[81]

Minister Hekia Parata responded that the government would consider the report and would be seeking a 'meaningful and constructive way forward'. This intent soon faltered and the relationship between Te Kōhanga Reo Trust Board and the Crown further deteriorated, with the minister insisting the Trust reform its governance as a prerequisite for settling the claim. This was in the aftermath of an audit and a Serious Fraud Office investigation that found 'wrongdoings amounting to gross financial mismanagement'.[82] Amid the furore, the minister made a direct approach to the 460 kōhanga reo, stating that she 'expected a new governance that was truly representative and auditable'.[83] In time changes were undertaken, but the relationship between the Trust and the Crown remained strained.

In 2018 Te Kōhanga Reo Trust Board lodged its claim again. The chair, Matua Hook, stated: 'We are trying to resolve a pathway forward … now with the new Labour Government, it's back on the table.'[84] The government's *He Taonga te Tamaiti – Every Child a Taonga: Strategic plan for early learning 2019–29* addressed one area of contention, recommending the co-design of an appropriate funding model with kōhanga reo. Iritana Tawhiwhirangi responded:

> The announcement is long overdue. Well, it's about time. It was about six years ago we were addressing this and no one noticed – in the end that's why we took a claim. Slowly [kōhanga reo] has been dragged away from the embrace of the Māori people into a government-regulated system that doesn't work for us all the time.[85]

This story is still unfolding; however, in a surprise post-budget announcement in June 2019, Associate Minister of Education Kelvin Davis announced a $32 million 'well-being' 'boost' as an investment, acknowledging 'the crucial role kōhanga reo play in the survival and revitalisation of te reo Māori'. Davis proclaimed: 'This is the start of what equality for kōhanga reo looks like.'[86]

REFRESHING TE WHĀRIKI

Fulfilling National's election promise in 2008, the Ministry of Education introduced national standards in primary schools as an assessment tool for the '3Rs' of reading, writing and arithmetic. Teachers protested en masse. Despite such resistance, national standards assessments were in place by 2010, with parents notified whether their child was meeting the expected standard or not. The consequence was an undermining of the holistic *New Zealand Curriculum* as teachers focused their teaching on the 3Rs. The early childhood sector voiced concern that national standards would undermine the empowering principles of Te Whāriki. A climate of anxiety caused some early childhood centres to introduce 'school time' and worksheets, and school entry tests categorised children as 'not up to standard' for not being able to count to 10, or not knowing some alphabet letters before starting school. Children's other domains of knowing and interests received scant attention.

The ongoing pedagogical story of Te Whāriki has been well documented, but less so the ongoing political story.[87] This section examines some of the political signposts around Te Whāriki during the timeframe of this chapter. Under the National government we saw a refreshed Te Whāriki; under Labour the immediate abolition of national standards; and during 2018 the conversation on 'Taking Te Whāriki to school' progressed.

Government policies that viewed children in terms of their vulnerability and deficits were at odds with the aspirations of Te Whāriki, which was based on principles of child agency. The ECE Taskforce in 2010 had considered whether to review Te Whāriki. There were strong submissions in support of the programme and the taskforce's view was that the framework of principles, strands and goals were robust, but it recommended a review of its implementation to better support teachers. Joce Nuttall wrote:

> Despite support for the centrality of Te Whāriki, [the taskforce] report is silent about the issue of children's universal human rights, including their rights to an optimal education. The language of rights is sidelined by the language of vulnerability and risk ... The language of Te Whāriki is not one of risk, vulnerability and competition. It speaks, instead of opportunity, respect and relationships.[88]

Concerns about implementation were shared by ERO, whose snapshot evaluation, *Working with Te Whāriki* (2013), showed that while 90% of centres were engaging with the principles and strands of Te Whāriki there was considerable variation in understanding and application by staff, with only 10% of centres 'engaging deeply' with the document.[89]

The *New Zealand Listener* (19 April 2014) waded into the debate, publishing a controversial article by Catherine Woulfe claiming: 'A "Massive Hole" in NZ's Early Learning Harms Life Chances'. Alongside commentary on government funding cuts, Woulfe crafted a story arguing that the curriculum was the deeper problem. Education researcher John Hattie urged more focus on early literacy and numeracy, '[which] at risk children aren't getting from ECE ... It's a scandal.' He called for a 'robust discussion about learning' in the sector. These concerns were shared by Ken Blaiklock, who was critical of the 'open and holistic' curriculum, which, he claimed, with its 'loose assessment', is 'a perfect storm'. Richie Poulton, a member of the ECE Taskforce and leader of the 'Growing Up in New Zealand' longitudinal study, was concerned at the lack of monitoring: 'If you're a consumer – if you're a parent – you're thinking your child is getting X yet they are getting Y.'[90] The *Listener* article drew a storm of letters to the editor, including one I re-titled in a letter of my own: '"The scandal" of uninformed commentary on ECE':

The views presented come from voices whose engagement in ECE, and whose scholarly or professional standing nationally or internationally in ECE is non-existent, fleeting or lightweight ... Professor Hattie's desire for a 'robust discussion about learning' indicates amnesia for the past 20 years and ignorance about Te Whāriki.[91]

After the 2014 election the new National Minister of Education, Hekia Parata, established an Advisory Group on Strengthening the Implementation of Te Whāriki. Dame Iritana Tawhiwhirangi was appointed to look after the interests of kōhanga reo. Mindful of the rhetoric of earlier heated debates, it was made clear in the terms of reference that rewriting Te Whāriki was 'out of scope'.[92] This was the stepping-stone to its eventual rejuvenation, and a signal that the principles of Te Whāriki could be accommodated in the current education environment. Sector support and international acclaim were key factors in keeping Te Whāriki safe. The original authors, Lady Tilly and Sir Tamati Reedy, Margaret Carr and myself were invited to meet the group. We were concerned to ensure that the philosophical underpinnings, principles, strands and goals of Te Whāriki remained intact. Margaret and I bravely proposed that national standards be abolished in junior classes and Te Whāriki be adopted and formally linked to *The New Zealand Curriculum*.

Te Whāriki had been showcased in many international forums and tenets of its aspirations and learning domains had seeped into the language and structure of curriculum documents in other countries. In 2013 the government hosted a meeting of the OECD Early Childhood Education and Care (ECEC) Network, preceded by, at the request of members, a conference on Te Whāriki.[93] It was an occasion to reflect on the origins of Te Whāriki in the presence of the Reedys, whose presentation, *Te Whāriki: A tapestry for life*, launched the conference and was fronted by their niece, Minister Parata. International delegates were told:

Te Whāriki is the first curriculum of its kind for Aotearoa-New Zealand. After 200 years of educational history, Māori were, for the first time, being given the opportunity to influence a new curriculum that would touch the minds of future New Zealanders.[94]

The *Report of the Advisory Group on Early Learning* (2015) cited the support for Te Whāriki and recommended an updated document and professional development programmes. In response to the idea of taking Te Whāriki to schools, the advisory group recommended that 'primary schools consider establishing reception classes for five-year-olds, with curriculum planning, assessment and evaluation based on Te Whāriki'.[95] Despite frequent requests for updates from the ministry's own ECE Research Policy Forum, this idea did not progress.[96]

In late 2016 the 'refresh' of Te Whāriki was under way with an expert group led by Nancy Bell, now in the Ministry of Education. There were tensions in the task, particularly balancing the opportunity to update and strengthen the document with the need to meet the minister's short timeline. Some were nervous about whether the task could be managed without political or pedagogical capture, and others were upset that no sector consultation was planned. The appointment of the four original writers as advisers was intended to reassure but the first draft shown to the advisers was *not* reassuring. In the wake of further feedback, Nancy Bell persuaded a reluctant minister that more time was needed and a consultation phase was necessary.

The final 'refreshed' draft was almost totally rewritten, with hands-on brokering by Bell, who met with concerned groups and sought specialist expertise. While the process had been tight and fraught, the task had engaged a whole new generation of teachers, researchers and scholars keen to participate in the 'refresh'. This was heartening and a reflection of an early childhood environment still stimulating pedagogical innovation. In April 2017 the ministry mounted a fanfare launch of 'Te Whāriki: Our world-leading early childhood curriculum'.[97] A gathering of officials, politicians, early childhood organisation representatives and those who had worked on the document endorsed the update, which gave a much stronger emphasis to a bicultural framework.

I spoke at the launch:

> Writing the original document with Sir Tamati and Lady Tilly Reedy that was named Te Whāriki in 1992 was an extraordinary journey of collaboration, aspiration, consultation and negotiation. We understood that a national curriculum document was not just a pedagogical statement on behalf of the profession. It was also a political document as a statement about the nation's children. The document has been through several political transformations and changes but Te Whāriki's overall principles of empowerment and relationships, its framework of mana, and its underpinning of children's rights and agency have remained unchallenged. Te Whāriki became something far more than we ever envisaged but there is still a journey ahead to realise these aspirations.[98]

Victoria University's Institute for Early Childhood Studies held a research seminar to explore the 'possibilities and realities' of Te Whāriki 2017 as 'an opportunity to think differently and therefore critically'.[99] The keynote presentations placed the new Te Whāriki under scrutiny. A number of comments identified challenges for its implementation, and a selection of these comments is reproduced here:

- Mere Skerrett urged the sector to 'avoid the constraints of conventional, colonial thinking'. She acknowledged the 'big ideas' around 'language culture and identity' but said: 'Let's put the pedagogical principles of Te Whāriki 2017 into linguistic play' by ensuring that te reo Māori becomes entrenched in the education system beyond early childhood.[100]
- Jenny Ritchie continued Skerrett's story of Te Whāriki's 'fantastic journey' to consider the challenges of increasing 'superdiversity in Aotearoa'. Ritchie cited the danger of 'tokenistic' practice in the sector, calling for 'more intervention in teacher education' and 'cohesive policy development and commitment to language regeneration, to equity and social justice'.[101]
- Sally Peters offered insights from research into the connections between Te Whāriki and *The New Zealand Curriculum*, highlighting the strengthened approaches to the transition process in the updated document.[102]

Professional development for the sector was seen as imperative. ERO subsequently released two reports from surveys conducted during 2017 reviewing the impact of the ministry's contracted programmes. While there was an 82% level of awareness of the updated document, only half of centres had begun to 'engage' with it. 'Their leaders and kaiako were unsure where to start.'[103]

In the weeks after the formation of the Labour-led coalition in late 2017, new Education Minister Chris Hipkins abolished national standards, with directions to implement *The New Zealand Curriculum* more fulsomely and creatively. There would need to be some 'unlearning' of past practices that might be a challenge to some teachers. There were implications too for early childhood and an opportunity to redress the mismatch across curricula settings.

NZEI–Te Riu Roa determined to kick off, with a one-day seminar in March 2018 titled 'Taking the Lead: Celebrating NZ curricula'.[104] Teachers were in a celebratory mood. I was asked to speak about Te Whāriki and determined that in 'new political times', to borrow the campaign words of Prime Minister Jacinda Ardern, we 'take Te Whāriki to school: LET'S DO THIS NOW!' I issued a plea for junior classes to return to a more playful child-centred learning environment.[105] Other speakers reminded teachers of the potential of realising the intentions of the school curriculum without national standards. The

Ministry of Education caught the optimistic mood and, with NZEI–Te Riu Roa, mounted six hui around the country.[106]

The idea of 'taking Te Whāriki to school' was powerfully illustrated by new entrant teacher Melissa Corbett, who demonstrated the playful possibilities with her own class at Victory School Nelson. However, the findings of Maggie Haggerty's doctoral thesis on curriculum and assessment priorities in transitioning to school, collected during the era of national standards, revealed a deeply embedded culture of conformity at odds with Te Whāriki. Haggerty's thesis challenged schools' privileging of the 'linguistically adept' child, arguing for space for 'other modes of being, doing, knowing'.[107] Taking Te Whāriki to school would be contested and likely subverted, but for some teachers the opportunity to rethink what kinds of learning are valued in the early years has been welcomed.

Te Whāriki has survived the political storms of the past decade, and been strengthened. Its future journeys in the early childhood sector and possibly within schools will depend upon the pedagogical infrastructure of support for teachers that is currently under review and negotiation. Its story so far is an example of cross-party political initiative and support, combined with scholarly and sector engagement from organisations and teachers. It is a unity of purpose across policy and practice not always achieved but characteristic of the New Zealand political playground.

AN OECD DRAMA

A parallel story on the world stage was the Ministry of Education's interest in participating in the OECD's International Early Learning Study (IELS) which, like the school-based Programme for International Assessment (PISA), would test five-year-olds. This was a undisclosed collaboration between OECD and the ministry, along with other officials, none of whom consulted early childhood organisations about the ethics and value of cross-national measurement. The idea had first been mooted in 2012 by the OECD ECEC network. By 2016 snippets of information were trickling out, particularly after a tender was issued to manage the project.[108] Concern began mounting internationally among early childhood policy and research leaders, many of whom had been supportive participants in OECD's *Starting Strong* (2001, 2006) projects investigating early childhood policy in cross-country contexts.[109] New Zealand was a foundation member of the ECEC network (formed in 2007), yet there had been no formal mention to early childhood organisations of this new study, as if government officials did not recognise the potential mismatch between national early childhood curricula and a cross-national testing regime.

By 2017 New Zealand's Ministry of Education was poised to affirm its interest in participating, despite only the most scant consultation. In my brief presentation at the launch of the updated Te Whāriki in April, amid the gathering of high-level ministry officials, I cautioned that the study might undermine Te Whāriki's holistic aspirations of empowerment across diverse settings.[110]

Two months later New Zealand withdrew from the first round of the project. It is useful to record the background politics of this 'almost happened' story, which illustrated the way in which international monetary agencies such as OECD and the World Bank are increasingly shaping the discourses of early childhood policy. New Zealand is renowned for its progressive early childhood policy, but Official Information Act (OIA) documents reveal that our country was a keen participant in the early development of IELS.[111]

For many years the ministry has convened two advisory groups: the Early Childhood Advisory Committee (ECAC) (comprising around 14 early childhood organisation representatives) and the ECE Research Policy Forum, a small group of researchers with long-term engagement in policy development. Meetings of both groups include government officials. ECE Research Policy Forum members were first briefed in 2014 about the IELS project and the ministry's interest in its development. However, it was not until February 2017 that ECAC was 'consulted', after individual forum members advised several ECAC members that they should be concerned. By then several forum members were engaged in an international campaign against a 'Preschool PISA'.

The ministry's view, expressed to forum members in 2014, was that it was important to 'be at the table' as the project developed. The forum was consulted about the domains and measures appropriate for early childhood,[112] but advised the ministry in turn that such assessment did not align with Te Whāriki (then under review), and that the resources would be better used to support this work. Hopes were dashed as it became clear that New Zealand was to participate in 'scoping' the development of learning outcomes.[113] In a briefing to the ministry's policy governance board in May 2015 Karl Le Quesne, senior early childhood policy manager, advised:

> Participating in the early learning outcomes survey will progress a key gap in our knowledge about the performance of the ECE system. While PISA,

TIMMS [reading literacy] and PIRLS [maths and science] correlates later achievement with ECE attendance, the information is not robust enough to make conclusive judgements on how well our system performs …[114]

Setting out New Zealand's position in June 2015, the ministry confirmed to the OECD's ECEC network it had endorsed an initiative linked to PISA designed to provide a 'stocktake' of the state of children's early learning and to assess its impact.[115] Financial imperatives were clearly at the forefront, with the ministry noting it 'invests heavily' in early childhood, having doubled its funding to $1.8 billion since 2008. The ministry wanted comparable information to that provided by national standards for primary school performance.[116]

Some advice from the forum did seep into ministry submissions, suggesting the study focus its measures not so such much on educational attainment but 'learning dispositions' and the 'learning domains that are most critical to later learning … and lifetime outcomes'.[117] In a second feedback document to the OECD's ECEC network, in August 2015, the ministry emphasised that its preferred domains were ones that 'relate well to the outcomes as specified in our ECE curriculum Te Whāriki, and the key competencies in our school curriculum'.[118] By early 2016 the ministry, now describing itself as 'one of the early initiators or the project', indicated the possibility of joining the proposed pilot intended to commence in 2017. Documents obtained under the OIA show the specific recommendation redacted, although the overall tone of the memo suggests it was more positive than simply having a presence 'at the table'.[119]

The intense round of meetings, travel, reports and submissions evident from the cache of OIA papers were entirely in-house within the ministry, with minimal information made available to the ECE Research Policy Forum. While there was an attempt to align the study with New Zealand contexts, there was no debate on the broader principles underlying cross-national assessment. In preparation for a forum meeting, Margaret Carr, with Linda Mitchell and Lesley Rameka from the University of Waikato, wrote a paper called 'Some thoughts about the value of an OECD international assessment framework for early childhood services in Aotearoa New Zealand'.[120] They quoted James Paul Gee's view that 'Many a standardized test can be perfectly "scientific" and useless at the same time; [and] in a worst case scenario, it can be disastrous' … 'the use of OECD standardised tests to evaluate our ECE sector, while they may be perfectly "scientific", could be disastrous for Te Whāriki'.[121]

Attending the meeting was Professor Stuart McNaughton, the chief education scientific adviser, an esteemed researcher in the field of early literacy. The overall view of the forum members was that the study should not proceed; this was an opportunity for robust debate. McNaughton responded, setting out the positives and dangers of participating in the study and concluded, 'Why would we NOT want to know this information?' He later reported that contractors had been appointed, the 'child domains were settled', and (oral language, numeracy, self-regulation and social-emotional) were 'able to be matched to the strands and learning outputs in Te Whāriki'.[122]

McNaughton was due to represent the ministry at the next OECD ECEC network meeting in Paris in September 2016. In due course he reported to Minister Parata on the meeting with forum members and the Paris meeting but his recommendation is redacted from the document obtained under the OIA. He noted the concerns about Te Whāriki and the risks, but said:

> the proposed measures have the potential to be consistent ... My view is that we can benefit from the three types of information such assessment can provide: system benchmarking, system diagnostics, and system performance over time.[123]

Meanwhile, individual forum members determined the issues needed wider debate. Collectively and rapidly, the issues galvanised the attention and concern of a broad group of researchers, scholars, teacher educators and union advocates:

- NZEI–Te Riu Roa mounted a celebration, 'Te Whāriki Turns 20', at its annual conference in Rotorua in September 2016, attended by the original writers. In a brief responding speech, Margaret Carr and I informed delegates of the ministry's involvement and our concerns with the idea of a 'Preschool PISA', urging NZEI engagement.
- At the Reconceptualising Early Childhood Education (RECE) conference in Taupo in October 2016 there was a similar celebration also attended by the writers. This time we presented the issues for an international audience. RECE's international board subsequently prepared a detailed formal response to the OECD that concluded: 'The use of research evidence to justify IELS is highly selective ... It raises fundamental questions about whose political or business interests are being privileged over research evidence.'[124]
- The NZ Association for Research in Education (NZARE) conference in November 2016 passed a resolution calling on the government not to

participate because 'OECD measures promote a "one-world" view with a focus on standardised outcomes … We risk a narrowing of the curriculum, loss of culturally valued outcomes, and the emergence of a pedagogy of compliance.'[125] The networking of the ECE NZARE Special Interest Group (SIG) of early childhood members was crucial in achieving this, reflecting the strength of the lively scholarly scene.

The breadth of activism was reassuring evidence that 'old style' advocacy of the pen, the voice and the person was still potent.

Meanwhile in London, Carr discussed her paper with Peter Moss, who decided an international debate should be mounted, with direct approaches to the OECD. Moss circulated a draft article, 'The OECD's International Early Learning Study: Opening for debate and contestation', around concerned researchers in OECD countries, citing eight co-authors. They outlined the OECD's arguments for such assessment, and reminded readers that education cannot be reduced to the technical exercise. Moss was critical of OECD's lack of awareness of the effects of power, stating: 'This new study is neither neutral nor unproblematic. It has important consequences for children, parents, practitioners, policy makers and others.' The final article was published in *Contemporary Issues in Early Childhood*,[126] as was the paper by Carr and colleagues.[127] Carr and Moss were both concerned that minority group communities and countries would be disadvantaged. Moss wrote:

> The IELS, and similar testing regimes, seek to apply a universal framework to all countries, all pedagogies and all services. This approach rests on the principle that everything can be reduced to a common outcome, standard and measure. What it cannot do is accommodate, let alone welcome, diversity – of paradigm or theory, pedagogy or provision, childhood or culture.[128]

Moss's article stirred wide commentary across the affected OECD countries.[129]

In December 2016 Clare Wells, a member of ECAC, formally requested that the ministry consult with the ECE sector. This generated a flurry of memos (most redacted) between the Secretary for Education and other senior managers, acknowledging that 'sector exposure to the study has been limited'.[130] Briefings on the study were subsequently provided to NZEI–Te Riu Roa and ECAC; both groups expressed their concern.

In the event only USA, England and Estonia joined the first round of the study. NZARE's Ipu Kererū blog by Alex Gunn (26 July 2017) reported: 'A near thing: The OECD's International Early Learning and Well-being Study will not reportedly be piloted in New Zealand.'[131] ECAC members were advised at their June meeting. There was no ministry communication with forum members. Ministry documents released under the OIA do not reveal the arguments surrounding their decision.

The OECD eventually published information about the study in *Early Learning Matters* (2017), including evidence that the duration of ECE participation is linked to better scores in PISA at age 15 years:

> The first study of its kind, it will provide countries with a common language and framework, encompassing a collection of robust empirical information and in-depth insights on children's learning development at a critical age.[132]

Moss, with Mathias Urban, president of the International Froebel Society, continued to report on the roll-out of IELS, including a London seminar on IELS in February 2018, attended by OECD, whose representative cited the study as the 'first wave' and said 'future waves' were envisaged after the publication of findings in 2020.[133] Despite low participation in the 'first wave', Moss and Urban warned of the wider dangers of the OECD hegemony:

> We find the IELS problematic and disturbing on its own, but far more problematic and disturbing when seen as a part of this spreading global web of measurement. The aim of this web appears to be the reduction of education to a purely technical exercise of producing common outcomes measured by common indicators, with the OECD acting as the global arbiter of what those outcomes and indicators should be … [and becoming] the global governor of education …[134]

There are lessons in this 'almost happened' drama, revealing that early childhood policy is situated in a global nexus of economic interests in education that can easily undermine the unique characteristics of our home-grown initiatives. Revealing, too, of the culture of secrecy within the Ministry of Education, evident also in earlier decades, although there have been times of positive engagement and collaboration with the sector. We also learn that sometimes the politics of the pen – through articles, submissions, resolutions, requests, collaboration and conversation – can make a difference.[135]

CHANGING WORLDS OF KINDERGARTEN AND PLAYCENTRE

Kindergarten and Playcentre are iconic 'do-it-yourself' Kiwi institutions and were once the mainstay of preschool education. In the postwar years they enjoyed huge growth and funding support from successive governments. Statistics presented earlier in this book reveal the declining enrolments for both kindergarten and Playcentre as other early childhood models emerged, trends that were hastened after the 1990 'Before Five' reforms, although seeded earlier amid the changing aspirations of women. In recent years the national body of each organisation – New Zealand Kindergartens Te Pūtahi Kura Pūhou o Aotearoa (NZK) and Te Whānau Tupu Ngātahi o Aotearoa – Playcentre Aotearoa (NZPF) – proposed amalgamating its local associations/branches and centres under the umbrella of the national body; a similar exercise was undertaken by the Plunket Society. Amalgamation proceeded in Plunket and Playcentre but not kindergarten.

Playcentre and kindergarten managed to keep internal disquiet about the planned restructuring out of the media. Radio NZ reported on 28 August 2018 that 'Kindys, Playcentres plan powerful multi-million-dollar national organisations to help create more financial clout and stem falling enrollments'. Plunket, however, faced a backlash as some communities protested against the well-publicised proposed shifting of local money into national coffers. The *New Zealand Listener* reported on 7 July 2018: 'Inside the Plunket Controversy: Why the volunteers are up in arms'. Local communities in regions such as Karori in Wellington objected to 'head office' closing its community crèche, and ownership of the local Plunket rooms, built on gifted land with funds raised by the community, being transferred to head office. 'What the whole thing smacks of to us is the corporatisation of communities. They've taken this much-loved 100-year-old brand and morphed it into a marketing company,' reported one aggrieved parent. But amalgamation was being forced upon Plunket by a government wanting to see 'measurable outcomes and a greater return on investment'.[136] At issue was the uneven delivery of services across the country, with well-off suburbs like Karori easily able to raise money and provide volunteers while less wealthy communities missed out.[137]

Fears of centralised control were common across the institutions whose roots lay in community initiative and huge volunteer effort. These endeavours were at the social heart of many local communities. But over the decades the services were increasingly professionalised. The concept of family life was changing, and women were spending fewer years, if any, 'at home' caring for preschool children. Unlike Plunket, with increasing demand for its services, kindergarten and Playcentre had declining enrolments as more parents chose alternative services that offered more hours and/or provided a particular cultural focus.

Most sorely affected was Playcentre, with centres closing or reopening as informal playgroups outside of licensing requirements. In 2018 there were 407 centres catering for 9734 children, a drop from 517 centres for 15,806 children in 2000.[138] Nevertheless there remains a loyal following of at-home mothers (mainly) for whom the small-scale parent cooperative part-day enterprise is perfect.

Playcentre faced deeper woes in an increasingly teacher-led environment. Suzanne Manning makes a case that under both Labour and National governments the interests of Playcentre have been sidelined and excluded from new funding streams.[139] The '20 hours free ECE' policy initially excluded Playcentre and kōhanga reo, on the assumption that their services, provided often by volunteer parents, were already 'free'. This was remedied in 2010. The higher funding subsidy to centres employing qualified teachers did not extend to Playcentre, which met the licensing qualification requirements with a proportion of parents collectively engaged in Playcentre training. Manning cites a deeper conflict:

> Playcentres are parent-cooperative … based on the philosophy that parents are 'the first and best educators of their children'. Much of current government social policy emphasises the role of parents as workers and providers for their families but does not emphasise their role as carers and educators.[140]

Manning analyses how each policy shift undermined the viability of parent-led services, to the extent that the ECE Taskforce recommended the exclusion of parent-led and home-based services from mainstream funding. (This recommendation was not implemented.) There were concerns too when the 2014 Advisory Group on Early Learning supported 100% qualified teachers as a baseline for effective implementation of Te Whāriki. These assumptions, Manning writes, flowed into the 2017 updated document:

> For the NZPF the biggest concern was the absence of acknowledgement of … the philosophy of parents as educators of their own children. The clear separation between parents and teachers, a discursive effect of the quality policies, continued to frame the thinking about adults in ECEC.[141]

In 2016 Playcentre Aotearoa launched a national roadshow to discuss its future, with the following imperative:

> The association model is not working, our funding model is not working, Playcentre's critical mass is shrinking. The Federation, Associations and Centres are at tipping point and we believe that if we fail to act now Playcentre as we know it will not be around for our grandchildren.[142]

This began a journey towards operational amalgamation of 32 associations under the federation, which would manage all operations. Legal amalgamation would be completed in 2018. Members were told: 'We are creating new ways of supporting centres, coupled with a sense of loss.' This loss was felt particularly by centres still thriving on traditional models of parent management and emergent leadership.

Playcentre's amalgamation was not embroiled in media commentary, but the process was not without internal controversy as associations wound up their operations and assets and debts were reallocated. Playcentre stalwart Sue Stover captures the sentiments:

> The democratic ethos and 'grassroots' empowerment built on the back of committed volunteers that have characterised Playcentre regionally and nationally for more than 50 years are being (noisily) shelved and replaced by commercially paid national staff, with six hubs (again with paid staff) supporting and monitoring what happens in Playcentres around the country. It is an open question how many Playcentres will survive under this model.[143]

Parents were assured that volunteers would remain an integral part of the organisation and that 'parents and whanau members will continue to be educators and make decisions about the running of their centre'.[144] However, as Stover explains, the group supervision model was also under threat:

> … it appears that Playcentre no longer has the clout to be allowed exemptions from requirements that disadvantage it … By 2020, all Playcentres will be required to have at least one person with a level 4 qualification – effectively a supervisor.

Stover's overall concern is the undermining of a model of community development for corporate accountability:

> The marginalising of Playcentres means the diminishing of what Playcentre offers better than any other early childhood service – a place for the growth of parents, especially women … There are thousands of stories [about] the adults who 'graduated' from Playcentre [who] have contributed to their communities and to the wider early childhood sector.[145]

The new structures were in place in 2018. It is too early to predict whether a centralised Playcentre model will trend towards sinking or swimming.

Between 2000 and 2018 kindergarten enrolments dropped from 45,869 to 29,048,[146] although the number of kindergartens increased from 606 in 2002 to 654 in 2018.[147] The waiting lists of previous decades are gone, but fewer children are staying longer hours. Kindergartens also began accepting two-year-olds, and most kindergartens shifted to full-day licences, offering parents the option of school day or half day hours. Some associations established childcare centres or absorbed struggling childcare centres, including, in Wellington, several Pasifika centres, although such diversification was not always favoured. There was much debate within kindergarten circles over the question 'what is distinctive about kindergarten?' now that all services could offer 'free ECE'. Other services could also boast a professionalised teacher-led programme including hours suited to working parents.

In 2005 NZK tabled a proposal to directly manage the kindergarten operations of the then 29 associations.[148] The argument was to create a stronger and more professional kindergarten organisation and better manage the consequences of the disparity in association sizes and variability in quality across associations.[149] Association members rejected the proposal but the idea simmered. In 2016 NZK mounted a three-day 'conversation': 'Designing the Future – Kindergarten 2026'. Unlike earlier 'conversations' conducted amidst a sense of crisis, the 2016 discussions occurred in a more positive space. NZK had its 'house' reasonably in order and was a proactive player at the political table. In a carefully managed process Clare Wells led the organisation towards amalgamation, with September 2018 set for a vote on a new entity comprising a governance board, a national office, and regional offices managing the operations of kindergartens.[150] Assurances were given that 'one organisation' did not mean 'one kindergarten model': 'the importance of local kindergarten identity is recognised and maintained: this is what kindergarten is all about – located within and reflecting each kindergarten'.[151] In June 2018 NZK's board published a booklet entitled *The Story*, outlining the external pressures facing kindergartens and arguing that the move had the potential to futureproof kindergarten to withstand shifts and changes, operate more efficiently, respond to competition, and lift teaching and learning with a new national strategy of pedagogy and practice.[152]

In the event smaller associations felt they had the most to lose and swayed a vote narrowly against the proposal. Larger associations that would have more broadly transformed into regional offices voted in favour. If the vote had been proportional to the number of kindergartens in each association there would have been overwhelming support for the proposal to amalgamate. Early indications are that the issue will be revisited. In the aftermath of the election of the 2018 Labour-led government, kindergarten is keen to position itself as the ideal institution to expand public provision of ECE.

There have been five significant policy blueprints for early childhood education (1947, 1971, 1988, 2002, 2011[153]), and currently under consideration is *He Taonga te Tamaiti – Every Child a Taonga: Strategic plan for early learning 2019–29*. The swings and roundabouts of the 'playground' of early childhood policy have been a rollercoaster of curtailment and gains. Broadly, Labour blueprints (1947, 1988, 2002) have extended government interest in early childhood services, whereas National blueprints (1971, 2002, 2011) have curtailed government responsibility. It is not always so neat. National governments have dampened Labour promises but usually embraced the broad direction. This final section gives an overview of the strategic planning under way.

Labour's 2017 election policy promised a new strategic plan for new demographics and economic times. Linda Mitchell described Labour's 'first 100 days of action' as offering 'exciting promise'.[154] Nonetheless, the early childhood sector was underwhelmed with the 2018 budget announcement of a 1.6% increase in operational funding after a nine-year freeze. Development of the strategic plan was by then under way and Minister Chris Hipkins possibly reasoned that the sector could tolerate a delay. A small ministerial advisory group, chaired by Professor Carmen Dalli, would take the lead. A reference group comprising members of ECAC and the ECE Research Policy Forum would provide feedback. There would also be sector consultation. This was a more collaborative approach than the ECE Taskforce, although ministry officials had a firm grasp on the pen and the process. Reference group member Linda Mitchell drafted an ambitious 'way forward' to 'turn the tide' towards a public and democratic system of early childhood intended to:[155]

- Improve the social context of childhood;
- Develop a democratic vision for children and the aims of ECEC;
- Retain Te Whāriki and sociocultural assessment approaches;
- Shift from a market approach to a 'partnership model' of ECEC provision;
- Provide free ECEC as an entitlement for all children; and
- Improve the qualifications, professional support and remuneration of all staff.

Keeping these aspirations on the table was a challenge amidst the diversity of interests.

The strategic plan also needed to stem the tide of scandals about failing centres, mistreatment of children, stressed teachers, rapacious fees and unsafe environments. ERO reviews and evaluations indicated a number of centres were poor quality and/or failing.[156] Timely doctoral research findings were released mid-year 2018 from Mike Bedford and Ann Pairman, whose long involvement in the sector lent credibility to their concerns. Bedford's background in public health framed his thesis: 'Cold and Crowded: Early childhood education environments study'.[157] He labelled early childhood education in New Zealand as a 'hazard to child and teacher health', with over-crowding, noise pollution and temperatures frequently below the 16 degree standard.[158] Bedford challenged the statement of Ministry of Education spokesperson Katrina Kasey on Radio New Zealand (7 October 2015) that New Zealand early childhood standards were the highest in the world.[159] The regulation of 2.5sq m of activity space per child is in fact near the bottom of OECD charts.

Pairman's research considered the lived experience of children in centres, raising questions about building architecture, staff/child ratios and total group size, which could extend to 100 children.[160] She found noise levels a particular concern – 'despite open doors and soundproof material on the walls the din reached every part of the room at times'; and multiple-use spaces for sleeping, meals and play caused regimentation of children.[161] These studies sparked media coverage, including an article in the *New Zealand Listener* by Catherine Woulfe (13 June 2018) that cited 'experts' arguing that 'lax regulations must change' because 'the country's early education centres are falling short'.[162] Minister Chris Hipkins acknowledged the issues:

> With a degree of urgency, we now need to shift the whole conversation [from lifting participation] to the quality of a child's experiences in early childhood education … The reality is with all these things that you [cannot] just turn around overnight and say 'right here's a whole new set of rules' … But with a 10-year plan you can actually put in place a timeframe for it all to happen.

Woulfe concluded that 'change is in the wind – maybe!'[163]

The release of the draft plan in November 2018 caused a brief flurry of media interest, particularly for its $3.5 billion price tag. The ministry began a consultation round and invited submissions. The draft plan contained 23 recommendations with indicative timeframes over 10 years, framed around five goals intended to 'advance the early learning sector forward'.[164] The economic language is absent and instead focuses on the 'here and now' of children's lives and their 'right to enjoy a good life as New Zealanders'.[165] The recommendation to 'incentivise for 100% [qualified teachers] and regulate for

80% in teacher-led centres, leading to regulation for 100%' reinstates what was previously halted. Less explicit are recommendations around funding, teacher supply and salaries. There are calls for improved staffing ratios for infants and toddlers, and advice to be developed on group size and physical environments. Stronger accountability measures around licensing, monitoring and establishment are sought to curtail poor-quality services, marketplace expansion and competition. As a nod towards the minister's goal to 'turn the tide' towards 'quality public education' are recommendations for better support for community centres, co-location of community services alongside schools, and a recommendation to '*consider* setting up three state-owned early learning services with an associated research programme'.

The sector's early response was broadly supportive. On behalf of the ECC, Peter Reynolds applauded the focus on quality but disagreed with selective support for community services, calling for 'a level playing field across the sector, and for all parts to be treated equally'.[166] For NZK, Clare Wells warned:

> The success of the plan will rely on the timely implementation of policies and while some may take some years to achieve, others such as improving ratios, regulating qualifications, improving employment conditions, and planning service provision cannot wait. It is untenable to think we would create the same situation as was the case for the 10-year plan developed in 2002, which was never fully implemented …[167]

The extensive consultation process yielded broad support for most of the draft plan's recommendations, although not without many questions, concerns and suggestions.[168] While this support will encourage the government towards adopting many of the recommendations, there is also some disappointment that the draft is not sufficiently brave to 'turn the tide' with incentives to establish community services and disincentives to corporate investors; and/or deliver pay parity for teachers in early childhood; and/or forge ahead on the design and regulation of better environments; and/or to enshrine the right for preschool children to receive early childhood education. For example, some of New Zealand's leading scholars at the Early Years Research Centre at the University of Waikato applauded the direction of the plan but labelled recommendations around child ratios, timeframes, regulation of qualification levels and a move towards planned provision of early childhood services as too timid.[169] An upfront concern for this group was the Ministry of Education's abandonment of the terms ECE or ECEC for the narrower term 'early learning', and the renaming of children as 'learners'. Early childhood 'is not just about early learning, it is education in its broadest sense … grounded in discourses of democracy, equitable opportunities for all children to care, education and development,' they wrote.[170] The new rhetoric around learning and learners, adopted in the later years of the National government term across the compulsory education sector, diminishes the actions, interests, abilities, agency and needs of the young child and potentially limits how children are viewed and what is valued by adults, institutions and government agencies.

The first and second editions of *Politics in the Playground* each concluded in 2000 (p. 258) and 2008 (p. 303) at a crossroad. In 2000 we were waiting for a newly elected Labour government to deliver on its promises. In 2008 we were in the midst of an economic crisis, with the election of a National government imminent. Writing this chapter in the early months of 2019 also feels like waiting at a crossroad. Positive directions have been signposted, but we cannot be certain there is the degree of political resolve required to implement the recommendations or 'turn the tide'. Other education sector groups are competing for government resources, and the government has also signalled spending priorities around mental health and well-being.

We are at an intergenerational crossroads too. As an older generation of ECE protagonists retires, an energetic new generation is coming to the fore and taking up the mantle in crafting new policy directions.

Much is riding on the government's ability to 'deliver' and win a second term in office. Will the sector move in a direction that realises the plan's aspirations for young children to 'enjoy a good life, learn and thrive'?[171] Major advances in the sector have always required political courage to counter those within the sector who are resistant to quality requirements and accountability, and also political opponents seeking to reduce state involvement. But when advances do happen, against the odds, once-contentious changes gradually become the new norm.

REFERENCES

REFERENCES TO INTRODUCTION

1   Helen May, *The Discovery of Early Childhood*, NZCER Press, Wellington, 2001, 2013.
2   www.educationcounts.govt.nz/statistics/early-childhood-education
3   Ellen S. Key, *The Century of the Child*, Putnam, New York and London, 1900.
4   Allison James and Alan Prout, *Constructing and Reconstructing Childhood: Contemporary issues in the sociological study of childhood*, Falmer Press, London and Philadelphia, 1997, p. 9.
5   Nikolas Rose, *Governing the Soul: The shaping of the private self*, Routledge, New York and London, 1990. p.121.
6   Allison James, Chris Jenks and Alan Prout, *Theorizing Childhood*, Polity Press, Cambridge, 1998, p.17.
7   Berry Mayall, *Children, Health and Social Order*, Open University Press, Buckinghamshire, 1996, p.52.
8   Sue Middleton and Helen May, *Teachers Talk Teaching 1915–1995*, Early Childhood, Schools and Teachers' Colleges, Dunmore Press, Palmerston North, 1997.
9   C.E. Beeby, *The Biography of an Idea*, New Zealand Council for Educational Research, Wellington, 1992, p.51.
10 May, *The Discovery of Early Childhood*, p.19.
11 *Report of the Consultative Committee on PreSchool Educational Services: Preschool Education*, Department of Education, Wellington, 1947.
12 David Lange, *Before Five: Early childhood care and education in New Zealand*, Government Printer, Wellington, 1988.
13 *Report of the Early Childhood Care and Education Working Group: Education to be more*, Wellington, 1988.
14 *Report of the Consultative Committee on Pre-School Educational Services*, p.9.
15 Ministry of Education, *Pathways to the Future –Ngā Huarahi Arataki: A ten-year strategic plan for early childhood education 2002–2012*, Ministry of Education, Wellington, 2002.
16 ECE Taskforce, *An Agenda for Amazing Children: Final report of the ECE Taskforce*, NZ Government, Wellington, 2011.
17 Ministry of Education, *Te Taonga te Tamaiti – Every Child a Taonga: Strategic plan for early learning 2019–29*, Ministry of Education, Wellington, 2018.
18 Helen May, *Minding Children, Managing Men: Conflict and compromise in the lives of postwar Pakeha women*, Bridget Williams Books, Wellington, 1992.
19 Helen May Cook, *Mind That Child: Childcare as a social and political issue in New Zealand*, BlackBerry Press, Wellington, 1985.
20 C.E. Beeby, 'The Place of Myth in Educational Change', *NZ Listener*, 8 November 1986, pp.53–56.
21 Jane Kelsey, *The New Zealand Experiment: A world model for structural adjustment?*, Auckland University Press/Bridget Williams Books, 1995.
22 J. Boston, R. Dalziel and S. St John, *Redesigning the Welfare State in New Zealand: Problems policies prospects*, Oxford University Press, Auckland, 1999.
23 https://treasury.govt.nz/information-and-services/state-sector-leadership/cross-agency-initiatives/social-investment
24 Helen May, *School Beginnings: A nineteenth century colonial story*, NZCER Press, Wellington, 2005; *'I am five and I go to school': The work and play of early education in New Zealand*, Otago University Press, Dunedin, 2011.

REFERENCES TO CHAPTER ONE

1 *The First Conference of the World Council for Early Childhood Education, Conseil Mondial pour l'Education Préscolaire, Svetova Rada Pro Presdskolni Vychoevu*, Charles University, Prague, 26–28 August 1948, p.4.

2 James L. Hymes, *Understanding Your Child*, Prentice-Hall, New York, 1952.

3 Beverley Morris, *Understanding Children*, A.H. and A.W. Reed, Wellington, 1967.

4 Erica Burman, *Deconstructing Developmental Psychology*, Routledge, London and New York, 1994, pp.164–65.

5 Elly Singer, *Child-care and the Psychology of Development*, Routledge, London, 1992.

6 Nikolas Rose, *Governing the Soul, The Shaping of the Private Self*, Routledge, New York and London, 1990.

7 Valerie Walkerdine, 'Developmental Psychology and the Child-centred Pedagogy: The Insertion of Piaget into Early Education', in J. Heinriques (ed.), *Changing the Subject*, Methuen, London and New York, 1984, pp.153–202; Burman, 1994; Chris Jenks, *Childhood*, Routledge, London and New York, 1996; Gail Sloan Cannella, *Deconstructing Early Childhood Education, Social Justice and Revolution*, Peter Lang Publishing, New York, 1997; Allison James and Alan Prout, *Constructing and Reconstructing Childhood*, Falmer Press, London and Washington, 1997.

8 Arnold Gesell and Frances L. Ilg, *Infant and Child in the Culture Today. The Guidance of Development in Home and Nursery School*, New York, 1943.

9 Ibid., p.xi.

10 Arnold Gesell, *The First Five Years of Life. A Guide to the Study of the Preschool Child*, Harper and Brothers, New York and London, 1942, pp.310–11.

11 Rose, 1990, p.142 and p.147.

12 Esther Thelen and Karen Adolph, 'Arnold L. Gesell: The Paradox of Nature and Nurture', *Developmental Psychology*, vol.28, no.3, 1992, p.375.

13 Erik Erikson, *Childhood and Society*, W.W. Norton, New York, 1950.

14 Helen May, *The Discovery of Early Childhood*, Auckland University Press/Bridget Williams Books with NZCER, 1997; Evelyn Weber, *Ideas Influencing Early Childhood Education. A Theoretical Analysis*, Teachers' College Press, New York, 1984.

15 Roma Gans, Celia Stendler and Milley Almy, *Teaching Young Children*, World Books, New York, 1952; Emma Sheehy, *The Fives and Sixes Go to School*, Henry Holt, New York, 1954.

16 Erik Erikson, 'A Healthy Personality for Every Child', *A Digest of the Fact Finding Report to the Midcentury White House Conference on Children and Youth*, 1951, pp.6–25.

17 May, 1997.

18 John Dewey in J.J. Findlay (ed.), *The School and the Child; being Selections from the Educational Essays of John Dewey*, Blackie and Son, London [n.d.].

19 Susan Isaacs, *The Nursery Years*, Routledge, London, 1929; *Social Development in Young Children*, Routledge, London, 1932; *Intellectual Growth in Young Children*, Routledge, London, 1933; Elizabeth Young-Breuhl, *Anna Freud*, Papermac, London, 1991.

20 Noeline Alcorn, *To the Fullest Extent of His Powers. C.E. Beeby's Life in Education*, Victoria University Press, Wellington, 1999.

21 Interview with C.E. Beeby, 1990, by Helen May.

22 H.G.R. Mason, *Education Today and Tomorrow*, Department of Education, Wellington, 1944, p.16.

23 *Report of the Consultative Committee on Pre-School Educational Services*, 1947, pp.6–8.

24 *The First Conference of the World Council for Early Childhood Education*, 1948, p.4.

25 Ibid., p.5.

26 Ibid., p.4.

27 Sue Middleton and Helen May, *Teachers Talk Teaching 1915–1995. Early Childhood, Schools and Teachers' Colleges*, Dunmore Press, Palmerston North, 1997.

28 Helen May, 'Learning Through Play: Women, Progressivism and Early Childhood Education 1920s–1950s', in S. Middleton and A. Jones (eds), *Women and Education in Aotearoa 2*, Bridget Williams Books, Wellington, 1992.

29 Interviews with C.E. Beeby, 1990, and Moira Gallagher, 1990, by Helen May.

30 Ibid.
31 NA, W2312, E16/1/13 Part 2, Consultative Committee, Kindergarten.
32 NA, W2312, E2 25/1/2, pp.2–3, Notes for Director, 5 March 1956.
33 Interview with Moira Gallagher, 1990.
34 NA, W2312, E2 25/1/6, Reports by Supervisors of Preschool Services.
35 Interview with Joyce Barnes, 1994, by Helen May.
36 Interview with Isobel Christison, 1995, by Helen May, cited in Middleton and May, 1997, p.129.
37 I.J. Christison, *Almost Half a Life Time*, speech to the NZ Free Kindergarten Union (NZFKU) annual conference, 1979, p.2.
38 NA, W2312, E2 25/1/6, Reports by Supervisors of Preschool Services, 1948–51.
39 Beryl Hughes, *Flags and Building Blocks, Formality and Fun. One Hundred Years of Free Kindergarten in New Zealand*, NZFKU, Wellington, 1989, p.52.
40 Interview with Isobel Christison, 1995, by Helen May, cited in Middleton and May, 1997, p.130.
41 Hughes, 1989, p.52.
42 *Nelson Evening Mail*, 21 February 1952.
43 *Timaru Herald*, 9 September 1959.
44 NA, W2312, E2 25/1/6, Reports by Supervisors of Preschool Services, Wellington, 1956.
45 NA, W2312, E2 25/1/6, Reports by Supervisors of Preschool Services, Hamilton, 1959.
46 Isobel Christison, 'A Survey of Preschool Educational Services in New Zealand', unpublished MA thesis, Victoria University of Wellington, 1965, p.25.
47 Auckland Playcentre Association, *25th Anniversary, 1970 Annual Report*, 1970; Ailsa Densem, *The Playcentre Way*, NZPCF, Auckland, 1980; Canterbury Playcentre Association, *Ups and Downs. 50 Years of the Canterbury Playcentre Association 1941–1991*, Christchurch, 1991; Sue Stover (ed.), *Good Clean Fun: New Zealand's Playcentre Movement*, NZPCF, Auckland, 1998.
48 ATL, NZPCF Archive, Wellington Nursery Play Centre Association, *How a Playcentre Works*, Wellington, 1945.
49 NA, W2312, E2 25/1/2, Correspondence.
50 Ibid.
51 Gwen Somerset, *I Play and I Grow*, NZPCF, Wellington, 1949, p.19.
52 *NZ Play Centre Journal*, 21st jubilee number, no.7, May 1962, p.11; Auckland Play Centre Association, 1970, p.88.
53 ATL, NZPCF Archive, no.24 (Acc. 88–10, Box 2), Playcentre Submissions to Government, Notes from a Meeting at the Department of Education, 7 May 1954.
54 ATL, NZPCF Archive, no.24 (Acc. 88–10, Box 2), The Definition of the Nursery Play Centre Field (submission to Government), 1954.
55 NA, W4262, 1261, 25/1/21, Letter from Director of Education to NZFKU, 22 September 1960. Playcentre–kindergarten relations 1960 –.
56 Geraldine McDonald, 'Educational Innovation: The Case of the New Zealand Playcentre', *NZ Journal of Educational Studies*, vol.9, no.2, pp.153–65.
57 Gwen Somerset, *The Beginnings of Parent Involvement. Hugs and Hassles, Parents and Children Growing Together – He Awhi He Porearoa*, NZPCF, Auckland, 1990, p.14.
58 Stover, 1998, pp.59–61.
59 ATL, NZPCF Archive, no.24 (Acc. 88–10, Box 2), The Nursery Play Centre in New Zealand (n.d.).
60 Jack Shallcrass, 'Changing Attitudes to Children in the Past 30 Years', in *New Zealand Children Yesterday, Today and Tomorrow*, 1972 Lectures Delivered to the Association for the Study of Childhood, Wellington, 1973, p.5.
61 Somerset, 1949, p.11.
62 Interview with Geraldine McDonald, 1999, by Helen May.
63 Interview with Val Burns, 1994, by Helen May, cited in Middleton and May, 1997, p.137.
64 John Bowlby, *Maternal Care and Mental Health*, World Health Organisation, Geneva, 1952.

65 Lex Grey, *Introducing Play Centre to Parents*, Auckland Play Centre Association, 1957, pp.23–24.
66 Interview with Betty Armstrong, 1984, by Helen May.
67 Molly Ladd-Taylor, 'Mother-Work: Women', in *Child Welfare and the State, 1890–1930*, University of Illinois Press, Urbana, 1994; Heather Knox, 'Feminism, Femininity and Motherhood in Post-World War II New Zealand', unpublished MA thesis, Massey University, 1995.
68 Helen May, *Minding Children, Managing Men. Conflict and Compromise in the Lives of Post-war Pakeha Women*, Bridget Williams Books, Wellington, 1992.
69 Densem, 1980, p.6.
70 Stover, 1998, p.49.
71 Helen May, 'The Early Post-war Years for Women. An Interview with Beverley Morris', *Women's Studies Journal*, vol.5 no.2, December 1989, p.73.
72 Lex Grey, *A Workshop on Leadership* and *Leading a Group*, Auckland Play Centre Association, Auckland, 1967.
73 Densem, 1980, pp.14–16.
74 Knox, 1995, p.82.
75 Stover, 1998, p.vii.
76 Geraldine McDonald, 'Educational Innovation: The Case of the New Zealand Playcentre', *NZ Journal of Educational Studies*, vol.9 no.2, 1974, p.160.
77 *NZ Herald*, 5 July 1956.
78 Kerry Bethell, 'Skirting the Boundaries. The Impact of Marriage and Domesticity on Women's Perceptions of Kindergarten and Primary Teaching as a Career in Postwar New Zealand', unpublished M.Ed. thesis, Massey University, 1998.
79 Kerry Bethell, 'Research Report: Skirting the Boundaries: Marriage, Motherhood and Kindergarten Teaching in New Zealand', *Early Education*, no.19, Autumn 1999, p.33.
80 Hughes, 1989, p.44.
81 Unsourced newspaper advertisement, circa 1960s, given to author from Phyllis Varcoe's clippings scrapbook, Dunedin.
82 *NZ Herald*, 5 July 1956.
83 NA, W2312, E2 25/1/2, Kindergarten General Correspondence.
84 Phyllis Varcoe, *New Zealand Kindergarten Teachers' Association Newsletter*, May 1958, p.2.
85 NA, W2312, E2 25/1/6, Reports by Supervisors of Preschool Services.
86 *Nelson Evening Mail*, 21 February 1952.
87 *Timaru Herald*, 12 July 1956.
88 'Preschool Education Recognised as Basis of Community Living', *Timaru Herald*, 12 July 1956.
89 Elsa Walters, *Activity and Experience in the Infant School*, National Froebel Foundation, London (1951), fifth edn, 1963, p.6.
90 Ibid., 1963, p.3.
91 Cathy Roxborough, 'The Developmental Approach to Learning – An Historical Survey from its Beginnings to the Present Day', unpublished paper, 1970, p.5.
92 Gesell and Ilg, 1943.
93 IECS, VUW, Moira Gallagher Papers.
94 Marie Bell, 'Working for Women, Working for Children, Working for Change', interview with Helen May, *Te Timatanga*, vol.10, no.2, Spring 1992, p.24.
95 Roxborough, 1970, p.6.
96 NA, AAAD.980, 7t, Submission relating to topic no.9, 1960.
97 NA, AAAD.980, 7t, Submission from the Combined Staff Wellington Teachers' College, Kelburn and Karori West Normal Schools, 1960.
98 NA, AAAD.980, 1c, Auckland Nursery Playcentre Supervisors, 1960.
99 Interview with Lex Grey, 1989, by Helen May.
100 Edna Mellor, *Education Through Experience in the Infant School Years*, Basil Blackwell, Oxford, 1950.
101 Interview with Val Burns, 1994, by Helen May, cited in Middleton and May, 1997, p.124.

102 Sue Kedgley, *Mum's the Word: The Untold Story of Motherhood in New Zealand*, Random House, Auckland, 1996.

103 Knox, 1995; Bronwyn Dalley, *Family Matters. Child Welfare in Twentieth-Century New Zealand*, Auckland University Press, 1998; Margaret McClure, *A Civilised Community. A History of Social Security in New Zealand 1898–1998*, Auckland University Press with the Historical Branch of the Department of Internal Affairs, Auckland, 1998.

104 Christina Hardyment, *Dream Babies. Child Care from Locke to Spock*, Jonathan Cape, London, 1983; Elizabeth Mellor, *Stepping Stones. The Development of Early Childhood Services in Australia*, Harcourt Brace Jovanovich, Sydney, 1990; Cathy Irwin and Elaine Sharland, 'From Bodies to Minds in Childcare Literature: Advice to Parents in Interwar Britain', in R. Cooter (ed.), *In the Name of the Child: Health and Welfare 1880–1940*, Routledge, London, 1942.

105 Truby King, *Feeding and Care of Baby*, Whitcombe & Tombs, Melbourne, 1937, p.180.

106 John Watson, *Psychological Care of the Infant and Child*, Allen and Unwin, London and New York, 1928.

107 Helen Deem and Nora Fitzgibbon, *Modern Mothercraft*, Royal New Zealand Society for the Health of Women and Children, Dunedin, 1945 and 1953.

108 Moira Gallagher, 'Other Important Aspects of Development', in Deem and Fitzgibbon, 1953, p.139.

109 Knox, 1995.

110 William Graebner, 'The Unstable World of Benjamin Spock: Social Engineering in a Democratic Culture, 1917–1950', *Journal of American History*, 1980, vol.67, no.3, pp.612–29.

111 *NZ Listener*, 11 September 1953.

112 Benjamin Spock, *The Common Sense Book of Baby and Child Care*, Duell, Sloan and Pearce, New York, 1946, p.267. Spock, like most advisers of childrearing then, wrote as if all children were male.

113 Ibid., pp.247–69.

114 Martha Wolfenstein, 'The Emergence of Fun Morality', *Journal of Social Issues*, 1951, vol.7, p.15.

115 IECS, VUW PCNZ Archive, Box 8.1, 1953–1960 Newspaper Clippings.

116 *New York Times*, 28 May 1968, p.46.

117 Spock, 1946, p.20.

118 Mary Dobbie, *The Trouble With Women. The Story of Parents' Centre New Zealand*, Cape Catley, Whatamonga Bay, 1990; Knox, 1995; IECS, VUW, PCNZ Archive, *Parents' Centre Bulletin* 1954–.

119 Dobbie, 1990, p.23.

120 May, 'Interview with Beverley Morris', 1989, p.68.

121 Ibid.

122 Dobbie, 1990, p.5.

123 Knox, 1995.

124 Cited by Helen Brew in many talks and submissions. Reprinted from *American Journal of Nursing*, October 1949.

125 Dobbie, 1990, p.2.

126 Maurice Bevan-Brown, 'The Foundations of Mental Health', *NZ Parent and Child*, vol.2, no.3, 1954–55, pp.28–29.

127 Bowlby, 1952.

128 Knox, 1995.

REFERENCES TO CHAPTER TWO

1 Helen May, *Minding Children, Managing Men. Conflict and Compromise in the Lives of Postwar Pakeha Women*, Bridget Williams Books, Wellington, 1992.

2 Margaret McClure, *A Civilised Community. A History of Social Security in New Zealand 1898–1998*, Auckland University Press with the Historical Branch of the Department of Internal Affairs, Auckland, 1998, p.153.

3 NA, W2312, E2 25/1/6, Reports by Supervisors of Preschool Services.

4 *The New Zealand Playcentre. Its Meaning and Working in the Wellington Play Centres' Association*, Wellington, 1964, p.2.

5 Maurice Bevan-Brown, *The Foundations of Mental Health*, The Caxton Press, Christchurch, 1956, p.10.

6 Talcott Parsons, *The Social System*, Routledge and Kegan Paul, London, 1951.

7 Bronwyn Dalley, *Family Matters. Child Welfare in Twentieth-Century New Zealand*, Auckland University Press, Auckland 1998, p.164.

8 Ibid., p.173.

9 Nikolas Rose, *Governing the Soul. The Shaping of the Private Self*, Routledge, New York and London, 1990.

10 Berry Mayall, *Children, Health and Social Order*, Open University Press, Buckinghamshire, 1996, p.6.

11 Parsons, 1951, p.207.

12 R.D. Laing, *The Politics of Experience*, Penguin, 1967.

13 May, *Minding Children, Managing Men*, 1992.

14 Department of Labour, *Women in the Workforce, Facts and Figures*, Wellington, 1980.

15 *Hansard*, vol.303, 24 June 1954.

16 *Hansard*, vol.303, 3 August 1954.

17 *Hansard*, vol.304, 16 September 1954.

18 NA, W2312, E2 25/1/6, Reports by Supervisors of Preschool Services.

19 John Bowlby, *Maternal Care and Mental Health*, World Health Organisation, Geneva, 1952, p.157.

20 Elly Singer, *Child-care and the Psychology of Development*, Routledge, London and New York, 1992, p.91.

21 Melanie Klein, *Love, Guilt and Reparation and Other Works 1921–1945*, Delacarete Press, S. Lawrence, New York, 1975.

22 Bowlby, 1952, p.53.

23 John Bowlby, *Child Care and the Growth of Love*, Pelican, London, 1953, p.11.

24 Ibid., p.76.

25 Bowlby, 1952, p.73.

26 *Dominion*, 21 September 1956.

27 Geraldine McDonald, 'Maternal Deprivation, Fact or Fallacy?', *Set 77*, no.1, item 3, 1977.

28 Michael Rutter, *Maternal Deprivation Reassessed*, Penguin, Harmondsworth, 1972; *Report of the Early Childhood Care and Education Working Group: Education to be More*, Wellington, 1988, p.11.

29 Anne Dally, *Inventing Motherhood. The Consequences of an Ideal*, Burnett Books, London, 1992.

30 Bruno Bettelheim, *Children of the Dream. Communal Child-rearing and its Implications for Society*, Macmillan, New York, 1969.

31 Sue Kedgley, *Mum's the Word. The Untold Story of Motherhood in New Zealand*, Random House, Auckland, 1996, p.180.

32 James Robertson, *Young Children in Hospital*, Tavistock, London, 1958, p.4.

33 Interview with Marie Bell, 1999, by Helen May.

34 Helen May Cook, *Mind That Child. Childcare as a Social and Political Issue in New Zealand*, BlackBerry Press, Wellington, 1985; Helen May, *The Discovery of Early Childhood*, Auckland University Press/Bridget Williams Books with NZCER, 1997.

35 Penny Fenwick, 'The New Zealand Family Planning Association, Its Growth and Development', unpublished MA thesis, Victoria University of Wellington, 1977.

36 *Report of the Consultative Committee on Pre-School Educational Services*, 1947, p.3.

37 NA, W2312, 1953, 35a. Part 2 Consultative Committee, Kindergarten.

38 May Cook, 1985.

39 *NZ Woman's Weekly*, 28 November 1946.

40 *NZ Woman's Weekly*, undated article in NZCA Clippings file, IECS, VUW NZCA Archive.

41 *Here and Now*, August 1952.

42 *NZ Woman's Weekly,* 28 November 1946.
43 May, 1997.
44 Auckland Playcentre Association, *25th Anniversary, 1970 Annual Report.*
45 Anne Frizelle, 'The Emergence of New Zealand Daycare Policy and the Role of Partisan Influence to the Present Day', unpublished paper, 1981.
46 *Here and Now,* August 1952.
47 *Hansard,* vol.304, 10 August 1951.
48 *Hansard,* vol.317, 30 July 1958.
49 *Hansard,* vol.316, 18 July 1958.
50 *Hansard,* vol.317, 6 August 1958.
51 *NZ Herald,* 21 August 1959.
52 Child Welfare Division, *Annual Report,* 1961, p.15.
53 NA, W1982, CW1 5/6/7 *Private Institutions, Provisional Licences.* 1961–
54 Child Welfare Division, *Annual Reports* E4. 1961–71.
55 Geraldine McDonald, 'The Politics of Childcare', *Research Papers '78, Women's Studies,* Rosemary Seymour (ed), Women's Studies Association, Hamilton, 1978, p.70.
56 IECS, VUW, NZCA Archive, NZACCC *First Conference Report, 1964.*
57 Sonja Davies, *Bread and Roses,* ANZ Book Co. Ltd with Fraser Books, Auckland, 1984, p.143.
58 Ibid.
59 IECS, VUW, NZCA Archive, NZACCC, *1964 President's Report.*
60 Interview with Sonja Davies, 1983, by Helen May.
61 IECS, VUW, NZCA Archive, speech by Sonja Davies, nd, circa 1964–69.
62 Davies, 1984, p.144.
63 Ibid., p.145.
64 Ibid.
65 IECS, VUW, NZCA Archive, *Report of Meeting of Nursery Care* by Jessie Donald, 1963, p.1.
66 Interview with Marge Williams, 1996, by Helen May.
67 Ibid.
68 Marge Williams, cited in Sue Middleton and Helen May, *Teachers Talk Teaching 1915–1995. Early Childhood, Schools and Teachers' Colleges,* Dunmore Press, Palmerston North, 1997, p.252.
69 Interview with Joan Kennett, by Helen May, 1994.
70 Joan Kennett, cited in Middleton and May, 1997, p.252.
71 Interview with Margaret Lamb, 1996, by Helen May, cited in Middleton and May, 1997, p.253.
72 IECS, VUW, NZCA Archive, NZACCC, *1967 President's Report,* p.2.
73 IECS, VUW, NZCA Archive, NZACCC, *1970 President's Report,* p.1.
74 Donald Winnicott, *The Child and the Family,* Tavistock Publications, 1957, pp.3–4.
75 Ibid., p.142.
76 Donald Winnicott, *The Child, the Family and the Outside World,* Pelican Books, Harmondsworth, 1964, pp.227–31.
77 This was probably the earlier report, 'Emotional Maladjustment in New Zealand School Children', *National Education,* March 1951, p.64.
78 Sandra Coney, *Every Girl. A Social History of the YWCA in Auckland,* YWCA, Auckland, 1986, p.251.
79 M. Bevan-Brown, *Mental Health and Personality Disorder,* Dunford Publications, Christchurch, 1961, p.211.
80 Ibid., pp.212–13.
81 New Zealand Government, *Report on Moral Delinquency in Children and Adolescents,* Government Printer, Wellington, 1954 (Mazengarb report).
82 *NZ Woman's Weekly,* 15 September 1955.
83 1956 Department of Education *Annual Report,* E1, pp.7–8.
84 *Hansard,* vol.306, 9 August 1955.

85 *Report of the Commission of Education in New Zealand 1962*, Government Printer, Wellington (Currie report).

86 Dugald J. McDonald, 'Children and Young Persons in New Zealand Society', in P. Koopman-Boyden (ed.), *Families in New Zealand Society*, Methuen, New Zealand, 1978, p.50.

87 Singer, 1992, p.99.

88 Dalley, 1998.

89 Anne Else, *A Question of Adoption. Closed Stranger Adoption in New Zealand, 1944–1974*, Bridget Williams Books, Wellington, 1991.

90 Ibid.

91 Bowlby, 1953, chapters 10–12.

92 Ibid., p.128.

93 NA, W1982, CW1 4/6, Unmarried Mother Policy, Report to Parliament by by Child Welfare Division, 1959.

94 Interview with Major Thelma Smith, 1999, by Helen May.

95 Anne Else, 'The Motherhood of Man Movement and Stranger Adoption', in B. Brookes, C. Macdonald and M. Tennant (eds), *Women in History 2*, Bridget Williams Books, Wellington, 1992, pp.225–53.

96 *New Zealand Listener*, 7 August 1964.

97 NA, W1982, CW1 4/6, Unmarried Mother Policy, undated clipping in reply to radio programme 'Out of Wedlock', August 1964.

98 Anne Else in Brookes, Macdonald and Tennant, 1992, p.226.

99 Interview with Major Eunice Eichler, 1999, by Helen May.

100 NA, W1982, CW1 4/6, Unmarried Mother Policy.

101 Interview with Major Thelma Smith, 1999, by Helen May.

102 NA, W1982, CW1 4/6, Unmarried Mother Policy, Report to Parliament by Child Welfare Division, 1960.

103 May, 1997.

104 NA, W1931, CW1 2/8/5, Infant Life Protection Returns 1959.

105 NA, W1988, CW1 3/1/6, Applications for Licensing under the Infant Act.

106 NA, W1988, CW1 4/5/2, Breaches of Act, 29/5/1958.

107 Else, 1991.

108 Ibid., p.68.

109 Anne Else, in Brookes, Macdonald and Tennant, 1992, p.247.

110 For example, Anglican St Barnabas Baby Home in Seatoun, Wellington; Salvation Army Nest in Hamilton.

111 Society for Research on Women, *The Unmarried Mother, Problems Involved in Keeping Her Child*, Wellington, 1969, p.43.

REFERENCES TO CHAPTER THREE

1 Ian Pool, *The Maori Population of New Zealand*, Oxford University Press and Auckland University Press, Auckland, 1977.

2 Department of Maori Affairs, *The Maori Today*, Wellington, 1949, p.5.

3 Ibid., p.4.

4 Ibid., p.1.

5 Ian Pool, *Te Iwi Maori. A New Zealand Population Past, Present and Projected*, Auckland University Press, Auckland, 1991.

6 Pool, 1977.

7 Fred M. Hechinger (ed.), *Preschool Education Today*, Doubleday and Company, New York, 1966; B.J. Bloom, A. Davis, and R. Hess, *Compensatory Education for Cultural Deprivation*, Holt, Rinehart and Winston, New York, 1965.

8 Basil Bernstein, 'Language and Social Class', *British Journal of Sociology*, vol.11, 1960.

9 William Labov, *The Study of NonStandard English*, National Council of Teachers of English, Illinois, 1968.

10 Jerome S. Bruner, *The Process of Education*, Harvard University Press, Cambridge, Mass., 1960; Maya Pines, *Revolution in Children's Learning. The Years from Birth to Five*, Allen Lane, Penguin Press, 1966.

11 H.G.R. Mason, *Education Today and Tomorrow*, Government Printer, Wellington, 1944.

12 Ibid., p.55.

13 Department of Maori Affairs, 1949, p.20.

14 In 1944 there were 156 native schools, mainly in rural Māori areas, catering for predominantly (but not exclusively) 11,300 Māori children. They were administered directly by the Department of Education. There were also 13,500 Māori children attending schools under the control of Education Boards (Mason, 1944).

15 Helen May, *The Discovery of Early Childhood*, Auckland University Press/Bridget Williams Books with NZCER, 1997.

16 NA, Acc W2312, E2 25/1/6, Reports by supervisors of preschool services.

17 AKA archives, Myers Park.

18 May, 1997, p.152.

19 E. Beaglehole and P. Beaglehole, *Some Modern Maoris*, NZCER, Wellington, 1946.

20 Ibid., pp.341–42.

21 Ailsa Densem, *The Playcentre Way*, NZPF, Auckland, 1980.

22 Ibid., p.343.

23 James E. Ritchie, *The Making of a Maori. A Case Study of a Changing Community*, A.H. and A.W. Reed, Wellington, 1963.

24 Pat Metekingi served with the Maori Battalion and was killed in Italy in 1944.

25 Margaret McMillan, *The Nursery School*, Dent, London, 1919; Susan Isaacs, *The Nursery Years*, Routledge, London, 1929.

26 Interview with Marie Bell, 1999, by Helen May.

27 Cedric Gardiner, 'Maori Infant Mortality', *New Zealand Medical Journal*, 1959, vol.58, pp.321–60.

28 Pool, 1977, p.181–85.

29 Department of Health, *The Maori Mother and Her Child*, Government Printer, Wellington, 1942, p.2.

30 Heather Knox, 'Feminism, Femininity and Motherhood in Post-World War II New Zealand', unpublished MA thesis, Massey University, 1995, pp.49-50.

31 *Report of the Consultative Committee on Infant and Pre-school Health Services*, Government Printer, Wellington, 1959.

32 Mira Szazy, quoted in V. Myers, *Head and Shoulders. Successful New Zealand Women Talk to Virginia Myers*, Penguin Books, Auckland, 1986, p.240.

33 Tania Rei, 'Maori Women's Welfare League, Te Ropu Wahine Maori Toko i te Ora', in A. Else (ed.), *Women Together. A History of Women's Organisations in New Zealand. Ngā Rōpū Wāhine o te Motu*, Daphne Brasell Associates and the Historical Branch, Dept. of Internal Affairs, Wellington, 1993, pp.34–38.

34 Tania Rei, 'Tatau Tatau – Let Us Be United!', in Sandra Coney (ed), *Standing in the Sunshine*, Viking, Auckland, 1993, pp.132–33.

35 Tania Rei, Geraldine McDonald and Ngahuia Te Awekotuku, 'Nga Ropu Wahine Maori – Maori Women's Organisations', in Else (ed.), *Women Together*, 1993, pp.3–14.

36 Ibid., also p.197. Geraldine McDonald later wrote: 'I have been told of Maori women who were involved in preschool work in the 1950s, but there is no official record of Maori participation.' See 'Preschool and Parent Education for Minorities', in *Equality of Opportunity Through Education*, Association for the Study of Childhood, 1972, p.58.

37 James Ritchie, 1963; Jane and James Ritchie, 'Children', in E. Schwimmer (ed.), *The Maori People in the Nineteen-Sixties*, Blackwood and Janet Paul, Auckland, 1968, pp.311–27; Jane and James Ritchie, *Child Rearing Patterns in New Zealand*, A.H. and A.W. Reed, Wellington, 1970.

38 Jane and James Ritchie in Schwimmer (ed.), 1968, p.316.

39 Ibid.

40 Jane and James Ritchie, 1970, p.40.

41 J.M. Barrington and T.H. Beaglehole, *Maori Schools in a Changing Society*, NZCER, Wellington, 1974, p.242.

42 Richard Benton, *The Flight of the Amokura*, NZCER, Wellington, 1981, p.16.

43 J.K. Hunn, *Report on the Department of Maori Affairs*, Government Printer, Wellington, 1960.

44 Ibid., p.15.

45 Department of Maori Affairs, *Integration of Maori and Pakeha*, no.1. Series of Special Studies, Government Printer, Wellington, 1962.

46 Maori Synod of the Presbyterian Church, *A Maori View of the 'Hunn Report'*, Maori Presbyterian Bookroom, Christchurch, 1961, p.7.

47 Hunn, *Report*, 1960, pp.22, 28.

48 Maori Education Foundation, second annual report, 1962, pp.10–11.

49 Richard Benton, *Research into the English Language Difficulties of Maori School Children 1963–64*, Maori Education Foundation, Wellington, 1966, p.96.

50 Ian H. Barham, *The English Vocabulary and Sentence Structure of Maori Children*, NZCER, Wellington, 1965, pp.57–58.

51 Benton, 1966; Richard Benton, 'E Rua Reo Ma te Kura? – Bilingual Preschool?', *Playcentre Journal*, no.28, 1973, pp.8–9.

52 Schwimmer (ed.), 1968, Chapter One.

53 Ibid., p.44.

54 Ibid., p.28.

55 Ibid., p.33, pp.56–57.

56 '"Sylvia", The Maori Infant Room, Organic Reading and the Key Vocabulary', *National Education*, 1 December 1955, p.392.

57 Personal communication, Sydney Clemens, 1990; Sydney Gurewitz Clemens, *Pay Attention to the Children. Lessons for Teachers and Parents from Sylvia Ashton-Warner*, Rattle OK Publications, California, 1996.

58 Lilian Katz, 'Preface', in Clemens, 1996, p.iv.

59 Clemens, 1996, p.7.

60 Lynley Hood, *Sylvia! The Biography of Sylvia Ashton-Warner*, Viking, Auckland, 1988, p.115.

61 Ibid., p.118.

62 Ibid.

63 Sylvia Ashton-Warner, *Teacher*, Penguin Books, Harmondsworth, 1963, p.206.

64 Interview with Arthur Fieldhouse, 1990, by Helen May.

65 Hood, 1988, p.143.

66 Jack Richards, 'Language Problems of Maori Children', *Comment*, no.36, October 1968, p.31.

67 G.A. (Alan) Simpson worked with Elwyn Richardson's art project in the far north, described in the book *In the Early World*, NZCER, Wellington, 1964.

68 G.A. Simpson, 'The Maori Child's First School Year', *Education*, no.1, vol.6, 1957, p.23.

69 NA, Acc W2312, E2 25/1/2/, Correspondence, Part 2, 1956–59.

70 AKA archives, clippings file, Press Assn, 'Kindergartens for Maoris urged', 6 July 1959.

71 Miria Pewhairangi, 'Maori Self Assertion in Pre-school Education 1961–1982', *Third Early Childhood Convention Papers*, Ngaruawahia, 1983, p.104.

72 Iriaka Ratana MP called both of these centres Playcentres in a report to parliament, 11 July 1961. Kaiwhaiki did not become a fully affiliated Playcentre until 1964. Putiki originally had associations with Playcentre, but soon became a private kindergarten on the marae. Centres calling themselves Playcentres do not necessarily tally with official Playcentre records.

73 Alison Stephenson, 'Taking Playcentre to the Pa. Reflections on the 1960s Initiative to Establish Playcentres in Maori Communities in the Wanganui Area', research essay for EDUC 528, Victoria University of Wellington, 1996.

74 NA, ABEP Preschool Accession, W4262, Box 1262, 25/1/22, Maori Education, Parts 1–5, 1961–81.

75 Geraldine McDonald, *Maori Mothers and Preschool Education*, NZCER, Wellington, 1973, p.2.
76 *Hansard*, vol.326, 11 July 1961.
77 Interview with Elaine Bray, in S. Stover (ed.), *Good Clean Fun. New Zealand's Playcentre Movement*, NZ Playcentre Federation, Auckland, 1988, p.164.
78 MEF second annual report, 1962, cited in Stephenson, 1996.
79 Kathleen Cameron-Chemis, *The Maori Education Foundation. A History and Analysis*, Delta Research Monograph no.5, Department of Education, Massey University, 1981.
80 Jane and James Ritchie, 'Pre-requisites for a Maori Pre-school Service', *Playcentre Journal*, 1962, no.7, p.22.
81 S. Stover et al., 'Voices from the Heartland of the Treaty', in Stover, 1998, pp.63–76.
82 Northland Playcentre Association AGM, October 1966, cited in Stover, 1998, p.66.
83 I.J. Christison, 'The Story Behind the Figures', *Maori Preschool Planning Conference Report*, NZ Maori Council, 1968, Appendix 1, pp.i–v.
84 Pewhairangi, 1982, p.104.
85 Stephenson, 1996.
86 NA, ABEP Preschool Accession, W4262, 25/1/22, Box 1262, Maori Education.
87 Christison, 1968.
88 Lex Grey, 'I Hope You Never Try to Teach a Child. But I Hope You will Spend your Time Learning from Children', in H. May and J. Mitchell (eds), *A Celebration of Early Childhood, Vol 2*, Department of Early Childhood Care and Education, University of Waikato, 1992, p.40.
89 NA, W4262, Box 1262 25/1/22, Maori Education, Part 1, Letter from Palmerston North Play Centres Association to Miss Gallagher, 2 September 1961.
90 Stover, 1998, p.70.
91 McDonald, 1973, pp.139–40.
92 Stover, 1998, p.68.
93 Benton, 1981.
94 Jane Ritchie, *Chance to be Equal*, Cape Catley, Whatamongo Bay, 1978, p.11.
95 Maureen Locke, 'I Was Born and Bred in Rotorua at Ohinemutu Among the Mudpools', in H. May and J. Mitchell (eds), *A Celebration of Women in Early Childhood*, Centre for Early Childhood, Hamilton Teachers College, 1989, pp.67–68.
96 Interview with Geraldine McDonald, 1999, by Helen May.
97 NA, W4262, 17/4/6/ Box 891, Maori Education, Report of the National Advisory Committee on Maori Education, 1970, p.4.
98 Pewhairangi, 1982, p.104.
99 NA, W4262, 25/1/22, Box 1262, Maori Education, Hine Potaka and Betty Brown, Te Roopu Awhina Tamariki, unsourced article
100 NA, W4262, 25/1/22, Box 1262, Maori Education, M.J. Holroyd (Senior Maori Welfare Officer Hamilton), Maori Family Education Association, 3 July 1974.
101 NA, W4262, 25/1/22, W4262, Box 1262, Maori Education, Submission to the Committee of Enquiry into Preschool Education, from the Maori Family Education (Waikato–Maniopoto).
102 Family Pre-school Groups, Appendix 3, *Maori Preschool Planning Conference Report*, NZ Maori Council, 1968.
103 Interview with Leone Shaw, 1994, by Helen May, cited in Sue Middleton and Helen May, *Teachers Talk Teaching 1915–1995. Early Childhood, Schools and Teachers' Colleges*, Dunmore Press, Palmerston North, 1997, pp.197–98.
104 Ibid.
105 Interview with Geraldine McDonald, 1999, by Helen May.
106 Interview with Georgina Kerr, 1994, by Helen May, cited in Middleton and May, 1997.
107 Middleton and May, 1997.
108 *The Commission on Education in New Zealand*, Government Printer, Wellington, 1962, p.429.

109 NA, W4262, 25/1/22, Box 1262, Maori Education Waiomio School Scheme Concerning Pre-school Children; A Statement Concerning the Attendance of Pre-school Children Aged Four and a Half Plus Years in Maori Infant Rooms, 15 August 1967.

110 Christison, 1968, p.iv.

111 *Hansard*, vol.352, 12 September 1967.

112 For example, Lex Grey, Miria Pewhairangi, Leone Shaw, Geraldine McDonald.

113 NA, ABEP Preschool Accession, W4262, holds various submissions from Maori Family Education Association, Te Roopu Awhina Tamariki, Maori Preschool Committee of the National Committee on Maori Education.

114 NA, W4262, 25/1/22, Box 1262, Maori Education, Letters, 16 August and 9 October 1967.

115 Jan Staffen, 'Taking the Initiative', *Te Kaunihera Maori*, January 1968, pp.45–47.

116 *Report of the Consultative Committee on Preschool Education*, Department of Education, 1971, p.37

117 Ibid., p.2.

118 Geraldine McDonald, *Maori Family Education Project, Report One*, NZCER, Wellington, 1976.

119 Anne Smith and David Swain, *Childcare in New Zealand. People, Programmes, Politics*, Allen and Unwin, Wellington, 1988, pp.117–18.

120 Geraldine McDonald, *Early Childhood Education in New Zealand. What is it? How Goes it for the Maoris?* NZCER, Wellington, 1976.

121 Ranginui Walker, 'Politics and Performance', *NZ Listener*, 11 June 1990, pp.98–99.

122 Jane and James Ritchie, in Schwimmer (ed.), 1968, p.327.

123 B.J. Bloom, *Stability and Change in Human Characteristics*, Wiley, New York, 1964; J.M. Hunt, *Intelligence and Experience*, Ronald Press, New York, 1961.

124 Nikolas Rose, *Governing the Soul. The Shaping of the Private Self*, Routledge, New York and London, 1990, p.184.

125 12 February 1965. Announcement reprinted in *Young Children*, September 1990, p.41.

126 Ibid., p.21.

127 Ibid., p.78.

128 Elly Singer, *Child-care and the Psychology of Development*, Routledge, London, 1992, p.110.

129 Bloom, David and Hess, 1965.

130 *Project Head Start* (nine titles), Office of Economic Opportunity, Washington DC, 1967.

131 Ibid., *The Staff*, p.3.

132 Ibid., *Daily Program 1*, p.9.

133 Ibid., *Daily Program 111*, p.46.

134 Westinghouse Learning Corporation, *The Impact of Head Start. An Evaluation of the Effects of Head Start on Children's Cognitive and Affective Development* (Report to the Office of Economic Opportunity), Clearinghouse for Federal, Scientific and Technical Information, Washington DC, 1969.

135 A.R. Jensen, 'How Much Can We Boost IQ and Scholastic Achievement?', *Harvard Educational Review*, 1969, vol.39, p.1.

136 E. Zigler and J. Valentine (eds), *Project Head Start. A Legacy of the War on Poverty*, The Free Press, New York, 1979, Part V.

137 Urie Bronfenbrenner, 'Is Early Intervention Effective?' *Day Care and Early Education 2*, November, 1974, pp.14–18. His optimism regarding the responsiveness of children to environmental change was ill-founded.

138 Urie Bronfenbrenner, 'Developmental Research, Public Policy and the Ecology of Childhood', *Child Development*, vol.45, no.1, pp.1–5; Urie Bronfenbrenner, *The Ecology of Human Development*, Harvard University Press, Cambridge, Mass., 1979.

139 Consortium for Longitudinal Studies, *As the Twig is Bent*, Erlbaum, London, 1983; L.J. Schweinhart, H.V. Barnes and D.P. Weikart, *Significant Benefits. The High/Scope Perry Preschool Study Through Age 27*, High/Scope Press, Ypsilanti, Mich., 1993.

140 Zigler and Valentine, 1979, p.xxiii.

141 M.D.S. Ainsworth, and S.M. Bell, 'Mother–Infant Interactions and the Development of

Competence', in K. Connolly and J. Bruner (eds), *The Growth of Competence*, Academic Press, London, 1974, p.116.

142 Kathie Irwin, 'Compensatory Education, Head Start and Affirmative Action. Implications for Maori Education in New Zealand', in D. Phillips, G. Lealand and G. McDonald (eds), *The Impact of American Ideas on New Zealand's Educational Policy, Practice and Thinking*, Wellington, NZ–US Educational Foundation/NZCER, 1989, pp.122–23.

143 Pines, 1966, p.26.

144 Ibid., p.31.

145 Barbel Inhelder and Jean Piaget, *The Growth of Logical Thinking*, Basic Books, New York, 1958.

146 Evelyn Weber, *Ideas Influencing Early Childhood Education. A Theoretical Analysis*, Teachers' College Press, New York, 1984, p.15.

147 Jean Piaget, 'Piaget Takes a Teacher's Look', *Learning*, vol.2, October 1973, p.2.

148 Louise Derman-Sparks, *A Developmental Approach. Implications for Teaching*, Pacific Oaks Occasional Papers, Los Angeles, 1970.

149 Millie Almy, 'Piaget in Action', *Young Children*, 31 January 1976, p.96.

150 Bruner, 1960, p.33.

151 Bloom, Davis and Hess, 1965.

152 Basil Bernstein, 'Language and Social Class', *British Journal of Sociology*, vol.XI, no.3, 1960, pp.15–21.

153 Pines, 1966, p.161.

154 *Maori Children and the Teacher*, Department of Education, Wellington, 1972, pp.34–37.

155 J.B. Pride, 'Maori Children and Bernstein: A Linguistic Appraisal', and Anne Salmond, '"Maori English" and the "Restricted Code"', *Education*, vol.23 no.9, 1974, pp.17–20 and pp.21–22.

156 Basil Bernstein, 'Education Cannot Compensate for Society', *New Society*, 26 February 1970.

157 Pines, 1966, p.163.

158 Kathie Irwin in Phillips, Lealand and McDonald (eds), 1989, p.125.

159 Pines, 1966, p.3.

160 Carl Bereiter and Siegfried Engelmann, *Teaching Disadvantaged Children in Preschool*, Prentice-Hall, Englewood Cliffs, NJ, 1966.

161 Carl Bereiter, Siegfried Engelmann, Jean Osborn and Philip A. Reidford, 'An Academically Oriented Pre-school for Culturally Deprived Children', in F. Hechinger (ed.), *Pre-school Education Today. New Approaches to Teaching Three, Four and Five-year-olds*, Doubleday, Garden City, NY, 1966, pp.105–35 (see p.107).

162 Pines, 1996, p.46.

163 Labov, 1968, p.1.

164 John E. Watson, *Accommodating the Polynesian Heritage of the Maori Child. A New Zealand Problem*, NZCER, Wellington, 1968.

165 Geraldine McDonald, 'Preschool Education for Culturally Different Children', unpublished paper, n.d.

166 Ibid., p.9.

167 Jane Ritchie, 1978, p.2.

168 Ibid.

169 Jane Ritchie, 'I Had Never Seen So Many Books in One Place', in May and Mitchell (eds), 1989, pp.38–39.

170 May and Mitchell (eds), p.3.

171 Ibid., p.78.

172 Nancy Gerrand, Book Programme, Working Paper no.11, *Te Kohanga Preschool Project*, Centre for Maori Studies and Research, University of Waikato, 1975.

173 Nancy Gerrand, Concepts Programme, Working Paper no.10, *Te Kohanga Preschool Project*, Centre for Maori Studies and Research, University of Waikato, 1975.

174 Ibid., p.127.

175 Jane Ritchie, 1989, p.38.

176 Jane Ritchie, 1978, p.134.
177 Jane Ritchie, 1989, p.38.
178 Joan Kennett, 'Project Atawhai', *Early Childhood Quarterly*, vol.1, no.3, summer 1976–77, pp.6–7.
179 Interview with Joan Kennett, 1994, cited in Sue Middleton and Helen May, *Teachers Talk Teaching*, Dunmore Press, Palmerston North, 1997, p.249.
180 Interview with Joan Kennett, 1994, by Helen May.
181 Jane Ritchie, 1978, p.150.

REFERENCES TO CHAPTER FOUR

1 For example, Eric Fromm, *The Fear of Freedom*, Routledge and Kegan Paul, London, 1962; Herbert Marcuse, *One Dimensional Man. Studies in the Ideology of Advanced Society*, Beacon Press, Boston, 1964; Edmund Leach, *A Runaway World*, The Reith Lectures, Oxford University Press, Oxford, 1967.
2 Helen May, *Minding Children, Managing Men. Conflict and Compromise in the Lives of Postwar Pakeha Women*, Bridget Williams Books, Wellington, 1992.
3 S. Hansen and J. Jenson, *The Little Red School Book*, New Zealand Edition, Alister Taylor, Wellington, 1972.
4 *NZ Listener*, 30 June 1979.
5 Anne Else, 'Politics in the Playpen', *Broadsheet*, no.113, October 1983, p.19.
6 Fraser McDonald, *NZ Woman's Weekly*, 12 November 1971.
7 Helen May, 'The Early Post-war Years for Women. An Interview with Beverley Morris', *Women's Studies Journal*, vol.5 no.2, December 1989.
8 D. McDonald, 1978, p.51.
9 Kate Birch, *Positive Parenting*, Methuen, Auckland, 1984, p.2.
10 Trish Gribben, *Pyjamas Don't Matter*, Heinemann Educational Books, Auckland, 1979; Jenny Phillips, *Mothers Matter Too*, A.H. and A.W. Reed, Wellington, 1983.
11 Karl du Fresne, 'Power to the Children', *NZ Listener*, 30 June 1979, p.15.
12 Nikolas Rose, *Governing the Soul. The Shaping of the Private Self*, Routledge, New York and London, 1990.
13 Nikolas Rose, *The Psychological Complex*, Routledge, London, 1985.
14 Department of Social Welfare, *Report on Child Abuse*, Wellington, 1972.
15 Bronwyn Dalley, *Family Matters. Child Welfare in Twentieth-Century New Zealand*, Auckland University Press, 1998, p.342.
16 Judith Duncan, *I Spy. Sexual Abuse Presention Policies. Protection or Harm?*, Institute for Early Childhood Studies, Victoria University of Wellington, 1998.
17 Jane and James Ritchie, *Child Rearing Patterns in New Zealand*, A.H. and A.W. Reed, Wellington, 1970, p.157.
18 Ibid., p.112.
19 Dugald J. McDonald, 'Children and Young Persons in New Zealand Society', in P. Koopman-Boyden (ed.), *Families in New Zealand Society*, Methuen, New Zealand, 1978, p.51.
20 *Parents' Centre Bulletin*, March 1970, p.8.
21 *Report of the Royal Inquiry into Social Security*, NZ Government, Wellington, 1972.
22 *Report of the Domestic Purposes Review Committee*, NZ Government, Wellington, 1977.
23 *NZ Woman's Weekly*, 9 May 1977.
24 Department of Education, *Report of the Committee of Inquiry into Pre-School Education*, Wellington, 1971.
25 W.B. Sutch, *For Children's Minds*, New Zealand Association of Childcare Centres, Wellington, 1971, p.15.
26 W.B. Sutch, *Women with a Cause*, Price Milburn, Wellington, 1973, p.150.
27 *Report of the Committee of Inquiry into Pre-school Education*, Department of Education, Wellington, 1971, p.17.
28 Ibid., p.29.

29 D.R. Mitchell and J.W. Mitchell, *Out of the Shadows. A Chronology of Significant Events in the Development of Services for Exceptional Children and Young Persons in New Zealand: 1850–1983*, Hamilton, published with assistance from the Department of Education, 1985.

30 David Barney, 'Education of the Atypical Preschool Child', in S. Havill and D. Mitchell (eds), *Issues in New Zealand Special Education*, Hodder and Stoughton, Auckland, 1972, pp.256–71.

31 Mitchell and Mitchell, 1985.

32 David Barney in Mitchell and Mitchell (eds), 1972, pp.268–69.

33 Celeste Litteck, 'Disability Paradigms in New Zealand Early Childhood Education', research essay for EDUC 528, Victoria University of Wellington, 1998.

34 Anne Meade, 'Public Participation in New Zealand Pre-school Education', *Occasional Papers in Sociology and Social Work*, no.4, 1981, Victoria University of Wellington, 1981.

35 *Hansard*, vol.379, 25 July 1972, Minister of Education, H.L. Pickering.

36 David Barney, *Who Gets to Pre-school?*, NZCER, Wellington, 1975.

37 *Hansard*, vol.401, 17 September 1972, Minister of Education, P. Amos.

38 Barney, 1975, p.281.

39 Ibid., p.282.

40 Helen May, 'Marie Bell: Working for Women, Working for Change', interview with Marie Bell, *Te Timatanga*, NZCA, Wellington, 1992, p.31.

41 Education Development Conference, *Educational Aims and Objectives*, Report of the Working Party on Aims and Objectives, Wellington, 1974, p.20.

42 Educational Development Conference, 1974.

43 *Hansard*, vol.400, 28 August 1975, P. Amos.

44 *Hansard*, vol.342, 4 June 1965, P. Amos.

45 *Hansard*, vol.375, 9 November 1971, C. Moyle.

46 Barney, 1975, Chapter 13.

47 AKA Archives, Myers Park, 1970s, No.1 Scrapbook, n.d. (around 1978).

48 Rae Julian, *The Forgotten Ones. An Evaluation of the Community Pre-school Workers and Itinerant Pre-school Teachers Schemes*, Department of Education, n.d. (around 1987), p.2.

49 C.P. Price, *A Review of the Staffing of the Correspondence School*, Department of Education, Wellington, 1989.

50 Rae Julian, *Special Pre-school Classes in Primary Schools. An Evaluation*, Department of Education, Wellington, 1987.

51 Penny Jamieson, 'Who Doesn't Get to Preschool in Newtown', *Set 1*, Item 13, 1979; D.M. Fergusson, L.J. Horwood and M.E. Gretton, 'Who Doesn't Get to Preschool?' *New Zealand Journal of Educational Studies*, no.16, 1984, pp.168–76; P. Fenwick, H. Norman and D. Leong, *Attendance at Preschool, Research Report Series*, no.31, Research and Statistics Division, Department of Education, Wellington, 1985.

52 *Pre-school Education*, vol.4, no. 2, 1974.

53 Rose Hanak, 'With Polynesian Children in Freeman's Bay', *Pre-school Education*, vol.3, no.2, 1972, p.3.

54 Julian, n.d. (around 1987), p.2.

55 Cathy Roxborough, 'Dunedin Teachers College Family Play-Group for Preschool. Polynesian Children and Their Families', unpublished paper, 5/4/1976, p.1.

56 Ibid., p.3.

57 Held by Cathy Roxborough, Morrinsville, one of the organisers.

58 Poko Morgan, 'Pacific Island Language Nests in New Zealand', unpublished paper, Anau Ako Pasifika, Tokoroa, 1988, pp.1–2.

59 Interview with Telesia McDonald and Iole Tagoilelagi, 1994, by Helen May.

60 Nicola Chisnall, 'Scripting the Role of Montessori in the Early Childhood Education Policy Play', unpublished research essay for EDUC 528, Victoria University of Wellington, 2000.

61 Ibid.

62 An expanded version of this section appeared in Sue Middleton and Helen May, *Teachers Talk Teaching 1915–1975. Early Childhood, Schools and Teachers Colleges*, Dunmore Press, Palmerston North, 1997, pp.258–68.
63 Interview with Ann Dickason, 1994, by Helen May, in Middleton and May, 1997, p.258.
64 Interview with Leone Shaw, 1994, by Helen May, in Middleton and May, 1997, p.258.
65 Interview with Ann Dickason, by Helen May, in Middleton and May, 1997, p.260.
66 Ibid.
67 Interview with Wendy Lee, 1994, by Helen May, in Middleton and May, 1997, p.260.
68 Interview with Georgina Kerr, 1994, by Helen May, 1994, in Middleton and May, 1997, p.261.
69 Interview with Heather Turner, 1994, by Helen May, 1994, in Middleton and May, 1997, p.262.
70 Interview with Leone Shaw, 1997, by Helen May, in Middleton and May, 1997, p.262.
71 Interview with Joan Brockett, 1994, by Helen May, in Middleton and May, 1997, p.263.
72 Interview with Margaret Carr, 1994, by Helen May, in Middleton and May, 1997, pp.263–34.
73 Interview with Wendy Lee, 1994, by Helen May, in Middleton and May, 1997, p.264.
74 Interview with Helen Bernstone, 1999, by Helen May.
75 Interview with Jill Wesselink, 1994, by Helen May, in Middleton and May, 1997, p.265.
76 Interview with Tony Holmes, 1994, by Helen May, in Middleton and May, 1997, p.266.
77 Ibid.
78 Middleton and May, 1997.
79 Interview with Anne Meade, 1999, by Helen May.
80 Meade, 1981.
81 Interview with Crispin Gardiner, 1999, by Helen May.
82 Report of the Select Committee on Women's Rights, *The Role of Women in New Zealand Society*, Government Printer, Wellington, June 1975, p.5.
83 Ibid., p.86.
84 Interview with Rosslyn Noonan, 1999, by Helen May.
85 Margaret Mead, 'Diversity of Choice for Women', *United Women's Convention 1975*, Wellington, 1976, pp.12–20.
86 *United Women's Convention 1975*, Wellington, 1976.
87 A Report on the National Conference in International Women's Year 1975, *Education and the Equality of the Sexes*, Department of Education, Wellington, 1976, p.7.
88 Ibid., p.17.
89 Anne Meade, 'Being Bold Pays Off', in N. Alcorn (ed.), *Conference Proceedings, Education and the Equality of the Sexes – Twenty Years On Conference, 2–4th July 1995*, University of Waikato, Hamilton, 1995, pp.24–33.
90 IECS, VUW, Education Papers, N.G. Leckie, *Report on the Education and Equality of the Sexes. Comments on Recommendations: Early Childhood Education'*, Confidential Report to Committee on Women and Education, Wellington, 1976.
91 Committee on Women, *Report on the Conference on Social and Economic Development, 11–12th March 1976*, Wellington, 1976, p.7.
92 Ibid., p.17.
93 Interview with Anne Smith, 1994, by Helen May.
94 W. Renwick, 'Early Childhood Education: A Moving Frontier', in B. O'Rourke and J. Clough (eds), *Early Childhood in New Zealand*, Heinemann Educational Books, Auckland, 1978.
95 Email communication to author from Geraldine McDonald, 11 February 2000.
96 Interview with Anne Smith,1994, by Helen May.
97 Interview with Anne Meade, 1999, by Helen May.
98 W.L. Renwick (ed.), *Early Childhood Care and Education. Papers from the New Zealand/ OECD Conference Held at Massey University, Palmerston North, 5–10 February 1978*, Department of Education, Wellington, 1980.
99 Ibid., 1980, pp.183–34.

100 Rosslyn Noonan and Wendy Lee, 'Childcare: The Case for Government Support', *Pre-school Education*, vol.7, no.1, April 1978, pp.20–22.

101 *Impact*, March 1980, p.3.

102 B.J. Lewis and P.M. Lockhart, *The I.Y.C. Report. A Resource for the Future*, New Zealand National Commission for the International Year of the Child, Wellington, 1979.

103 Urie Bronfenbrenner, 'Who Cares for Children?', opening address to the second Early Childhood Care and Development Conference, Christchurch, August 1979.

REFERENCES TO CHAPTER FIVE

1 *NZ Herald* photograph [n.d.], Reproduced in *Childcare Quarterly*, vol.7, no.1, 1986, p.11, with permission of Pam Croxford.

2 Helen May, *Minding Children, Managing Men. Conflict and Compromise in the Lives of Postwar Pakeha Women*, Bridget Williams Books, Wellington, 1992; Sue Kedgley, *Mum's the Word. The Untold Story of Motherhood in New Zealand*, Random House, Auckland, 1996.

3 IECS, VUW, NZCA archive, *President's Report*, 1971, p.1.

4 Sonja Davies, *Bread and Roses*, Australia and New Zealand Book Co., Auckland, 1984; *Marching On …*, Random House, Auckland, 1997.

5 Geraldine McDonald, 'The Politics of Childcare', in Rosemary Seymour (ed.), *Research Papers '78. Women's Studies*, Women's Studies Association, 1978, p.71.

6 W. Renwick, 'Early Childhood Education: A Moving Frontier', in B. O'Rourke and J. Clough (eds), *Early Childhood in New Zealand*, Heinemann Educational Books, Auckland, 1978, p.235.

7 *Hansard*, vol.378, 20 June 1972.

8 *Hansard*, vol.381, 4 October 1972.

9 Davies, 1984, p.224.

10 *Evening Post*, 21 May 1972.

11 *Evening Post*, 2 May 1972.

12 *Parents' Centre Bulletin*, June, 1972, p.8.

13 *Parents' Centre Bulletin*, March, 1973, p.8.

14 IECS, VUW, NZCA Archive, NZCA Clippings File, Richard Neville, *Govt. Taking Conservative Line on Childcare Centres*, n.d. (early 1973).

15 Ibid.

16 IECS, VUW, NZCA Archive, NZCA Clippings File, NZ Press Association, October 1973.

17 In 1973 this was $33,000; 1978 – $98,000; 1979 – $157,340. The scheme was then stopped until the 1980s.

18 The Family Life Education Council had been established in Wellington in 1965. Among its members were Beverley Morris and Helen Brew.

19 IECS, VUW, PCNZ Archive, Box, 4.1, Helen Brew, Newsletter no.1, 25 November 1973, p.2.

20 *Hansard*, vol.394, 8 August 1974.

21 IECS, VUW, NZCA Archive, President's Report, 1974.

22 IECS, VUW, NZCA Archive, Conference Report, 19 January 1974.

23 Department of Social Welfare, *Annual Reports* 1971–1981.

24 Cate Anderson, *Report on Childcare in Wellington*, Community Services Office, Wellington City Council, 1981.

25 Helen May Cook, *Mind that Child. Childcare as a Social and Political Issue in New Zealand*, BlackBerry Press, Wellington, 1985, p.35.

26 Crispin Gardiner, 'Suggested Guidelines for Administration of the Capitation Subsidy', *Early Childhood Quarterly*, vol.2, no.2, 1976, pp.16–18.

27 John Bowlby, *Attachment and Loss: Vol. 1. Attachment*, Basic Books, New York, 1969; *Vol. 2. Separation: Anxiety and Anger*, Basic Books, New York, 1973.

28 Elly Singer, *Child-care and the Psychology of Development*, Routledge, London and New York, 1992, p.123.

29 M.S. Ainsworth and S.M. Bell, 'Attachment, Exploration and Separation: Individual Differences in Strange-situation Behaviour of One-year-olds', *Child Development*, no.41, 1970, pp.49–67.
30 Kedgley, 1996, p.259.
31 Television interview with Claire Henderson, *On Camera*, 1 May 1973.
32 Singer, 1992, p.135.
33 Ibid.
34 A. Clarke-Stewart and G. Fein, *Day Care in Context*, Wiley, New York, 1973; A. Clarke-Stewart, *Child Care in the Family, a Review of Research and Some Propositions*, Academic Press, New York, 1977.
35 IECS, VUW, PCNZ Archive, Box, 4.1, Helen Brew's Report, 3 November 1973, p.1.
36 Ibid.
37 James and Joyce Robertson, *Young Children in Brief Separation. Fresh Look*, Quadrangle Books, New York Times, New York, 1971; *Young Children in Brief Separation*, films on foster care and residential nursery care, Tavistock Child Development Research Unit, London.
38 Kedgley, 1996, p.260.
39 IECS, VUW, PCNZ Archive, Box 4.2, transcribed tapes from James and Joyce Robertson.
40 *Nova Magazine*, July 1970, pp.9–11.
41 Helen May, 'Childcare Activism in the Seventies: An Interview with Duilia Rendall', *Childcare Quarterly*, vol.7, no.2, 1987, p.28.
42 IECS, VUW, PCNZ Archive, Box 4.1, undated clipping.
43 FNZPC Submission to the Select Committee on Women's Rights, 1974.
44 *Dominion*, 9 May 1974.
45 IECS, VUW, PCNZ Archive, Boxes 4.2, 4.3.
46 IECS, VUW, PCNZ Archive, Box 4.3, Working Party for Children in Separation.
47 Ibid.
48 Ibid., Policy Statement on Childcare.
49 Anne Smith and David Swain, *Childcare in New Zealand. People, Programmes and Politics*, Allen and Unwin/Port Nicholson Press, Wellington, 1988, p.77.
50 May Cook, 1985; Smith and Swain, 1988.
51 Interview with Helen Orr, 1994, by Helen May.
52 Helen May, 'Childcare Herstory: Interview with Heather Lintott', *Childcare Quarterly*, vol.7, no.4, 1988, p.30.
53 Interview with Joan Kennett, 1994, by Helen May.
54 May, 1987, p.28.
55 Ibid., p.30.
56 Janet McCallum, 'A Brief History of the Wellington Community Childcare Association', *Te Karere*, Issue 2, December 1993, pp.8–9.
57 Helen May, 'Childcare Herstory: Interview with Cathy Lythe', *Childcare Quarterly*, vol.7, no.1, 1986 p.17.
58 Interview with Margaret Lamb, Sue Middleton and Helen May, *Teachers Talk Teaching*, Dunmore Press, Palmerston North, 1997, pp.257–58.
59 Interview with Anne Smith, in Middleton and May, 1997, p.256.
60 Anne Smith, 'The Case for Quality Day Care in New Zealand – Liberation of Children and Parents', in O'Rourke and Clough (eds), 1978, p.248.
61 Bettye Caldwell, 'What is the Optimal Learning Environment for the Young Child?', *American Journal of Orthopsychiatry*, no.37, 1967, pp.8–22; G.G. Fein and A. Clarke-Stewart, *Day Care in Context*, John Wiley and Sons, London, 1973; S.C. Schwarz, G. Krolick and R.G. Strickland, 'Effects of Early Day Care Experience on Adjustment to a New Environment', *American Journal of Orthopsychiatry*, vol.40, no.3, 1973, pp.340–46.
62 Michael Rutter, *Maternal Deprivation Reassessed*, Penguin, Middlesex, England, 1972, p.64.
63 Anne Smith, in O'Rourke and Clough (eds), 1978, pp.251–52.
64 Interview with Anne Smith, cited in Middleton and May, 1997, p.256.
65 Anne Smith, 'The Dunedin Community Childcare Association', unpublished paper, n.d.
66 Interview with Pat Hubbard, in Middleton and May, 1997, p.256.

67 Bettye Caldwell, 'Can Young Children have a Quality Life in Daycare?', foundation lecture, Pacific Oaks College, Pasadena, California, 1972.

68 Consortium of Longitudinal Studies, *As the Twig is Bent*, Erlbaum, London, 1983.

69 Caldwell, 1967.

70 A.S. Honig and J.R. Lally, *Infant Caregiving. A Design for Training*, Syracuse University Press, New York, 1972.

71 IECS, VUW, NZCA Archive, Box 32, Bettye Caldwell correspondence.

72 Margaret Lamb, 'A Message from the President', *Early Childhood Quarterly*, vol.1, no.4, 1978, p.3.

73 Urie Bronfenbrenner, *The Ecology of Human Development*, Harvard University Press, Cambridge, Mass., 1979, p.19.

74 *NZ Listener*, 27 October 1979.

75 Committee on Women, *Child-care: Facts, Principles and Problems*, IWY76-Synd 2-1; *Report on the Conference on Women in Social and Economic Development*, Wellington, 1976, p.3.

76 Committee on Women, *Report on the Conference on Women in Social and Economic Development*, Wellington, 1976, p.8.

77 Statement prepared by the Department of Social Welfare, cited in *National Business Review*, 21 September 1977.

78 *National Business Review*, 21 September 1977.

79 *National Party Manifesto*, 1978.

80 Society for Research on Women, *Urban Women*, 1972; *Childcare in a Wellington Suburb*, 1975; *Childcare in a Waikato Town*, 1979.

81 May, 1992.

82 Ann Oakley, *The Sociology of Housework*, Robertson, London, 1974; New Zealand Federation of University Women, *Women at Work*, 1968; Wellington Branch, *Women at Home*, 1976.

83 Claire Hadfield, *Childcare in Newtown. A Study of Working Mothers and Their Families*, Occasional Paper no.3, Department of Sociology and Social Work, Victoria University of Wellington, 1981.

84 Committee of Women (eds), *What's Been Done?*, Wellington, 1978.

85 *Dominion Sunday Times*, 19 October 1975.

86 Committee of Women, *What's Been Done?*, 1978, p.93, p.34.

87 Working Women's Council, *Working Women's Charter*, 1978.

88 *Auckland Star*, 15 October 1980; *Evening Post*, 15 October 1980.

89 Ibid.

90 IECS, VUW, NZCA Archive, NZCA Clippings File.

91 Sonja Davies, 'What Price Quality?', *Early Childhood Quarterly*, vol.3, no.2, pp.3–5.

92 *Sunday Times*, 4 September 1980.

93 Report of the State Services Commission Working Group, *Early Childhood Care and Education*, Wellington, 1980.

94 Geraldine McDonald, 'The Story of a Recommendation about Early Childhood Care and Education', in M. Clark (ed.), *The Politics of Education in New Zealand*, NZCER, Wellington, 1981.

95 Ibid., p.161.

96 Interview with Geraldine McDonald, 1998, by Helen May.

97 Committee on Women, *Report of the Conference on Women in Social and Economic Development*, Wellington, 1976, p.17.

98 Geraldine McDonald, in Clark (ed), 1981, p.162.

99 IECS, VUW, NZCA Archive, Box 24, Report of meeting with the Minister, 14 July 1978, by Duilia Rendall.

100 Geraldine McDonald, in Clark (ed), 1981, p.167.

101 Val Burns, 'Policy Developments in Early Childhood Care and Education in New Zealand', unpublished paper presented to Australian Early Childhood Association 17th National Conference, Brisbane, Queensland, 1985.

102 PCCF was set up in 1980 and tabled a contentious, but later withdrawn, remit at the 1981 NZCA conference in Auckland calling for the endorsement of profit making (May Cook, 1985).

103 Playcentre submission to the State Services Commission, 1981.

104 National Council of Women submission to the State Services Commission, 30 August 1981.

105 IECS, VUW Archive, undated Feminists for Life pamphlet.

106 *NZ Listener*, 18 September 1982.

107 *Hansard*, vol. 446, 8 September 1982.

108 *Evening Post*, 9 June 1982.

109 *Auckland Star*, 16 June 1982.

110 *NZ Herald*, 10 June 1982.

111 Minister of Social Welfare, news release, 28 July 1983; Address by Minister of Social Welfare Venn Young to the Third Early Childhood Convention at Ngaruawahia, 1983.

112 *Roundabout*, August 1983.

113 *Labour Party Manifesto*, Women's Policy, 1984.

114 Minister of Women's Affairs, news release, 10 October 1984.

115 *Evening Post*, 30 March 1985.

116 Social Advisory Council, *Childcare Services. Impact and Opportunities*, Government Printer, Wellington, 1985, p.32.

REFERENCES TO CHAPTER SIX

1 Geraldine McDonald, 'Early Childhood Education in New Zealand', unpublished position paper, 1975, p.4.

2 Ibid.

3 Helen May Cook, 'Early Childhood Education: A Woman's Sphere in a Man's World', in J. Codd, R. Harker and R. Nash (eds), *Political Issues in New Zealand Education*, Dunmore Press, Palmerston North, 1985, pp.205–16.

4 Ruth Beaglehole and Vera Levett, 'The Myths of Motherhood', *NZ Listener*, 24 May 1975.

5 Ann Oakley, *Becoming a Mother*, Robertson and Co., London, 1979; Simone de Beauvoir, *The Second Sex*, Penguin, Harmondsworth, 1972.

6 Juliet Mitchell, *Woman's Estate*, Penguin, Harmondsworth, 1971.

7 Reported in the *NZ Herald*, cited in Sue Kedgley, *Mum's the Word. The Untold Story of Motherhood in New Zealand*, Random House, Auckland, 1996, p.233.

8 Shulamith Firestone, *The Dialectic of Sex. The Case for Feminist Revolution*, The Women's Press, London, 1979, p.193.

9 Kedgley, 1996, p.233.

10 Kay Goodger, *A Strategy for Women's Liberation*, Pilot Books, Auckland, 1974.

11 Firestone, 1971, p.91.

12 Robin McKinlay, '"Mothers: Where Would We be Without Them?" Motherhood and Self Definition in New Zealand', unpublished PhD thesis, Victoria University of Wellington, 1983.

13 Jane and James Ritchie, *Growing Up in New Zealand*, Allen and Unwin, Auckland, 1978.

14 *Above Rubies*, April 1978, p.1.

15 Kedgley, 1996, p.266.

16 *Parents' Centre Bulletin*, Winter 1982.

17 New Zealand Federation of University Women, *Women at Home*, Wellington, 1976.

18 National Council of Women, *Women and Change. A Study of New Zealand Women*, Wellington, 1985.

19 Helen May, *Minding Children, Managing Men. Conflict and Compromise in the Lives of Post-war Pakeha Women*, Bridget Williams Books, 1992.

20 Deirdre Dale, 'Changes Changes', *Playcentre Journal*, no.48, 1978, p.3.

21 *Playcentre Journal*, no.29, 1974.

22 Deirdre Dale, 'Changes Changes', *Playcentre Journal*, no.48, 1978, p.3.

23 Interview with Kerry Bethell, in Sue Middleton and Helen May, *Teachers Talk Teaching*, Dunmore Press, Palmerston North, 1997, p.266.

24 Interview with Carol Hamer, in Middleton and May, 1997, p.267.

25 Geraldine McDonald, 'Education Innovation: The Case of the New Zealand Playcentre', *NZ Journal of Education Studies*, vol.9 no.2, 1974.

26 Interview with Carol Garden, 1995, by Helen May.

27 Ailsa Densem, *The Playcentre Way*, NZPCF, Auckland, 1980, p.16.

28 Jean Goldschmidt, 'How Leadership Emerged in Playcentre', in Sue Stover (ed.), *Good Clean Fun: New Zealand's Playcentre Movement*, NCPCF, Auckland, 1998, pp.39–45.

29 Helen Bernstone, in Stover, 1998, p.87.

30 Interview with Fay Clarke, 1984, by Helen May.

31 Anne Meade, *Public Participation in New Zealand Pre-school Education*, Occasional Papers in Sociology and Social Work No. 4, Victoria University, Wellington, 1981.

32 Geraldine McDonald, *Working and Learning: A Participatory Project on Parent-helping in the New Zealand Playcentre*, NZCER, Wellington, 1982.

33 J.M. Williams, *Playcentre in a Changing World*, Hutt Wairarapa Playcentre Assn., 1978, p.44.

34 Dale, 1978, p.3.

35 Llewelyn Richards, 'Population Trends and Preschool Ends', paper presented to NZARE conference, 1980.

36 Beverly Morris, 'The Continuing Education of Holders of the National Playcentre Supervisor's Certificate', paper presented to NZARE conference, 1981.

37 Interview with Carol Nicholson, 1994, by Helen May.

38 Society for Research on Women, *Child Care in a Wellington Suburb*, Wellington, 1975; *Child Care in a Waikato Town*, Hamilton, 1979.

39 Helen May, *The Discovery of Early Childhood*, Auckland University Press/Bridget Williams Books with NZCER, 1997.

40 Rae Julian, *Brought to Mind*, NZCER, Wellington, 1981, p.7.

41 Ibid., p.11.

42 B. Ward, *The Home of Man*, Penguin, London, 1976, p.123, in C.I. St Johanser, 'Family Daycare in New Zealand', unpublished MA thesis, Victoria University of Wellington, 1980.

43 D. Myrian and I. Lezine, *Early Child Care in France*, Gordon and Beach, London, 1975, p.78.

44 M. Wagner and M. Wagner, *The Danish National Child Care System*, Westview, Colorado, 1976; R. Berfenstein et al, *Early Child Care in Sweden*, Gordon and Beach, London, 1973.

45 M. O'Brien Steinfels, *Who's Minding the Children? The History and Politics of Day Care in America*, Simon and Schuster, New York, 1973, p.154.

46 Australian Council for Social Services, *Family Day Care in New South Wales*, Sydney, ACOSS and NSWCOSS, 1976.

47 'Extended Family Daycare', *Early Childhood Quarterly*, vol.1, no.3, summer, 1976–77, pp.4–5.

48 Mary Collie-Holmes, *Where the Heart Is. A History of Barnardos in New Zealand 1866–1991*, Barnardos, Wellington, New Zealand, 1991.

49 B. Brown, L. Duurloo, J. Cameron, 'Family Day Care Report', *Early Childhood Quarterly*, vol.2, no.3, spring 1979, pp.14–16.

50 Anne Smith and David Swain, *Childcare in New Zealand. People, Programmes and Politics*, Allen and Unwin/Port Nicholson Press, Wellington, 1988.

51 Elizabeth Everiss, 'Time to Move On? A Study of Training Participation by Caregivers Working in Chartered Home-based Schemes in Aotearoa–New Zealand', unpublished MA thesis, Victoria University of Wellington, 1998.

52 Brown et al., 1979.

53 Department of Education, *Family Day Care. Current Issues and Future Developments. Report of the National In-Service Course held at Lopdell Centre*, Department of Education, April 1988.

54 Smith and Swain, 1988, p.102.

55 *Broadsheet*, May 1980, p.6.
56 Ibid., p.7.
57 St Johanser, 1980.
58 *Broadsheet*, September 1980, pp.2–3.
59 Interview with Pam Croxford, in May Cook, 1985, p.38.
60 Lois Duurloo, 'Family Day Care – the Realities', *Early Childhood Quarterly*, vol.3, no. 4, winter, 1980–81, p.17.
61 Interview with Joyce Barns, 1994, in Middleton and May, 1997, p.199.
62 Interview with Cushla Scrivens, 1994, by Helen May.
63 *Report of the Committee of Inquiry into Pre-school Education*, Department of Education, Wellington, 1971, p.91.
64 Betty Cosson, 'End of an Era', *Pre-school Education*, vol.4, no.4, May 1975, pp.8–10.
65 At Christchurch, where there was an adjoining site, there were close links with primary college and some shared courses. At the Hamilton and North Shore Teachers' Colleges, small preschool units were established in 1973 and at Palmerston North in 1974 (Audrey Mayo-Haggitt, 'Early Childhood Preparation: Christchurch Teachers' College', *Pre-School Education* (NZFKTA), vol.5, no.2, May 1976, pp.10–14.)
66 Department of Education, *Working Party Report on Teacher Preparation for Early Childhood*, Hogben House, Christchurch, May 1974.
67 Joan Brockett, 'Towards an Evaluation of Kindergarten Teacher Training', in G. McDonald and P.E. Dinniss (eds), *Young Children and Early Childhood Services. Some New Zealand Research*, NZCER, Wellington, 1978, pp.163–70.
68 Phyllis M. Varcoe, 'Integration', *Kindergarten Education* (NZFKU), June 1975, pp.6–7.
69 Interview with Val Burns, 1995, by Helen May.
70 Beryl Hughes, *Flags and Building Blocks, Formality and Fun. One Hundred Years of Free Kingergarten in New Zealand*, NZFKU, Wellington, 1989, p.44.
71 Jean Simpson, 'New Zealand Free Kindergarten Teachers' Association', in Anne Else (ed.), *Women Together. A History of Women's Organisations in New Zealand, Ngā Rōpū Wāhine o te Motu*, Daphne Brasell Associates and the Historical Branch, Dept of Internal Affairs, Wellington, 1993, pp.345–47.
72 Interview with Wendy Lee, 1994, by Helen May.
73 Wendy Lee, President's Address, *Pre-School Education*, vol.4, no.1, November 1973, pp.5–6.
74 *Otago Daily Times* (undated clipping – probably shortly after 21 August 1973), Phyllis Varcoe, clippings book.
75 Simpson, 1993.
76 Wendy Lee Papers, *The Workload and Duties of a Kindergarten Teacher*, Paper no.4, IECS, VUW archive.
77 Janice Burns, *Kindergarten and Primary Teachers. A Comparison of their Work*, NZEI, Riu Roa, Wellington, 1999.
78 Interview with Wendy Lee, 1994, by Helen May.
79 Interview with Lynne Bruce, 1999, by Helen May.
80 Interview with Georgina Kerr, 1994, by Helen May.
81 Interview with Rosslyn Noonan, 1999, by Helen May.
82 Rosslyn Noonan, 'Play-Doh and Power Politics. The Kindergarten Service – A Women's Movement from the Beginning', *Broadsheet*, no.50, June 1977, pp.32.
83 *Broadsheet*, no.70, June 1979, p.4.
84 Interview with Lynne Bruce, by Helen May, 1999.
85 *Auckland Star*, 15 July 1982.
86 Belinda Montgomery and Kate Clark, 'Kindy Teachers Rebel', *Broadsheet*, October 1982, p.5.
87 *Evening Post*, 22 July 1983.
88 Minister of Education, Press Statement, 19 February 1984.
89 *Labour Party Manifesto*, Women's Policy, 1984.
90 Department of Education, *Report of the Working Party of Three Year Training for Kindergarten Teachers*, April 1986.

91 Maris O'Rourke, 'Day Care Policy', *Early Childhood Quarterly*, vol.2, no.4, 1979/80, p.7.
92 Estelle Von Sturmer and Jackie Carpenter, *Childcare Assessment and Training in New Zealand*, New Zealand Childcare Association, Wellington, 1981.
93 Helen May Cook, in Codd, Harker and Nash (eds), 1985; IECS, VUW NZCA archive, Training reports.
94 *Sunday Times*, 1 February 1980.
95 Sonja Davies, 'What Price Quality?' *Early Childhood Quarterly*, vol.3. no.2, 1980, p.5.
96 R. Roupp, J. Travers, F. Glantz and C. Coelen, *Children at the Centre. Final Report of the National Day Care Study*, Department of Health, Education and Welfare, Washington DC, 1979.
97 Smith and Swain, 1988.
98 Helen May Cook, 'The Early Childhood Workers' Union: An Analysis of Collective Consciousness and Praxis', *New Zealand Industrial Relations Journal*, vol.9, no.1, 1984, pp.5–9; Helen May, 'The Early Childhood Workers' Union', in Anne Else (ed.), 1993, pp.235–37; Helen May, 'Fighting for Recognition: the Development of the Early Childhood Workers' Union', in Pat Walsh (ed.), *Trade Unions, Work and Society*, Dunmore Press, Palmerston North, 1994, pp.177–98.
99 *Early Childhood Quarterly*, vol.1, no.3, 1976, pp.18–19.
100 Helen May, in Walsh (ed), 1994.
101 Helen May, in Walsh (ed), 1994, p.183.
102 In Wellington there were Yvonne Van Dongen, Hillary Watson and, after registration, Rose Ryan and Belinda Montgomery; in Auckland Glenda Hinchey, Pippa Cubey and Nicky Treadwell; and in Christchurch Elizabeth Nurse. They were all paid union organisers at various times. Each of these women contributed much to the establishment and survival of ECWU in the early years.
103 *Childcare: A Step Towards Equality*, PSA Discussion Paper no.17, PSA, Wellington, 1982.
104 *National Business Review*, 26 July 1982
105 *Otago Daily Times*, 22 November 1982.
106 *NZ Listener*, 7 May 1983.
107 *Auckland Star*, 2 February 1983.
108 IECS, VUW, ECWU papers, President's Report, July 1993.
109 *Childcare: A Step Towards Equality*, 1982.
110 Federation of Labour Conference Minutes, 1984, p.74.
111 *Labour Party Manifesto*, 1984.

REFERENCES TO CHAPTER SEVEN

1 Michael King, *Maori: A Photographic and Social History*, Reed, Auckland, 1996.
2 Government Review Team, *Report of the Review of Te Kohanga Reo. Language is the Life Force of the People*, Wellington, 1988, p.16.
3 Kuni Jenkins (with Tania Kai`ai), 'Maori Education: A Cultural Experience and Dilemma for the State – A New Direction in Maori Society', in E. Coxon, K. Jenkins, J. Marshall and L. Massey (eds), *The Politics of Learning and Teaching in Aotearoa–New Zealand*, Dunmore Press, Palmerston North, 1994, pp.148–79.
4 Graham Ihingangaroa Smith and Linda Tuhiwai Smith, 'Ki te whai ao, ki te ao marama: Crisis and Change in Maori Education', in A. Jones, G. McCulloch, J. Marshall, G.H. Smith and L. Smith (eds), *Myths and Realities. Schooling in New Zealand*, Dunmore, Palmerston North, 1990, pp.123–56.
5 Bernard Spolsky, *Report to the Department of Education on Bilingual Education*, Government Printer, Wellington, 1985.
6 Sue Middleton and Helen May, *Teachers Talk Teaching. Early Childhood, Schools and Teachers' Colleges*, Dunmore Press, Palmerson North, 1997, pp.240–51.
7 Manuka Henare and Edward Douglas, *Te Reo o Te Tiriti Mai Rano*, Report of the Royal Commission on Social Policy, Volume III, Part One, Government Printer, Wellington, 1988, pp.79–220.

8 Government Review Team, *Report of the Review of Te Kohanga Reo*, 1988.
9 Kara Puketapu, *Reform from Within*, Department of Maori Affairs, Wellington, 1982, cited in Government Review Team, *Report of the Review of Te Kohanga Reo*, 1988.
10 Iritana Tawhiwhirangi, 'The Origins of Te Kohanga Reo', 1991, cited in Anne Else (ed.), *Women Together. A History of Women's Organisations in New Zealand. Ngā Rōpū Wāhine o te Motu*, Daphne Brasell Associates and the Historical Branch, Dept of Internal Affairs, Wellington, 1993, p.42.
11 Richard Benton, *The Maori Language in the Nineteen Seventies*, Maori Research Unit, NZCER, Wellington, 1979.
12 Kathie Irwin, 'The Politics of Kohanga Reo', in S. Middleton, J. Codd and A. Jones (eds), *New Zealand Education Policy Today*, Allen and Unwin, Wellington, 1990, pp.110–20.
13 Ibid., p.115.
14 Government Review Team, 1988, p.18.
15 Tania M. Ka`ai, 'Te Hiringa Taketake: Mai i te Kohanga Reo ki te Kura. Maori Pedagogy. Te Kohanga Reo and the Transition to School', unpublished M. Phil thesis in education, University of Auckland, 1990.
16 Ibid., p.6.
17 Interview with Iritana Tawhiwhirangi, kōhanga reo organiser, *North and South*, October 1994, p.78.
18 Kuni Jenkins (with Tania Ka`ai), in Coxon, Jenkins, Marshall and Massey (eds), 1994, p.153.
19 *Maori Educational Development Conference – Nga Tumanako*, report to the Centre for Continuing Education, University of Auckland, Auckland, 1984.
20 Judith Simon, 'The Ideological Rationale for the Denial of Maoritanga', paper presented at Maori Educational Development Conference – Nga Tumanako, 23–25 March 1984, Tūrangawaewae Marae, Ngaruawahia; 'Policy, Ideology and Practice: Implications of the Views of Primary School Teachers of Maori Children', unpublished MA thesis, University of Auckland, 1984.
21 Donna Awatere, 'Maori Sovereignty Part One', *Broadsheet*, no.100, June 1982, p.41.
22 Hilda Halkyard, 'Te Kohanga Reo', *Broadsheet*, no.113, October 1983, p.16.
23 Helen May, *The Discovery of Early Childhood*, Auckland University Press/Bridget Williams Books with NZCER, 1997, p.35.
24 Robert Muldoon, speech to the Tu Tangata Wananga Whakatauira, Legislative Chamber, Parliament, Wellington, 13 July 1982.
25 Donna Awatere, 'Te Mana Maori Motuhake. Maori Sovereignty Part Three', *Broadsheet*, no.106, Jan/Feb 1983, p.13.
26 Mason Durie, 'Understanding Biculturalism', paper presented to Kokiri Tahi conference, Gisborne, September 1994.
27 Te Kōhanga Reo Wānanga, No Compromise, Legislative Chamber, Parliament Buildings, Wellington, 14–15 July 1982.
28 Government Review Team, *Report of the Review of Te Kohanga Reo*, 1988.
29 Ibid; Department of Maori Affairs, *Annual Report 1985*, Government Printer, Wellington, 1985.
30 Interview with Iritana Tawhiwhirangi, Te Puna Wai Korero, National Radio, 13 November 1993.
31 Ibid.
32 John Rangihau, 'Te Kohanga Reo', unpublished paper presented to the Kōhanga Reo National Hui, Tūrangawaewae Marae, Ngaruawahia, 19 January 1984, p.5.
33 *NZ Listener*, 24 July 1982.
34 *North and South*, October 1994, p.79.
35 Arapera Royal Tangaere, 'Te Kohanga Reo: More than a Language Nest. The Future of Te Reo Maori, Te Iwi Maori and a People's Soul', Dame Jean Herbison Lecture, *Proceedings of the NZ Association for Research in Education Conference*, Nelson, 5–8 December 1996, NZARE, Wellington, 1996, p.42.
36 John Bennett, 'Early Childhood Care and Education. Te Kohanga Reo', *Proceedings of the*

Early Childhood Care and Education Forum, Legislative Chamber, Parliament, Wellington, 4–5 December 1985, Keynote Papers, pp.2–3.

37 Ibid., p.3.

38 Ka`ai, 1990, pp.6–9.

39 Ibid., p.9.

40 *Te Kohanga Reo ... the language nest*, Dept of Maori Affairs and MEF, n.d. [1982], p.6.

41 *NZ Listener*, 24 July 1982.

42 Government Review Team, 1988, pp.23–24.

43 Interview with Rita Walker, 1995, cited in Middleton and May, 1997, p.299.

44 *Te Kohanga Reo Trust Certificate*, Government Printer, Wellington, 1984.

45 Tu Tangata Wananga Whakatauira, *Te Kohanga Reo: Guidelines for Wananga*, Department of Maori Affairs, Wellington, 1983.

46 Bennett, 1985.

47 Mere Mitchell, in Middleton and May, 1997, p.300.

48 Te Kohanga Reo Trust, *Report of the Kohanga Reo National Wananga*, Te Kohanga Reo National Trust, Wellington, 1984; *Te Kohanga Reo National Wananga, Resource Manual*, Tūrangawaewae Marae, Ngaruawahia, 1985.

49 *Maori Educational Development Conference – Nga Tumanako*, 1984, pp.16–17.

50 Ibid., p.5.

51 William Renwick, 'Picking up the Challenge', in *Maori Educational Development Conference – Nga Tumanako*, 1984, p.15.

52 Waitangi Tribunal Report, *Findings of the Waitangi Tribunal Relating to Te Reo Maori and a Claim by Huirangi Waikerepuru and Nga Kete Wananga*, Wellington, 1985.

53 IECS, VUW, Education, papers, Department of Education response to the Cabinet Social Equity Committee regarding the recent findings of the Waitangi Tribunal on the Language Claim, 1 May 1986.

54 Government Review Team, *Report of the Review Team of Te Kohanga Reo*, 1988.

55 Interview with Iritana Tawhiwhirangi, Te Puna Wai Korero, National Radio, 13 November 1993.

56 Patricia Maringi Gina Johnston, 'Examining a State Relationship: Legitimation and Te Kohanga Reo – The Return of the Prodigal Child', paper presented to the NZARE Conference, University of Waikato, December 1993.

57 Government Review Team, *Report of the Review Team of Te Kohanga Reo*, 1988.

58 Ibid., p.7.

59 *NZ Listener*, 24 July 1982.

60 *Hansard*, vol.454, 25 October 1983.

61 IECS, VUW, Education, papers, Minister of Education, Kohanga Reo and the Primary School, draft document prepared for the Cabinet Committee on Expenditure, 12 July 1984.

62 IECS, VUW, Education, papers, Letter from the Office of the Minister of Finance to the Minister of Education, 2 November 1984.

63 Government Review Team, *Report of the Review Team of Te Kohanga Reo*, 1988, p.43.

64 Ibid., p.44.

65 *NZ Herald*, 16 September 1985.

66 Smith and Smith (eds), 1990, p.148.

67 Department of Education, *A Guide Towards Bilingual Education for New Zealand Schools*, Maori and Island Division, Wellington, 1987, p.3.

68 Kuni Jenkins, (with Tania Ka`ai), in Coxon, Jenkins, Marshall and Massey (eds), 1994, p.158.

69 Interview with Rita Walker, 1995, cited in Middleton and May, 1997, p.302.

70 Ibid.

71 David Barney, *Who Gets to Preschool?*, NZCER, Wellington, 1975, p.198. Barney notes that this figure is presented with some caution, given the poor statistics of the period.

72 IECS, VUW, Education, papers, Hine Potaka, Pre-school Education – Maori Education Foundation Report of Findings in the Waiariki District 1978–82, 1983; Maori Education Foundation, Pre-School Officer's Report of Findings in Waiariki Area 1982, n.d.

73 Hine Potaka, 'Awhina Whanau Kaupapa, Family Support Philosophy', in *Proceedings of the Australian Early Childhood Association, 19th Annual Conference*, Adelaide, pp.270–87.
74 IECS, VUW, D Education, papers, Hine Potaka, Maori Education Foundation, Pre-School Officer's Report of Findings in Waiariki Area 1982. n.d., p.8.
75 Ministry of Education, 'Trends in Early Childhood Education', *Education Trends Reports*, vol.5, no.1, 1992.
76 William Renwick, Foreword, *Nga Tamariki Iti o Aotearoa – The First Steps in the Introduction of Maori Studies for Preschool Children*, Department of Education, Wellington, 1980, p.2.
77 Interview with 'Dawn Ellis' (not her real name), by Helen May, 1994.
78 Kathie Irwin, 'The Pakeha Response to Kohanga Reo', in *Proceedings of the Fourth Early Childhood Convention*, Wellington, 1987, pp.27–31.
79 Ibid., pp.29–30.
80 Arapera Royal Tangaere, 'Kei Hea te Komako e Ko? Early Childhood Education, a Maori Perspective', in L. Foote, M. Gold and A. Smith (eds), *Fifth Early Childhood Convention Papers*, Dunedin, 1991, p.87.
81 Department of Education, *Te Ripoata, Taha Maori in Early Childhood Education*, Lopdell Centre, Auckland, September 1988.
82 Department of Education, *Awareness of Racism and Anti-Racist Strategies for Early Childhood Education*, Lopdell Centre, Auckland, February 1989.
83 Interview with Jenny Ritchie, 1994, cited in Middleton and May, 1997, p.305.
84 Interview with 'Lesley Howes' (not her real name), cited in Middleton and May, 1997, p.304.
85 Interview with Georgina Kerr, 1994, by Helen May.
86 Interview with Georgina Kerr, 1994, cited in Middleton and May, 1997, p.312.
87 Maureen Locke, 'I was Born and Bred in Rotorua at Ohinemutu among the Mudpools', in H. May and J. Mitchell (eds), *A Celebration of Women in Early Childhood*, Centre of Early Childhood, Hamilton Teachers' College, 1989.
88 IECS, VUW, NZCA Archive, NZCA Report to 25th Annual Conference, 12–14 August 1988; Elena Ilalio, 'NZCA – A Bicultural Association', *Childcare Quarterly*, vol.8, no.3, 1989, pp.13–27.
89 Rahera Barrett-Douglas, 'Equality of Opportunity or Equality of Outcome: Ko te taurite o nga huarahi, ko te taurite ranei o nga hua', in *Hugs and Hassles – He Awhi he Porearea*, NZ Playcentre Federation, Auckland, 1989, p.65.
90 *Whanau Tupu Ngatahi. Families Growing Together*, report to the NZ Playcentre Federation from the Working Party on Cultural Issues, Ropu Hanga Tikanga, NZ Playcentre Federation, Auckland, 1990.
91 Interview with Jill Wesselink, 1994, cited in Middleton and May, 1997, p.303.
92 Penny Jamieson, 'Who Doesn't Get to Preschool in Newtown', *Set I Item 13*, NZCER, Wellington; D.M. Fergusson, L.J. Horwood, M.E. Gretton, 'Who Doesn't Get to Preschool?', *New Zealand Journal of Education Studies*, 16, 1984, pp.168–76.
93 P. Fenwick, H. Norman, and D. Leong, *Attendance at Preschool*, Research Report Series No. 26, Department of Education.
94 Early Childhood Development Unit (ECDU), 'Pacific Island Early Childhood Education', unpublished paper, Wellington, 1991, p.6.
95 Poko Morgan, 'Pacific Islands Language Nests', Anau Ako Pasifika, unpublished paper, 1998.
96 Interview with Iole Tagoilelagi, 1995, by Helen May.
97 Jacqueline Leckie, 'Pacific Islands Women's Organisations', in Anne Else (ed.), *Women Together. A History of Women's Organisations in New Zealand – Ngā Rōpū Wāhine o te Motu*, Daphne Brasell Associates with the Historical Branch, Department of Internal Affairs, 1993, pp.521–29.
98 Diane Lysette Mara, Te Puai No Te Wahine: Pacific Island Education Policy and Education Initiatives in Aotearoa/New Zealand, a Critique', unpublished M.Lit. thesis in Education, University of Auckland, 1995.
99 Jacqueline Leckie, in Else (ed.), 1993.

100 Fereni Pepe Ete, 'Pacific Island Early Childhood Centres. The Role of the Church in Promoting Early Childhood Education in Aotearoa', in V. Podmore (ed.), *What is Government's Role in Early Childhood Education. Papers Presented at the 1993 NZCER Invitational Seminar*, NZCER, Wellington, 1993, p.91.
101 Ibid., p.91.
102 Feaua`i Burgess, 'Starting with the Samoan Language', unpublished paper, Wellington Multicultural Resource Centre, 1988, pp.2–3.
103 Mara, 1995, p.113.
104 ECDU, 'Pacific Island Early Childhood Education', 1991, p.1, based on Department of Education 1986 statistics.
105 Feaua`i Burgess, 'Recent Developments in Pacific Island Language Nests', unpublished paper, Wellington Multicultural Resource Centre, 1990, p.9.
106 Interview with Telesia McDonald, 1995, by Helen May.
107 Mara, 1995.
108 Diane Mara, *Progress Towards Licensing and Chartering Pacific Island Early Childhood Centres in New Zealand*, NZCER, Wellington, 1988.
109 Interview with Iole Tagoilelagi, 1995.
110 IECS, VUW, NZCA archive, Report to 25th Annual Conference, 1989, p.8.
111 IECS, VUW, NZCA archive, Report to 27th Annual Conference, 1990, p.11.
112 Burgess, 1990.
113 Jacqueline Leckie, in Else (ed.), 1993.
114 Mara, 1995.
115 Poko Morgan, 'We Encourage Our Parents to Tell Stories, to Tell the Stories of Samoa, to Tell the Stories of Rarotonga', in H. May and J. Mitchell (eds), *A Celebration of Women in Early Childhood*, Vol.II, Department of Early Childhood Care and Education, University of Waikato, 1992, p.29.
116 'Ana Koloto, The Home-Based Project, *Working Papers 1–3*, Anau Ako Pasifika Project, Tokoroa, 1991; 'Ema Wolfgamm, The Home-Based Project, *Working Paper 4*, Anau Ako Pasifika Project, Tokoroa, 1991; Diane Mara, *Evaluation Report of the Anau Ako Pasifika Project*, Anau Ako Pasifika, Tokoroa, 1996.

REFERENCES TO CHAPTER EIGHT

1 Jane Kelsey, *The New Zealand Experiment. A World Model for Structural Adjustment?*, Auckland University Press/Bridget Williams Books, Auckland, 1995.
2 Colin James, *The Quiet Revolution*, Allen and Unwin, Wellington, 1986.
3 Val Burns, 'Early Childhood Education in New Zealand: The "Quiet Revolution"', unpublished paper presented to L'Organisation Mondiale pour l'Education Préscolaire, XIX Assembly and Congress, London, 12 July 1989, pp.1–2.
4 Anne Meade, 'Major Policy Developments for Early Childhood Services in New Zealand', unpublished paper presented at the International Conference on Early Education and Development, Hong Kong, 31 July to 4 August 1989.
5 Kelsey, 1995.
6 Taskforce to Review Education Administration, *Administering Education – Effective Administration in Education* (Picot report), Department of Education, Wellington, 1988.
7 Gerald Grace, 'The New Zealand Treasury and the Commodification of Education', in S. Middleton, J. Codd and A. Jones (eds), *New Zealand Education Policy Today. Critical Perspectives*, Allen and Uniwn/Port Nicholson Press, Wellington, 1990, pp.27–39; Hugh Lauder, 'The New Right Revolution and Education in New Zealand', in Middleton et al, 1990.
8 Ministry of Education, *Education for the Twenty–First Century*, Wellington, 1994.
9 Jean Anyon, 'Intersections of Gender and Class: Accommodation and Resistance by Working-class and Affluent Females to Contradictory Sex-role Ideologies', in S. Walker and L. Barton (eds), *Gender Class and Education*, Falmer, Barcombe, pp.19–37.

10 *NZ Herald*, 12 February 1985.
11 Interview with Val Burns, cited in Sue Middleton and Helen May, *Teachers Talk Teaching*, Dunmore Press, Palmerston North, 1997, pp.283–84.
12 Office of the Ministry of Women's Affairs, press statement, 10 October 1984.
13 Department of Education and Department of Social Welfare, *Childcare in Transition. A Discussion Document*, Wellington, April 1985.
14 Interview with Anne Meade, 2000, by Helen May.
15 John Bennett, 'Early Childhood Care and Education. Te Kohanga Reo', *Proceedings of the Early Childhood Care and Education Forum*, Legislative Chamber, Parliament, Wellington, 4–5 December 1985, Keynote Papers, pp.2–3
16 Donna Awatere, 'Challenges in the Future, panel presentation', Early Childhood Care and Education (ECCE) Forum, Legislative Chamber, Parliament, 5 December 1985, Forum Papers 1 (no page numbers).
17 David Lange, speech notes, ECCE Forum, 1985.
18 Maris O'Rourke, panel presentation, ECCE Forum, 1985.
19 Rosslyn Noonan, panel presentation, ECCE Forum, 1985.
20 Geraldine McDonald, summing up, ECCE Forum, 1985.
21 Interview with 'Dawn Ellis', 1994, by Helen May.
22 IECS, VUW, NZCA Archive, Clippings book 1983–1990, unsourced clipping, 1986.
23 *Report of the Joint Ministerial Working Party for the Transition of Administration of Childcare from the Department of Social Welfare to the Department of Education*, New Zealand Government, Wellington, November 1985.
24 Helen May, 'Fighting for Recognition of Childcare as Real Work: The Development of the Early Childhood Workers Union', in Pat Walsh (ed.), *Trade Unions, Work and Society. The Centenary of the Arbitration System*, Dunmore Press, Palmerston North, 1994, pp.177–98.
25 *Report of the Working Party on Three Year Training for Kindergarten Teachers*, Department of Education, Wellington, April 1986.
26 *Report of the Working Party on Childcare Training*, Department of Education, Wellington, December 1986.
27 M.D.R. Irwin, 'Integrated Early Childhood Training', Treasury paper to the Minister of Finance, 16 June 1987, T 62/9/5, T4/2/11, FS:NP.
28 R.J. Renwick, 'Integrated Training for Early Childhood Education', Department of Education Paper to the Minister of Finance, (n.d.).
29 Margaret Carr, Helen May and Jane Mitchell, 'The Development of an Integrated Early Childhood Training Programme', in L. Foote, M. Gold and A. Smith, *Fifth Early Childhood Convention Papers*, Dunedin, September 1991, pp.212–35.
30 Helen May, 'The Politics of Provision and Funding', in *Proceedings of the Fourth Early Childhood Convention*, Early Childhood Convention, Wellington, 1987, pp.31–32.
31 Trudy Keenan, 'Who Pays for Early Childhood Services and Who Benefits? Some Economic Aspects of Early Childhood Services', Early Childhood Care and Education Forum, Legislative Chamber, Parliament, Wellington, 4–5 December 1985, Keynote papers; *The Economics of Childcare*, NZ Institute of Economic Research, Wellington, 1985; NZ Public Service Association (PSA), 'Measuring the Costs and Benefits of Childcare', *Economic Information, PSA*, vol.9, no.1, February 1986, pp.1–4.
32 *Waikato Times*, 30 January 1987.
33 L.J. Schweinhart, D.P. Weikart, and M.B. Larner, *A Report on the High/Scope Preschool Curriculum Comparison Study: Consequences of Three Preschool Curriculum Models Through Age 15*, High/Scope Educational Research Foundation, Ypsilanti, Mich., 1986; David Weikart, keynote address, in *Proceedings of the Fourth Early Childhood Convention*, 1987, Wellington, pp.11–21.
34 *Dominion*, 3 February 1987.
35 *Dominion*, 9 February 1987.
36 *Evening Post*, 10 September 1986; Department of Justice, *Report of the Ministerial Committee of Inquiry into Violence* (Roper report), Wellington, 1987.

37 Cathy Wylie, *In the Country of the Blind the Sighted Have No Proof. An Assessment of Treasury's Case Against Preschool Education*, NZCER, Wellington, 1988; H. Lauder, S. Middleton, J. Boston and C. Wylie, 'The Third Wave: A Critique of the New Zealand Treasury's Report on Education', *NZ Journal of Education Studies*, vol.23, no.1, 1988, pp.15–43; Middleton et al (eds), 1990.

38 The Treasury, *Government Management. Brief to the Incoming Government*, Wellington, 1987, pp.32–33.

39 Ibid., pp.40–41.

40 Harvey McQueen, *The Ninth Floor. Inside the Prime Minister's Office. A Political Experience*, Penguin Books, Auckland, 1991.

41 Clare Wells, 'The Impact of Change, Against the Odds', in Foote, Gold and Smith (eds), 1991, pp.115–27.

42 Royal Commission on Social Policy, *Towards a Fair and Just Society*, vols. 1–4, Wellington, 1988.

43 Anne Meade, 'Women and Young Children Gain a Foot in the Door', *Women's Studies Journal*, vol.6, no.1, 1990, pp.38–46.

44 P. Moss and A. Pence (eds), *Valuing Quality in Early Childhood Services*, Paul and Chapman Publishing, London, 1994; P. Moss and H. Penn, *Transforming Nursery Education*, Paul Chapman, Publishing, London, 1996.

45 *Early Childhood Care and Education. A Report of the States Services Commission Working Group*, State Services Commission, Wellington, 1988, p.6.

46 Interview with Anne Meade, 1999, by Helen May.

47 Ibid.

48 The Treasury, T62/9/5/3, *Early Childhood Care and Education. Report of the Working Group*, September 1988, p.1.

49 Interview with Anne Meade, 1997, by Helen May.

50 Meade, 1990, p.42.

51 *Towards 1990 and Beyond – a Tangata Whenua Response to 'Education to be More'*, Te Poho-Rawiri Kōhanga Reo and Te Whakaruruhau Kōhanga Reo, Gisborne, 1988, p.1.

52 Department of Education, *Responses to 'Education to be More'*, Department of Education, Wellington, October 1988.

53 *New Zealand Sunday Times*, 9 October 1988.

54 Linda Mitchell, 'Influencing Policy Change Through Collective Action', unpublished paper, NZEI, Wellington, 1997.

55 *Dominion* interview with Rosslyn Noonan, 1999, by Helen May.

56 Meade, 1990, p.42.

57 Helen May, 'After Before Five. The Politics of Early Childhood Education in the Nineties', *Women's Studies Journal*, vol.8, no.2, 1992, pp.85–86.

58 David Lange, *Before Five. Early Childhood Care and Education in New Zealand*, Government Printer, 1988, p.iii.

59 Department of Education, *Report of the Awareness of Racism and Anti-Racist Strategies for Early Childhood*, Lopdell Course, 7–10 February 1989. Appendix 3, memorandum.

60 Before Five Implementation Working Group, *Report of the Qualifications Working Group*, Department of Education Implementation Unit, Wellington, 1989.

61 Before Five Implementation Working Group, *Report of the Bulk Funding Working Group*, Department of Education Implementation Unit, Wellington, 1989.

62 Before Five Implementation Working Group, *Report of the National Guidelines, Minimum Standards and Charters Working Group*, Department of Education Implementation Unit, Wellington, 1989.

63 Meade, 1990, p.44.

64 David Lange, editorial, 1989, unsourced and undated, IECS–VUW, Clippings book 1983–90.

65 *Dominion Sunday Times*, 13 August 1989.

66 *Roundabout*, May 1989.

67 Anne Smith, 'Preschool Foresight Deserves Credit', unsourced undated article, 1990, IECS, VUW, Clippings book 1983–90.
68 Interview with Anne Smith, 1994, by Helen May.
69 Helen May, 'The Price of Partnership. The Before Five Decade', in M. Thrupp (ed.), 'A Decade of Reform in New Zealand Education. Where to Now?' *NZ Journal of Educational Studies*, vol.34, no.1, 1999, pp.18–27.
70 Helen May, 'From a Floor to a Drawer. A Post-Meade Reflection on Early Childhood Policy', *Te Timatanga*, vol.9, no.2, 1991, p.4.
71 Ministry of Education, *'Purple' Management Handbook*, Wellington, 1989.
72 Sue Stover (ed.), *Good Clean Fun: New Zealand's Playcentre Movement*, NZPCF, Auckland, 1998; *Whanau Tupu Ngatahi. Report to the New Zealand Playcentre of the Working Party on Cultural Issues*, New Zealand Playcentre Federation, Wellington, 1990; NZCA, *Policy Document*, NZCA, Wellington, June 1990.
73 *Roundabout*, September 1989.
74 *Roundabout*, November 1989.
75 *Doubletake*, November 1990.
76 May, 'From a Floor to a Drawer', 1991.
77 *NZ Herald*, 13 November 1990.
78 Crispin Gardiner, 'Childcare Funds and the Ministry', letter to *NZ Sunday Times*, 28 August 1990.
79 'Tiny Tot Fees Become Growing Problem', *NZ Herald*, 13 November 1990.
80 Linda Mitchell, 'Before Five, The Price of Partnership', unpublished paper for conference on A Decade of Reform in New Zealand, University of Waikato, Hamilton, 10–11 June 1999, p.6.
81 Childcare Employee Project, *National Childcare Staffing Study in the USA*, Berkeley, California, 1990.
82 Ministry of Education, *Conditions for the Receipt of Early Childhood Bulk Funding*, Wellington, 1990, 1991.
83 Ministry of Education, 'Accountability in Early Childhood Centres', *Education Gazette*, vol.70, no.19, 15 October 1991, p.1; John Gill, 'Early Childhood Education Centres – Financial Planning and Accountability', *Accountants' Journal*, December 1991, pp.51–55; Ministry of Education, *Early Childhood Education: Accountability for Government Funding for Private Providers*, Wellington, 20 March 1992.
84 Ministry of Education, 'Early Childhood Charter Guidelines. A Statement of Desirable Objectives and Practices', a supplement to the *Education Gazette*, 14 December 1990.
85 A. Smith and S. Farquhar, 'The New Zealand Experience of Charter Development in Early Childhood Services', in Moss and Pence, (eds), 1994, pp.123–41.
86 *Report of the Change Team on Targeted Social Assistance*, Prime Minister's Office, Wellington, 1991.
87 Lockwood Smith, press statement, 22 January 1991.
88 Anne Meade, 'Boffins in Early Childhood Services', in L. Foote, M. Gold and A. Smith (eds), 1991, pp.55–67.
89 Ministry of Education, *A Summary of the Submissions on the Early Childhood Reviews, February 1991*, Research and Statistics, Ministry of Education, Wellington, 1991.
90 Crispin Gardiner, *Review of Early Childhood Funding: An Independent Report*, University of Waikato, Hamilton, 1991.
91 *Dominion*, 3 May 1991.
92 Prime Ministerial Committee on Reform of Social Assistance, *Early Childhood Care and Education Funding Review*, Wellington, May 1991.
93 Lockwood Smith, *Education Policy: Investing in People Our Greatest Asset*, Ministry of Education, Wellington, July 1991, p.18.
94 CECUA, *Survey of Childcare Centre Managers, Reduction in Funding for Under Two Year Olds in Childcare Centres: Effects on Quality, Access and Centre Operation*, Wellington, 1991.
95 Anne Meade and Carmen Dalli, 'Review of the Early Childhood Sector', in Ian Living-

stone (ed.), *New Zealand Annual Review of Education 1, 1991*, Education Department, VUW, 1992, pp.113–32.

96 Cited in Lockwood Smith and Jenny Shipley, *Targeted Assistance to Low Income Users of Early Childhood Services*, Cab (91) M 28/18 ref., Paper to Prime Ministerial Committee on Reform of Social Assistance, 9 October 1991, p.1.

97 Ibid., p.3.

98 Ministry of Education, *Review of Early Childhood Funding Terms of Reference*, Wellington, 6 July 1993.

99 Ministry of Education, *Review of Early Childhood Funding: Summary of Submissions*, Economic and Funding Policy Section, Wellington, December 1993.

100 Ministry of Education, *A Report of the 1994 Speaking Directly Early Childhood Education Conference*, Wellington, 1994.

101 Carmen Dalli, 'Is Cinderella Back Among the Cinders? A Review of Early Childhood Education in the 1990s', in H. Manson (ed.), *New Zealand Annual Review of Education 3, 1993*, Faculty of Education, Victoria University of Wellington, 1994, p.226–27.

102 Quality Funding Working Group, *Criteria for Eligibility for Quality Funding. Report to the Associate Minister of Education*, Ministry of Education, Wellington, 1995; Ministry of Education, *Criteria for Funding Rate from 1 March 1996*, Wellington, 1996.

103 Helen May, in Walsh (ed.), 1994.

104 Linda Mitchell, 'Crossroads – Early Childhood in the Mid-1990s', in Ian Livingstone (ed.), *New Zealand Annual Review of Education 5, 1995*, VUW Faculty of Education and NZCER, Wellington, 1996, pp.75–92.

105 Clare Wells, 'Future Directions: Shaping Early Childhood Policy for the 21st Century – A Personal Perspective', in Ian Livingstone (ed.), *New Zealand Annual Review of Education 8, 1988*, VUW School of Education and NZCER, Wellington, 1999, pp.45–60.

106 Early Childhood Education Project, *Future Directions: Early Childhood Education in New Zealand. Final Report*, NZEI–Te Riu Roa, Wellington, 1996, p.1.

107 Clare Wells, in Livingstone (ed.), 1999.

108 NZEI–Te Riu Roa, 'May Day May Day – Red Alert, Early Childhood Funding Campaign', Wellington, 1997.

109 Clare Wells, in Livingstone (ed.), 1999, p.56.

110 Nick Smith, opening address to 7th Early Childhood Convention, Nelson, 27 September 1999.

111 J. Walmsley and J. Margolis, *Hot House People. Can We Create Super Human Beings?* Pan Original, London, 1987.

112 S. Vartulli and M. Winter, 'Parents as First Teachers', in M.J. Fine (ed.), *The Second Handbook on Parent Education*, Academic Press, San Diego, 1989, p.99.

113 Walmsley and Margolis, 1987; Statement from Lockwood Smith, *Sunday Star*, 6 May 1990.

114 *Hansard*, vol.46, 4 June 1992, John Luxton.

115 Lesley Max, *Children: Endangered Species?*, Penguin Books, Auckland, 1990.

116 Lockwood Smith, speech notes, 2nd NZ Conference on Research and Policy, Wellington, 31 August 1990, p.10.

117 *Daily News*, undated clipping, 1990, 'Massive Wastage', IECS–VUW, Clippings book 1990–1995.

118 Ibid.

119 Douglas Powell, 'Home Visiting in the Early Years: Policy and Program Design Decisions', *Young Children*, vol.45, no.6, 1990, p.72.

120 Carmen Dalli, 'Policy Agendas for Children's Lives', *NZ Educational Studies Journal*, vol.27, no.1, 1992, p.60.

121 L. Wallace, F. Burgess and P. Robertson, letter to Lockwood Smith, 1 August 1980.

122 Leonie Pihama, 'Tungia te ururua, kia tupu whakaritorito te tupu o harekeke: A Critical Analysis of Parents as First Teachers', unpublished MA thesis, Victoria University of Wellington, 1993, p.143.

123 Bruce McMillan, 'Parents as First Teachers', unpublished paper presented at a seminar for the Children's Issues Centre, University of Otago, Dunedin, 16 October 1995, p.7.

124 Bruce McMillan, letter to Lockwood Smith, 27 May 1990.

125 Jill Mitchell and Val Ford, 'Intervening Early: The Use and Adaptation of a Parents as First Teachers Programme in New Zealand/Aotearoa', paper presented at Inclusive Education, Inclusive Society, First International Conference on Special Education, Brunei, 21–26 July 1997.

126 K. Campbell and P. Sylva, *PAFT Pilot Project Evaluation. Preliminary Report on Phase 111: Subject Recruitment and Initial Data Collection*, University of Otago Medical School, Dunedin, 1994; A. Boyd and H. Dixon, *Parents as First Teachers Pilot Project*, Auckland Uniservices for the Ministry of Education, Auckland, 1995.

127 Ministry of Education, *Education for the Twenty-first Century*, Ministry of Education, Wellington, 1994.

128 Interview with Mere Mitchell, 1994, cited in Middleton and May, 1997, pp.321–22.

129 Mitchell and Ford, 1997, p.6.

130 Sharyn Devereux Blum, 'Parents as First Teachers in New Zealand', paper presented at Australian Early Childhood Association conference, Children in the Balance, Melbourne, September 1997, p.9.

131 Ian Livingstone, *Parents as First Teachers, Summary Report, Evaluation of Pilot Project*, Ministry of Education, Wellington, 1998, p.43.

132 Early Childhood Development (ECD), *Parents as First Teachers. Progress Report*, ECD, Wellington, 1999.

133 Cathy Wylie, *First Impressions. The Initial Impact of Salary Bulk Funding on New Zealand Kindergartens*, NZCER, Wellington, 1992.

134 Claire Davison, *The Sinking of the Early Childhood Education Flagship. Government's Plan to Privatise Kindergartens. The Bulk Funding Story*, occasional paper no.3, Institute for Early Childhood Studies, Victoria University of Wellington and Wellington College of Education, Wellington, 1997.

135 John Luxton, speech to the NZFKTA annual conference, Wellington, 1994, p.4.

136 Davison, 1997, p.20.

137 John Luxton, speech to the NZFKTA annual conference, Wellington, 1995, p.6.

138 Ministry of Education, Education and Science Select Committee Briefing Notes, 28 November 1995.

139 Linda Mitchell, in Livingstone (ed.), 1996; Davison, 1997.

140 Claire Davison, 'Kindergartens and the State Sector Act', in Ian Livingstone (ed.), *New Zealand Annual Review of Education 1997*, VUW School of Education and NZCER, Wellington, 1998, p.156.

141 *NZ Herald*, 'Kindergartens Feel Pressure with Bulk Grant', 7 August 1992.

142 Wylie, 1992; *The Impact of Salary Bulk Funding on New Zealand Kindergartens. Results of the Second National Survey*, NZCER, Wellington, 1993; U. Dougherty, 'Kindergarten Bulk Funding, Teacher and Parent Perceptions of Salary Bulk Funding and its Effect on the Quality of Care and Education', unpublished M.Ed thesis, Massey University, 1994; R. Houghton and A. Wilson, *The Introduction of Bulk Funding Including Salaries of Kindergartens: Financial and Operational Impacts for 1993 and 1994*, University of Otago, Dunedin, 1995.

143 Houghton and Wilson, 1995, p.vi.

144 Judith Duncan and Lee Rowe, 'Don't be Too Polite Girls, Don't be Too Polite: Kindergarten Teachers and Employment Contracts', in Ian Livingstone (ed.), *New Zealand Annual Review of Education 1996*, VUW Faculty of Education and NZCER, Wellington, 1997, pp.157–80.

145 Linda Mitchell, *Closing the Gap*, NZ Council of Trade Unions, 1997, p.9.

146 Briefing to Wyatt Creech, Minister of Education, released under the Official Information Act, n.d., p.2.

147 The Treasury, T97C/986, Cabinet Agenda item 14: State Sector Amendment Bill (Kindergarten Associations), 18 April 1997; Ministry of Education, *State Sector Act Amendment: Policy Issues*, Wellington, 24 April 1997.

148 Cabinet Committee on Legislation and House Business, Leg (97) 25, State Sector Amendment Bill (Kindergarten Associations), 16 April 1997, p.2.

149 Linda Mitchell, 'Before Five', 1999.

150 'Kindergarten Cop-out', *NZ Education Review*, 7 May 1997.

151 *Hansard*, 29 April 1997.

152 Linda Mitchell, 'Before Five', 1999.

153 *Evening Post*, 4 April 2000.

154 Janice Burns, *Kindergarten and Primary Teachers. A Comparison of Their Work*, NZEI, NZFKA, AKA and NZEI–Te Riu Roa, Wellington, 1999, p.5.

155 Labour Party, *Better Beginnings, Labour in Education*, Wellington, 1999.

156 Allan Wendelborn, 'The Employment Relations Bill', *Executive Diary, Confidential Journal to Members of Early Childhood Council*, 14 April 2000, pp.1–3.

REFERENCES TO CHAPTER NINE

1 Anne Smith, 'Early Childhood Educare in New Zealand: The Search for Quality', unpublished talk, Wellington, 8 June 1993.

2 Te Kōhanga Reo National Trust Board, *Te Korowai*, Te Kōhanga Reo National Office, Wellington, 1995, described in Arapere Royal Tangaere, 'A Framework for Developing Quality in Early Childhood Centres in Aotearoa', in A.B. Smith and N.J. Taylor (eds), *Assessing and Improving Quality in Early Childhood Centres, National Seminar Proceedings*, Children's Issues Centre, University of Otago, Dunedin, 1996, pp.11–18; Ministry of Education, *The Quality Journey, He Haerenga Whai Hua*, Learning Media, Wellington, 1999.

3 Te Tari Puna Ora O Aotearoa–NZCA, *Quality Register for Early Childhood Education and Care Centres*, Wellington, 1996.

4 Early Childhood Development Unit, *A Procedural Guide for Sexual Abuse and Care in Early Childhood*, Wellington, 1990; Ministry of Education, *Prevent Child Abuse: Guidelines for Early Childhood Education Services*, Learning Media, Wellington, 1993.

5 Judith Duncan, *I Spy: Sexual Abuse Prevention Policies – Protection or Harm?* Wellington College of Education, 1998.

6 Anne Smith, 'The Case for Quality Day Care in New Zealand – Liberation of Children and Parents', in B. O'Rourke and J. Clough (eds), *Early Childhood in New Zealand*, Heinemann Educational Books, Auckland, 1978, p.235.

7 R. Roupp, J. Travers, F. Glantz and C. Coelen, *Children at the Centre. Final Report of the National Day Care Study*, Department of Health Education and Welfare, Washington DC, 1979; M. Whitebook, C. Howes and D. Phillips, *Who Cares? Child Care Teachers and the Quality of Care in America. Final Report of the National Child Care Staffing Study*, Child Care Employee Project, Oakland, CA, 1989; Costs, Quality and Child Outcomes Study Team, *Costs, Quality and Child Outcomes in Childcare Centres. Public Report*, Department of Economics, Center for Research in Economics and Social Policy, University of Colorado at Denver, 1995.

8 Gail Sloan Cannella, *Deconstructing Early Childhood Education. Social Justice and Revolution*, Peter Lang Publishing, New York, 1997.

9 Interview with Heather Te Huia, 1996, cited in Sue Middleton and Helen May, *Teachers Talk Teaching*, Dunmore Press, Palmerson North, 1997, p.315.

10 Linda Mitchell, 'Before Five: The Price of Partnership', unpublished paper for conference A Decade of Reform in New Zealand, University of Waikato, Hamilton, 10–11 June 1999.

11 Gunilla Dahlberg, Peter Moss and Alan Pence, *Beyond Quality in Early Childhood Education and Care. Postmodern Perspectives*, Falmer Press, London, 1999, p.4.

12 Ibid., pp.1–2.

13 Martin Woodhead, *In Search of the Rainbow: Pathways to Quality in Large Scale Programmes for Young Disadvantaged Children*, Bernard van Leer Foundation, The Hague, 1996.
14 P. Moss and A. Pence (eds), *Valuing Quality in Early Childhood Services*, Paul Chapman Publishing, London, 1994.
15 Sarah-Eve Farquhar, 'Quality in Early Education and Care: What Do We Mean?' *Early Development and Care*, vol.64, 1990, pp.71–83.
16 Martin Woodhead, '"Quality" in Early Childhood Programme – A Contextually Appropriate Approach', *International Journal of Early Years Education*, vol.6, no.1, 1998, pp.15–16.
17 Moss and Pence, 1994, p.172.
18 Anne Smith, 'Is Quality a Subjective or Objective Matter?' in A.B. Smith and N.J. Taylor (eds), 1996, p.87.
19 Ibid.
20 S.J. Barraclough and A.B. Smith, 'Do Parents Choose and Value Quality Child Care in New Zealand?', *International Journal of Early Years Education*, vol.4, no.1, pp.5–26.
21 Anne Smith, in Smith and Taylor (eds), 1996, p.87.
22 *Dominion*, 5 May 2000.
23 Cathy Wylie, *Five Years Old and Competent*, NZCER, Wellington, 1996; Cathy Wylie with Anne Else, *Six Years Old and Competent*, NZCER, Wellington, 1998; C. Wylie, J. Thompson and C. Lythe, *Competent Children at Eight. Families, Early Childhood Education and Schools*, NZCER, Wellington, 1999.
24 Interview with Helen Orr, 1994, cited in Middleton and May, 1997, p.317.
25 Ministry of Education, 'Revised Statement of Desirable Objectives and Practices (DOPs) for Chartered Early Childhood Services in New Zealand', *Education Gazette*, 3 October 1996.
26 NZEI–Te Riu Roa, *Response to the ERO Evaluation Report 'What Counts as Quality in Childcare'*, NZEI, Wellington, [n.d.], p.10.
27 Data Analysis and Management Division, *Early Childhood Statistics: Education Statistics News Sheet*, vol.10 no.1, May 2000, Ministry of Education, Wellington.
28 Linda Mitchell, 'Before Five', 1999, p.9.
29 Ministry of Education, *The Quality Journey*, 1999.
30 Data Analysis and Management Division, *Early Childhood Statistics*, 2000.
31 Linda Mitchell, 'The Cost of Quality?', in Smith and Taylor (eds), 1996, pp.91–102; Helen May, 'The Price of Partnership. The Before Five Decade', in M. Thrupp (ed.), 'A Decade of Reform in New Zealand Education. Where to Now?', *NZ Journal of Educational Studies*, vol.34, no.1, 1999.
32 Data Analysis and Management Division, *Summary of Children on Regular Rolls of Early Childhood Services*, Ministry of Education, Wellington, 1999.
33 Data Analysis and Management Division, *Early Childhood Statistics*, 2000.
34 Ibid.
35 ECDU, *Meeting the Needs of Young Children with Special Developmental Needs. A Resource Booklet for Charter Development in Early Childhood Settings*, ECDU, Wellington, 1990, Frontpiece.
36 'Montessori School. A Profile', *Education Review*, 19 June 1996, pp.12–13.
37 Ministry of Education, 'Growth in Early Childhood', *Education Trends Report*, vol.7, no.1, Wellington, 1993.
38 Ministry of Education, *Introducing the Resourcing Division*, Circular no.1999/19, 1999.
39 Ministry of Education, 'Growth in Early Childhood', 1993; Data Analysis and Management Division, *Education Statistics News Sheet*, 1997, 1999.
40 Diane Mara, *Implementation of Te Whāriki in Pacific Island Centres. Final Report to the Ministry of Education*, NZCER, Wellington, 1998.
41 Ministry of Education, *Ko e Ako `a e Kakai Pasifika*, Wellington, 1996.
42 New Zealand Labour Party, *Better Beginnings, Labour on Early Childhood Education*, Wellington, 1999.
43 Iritana Tawhiwhirangi, 'Kohanga Reo and the Tino Rangatiratanga Training Programme', in G. Maxwell, I. Hassel and J. Robertson (eds), *Towards a Child and Family Policy for New*

Zealand, Office of the Commissioner for Children, Wellington, 1991, pp.359–64; Arapera Royal Tangaere, 'Te Kohanga Reo – More than a Language Nest. The Future of Te Reo Maori, Te Iwi Maori and a People's Soul', keynote address to the NZARE Conference, Nelson, 1996.

44 *NZ Education Review*, July 1999.

45 Iritana Tawhiwhirangi, Foreword, in D. Waiti and A. Royal Tangaere (eds), *Pono ke te Kaupapa Puna ko te Reo. A Study of Early Kohanga Reo and Their Whanau*, NZCER and Te Kohanga Reo National Trust, Wellington, in press.

46 Paul Callister and Val Podmore, *Striking the Balance: Families, Work and Early Childhood Education*, Paul Callister and Associates and NZCER, Wellington, 1995.

47 Report of the Prime Ministerial Task Force on Employment, *An Education, Training and Employment Policy for Young People*, Wellington, 1994.

48 Department of Labour and National Advisory Council on the Employment of Women, *New Zealand Childcare Survey 1998: A Survey of Early Childhood Education and Care Arrangements for Children*, Wellington, 1999.

49 Margaret Carr and I have written extensively in this topic. This section is culled from joint writing.

50 Ministry of Education, *He Whāriki Matauranga mo nga Mokopuna o Aotearoa. Te Whāriki: Early Childhood Curriculum*, Learning Media, Wellington, 1996.

51 Ministry of Education, 'Revised Statement of Desirable Objectives and Practices', 1996.

52 Margaret Carr and Helen May, 'The Role of Government in Early Childhood Curriculum', in V. Podmore (ed.), *What is Government's Role in Early Childhood Education?*, NZCER, Wellington, 1993, pp.42–50; 'Choosing a Model: Reflecting on the Development Process of Te Whāriki, National Early Childhood Curriculum Guidelines in New Zealand', *International Journal of Early Years Education*, vol.1, no.3, 1993, pp.7–22; 'Weaving Patterns: Developing National Early Childhood Curriculum Guidelines in Aotearoa–New Zealand', *Australian Journal of Early Childhood Education*, vol.19, no.1, 1994, pp.25–33; 'Te Whāriki, Making a Difference for the Under Fives? The New National Early Childhood Curriculum', *International Journal of Early Years Education*, vol.5, no.3, 1997, pp.225–36; Te Whāriki: Curriculum Voices', in Helen Penn (ed.), *Early Childhood Services. Theory, Policy and Practice*, Open University Press, Buckingham, pp.53–73; 'Empowering Children to Learn and Grow – Te Whāriki, the New Zealand National Early Childhood Curriculum', in J. Hayden (ed.), *Landscapes in Early Childhood. Cross-National Perspectives on Empowerment*, Peter Lang, New York, 2000, pp.153–70.

53 Ministry of Education, *Te Whāriki: Draft Guidelines for Developmentally Appropriate Programmes in Early Childhood Services*, Learning Media, Wellington, 1993.

54 Kathleen Murrow, *Early Childhood Workers' Opinion on the Draft Document Te Whāriki*, Research Section Report Series no.5, Ministry of Education, Wellington, 1995.

55 Dunedin College of Education, *Te Whāriki Curriculum Trial*, Ministry of Education, Wellington, 1994; M. Haggerty and P. Hubbard, *Te Whāriki Trial: Five Wellington Centres Work on an Agreed Basis for Curriculum in Early Childhood in Aotearoa New Zealand*, Ministry of Education, Wellington, 1994.

56 Margaret Carr, *Assessing Children's Experiences. Final Report to the Ministry of Education*, University of Waikato, Hamilton, 1998; Val Podmore and Helen May, *Evaluating Early Childhood Programmes Using Te Whāriki: Final Report of Phases One and Two to the Ministry of Education*, NZCER, Wellington, 1998; Mara, 1998; Margaret Carr, Helen May and Val Podmore, *Learning and Teaching Stories: Action Research on Evaluation in Early Childhood Centres. Final Report to the Ministry of Education*, NZCER, Wellington, 2000.

57 Ministry of Education, *The National Curriculum of New Zealand: A Discussion Document*, Learning Media, Wellington, 1991, p.1.

58 Ministry of Education, *The New Zealand Curriculum Framework*, Learning Media, Wellington, 1993.

59 May and Carr, 'Choosing a Model', 1993.

60 Department of Education, *The Curriculum: An Early Childhood Statement, Report of the Lopdell Working Group*, Wellington, 1988.
61 Tilly Reedy, 'I Have a Dream', *Proceedings of the Combined Early Childhood Union of Aotearoa (CECUA) Early Childhood Conference*, CECUA, Christchurch, 1993, pp.1–7; 'Knowledge and Power Set Me Free', *Proceedings of the Sixth Early Childhood Convention*, Convention Committee, Auckland, vol.1, 1995, pp.13–32.
62 Reedy, 1995, p.13.
63 Erik Erikson, *Childhood and Society*, W.W. Norton, New York, 1950; Barbel Inhelder and Jean Piaget, *The Growth of Logical Thinking*, Basic Books, New York, 1958.
64 Urie Bronfenbrenner, *The Ecology of Human Development*, Harvard University Press, Cambridge, Mass., 1979; L.S. Vygotsky, *Mind in Society: the Development of Psychological Processes*, Harvard University Press, Cambridge, Mass., 1978.
65 J.S. Bruner, *Acts of Meaning*, Harvard University Press, Cambridge, Mass., 1990.
66 Anne Meade, 'Good Practice to Best Practice in Early Childhood Education: Extending Policies and Children's Minds', unpublished paper for Start Right conference, London, September, 1995, p.14.
67 Anne Smith, 'The Early Childhood Curriculum from a Sociocultural Perspective', *Early Childhood Development and Care*, no.115, 1995, p.56.
68 Jenny Ritchie, 'The Bicultural Imperative Within the New Zealand Draft Curriculum Guidelines for Early Childhood Education, Te Whāriki', *Australian Journal of Early Childhood*, vol.21, no.3, p.31.
69 Feaua`i Burgess, 'Blending Te Whāriki and the Ta`iala in Early Childhood Education Programmes for Bilingual Children', unpublished paper presented at the Sixth National Conference on Community Languages and ESOL, Palmerston North, September 1998; Mara, 1998.
70 Reedy, 1995.
71 Dunedin College of Education, *Te Whāriki Curriculum Trial*, 1994; Haggerty and Hubbard, 1994.
72 Education Review Office, *Use of Te Whāriki*, Wellington, December 1998.
73 Mara, 1998.
74 Maggie Haggerty, 'Sighting, Citing and Siting Te Whāriki: Exploring the Use of Video Feedback as a Tool for Critical Pedagogy', unpublished M.Ed thesis, Victoria University of Wellington, 1998; Anne Smith, 'The Role of Early Childhood Curriculum: Promoting Diversity Versus Uniformity', unpublished paper presented at Enhancing Quality in the Early Years conference, Dublin, Ireland, November 1999.
75 Joy Cullen, 'The Challenge of Te Whāriki for Future Development in Early Childhood Education', *Delta*, vol.48, issue 1, 1996, p.118.
76 Joy Cullen, 'Raising the Profile of Infant and Toddler Education', *The First Years*, vol.2. issue 1. April 2000, p.6.
77 Svend Ove Olsen, *Verdens Bedste Folkskole! – vi kan loere af det New Zealandske Skolesystem*, Dafolo Forlag, Copenhagen, 1996; Penn, 1999; Hayden, 2000.
78 Cathy Nutbrown, *Respectful Educators – Capable Learners: Children's Rights and Early Education*, Paul Chapman, London, 1996.
79 Frode Sobstad, 'National Program for the Kindergarten in Norway: A Framework for Reflection in Action', unpublished paper presented at a curriculum seminar, Queen Maude College of Early Education, Norway, December 1997, p.11.
80 Early Childhood Forum, *Quality in Diversity in Early Learning. A Framework for Practitioners*, National Children's Bureau, Goldsmith College, London, 1997. This is the draft version. The final version appeared in 1999.
81 The School Curriculum and Assessment Authority, *Nursery Education: Desirable Outcomes for Children's Learning on Entering Compulsory Education*, Her Majesty's Government, London, 1996.
82 Tina Bruce, 'Weaving Links Between New Zealand and the United Kingdom', unpublished paper presented at Beyond Desirable Objectives Seminar, Pen Green Research, Development and Training Base, November 1996, p.11.

83 Margaret Carr, *Assessing Children's Learning in Early Childhood Settings, Three Videos and Workshop Programme*, NZCER, Wellington, and VIDEOCAMPUS, Auckland, 1998.

84 Anne Meade, Val Podmore, Helen May, Sarah Te One and Rachel Brown, *Options Paper, Early Childhood Qualifications and Regulations Project. Final Report to the Ministry of Education*, University of Waikato and NZCER, Wellington, 1998; Anne Smith, 'The Quality of Childcare Centres for Infants in New Zealand', *NZARE Monograph*, no.4, 1996, New Zealand Association for Research in Education, Palmerston North.

85 Data Management and Analysis Division, *Education Statistics News Sheet*, 1997.

86 Early Childhood Education Project, *The Workload of Volunteers in Early Childhood Services*, NZEI–TRR, Wellington, 2000.

87 Ministry of Education, *Early Qualifications and Training: A Blueprint for the Future*, Ministry of Education, Wellington, 1990.

88 Anne Meade and Carmen Dalli, 'Review of the Early Childhood Sector', *NZ Annual Review of Education 1. 1991*, Department of Education, VUW, 1992, pp.113–32; Carmen Dalli, 'Is Cinderella Back Among the Cinders? A Review of Early Childhood Education in the 1990s', *NZ Annual Review of Education 3. 1993*, Faculty of Education, VUW, 1994.

89 Anne Meade, 'Before Five – 5 Years On', unpublished keynote address to NZARE special seminar, University of Auckland, August 1994, p.7.

90 Data Management and Analysis Division, *Early Childhood Statistics*, 2000.

91 Ministry of Education, *Pathways Programme*, letter to management and staff of Early Childhood Services, National Early Childhood Organisations and Training Providers, Wellington, 30 August 1996.

92 New Zealand Qualifications Authority, *Early Childhood Education Policies*, Wellington, 1996.

93 Meade et al, *Early Childhood Qualifications and Regulations Project*, 1998.

94 Data Management and Analysis Division, *Early Childhood Statistics*, 2000.

95 New Zealand Qualifications Authority, *Skill New Zealand. Life Long Education and Learning*, Wellington, 1993, p.63.

96 Helen May, 'The Politics and Pitfalls of Teacher Education Unit Standards for the New Qualification Framework: Early Childhood Issues', unpublished paper presented at the NZARE conference, Hamilton, December 1993.

97 Margaret Carr, 'Competency or Teacher Change', unpublished paper, University of Waikato, 1993.

98 Margaret Carr and Helen May, *The Development of Unit Standard Titles for Qualifications in Early Childhood Settings. Report to the Ministry of Education*, University of Waikato, Hamilton, November 1993.

99 Linda Mitchell, 'Before Five', 1999.

100 Helen May, 'Discoveries: Triumphs, Trials and Talk of Early Childhood Teachers' Education', Inaugural Lecture at Victoria University of Wellington, Institute for Early Childhood Studies, Victoria University and Wellington College of Education, May 1997.

101 PORSE, *When Nanny's Here. Affordable Home Childcare in Partnership with Families*, PORSE Network, Hastings, n.d.

102 Ministry of Education, *Education for the Twenty-first Century*, Learning Media, Wellington, 1994.

103 Eileen Ledger, 'Do I Go To School to Get a Brain?', *Childrenz Issues Journal*, vol.2. no.1, 1998, pp.7–11; Jennifer Ann Norris, 'Transforming Masculinities: Boys Making the Transition to School', unpublished MA thesis, Victoria University of Wellington, 1999; Sally Peters, 'Planning for Transition. Early Childhood Teachers' Role in Enhancing Children's Transition to School', paper presented at the 7th Early Childhood Convention, Nelson, September 1999; 'Continuity and Discontinuity. Issues for Parents and Teachers to Enhance Children's Transition to School', paper presented at the Warwick Early Years Conference, University of Warwick, Coventry, England, April, 1999.

104 Tony Holmes, 'Transition to School', *Childrenz Issues Journal*, vol.2, no.1, 1998, p.51.

105 Ledger, 1998; Norris, 1999; Peters, 1999; Stuart McNaughton, *Patterns of Emergent Literacy: Processes of Development and Transition*, Auckland University Press, Auckland,

1995; L.M. Sauvao, L. Mara and V. Podmore, *Transition to School from Pacific Islands Early Childhood Services*, NZCER, Wellington, 2000.

106 Middleton and May, 1997.

107 Mary Eming-Young (ed.), *Early Child Development: Investing in Our Children's Future. Proceedings of a World Bank Conference on Early Child Development: Investing in the Future*, World Bank, Atlanta, Georgia, 1996.

108 Ministry of Education, 1993.

109 Carr, 1998.

110 Helen May, 'The Price of Partnership: The *Before Five* Decade', *NZ Journal of Educational Studies*, vol. 34 no.1, 1999.

111 Linda Mitchell, 'Before Five: The Price of Partnership', unpublished paper for conference on A Decade of Reform in New Zealand, University of Waikato, Hamilton, 10–11 June 1999.

112 Linda Mitchell, 'A New Debate About Childhood. Can It Make a Difference?' Proposal for a PhD thesis, Victoria University of Wellington, 1999.

113 New Zealand Government, *Towards a Social Code of Responsibility. A Public Discussion Document*, Department of Social Welfare, Wellington, 1998.

114 Mitchell, 1999, 'A New Debate About Childhood', p.16.

115 Cannella, 1997.

116 National Working Group, *Early Childhood Education Code of Ethics for Aotearoa/New Zealand*, NZEI Te Riu Roa, Wellington, 1995; Carmen Dalli and Linda Mitchell, *The Early Childhood Code of Ethics. Dealing with the Hard Issues*, proceedings of the 6th Early Childhood Convention, Auckland Convention Committee, Auckland, vol.1, September 1995, pp.63–76.

117 Dahlberg, Moss and Pence, 1999, p.73.

118 Mitchell, 1999, 'A New Debate About Childhood', p.18.

REFERENCES TO CHAPTER TEN

1 Editorial, 'Nanny tax cuts or nanny state', *Dominion Post*, 13 July 2005.

2 'Helen May, 'Election year politics, 2005, and the "Nanny" State' in I. Livingston (ed), *New Zealand Annual Review of Education 15*, 2005, School of Education Studies, Victoria University Wellington, 2006, pp.133–52.

3 Strategic Plan Working Group, *Consultation document for the development of the strategic plan for early childhood education*, Ministry of Education, Wellington, 2001.

4 Early Childhood Education Project, *Future Directions. Early childhood education in New Zealand. Final report*, NZEI-Te Riu Roa, Wellington, 1996.

5 Strategic Plan Working Group, 2001, p.5.

6 Helen May. '"Blue skies" talk in the "playground"', *Delta*, vol. 54, nos. 1/2, 2002, pp.9–28.

7 Minister of Education, Trevor Mallard, Speech notes, 10 July 2001.

8 Strategic Plan Working Group, *Final version. Strategic plan for early childhood education*. Ministry of Education, Wellington. 2001.

9 Brenda Bushouse, *Early childhood education policy in Aotearoa-New Zealand. The creation of the 20 hours free programme*, Fulbright New Zealand, Wellington, 2008, p.38.

10 Helen May, 'The politics of free early childhood education. A New Zealand case study', paper presented at the European Early Childhood Research Association Conference, Prague, Czech Republic, 29 August–2 September 2007.

11 Helen May, 'Mapping Some Landscapes of Colonial-Global Childhood', *European Early Childhood Research Journal*, vol. 9, no. 2, 2001, pp.5–20.

12 Helen May, 'Towards Citizenry Rights in Early Childhood', *Delta*, vol.56, no. 1, 2004, pp.75–91; 'A right as a citizen to a free [early childhood] education 1930s–2000s', *Childrenz Issues. Journal of the Children's Issues Centre*, vol. 9, no. 2, 2005, pp.20–24.

13 Peter Fraser, 'Education Department, Annual Report' *Appendices to the Journal of the House of Representatives*, 1939, E.1, p.2.

14 Carmen Dalli, 'Becoming a profession. A New Zealand story of advocacy, strategy and

challenge' Keynote address, European Conference on quality employment in care work with young children, Kind & Gezin, Brussels, 21–22 April 2008, p.1.

15 Ministry of Education, *State of New Zealand Education 2007*, Learning Media, Wellington, 2008.
16 Social Policy and Parliamentary Unit, *What does it profit us? A state of the nation report from the Salvation Army*, The Salvation Army, Wellington, 2008, p.6.
17 Ministry of Education, 2008.
18 *Licensed services and Licensed exempt groups 2007*, Education Counts, Ministry of Education: www.educationcounts.govt.nz/statistics/ece/ece_staff_return/licensed_services_and_licence-exempt_groups/17812
19 L. Smith, C. Wylie & M. Carr, *Outcomes of Early Childhood Education: Literature Review. Report to the Ministry of Education*, Research Division, Ministry of Education, Wellington, 2008.
20 Iris Duhn, 'Cartographies of childhood: Mapping the modern/global child', Unpublished PhD thesis, University of Auckland, 2006; Andrew Gibbons, 'Playing the ruins: the philosophy of care in early childhood education', *Contemporary Issues in Early Childhood*, vol. 8, no. 2, 2007, pp.123–32; Sandy Farquhar, 'Narrative identity: Ricoeur and early childhood education', unpublished PhD thesis, University of Auckland, 2008.
21 Sarah Farquhar, 'Assessing the evidence on early childhood education/childcare' (2008): www.childforum.com, p.1.
22 C. Wylie & E. Hogan, *Competent Learners @ 16: Competency levels and development over time*, New Zealand Council for Educational Research for the Ministry of Education, Wellington, 2007.
23 Ibid., p.15.
24 OECD, 'Early childhood education and care – history and context of the reviews', OECD, Paris, 2004: www.oecd.org.document 63/0
25 OECD, *Starting Strong. Early childhood education and care*, OECD, Paris, 2001.
26 Helen May, 'Te Whāriki – A woven mat for all to stand on', in J. Bennett (ed), *Starting Strong. Curricula and pedagogy in early childhood care and education. Five Curriculum*, OECD, Paris, 2004, pp.14–20.
27 OECD, *Starting Strong II. Early childhood education and care*, OECD, Paris, 2006.
28 OECD, *Babies and Bosses – Reconciling work and family life* (Vol.3): *New Zealand, Portugal, Switzerland*, OECD, Paris, 2004; *Babies and Bosses – Reconciling work and family life: A synthesis of findings for OECD counties*, OECD, Paris, 2006.
29 Trevor Mallard, Foreword, *Pathways to the Future. Ngā Huarahi Arataki. A ten year strategic plan for early childhood education*, Learning Media, Wellington, 2002, p.1.
30 Clare Wells, 'Future Directions: Shaping early childhood education policy for the 21st century. A personal perspective' in I. Livingston (ed), *New Zealand Annual Review of Education 1998:8*, School of Education, Victoria University of Wellington, 1999, p.45.
31 Early Childhood Education Project, *Future Directions. Early childhood education in New Zealand. Final report*, NZEI–Te Riu Roa, Wellington, 1996.
32 Linda Mitchell, 'Currents of change: Early childhood education in 2001', in I. Livingston (ed), *NZ Annual Review of Education 11*, 2001, School of Education, Victoria University Wellington, 2002, pp.123–43; C. Dalli and S. Te One, 'Early childhood education in 2002. Pathways to the future', in I. Livingston (ed), *NZ Annual Review of Education 12*, 2002, School of Education, Victoria University Wellington, 2003, pp.177–202
33 Strategic Plan Working Group, *Consultation document for the development of the strategic plan for early childhood education*, Ministry of Education, Wellington, 2001.
34 Victoria Carter, 'All talk and no walk – Let's get on and actually make something happen', *NZ Education Review*, 24 August 2001.
35 Ministry of Education, *Pathways to the Future. Ngā Huarahi Arataki. A ten year strategic plan for early childhood education*, Learning Media, Wellington, 2002, p.5.
36 Minister of Education Trevor Mallard, Speech notes, 10 July 2001.
37 Deborah Montgomery, 'The other teacher crisis', *Listener*, 27 April 2002, pp.27–31.
38 Carmen Dalli, 'The new teacher in New Zealand', in L.K. Miller & C. Cable (eds),

Professionalism in the Early Years, Hodder Arnold, 2008 (forthcoming)
39 Ministry of Education, *State of New Zealand Education 2007*, Learning Media, Wellington, 2008.
40 Verbal report from Rose Cole and Karl Le Quesne to the Ministry of Education Early Childhood Advisory Committee, 5 March 2008.
41 Dalli, 'The new teacher in New Zealand'.
42 C. Dalli and S. Cherrington, 'Pedagogical style and professionalism: Practitioner perspectives', paper presented at the Asia Pacific Conference of L'Organisation Modiale pour l'Education Préscholaire OMEP) Aotearoa New Zealand, 3 December 2005.
43 Dalli, 'The new teacher in New Zealand'.
44 Anne Meade (ed), *Riding the Waves. Innovation in early childhood education*. NZCER Press, Wellington, 2006, p.45.
45 C. Wylie & J. Thompson, 'The long-term contribution of early childhood education to children's performance – evidence from New Zealand', *International Journal of Early Years Education*, vol.11, no. 1, 2003, pp.69–78; Anne Smith and Helen May, 'Early childhood care and education in Aotearoa-New Zealand,' in E. Melhuish (ed), *Preschool Care and Education. International perspectives*, Routledge, London, 2006, pp.144–76; L. Smith, C. Wylie & M. Carr, *Outcomes of Early Childhood Education; literature review. Report to the Ministry of Education*, Research Division, Ministry of Education, Wellington, 2008.
46 Ministry of Education, *Early Childhood Education Funding Handbook*, Resourcing Division, Ministry of Education, Wellington, 2005.
47 Linda Mitchell, 'A new debate about children and childhood. Can it make a difference to early childhood pedagogy and policy', unpublished PhD. thesis, Victoria University Wellington, 2007.
48 Ministry of Education, *Review of regulations and funding – of early childhood education (ECE) – consultation document*, Wellington, 18 March 2003; *Review of regulations and funding – Cabinet paper for release of consultation document*, Wellington, 1 April 2003.
49 The Treasury, 'Aide memoire. Early childhood education – proposed funding options', Wellington, 12 September 2003.
50 Mitchell, 'A new debate about children and childhood', p.187; Ministry of Education, *Update on funding and regulatory reviews of ECE*, Wellington, 12 May 2003.
51 Harvey McQueen with Anne Else, *A question of shoes size. The campaign for pay parity for primary teachers 1994–1998*, NZEI-Te Riu Roa, Wellington, 2001.
52 Janette Kelly, 'Sally's shoe size still shouldn't shape salaries', paper presented at Te Tari Puna Ora o Aotearoa, NZCA (TTPOoA-NZCA) Annual Conference, Queenstown, 29 May 2004.
53 Trevor Mallard, 'Kindergarten teachers to return to State Sector', Media Release, 13 March 2000.
54 *Dominion Post*, 17 August 2002.
55 Helen May, *Twenty years of Consenting Parties. The politics of 'working' and 'teaching' in childcare 1985–2005*, NZEI-Te Riu Roa, Wellington, 2005.
56 NZEI–TRR, Media Release, 12 December 2003.
57 NZEI–TRR, Media Release, 24 May 2004.
58 Kelly, 'Sally's shoe size still shouldn't shape salaries'.
59 Ministry of Education, *Guide to the New Early Childhood Funding System – Implementing Pathways to the Future – Ngā Huarahi Arataki*, Wellington, 2004, p.12
60 *NZEI Rourou*, 8 November 2004.
61 NZEI–TRR, Media Release, 18 October 2004.
62 TTPOoA–NZCA, Addendum, Flyer, 10 November 2004.
63 Ministry of Education, *Early Childhood Education Funding Handbook*, Wellington, 2005, Ch. 3, p.15; Ch. 8, p.12.
64 Ministry of Education, 'Circular 2005/5 – Early Childhood Education Funding – Attestation: Registered Teachers' Salaries', p.2.
65 Letter from Nancy Bell to Trevor Mallard, Minister of Education, 1 April 2005.
66 Nancy Bell, *Itirearea*, no. 2, April 2005.

67 Minister of Education Trevor Mallard, Speech notes, 12 April 2005.
68 Email communication, Nancy Bell, chief executive of TTPOoA-NZCA, 15 May 2008.
69 *NZ Herald*, 3 March 2008.
70 Report to Members from ECAC from Nancy Bell, Chief Executive of TTPOoA–NZCA, 5 March 2008.
71 Email communication, Nancy Bell, Chief Executive of TTPOoA–NZCA, 15 May 2008.
72 NZEI–Te Riu Roa, *Report to the NZEI Annual Meeting 2007. Quality public ECE. A vision for 2020*, NZEI–Te Riu Roa, Wellington, 2007.
73 *NZ Herald*, 29 February 2008.
74 Cited in Diana Burns, 'The kids business', *Unlimited Inspiring Business*, Issue 82, Monday, 1 May 2006, p.1: http://unlimited.co.nz.nsf/default/77ACCC2AC84CC2571540006EFA7
75 Email communication, Julian Cook, Associate Director, Macquarie Bank, 8 March 2008.
76 Cited in Burns, 'The kids business', 2006.
77 Ibid.
78 Maria Slade, 'Child's play making a decent living', 3 March 2008: www.nzherald.co.nz/section/3/print/cfm7c_id
79 Cited in Burns, 'The kids business', 2006, p.1.
80 Deborah Brennan, 'The ABC of child care politics', *Australian Journal of Social Issues*, vol. 47, no.2, 2007, p.217.
81 Cited in Brennan, 'The ABC of child care politics', 2007.
82 *The Melbourne Age*, 15 September 2007.
83 Child Care Advocacy Association of Canada: www.ccaac.ca/campaign/index.php
84 Martha Friendly and Margaret McCain, 'Child care must serve kids not corporate shareholders', 7 March 2008: www.thestar.com/printArticle/310203
85 NZEI–Te Riu Roa, 'Quality public ECE. A vision for 2020, NZEI', 2007, p.5.
86 G. Cleveland, B. Forer, D. Hyatt, C. Japel and M. Krashinsky, *Final Report. An economic perspective on the current and future role of non-profit provision of early learning and childcare services in Canada*, University of Toronto, Canada, 2007.
87 Ibid., p.131.
88 Gordon Cleveland, 'Brief Summary of Findings in Non-Profit Child Care Project', 2007: www.childcarepolicy.net
89 A.B. Smith, V.E. Ford, P. Hubbard and J. White, *Working in infant childcare centres. Final Research Report to Ministry of Education*, University of Otago, Dunedin, 1995.
90 Linda Mitchell. *Differences between community owned and privately owned early childhood education and care centres. A review of the evidence.* NZCER Occasional Paper, 2002/2, Wellington.
91 L. Mitchell and K. Brooking, *First NZCER national survey of early childhood education services 2003–2004*, NZCER, Wellington, 2007.
92 Burns, 'The kids business', 2006.
93 *Dominion Post*, 13 September 2002.
94 *Sunday Star Times*, 6 May 2007.
95 ABC Learning Centres Limited, 'So much more than childcare. Half yearly results as at 31 December 2007', power-point, p.37.
96 Email communication, Julian Cook, 15 April 2008.
97 *Herald Sun*, 29 February 2008.
98 *Brisbane Times*, 27 February 2008.
99 *NZ Herald*, 29 February 2008.
100 Frances Nelson, NZEI–Te Riu Roa Media Release, 29 February 2008.
101 Nikki Todd, 'Groves to face ABC Learning directors', 8 March 2008: www.news.com.au/story/0,23599,23342954-29277,00.html
102 *The Age*, 29 February 2008.
103 M. Friendly and M. McCain, 'Child care must serve kids not corporate shareholder', 2008, p.2.
104 Ibid.

105 'Report on ECAC meeting held March 5, 2008', Email to members, 6 March 2008 from Nancy Bell, Chief Executive of Te Tari Puna Ora o Aotearoa/NZ Childcare Association.

106 Editorial, *Dominion Post*, 13 July 2005.

107 Helen May, 'Election year politics, 2005, and the "Nanny" State' in I. Livingston (ed.), *New Zealand Annual Review of Education 15, 2005*, School of Education Studies, Victoria University Wellington, 2006, pp.133–52.

108 Jane Clifton, Editorial, *Listener*, 23 July 2005, pp.20–21.

109 Linda Mitchell, *Putting children first: A well qualified early childhood teaching workforce*, NZCER, Wellington, 2004; NZ Institute of Economic Research, *Putting children first. Early childhood education policies for a new tomorrow*, NZIER, Wellington, 2005.

110 Mitchell, 'Putting children first', 2004, p.1.

111 A. Smith, G. Grima, M. Gaffney, K. Powell, L. Masse and S. Barnett, *Strategic research initiative literature review. Early childhood education*, Ministry of Education, Wellington, 2000.

112 C. Lee-Smith, 'Preschools face mass closure', *Sunday Star Times*, 8 February 2004, A5.

113 Education Review Office, *Readiness for new qualification requirements in early childhood education*, Wellington, 2003; C. Harkness, *Qualifications and registration in the early childhood education teacher-led workforce*, Demographic and Statistical Analysis Unit, Ministry of Education, Wellington, 2004.

114 Mitchell, 'Putting children first', 2004, p.2.

115 NZIER, 'Putting children first', 2005, p.2.

116 Ibid., p.3.

117 *Listener*, 29 October 2005.

118 *Listener*, 12 November 2005.

119 Therese Sayers, 'Macquarie Bank invests in NZ early childhood education', *Subtext. The newsletter of the Education Forum*, September 2005.

120 Michelle Quirke, 'Aussie bank buys Kiwi preschool', *Dominion Post*, 30 September 2005.

121 Garry Sheeran 'Kidicorp's growing up fast', *Sunday Star Times*, 20 November 2005.

122 Sarah Farquhar, 'Behind the early childhood policies – some thoughts': www.childforum.com/article_details.asp?, 2005, p.2.

123 Ibid.

124 Editorial, 'Minister sees "public value" as touchstone for future policy', *Itirearea*, no. 6, December 2005, p.1.

125 New Zealand Institute for Economic Research, *Early Childhood Participation. Is 20 hours free the answer? Key findings*, NZIER, Wellington, p.2.

126 David Lange, quoted in documentary for childcare produced by Anna Simmons for *Frontline*, TV One, June 1987, day unknown.

127 Peter Fraser, *AJHR*, E1, 1939, p.2.

128 Helen May, 'A right as a citizen to a free [early childhood] education 1930s–2000s', 2005.

129 These papers were collected by Linda Mitchell and passed to the author in 2008.

130 Ministry of Education, 'Update on funding and regulatory reviews of ECE', File No: FP25/07/1, LG10/07/1, 12 May 2003, Wellington. Released under the Official Information Act. Submission No. S02/1909.

131 Ibid., p.2.

132 Ministry of Education to the Minister of Education, 'Aide Memoire: meeting on costing model for review of early childhood funding', 30 July 2003, Wellington, File No: FP25/07/02/2. Released under the Official Information Act. Submission No SO3/0207.

133 Ibid., p.29.

134 Ministry of Education to the Minister of Education, 'ECE funding review: options for consultation and further information', 5 September 2003, Wellington, File No: FP25/07/00/1. Released under the Official Information Act. Submission No: SO3/0469.

135 Ibid., pp.5–6.

136 Treasury Report, 'Options for ECE funding – Meeting with the Minister of Education and the Minister of Social Development', 3 October 2003, Wellington. Treasury: 564044v1. Released under the Official Information Act.

137 Cabinet Social Development Committee, 'Review of early childhood education funding: public consultation', 9 February 2004, SDC(04)6, Cabinet Office. Released under the Official Information Act; Cabinet Policy Committee, 'Minute of decision, Early childhood funding: proposed new system', 31 March 2004, Cabinet Office. Released under the Official Information Act; Cabinet, 'Minute of Decision, 2004 Budget Package: Vote Education'. CAB Min (04) 13/3(24. Cabinet Office. Released under the Official Information Act.

138 Cabinet Policy Committee, 'Minute of decision, Early childhood funding: proposed new system', 31 March 2004, Cabinet Office, p.9. Released under the Official Information Act.

139 Brenda Bushouse, 'Early childhood education policy in Aotearoa–New Zealand', 2008.

140 *Dominion Post*, 28 May 2004.

141 John Gadsby, *Listener*, 12 June 2004.

142 *Dominion Post*, 28 May 2004.

143 *NZ Herald*, 17 June 2004.

144 *Dominion Post*, 19 June 2004.

145 *Education Review*, 2–8 June 2004.

146 Ministry of Education, 'Memo. ECE funding Review – Approaches to answering questions from the sector', Wellington, 2 June 2004, File FP25/07/00/2, pp.2–3. Released under the Official Information Act.

147 Trevor Mallard, Press Release, 22 August 2005.

148 Cited in Brenda Bushouse, 'Early childhood education policy in Aotearoa–New Zealand', 2008, p.40.

149 Carmen Dalli, 'Becoming a profession. A New Zealand story of advocacy, strategy and challenge', Keynote address, European Conference on quality employment in care work with young children, Kind & Gezin, Brussels, 21–22 April 2008, p.11.

150 Ministry of Education, *Travelling pathways to the future. Ngā huarahi arataki. Early childhood education symposium proceedings 2–3 May 2007*, Ministry of Education, Wellington.

151 A. Meade and P. Royal-Tangaere, 'Travelling pathways to 2007', in *Travelling pathways to the future: Ngā huarahi arataki. Early childhood education symposium proceedings 2–3 May 2007*, Ministry of Education, Wellington, pp.12–21.

152 Peter Moss, 'Leading the wave. New Zealand in an international context', in *Travelling pathways to the future: Ngā huarahi arataki. Early childhood education symposium proceedings 2–3 May 2007*, Ministry of Education, Wellington, p.33.

153 Ibid., p.35.

154 Statistics New Zealand, 'Consumer Price Index: September 2007 quarter', *Hot off the press. Latest statistics from New Zealand*. Wellington, 15 October 2007.

155 Ministry of Education, 'Preliminary findings from early effects study', unpublished paper released to ECE Research Policy Forum, Wellington, 13 June 2000.

156 Ministry of Education, 'Free ECE Monthly Monitoring Report', 4 February 2008: www.minedu.govt.nz/index.cfm?layout=document&doc

157 Ministry of Education, 'Preliminary findings from early effects study', unpublished paper released to ECE Research Policy Forum, Wellington, 13 June 2000.

158 Barnardo's, Media Release, 19 January 2007.

159 *NZ Herald*, 17 January 2007.

160 Early Childhood Council, 'Free Early Childhood Education. Why your child might miss out? Information for parents', pamphlet, Auckland, 2007.

161 http://20hoursfree.blogspot.com/

162 *Sunday Star Times*, 17 June 2007.

163 Interview on *Nine to Noon*, Radio New Zealand, 13 June 2007.

164 Paula Bennett, National Policy 2008: Education, 'Early childhood care and education', 11 July 2008: www.national.org.nz/Article.aspx?ArticleID=28202

165 *NZ Herald*, 27 April 2007.

166 Linda Mitchell, 'Currents of change', 2002, 'Crossroads – Early childhood education in the mid-1990s', 2005.

167 L. Mitchell & K. Brooking, 'First NZCER national survey of early childhood', 2007.

168 Ministry of Education, 'Update on the ECE regulatory review', Wellington, September 2007: www.minedu.govt.nz/index.cfm?layout=index&indexid=882

169 *NZ Herald*, 17 June 2007.

170 Statistics New Zealand, Consumer Price Index: September 2007.

171 Ministry of Education, 'Preliminary findings from early effects study', unpublished paper released to ECE Research Policy Forum, Wellington, 13 June 2000.

172 *Otago Daily Times*, 19 February 2008.

173 *Otago Daily Times*, 1 March 2008.

174 Sarah Farquhar (ed.) *The future for children's early care and education. Proceedings of the National Forum*, 11 February 2008, National Library, Wellington: www.childforum.com

175 Sarah Farquhar, '20 hours free ECE policy not a good thing for children', 26 June 2007: childforum.com/articles.asp

176 Sarah Farquhar, 'The future for children's early care and education', 2008.

177 Ibid.

178 Farquhar (ed.), *The future for children's early care and education. Proceedings of the National Forum*, 2008, p.7.

179 Maureen Woodham, 'Looking a gift horse in the mouth: Examining Labour's "20 Hours Free" early childhood education policy', I. Livingstone (ed.), *New Zealand Annual Review of Education 17:2007*, School of Education Studies, Victoria University of Wellington, 2008, p.169.

180 Trevor Mallard, Foreword, *Pathways to the Future: Ngā Huarahi Arataki*, Ministry of Education, Wellington, 2002, p.1.

181 Helen May, 'Towards citizenry rights in the early childhood sector', 2004.

182 Alan Prout, 'Children, representation and social change', Address to European Early Childhood Research Association Conference, Glasgow, September 2003, p.3.

183 Frances Press, '(Re)positioning the child in the policy/politics of early childhood', *Educational philosophy and theory, Special Issue: Philosophy of early childhood education*, vol.39, no.3, June 2007, p.323.

184 Sarah Te One, 'Citizenry rights and early childhood policies', 2005, p.178.

185 *United Nations Convention on the Rights of the Child*, United Nations Committee on the Rights of the Child, New York.

186 Sandy Farquhar, 'Narrative identity: Ricoeur and early childhood education', 2008, p.30.

187 Margaret Carr, *Assessment in Early Childhood Settings*, Paul Chapman, London, 2001.

188 Rita Walker and Lesley Rameka, 'Te Whatu Pōkeka – (Weaving the Baby Carrier)', Paper presented at the 16th International Reconceptualising Early Childhood Education Conference: Weaving within and across paradigms and traditions, University of Victoria, British Columbia, Canada, 2–6 June 2008, Abstract.

189 John Bennett (ed.) *Starting Strong. Curricula and pedagogy in early childhood care and education: Five Curriculum*, OECD, Paris, 2004.

190 Joce Nuttall, *Weaving Te Whāriki. Aotearoa New Zealand's early childhood curriculum document in theory and practice*, NZCER, Wellington, 2003.

191 Joce Nuttall, 'Why don't you ask someone who cares? Teacher identity, intersubjectivity and curriculum negotiation in a New Zealand childcare centre', unpublished PhD thesis, Victoria University of Wellington.

192 Alison Stephenson, 'Skirmishes on the border: How children experienced, influenced and enacted the boundaries of curriculum in an early childhood education centre setting', PhD thesis (nearing completion), Victoria University of Wellington.

193 Alison Stephenson, 'Skirmishes on the border'; Te One, 'Interwoven, interrelated, interdependent. Perceptions of children's rights in three early childhood settings' PhD thesis (nearing completion), Victoria University of Wellington; Margaret Brennan, '"They just want to be with us". Young children: Learning to live the culture: A post-Vygotskian analysis of young children's enculturation into a childcare setting', unpublished PhD thesis, Victoria University Wellington, 2005.

194 Andrew Neil Gibbons, 'The matrix ate my baby', 2005, p.6.
195 Iris Duhn, 'Cartographies of childhood', 2006, p.149.
196 Sandy Farquhar, 'Narrative identity', 2008, p.175.
197 Ibid., p.204.
198 Ibid., p.152.
199 NZEI-Te Riu Roa, 'Quality public ECE. A vision for 2010', 2007.
200 Ibid., p.2.
201 Mitchell, 'A new debate about children and childhood', 2007, p.224.
202 *Press*, 7 October 2008.

REFERENCES TO CHAPTER ELEVEN

1 Jonathan Boston and Derek Gill, *Social Investment: A New Zealand policy experiment*, Bridget Williams Books, Wellington, 2018.

2 Helen May, 'New Zealand Case Study: A narrative of shifting policy directions for early childhood education and care', in L.F. Gambaro, K. Stewart and J. Waldfogel (eds), *An Equal Start? Providing quality early childhood education and care for disadvantaged children*, Policy Press, London, 2014, pp.147–70.

3 Helen May, *Ngā Āhuatanga Hurihuri o te Tiaki Tamariki: The changing fortunes of childcare 2003–2013*, Te Tari Puna Ora o Aotearoa New Zealand Childcare Association, Wellington, 2013, p.v.

4 Linda Mitchell, 'Shifting Directions in ECEC Policy in New Zealand: From a child rights to an interventionist approach', *International Journal of Early Years Education*, vol. 23, no. 3, 2015, pp.299–300.

5 https://treasury.govt.nz/information-and-services/state-sector-leadership/cross-agency-initiatives/social-investment

6 Thomas Coughlan, 'What becomes of Social Investment?', 5 February 2018: www.newsroom.co.nz/2018/02/04/80935/what-becomes-of-social-investment

7 Ministry of Education, 'Terms of Reference: Development of a 10-year strategic plan for early learning', 2018.

8 Ministry of Education, *Te Taonga te Tamaiti – Every Child a Taonga: Strategic plan for early learning 2019–29*, Wellington, 2018.

9 www.educationcounts.govt.nz/__data/assets/pdf_file/0009/192942/ECE-Summary-page-1Attendance-in-2018.pdf

10 This is a lower figure than the one presented in Chapter 10 on p.264, which had been inflated by dual enrolment in services.

11 Cited in Linda Mitchell, *Democratic Policies and Practices in Early Childhood Education: An Aotearoa New Zealand case study*, Springer, Singapore, 2018, p.32.

12 www.growingup.co.nz/en/research-findings-impact/study-reports.html#97368894a33903 262822d5ac16e78c12

13 www.growingup.co.nz/en/research-findings-impact/study-reports.html#a68ade4654cd87a 92487d7efb2160116

14 https://cdn.auckland.ac.nz/assets/growingup/research-findings-impact/GUiNZ_Now%20 we%20are%20four%20report.pdf

15 Peter Moss, 'Leading the Wave: New Zealand in an international context', in Ministry of Education, *Travelling Pathways to the future – Ngā Huarahi Arataki: Early childhood education symposium proceedings 2–3 May 2007*, Wellington, p.33.

16 Peter Moss, 'Beyond Childcare, Markets and Technical Practice: Re-politicising early childhood', *Proceedings of Early Childhood Care and Education Seminar Series 2*, Centre for Social and Educational Research, Dublin, 2008, pp.7–8.

17 Anne Tolley, speech to NZK conference, 8 August 2009, Office of the Minister of Education.

18 A. Morrison, *Likely Reasons for Low Participation in Early Childhood Education in the Low Participation Areas of County-Manukau*, Ministry of Education, Wellington, 2009.

19 L. Mitchell, P. Meagher Lundberg, D. Mara, P. Cubey and M. Whitford, *Locality-based Evaluation of Pathways to the Future – Ngā Huarahi Arataki*, Ministry of Education, Wellington, 2011.

20 *New Zealand Herald*, 22 and 23 May 2010.

21 NZK, *Quality ECE: Worth the investment*, Wellington, 2010.

22 Anne Tolley, speech to the Childforum Seminar, 4 April 2011, Office of the Minister of Education.

23 Hekia Parata, 'Raising Achievement for All in the Budget', speech notes, 16 May 2012, Office of the Minister of Education.

24 TTPOoA NZCA, 'Erosion of Early Childhood Funding Causes Concern', media release, 24 May 2012.

25 Margaret Carr and Linda Mitchell, 'Qualified Teachers in Early Childhood Centres: Do We Need Them?', occasional paper, University of Waikato, Hamilton, 2010, pp.1–4.

26 A. Meade, L. Robinson, S. Smorti, M. Smart and J. Williamson, *Early Childhood Teachers' Work in Education and Care Centres*, TTPOoA NZCA, Wellington, 2012, p.xii.

27 Nancy Bell, Opening speech, TTPOoA NZCA 49th Annual Conference, Dunedin, 30 June 2012.

28 ECE Taskforce, *An Agenda for Amazing Children: Final Report of the ECE Taskforce*, NZ Government, Wellington, 2011.

29 Ibid., p.176.

30 NZCA, 'Early Childhood Taskforce Established Without Consultation', media release, October 2010.

31 TTPOoA NZCA, 'Submission to ECE Taskforce', 11 March 2011, p.1.

32 Michael Mintrom, 'Broader Perspectives', in Boston and Gill (eds), *Social Investment*, 2018, p.81.

33 Anne Smith, unpublished 'Position Paper on Essay 3: Reforming Funding Mechanisms', May 2011; unpublished 'Position Paper on Early Childhood Education to the ECE Taskforce and the Minister of Education', November 2010.

34 ECE Taskforce, *An Agenda for Amazing Children*, pp.14–15.

35 *Pathways to the Future – Ngā Huarahi Arataki*, Ministry of Education, Wellington, 2002.

36 Smith, unpublished 'Position Paper on Early Childhood Education', p.2.

37 Smith, unpublished 'Position Paper on Essay 3', pp.2–3.

38 Email, Anne Smith to Michael Mintrom, 5 May 2011, Anne Smith papers, Hocken Collections (HC), University of Otago. Reprinted with permission.

39 www.childcarepolicy.net/105-2/

40 Email, Anne Smith to Gordon Cleveland, 3 June 2011, HC. Reprinted with permission.

41 Email, Anne Smith to Michael Mintrom, 23 February 2011, HC. Reprinted with permission. The report referred to is L. Mitchell, P. Meagher-Lundberg, D. Mara, P. Cubey and M. Whitford, 'Locality-based Evaluation of Pathways to the Future – Ngā Huarahi Arataki', 2011: www.educationcounts.govt.nz/publications/ece/locality-based-evaluation-of-pathways-to-the-future-ng-huarahi-arataki

42 Anne Smith, 'Defining Quality, Implementing it and Holding on to it', keynote address, NZEI–TRR conference, Auckland, 19 October 2013, HC.

43 Helen May and Kerry Bethell, *Growing a Kindergarten Movement: Its people, purposes and politics*, NZCER Press, Wellington, 2017.

44 NZK, 'Critical Issues and Key Messages' from participant discussion at the AGM, 13–14 May 2011, Wellington.

45 NZK meeting with Minister of Education, 15 August 2011, cited in May and Bethell, *Growing a Kindergarten Movement*, 2017.

46 ECE Taskforce, *An Agenda for Amazing Children*, p.58

47 Ibid., p.45.

48 *ECE Sector Advisory Group Report: Quality for under-twos; ECE Sector Advisory Group Report: Quality ECE*, Ministry of Education, Wellington, 2012.

49 NZ Treasury, briefing to the incoming minister, 2012: www.beehive.govt.nz/sites/all/files/MinEdu_BIM.pdf

50 State Services Commission, *Better Service Results: Targets and public communication*, Office of the Minister of State Services, 25 June 2012.

51 Education Counts, 'ECE Participation Programmes Evaluation Reports', Ministry of Education, Wellington, 2012: www.educationcounts.govt.nz/publications/ECE

52 L. Mitchell, P. Meagher Lundberg, M. Taylor, T. Caulcutt, T. Kalavite, H. Kara and V. Paki, *ECE Participation Programme Evaluation: Baseline report*, 2013: www.educationcounts. govt.nz/publications/ECE/ece-participation-programmeevaluation; L. Mitchell, P. Meagher Lundberg, M. Taylor, T. Caulcutt, M. Taylor, S. Archard, H. Kara and V. Paki, *ECE Participation Programme Evaluation: Delivery of the ECE participation initiatives, Stage 2*, 2014: www.educationcounts.govt.nz/publications/ECE/148513; L. Mitchell, P. Meagher-Lundberg, C. Davison, H. Kara & T. Kalavite, *ECE Participation Programme Evaluation Stage 3*, 2016: www.educationcounts.govt.nz/publications/ECE/ece-participation-programmeevaluation-delivery-of-ece-participation-initiatives-stage-3

53 Linda Mitchell, *Democratic Practices and Processes in Early Childhood Education: An Aotearoa New Zealand case study*, Springer, Singapore, 2019.

54 Ibid., p.99.

55 Ministry of Social Development, *Green Paper on Vulnerable Children: Every child thrives, belongs, achieves*, NZ Government, Wellington, 2011: www.childrensactionplan.govt.nz/green-paper

56 Ministry of Social Development, *White Paper on Vulnerable Children*, NZ Government, Wellington, 2012, p.4: www.childrensactionplan.govt.nz/whitepaper

57 NZK, *Increasing Participation*, Wellington, 2013.

58 Author interview with Amanda Coulston, 2016.

59 UNICEF, 'Collective Voice for New Zealand's Children', media release, 12 July 2012.

60 Linda Mitchell, 'A New Debate about Children and Childhood: Can it make a difference to early childhood pedagogy and policy?', unpublished PhD thesis, Victoria University of Wellington, 2007.

61 Mitchell, *Democratic Practices and Processes*, 2019.

62 J. Randall, 'Impacts of Early Childhood Education Social Obligations on Families and Whanau', unpublished MEd thesis, University of Waikato, 2015.

63 New Zealand National Party, media release, 29 January 2018: www.scoop.co.nz/stories/PA1801/S00084/public-services-targets-to-continue-without-govt.htm

64 Waitangi Tribunal, *Matua Rautia: The report on the Kōhanga Reo claim*, Wellington, 2013, p.6: https://forms.justice.govt.nz/search/Documents/WT/wt_DOC_68775144/Matua%20Rautia%20W.pdf

65 Mai Chen, 'Submission of Council for the Claimant', WAI 2336, 3.3.1, Waitangi Tribunal, pp.7–8.

66 Ibid., p.8.

67 'Opening Submissions of the Crown', WAI 2336, 3.3.2 Waitangi Tribunal, p.2.

68 Richard Whalley, Ministry of Education, WAI 2336, A062, Waitangi Tribunal.

69 WAI 2336, A062, p.8.

70 WAI 2336, 3.3.2, p.13, and see Whalley, WAI 2336, A062, p.3.

71 Anne Meade, WAI 2336, A066, Waitangi Tribunal, p.5.

72 Ibid., p.11.

73 Cited in Meade, WAI 2336, A066, p.13.

74 Ibid. p.19.

75 Iritana Tawhiwhirangi, WAI 2336, A078, Waitangi Tribunal, p.9.

76 Ibid., p.17.

77 Mai Chen for Arapera Royal Tangaere, WAI 2336, A096, p.1.

78 Ibid., p.2.

79 Ibid.

80 Waitangi Tribunal, *Matua Rautia*, 2013, p.326

81 Ibid., p.327.

82 www.minedu.govt.nz/theMinistry/InformationReleases/TeKohangaReoNationalTrust PublicFundingReview.aspx

83 'Minister Sidelines Kōhanga Reo Board', Radio NZ, 31 August 2015.

84 'Kōhanga Reo Claim Back on the Table', *NZ Herald*, 28 May 2018.

85 'Underfunded Kōhanga Reo Means Staff Earning Minimum Wage', Radio NZ, 21 November 2018.

86 NZ Government, press release, 4 June 2019: www.scoop.co.nz/stories/PA1906/S00016/wellbeing-budget-recognises-the-importance-of-kohanga-reo.htm

87 W. Lee, M. Carr, B. Soutar and L. Mitchell, *Understanding the Te Whāriki Approach*, David Fulton, United Kingdom, 2012; Joce Nuttall, *Weaving Te Whāriki: Aotearoa New Zealand's early childhood curriculum document in theory and practice*, NZCER Press, Wellington, 2013 (2nd edn).

88 Nuttall, ibid., p.2.

89 ERO, *Working with Te Whāriki*, Wellington, 2013.

90 Catherine Woulfe, 'Early Warnings', *NZ Listener*, 19 April 2014, pp.20–22.

91 Helen May, Letter to the Editor, *NZ Listener*, 26 April 2014.

92 Ministry of Education, 'Terms of Reference – Advisory Group on Early Learning', Wellington, 2014, p.1.

93 Anne Meade, 'The Impact of New Zealand's Early Childhood Curriculum and Pedagogy on Learning Outcomes', presentation to the OECD ECEC Network, 10 December 2013, Wellington; Helen May, 'Developing and Implementing Te Whāriki: An overview over two decades', keynote address to New Zealand conference on ECEC in co-operation with the OECD ECEC Network, *Curriculum Implementation in ECEC: Te Whāriki in International Perspective*, 9 December 2013, Wellington.

94 T. Reedy and T. Reedy, 'Te Whāriki: A tapestry of life', keynote address to New Zealand conference on ECEC in co-operation with the OECD ECEC Network, *Curriculum Implementation in ECEC: Te Whāriki in International Perspective*, 9 December 2013, Wellington, p.1.

95 Ministry of Education, *Report of the Advisory Group on Early Learning*, Wellington, June 2015, p.7.

96 ECE Research Policy Forum minutes 2015–16.

97 Ministry of Education, media release, 12 April 2017.

98 Helen May, speech at 'Te Whāriki 2017 launch', Ministry of Education, Wellington, 13 April 2017. Reprinted in *Childspace*, no. 48, winter 2017, pp.4–5.

99 Linda Mitchell, 'Comment', *Early Childhood Folio*, vol. 22, no. 1, 2018, p.1.

100 Mere Skerrett, 'Pedagogical Intentions: Enacting a "refreshed" bicultural curriculum positioned at the crossroads of colonial relations, bicultural education and critical literacy', *Early Childhood Folio*, vol. 22, no. 1, 2018, pp.7–8.

101 Jenny Ritchie, 'A Fantastical Journey: Reimagining Te Whāriki', ibid., p.11.

102 Sally Peters, 'Exploring New Approaches to Pathways from Early Childhood Education to School', ibid., pp.21–27.

103 ERO, *Awareness and Confidence to Work with Te Whāriki*, July 2018; *Engaging with Te Whāriki*, November 2018, p.8.

104 NZEI Te Riu Roa, 'Taking the Lead: Celebrating NZ curricula', Wellington, 9 March 2018.

105 Helen May, *'I am Five and I Go to School': The work and play of early education in New Zealand*, Otago University Press, Dunedin, 2011.

106 Ministry of Education and NZEI-TRR, 'Growing Strong Foundations: Exploring the potential of the national curricula for all students', June 2018.

107 Maggie Haggerty, 'Navigating the Entanglements: Curriculum and assessment priorities in transitioning to school in Aotearoa–New Zealand', unpublished PhD thesis, Victoria University Wellington, 2019.

108 OECD, *Call for Tenders: International early learning study*, Paris, 2015: www.oecd.org/callsfortenders/CfT%20100001420%20International%20Early%20Learning%20Study.pdf

109 OECD, *Starting Strong I*, Paris, 2001; *Starting Strong II*, Paris, 2006.

110 Helen May, 'Te Whāriki 2017 Launch', *Childspace*, no. 48, 2017, pp.4–5.

111 OIA 1043294, 31 documents between 2 February 2017 and 22 April 2015, supplied to NZK by the Ministry of Education.

112 OECD, 'International Learning Assessment: Background information for the tele-conference with members of the ECE Research Policy Forum', 14 October 2015, OIA 1043294.

113 Memo from Karl Le Quesne to the Policy Governance Board, 22 May 2015, OIA 1043294.

114 Ibid., p.2.

115 Ministry of Education, 'An International Assessment of Early Learning Outcomes: Background document for scoping. Comments from the Ministry of Education, New Zealand', 11 June 2015, OIA 1043294.

116 'Background Note on OECD Early Learning Assessment', 6 April 2016, OIA 1043294, p.2.

117 Ministry of Education, 11 June 2015, p.2.

118 Ministry of Education, 'An International Assessment of Early Learning Outcomes: Background document for scoping. Comments from the Ministry of Education, New Zealand', 25 August 2015, OIA 1043294, p.2.

119 Memo, 'NZ's Contribution to the OECD Early Learning Assessment Project', 2 February 2016, OIA 1043294, p.1.

120 M. Carr, L. Mitchell and L. Rameka, 'Some Thoughts About the Value of an OECD International Assessment Framework for Early Childhood Services in Aotearoa New Zealand: A paper to contribute to the ECE Research Policy Advisory Forum discussions', July 2016, tabled at the 6 September 2016 meeting.

121 James P. Gee, 'Reflections on Assessment from a Sociocultural-situated Perspective', in *Yearbook of the National Society for the Study of Education*, vol. 106, issue 1, April 2007, p.364.

122 Stuart McNaughton, 'Early Learning (for Child Well-being) Study, 26–27 September 2016, OECD, Paris, OIA 1043294, p.1.

123 Briefing note to update Minister Hekia Parata on recent activities: 'Update from Professor Stuart McNaughton', 30 November 2016, OIA 1043294, p.1.

124 Mattias Urban and Beth Blue, 'Democratic Accountability and Contextualised Systems: A comment on the OECD initiative to launch an International Early Learning Study', December 2016, p.9. Later published in *International Critical Childhood Policy Journal*, vol. 6, no. 1.

125 Alex Gunn, 'Paper and Motion to the 2016 AGM of the New Zealand Association for Research in Education: OECD International Early Learning and Child Well-being Study', p.2.

126 P. Moss [UK], G. Dahlberg [Sweden], S. Grieshaber [Australia], H. May [New Zealand], S. Mantovani [Italy], A. Pence [Canada], S. Rayna [France], E. Swadener [USA], M. Vandenbroek [Belgium], 'The Organisation for Economic Co-operation and Development's International Early Learning Study: Opening for debate and contestation', *Contemporary Issues in Early Childhood*, vol, 17, no. 3, 2016, pp.343–51.

127 M. Carr, L. Mitchell and L. Rameka, 'Some Thoughts about the Value of an OECD International Assessment Framework for Early Childhood Services in Aotearoa New Zealand, *Contemporary Issues in Early Childhood*, vol. 17, no. 4, 2016, pp.450–54.

128 Moss et al., 2016, p.344.

129 Alan Pence, 'Baby PISA: Dangers that can arise when foundations shift', *Journal of Childhood Studies*, vol. 44, no. 43, 2016, pp.54–58; H. Wasmuth, 'Baby PISA is Just Around the Corner: So why is no one talking about it?', *ECE Policy Matters*, 2017: http://ecepoli-cyworks.com/blog/page/2

130 Memo to Iona Holsted, Secretary for Education, from Siobhan Murray, senior policy manager Early Learning, 12 December 2017, OIA 1043294, p.1.

131 Alex Gunn, *Ipu Kerurū*, 26 July 2017: https://nzareblog.wordpress.com/2017/07/26/oecd-T/

132 OECD, *Early Learning Matters*, Paris, 2017, p.14.
133 P. Moss and M. Urban, 'The Organisation for Economic Co-operation and Development's International Early Learning Study: What happened next?', *Contemporary Issues in Early Childhood*, vol. 18, no. 2, 2017, pp.250–58; 'The Organisation for Economic Co-operation and Development's International Early Learning Study: What's going on', *Contemporary Issues in Early Childhood*, vol. 20, no. 2, 2018. pp.207–12.
134 Moss & Urban, 2018, ibid., p.211.
135 Helen May, 'Power of the Pen: Personal journeys, political stories. documenting the politics of early childhood in Aotearoa', lecture in Education Seminar Series *The Road Ahead*, Stout Centre, Victoria University Wellington, 12 April 2017.
136 www.plunket.org.nz/assets/strategy/Plunket-Strategy-2016-2021-9Feb2017.pdf, p.3
137 www.noted.co.nz/the-listener/july-7-2018/
138 www.educationcounts.govt.nz/__data/assets/pdf_file/0009/192942/ECE-Summary-page-1Attendance-in-2018.pdf
139 Suzanne Manning, '"Playcentre is Special": Playcentre parenting and policy', unpublished PhD thesis, University of Auckland, 2018.
140 Ibid., pp.5–6.
141 Ibid., p.231.
142 Reprinted in 'Redesigning Playcentre', *Playcentre Journal*, Autumn 2016, pp.10–11.
143 Sue Stover, 'Editorial: Moving on looking back', *Early Years Journal*, vol. 64, spring/summer 2018, p.4.
144 Te Whānau Tupu Ngātahi o Aotearoa Playcentre Aotearoa, 'Revised Operational Restructure Project', 17 February 2016, p.9.
145 Stover, 'Editorial: Moving on looking back', p.4.
146 Education Counts, 'ECE enrolments time series 2000–2018': www.educationcounts.govt.nz/statistics/early-childhood-education/services
147 Ibid.
148 This excluded the four North Island associations belonging to Early Childhood Leadership, which exited from the then NZ Free Kindergarten Union in 1991.
149 Sherryll Wilson, Discussion Paper: 'A Single Organisation for Kindergartens in New Zealand', May 2005, NZK, Wellington.
150 NZK brochure, 'Kindergarten 2026 and Beyond', nd.
151 NZK brochure, 'One Organisation Functions Summary', nd.
152 NZK, *The Story*, Wellington, June 2018.
153 *Report of the Consultative Committee on Pre-School Educational Services*, 1947; Department of Education, *Report of the Committee of Inquiry into Pre-School Education*, Wellington, 1971; David Lange, *Before Five: Early childhood care and education in New Zealand*, 1988, Ministry of Education, Wellington; *Pathways to the Future: Ngā Huarahi Arataki 2002–2012*; ECE Taskforce, *An Agenda for Amazing Children: Final report of the ECE Taskforce*, NZ Government, Wellington, 2011.
154 Mitchell, *Democratic Practices and Processes*, p.156.
155 Ibid., pp.156–62.
156 For example ERO, *Engaging with Te Whāriki*, 2017; *Awareness and Confidence to Work with Te Whāriki*, July 2018; *Meeting Requirements for Children's Safety and Well-being in ECE*, 2016; *Infants and Toddlers Competent and Confident Communicators and Explorers*, 2015.
157 Mike Bedford, 'Cold and Crowded: Early childhood education environment's study', unpublished PhD thesis, University of Otago (under examination 2019).
158 M. Bedford, S. Bates, W. Page and S. McLaren, 'ECE in New Zealand: A hazard to child and teacher health', public presentation, University of Otago Medical School, 8 June 2018.
159 www.radionz.co.nz/news/national/286327/it-is-like-factory-farming-for-children
160 Ann Pairman, 'Living in this Space: Case studies of children's lived experiences in four spatially diverse early childhood centres', unpublished PhD thesis, Victoria University of Wellington, 2018.
161 Interviewed by Catherine Woulfe, 'Look and Learn', *NZ Listener*, 13 June 2018, p.27.

162 Ibid., p.22.
163 Ibid., p.28.
164 Nancy Bell, Consultation Hui presentation, Wellington, 7 February 2019.
165 Ministry of Education, *Te Taonga te Tamaiti*, 2018, p.11.
166 ECC, 'Early Learning Strategic Plan Ambitious', media release, 20 November 2018.
167 NZK, 'High Quality ECE – a right for every child', media release, 20 November 2018.
168 Martin Jenkins, *The Kōrero Mātauranga: Draft Early Learning Strategic Plan Submission Analysis*, Wellington, April 2019.
169 'Early Years Research Centre Submission on Strategic Plan for Early Learning 2019–2029,' University of Waikato, 11 March 2019.
170 Ibid., p.6.
171 Ministry of Education, *Te Taonga te Tamaiti*, 2018, p.11.

ABBREVIATIONS

ACC	Associated Childcare Council
AKA	Auckland Kindergarten Association
ATL	Alexander Turnbull Library
CECUA	Combined Early Childhood Union of Aotearoa
CEO	Chief Executive Officer
COI	Centre of Innovation
CPA	Consenting Parties Agreement
DOPs	*Statement of Desirable Objectives and Practices*
DPB	Domestic Purposes Benefit
ECC	Early Childhood Council
ECDU	Early Childhood Development Unit
ECD	Early Childhood Development
ECE	early childhood education
ECEC	Early Childhood Education and Care
ECECA	Early Childhood Education Collective Agreement
ECWU	Early Childhood Workers' Union
ERO	Education Review Office
FOL	Federation of Labour
FNZPC	Federation of New Zealand Parents' Centres
HIPPY	Home Instruction for Pre-School Youngsters
IDP	Individual Development Plan
IHC	Intellectually Handicapped
IECS, VUW	Institute for Early Childhood Studies, Victoria University Wellington
IELS	International Early Learning Study
IWY	International Women's Year
IYC	International Year of the Child
KTA	Kindergarten Teachers' Association
LCCF	Licensed Childcare Centres Federation
MEF	Maori Education Foundation
MWWL	Maori Women's Welfare League

NA	National Archives
NACPSE	National Advisory Council on Pre-School Education
NZACCC	New Zealand Association of Childcare Centres
NZCA	New Zealand Childcare Association Te Tari Puna Ora o Aotearoa (was NZACCC)
NZCER	New Zealand Council for Educational Research
NZEI	New Zealand Educational Institute
NZEI–TRR	New Zealand Educational Institute – Te Riu Roa
NZFKTA	New Zealand Free Kindergarten Teachers' Association
NZFKA	New Zealand Free Kindergarten Association
NZFKU	New Zealand Free Kindergarten Union
NZK	New Zealand Kindergartens Te Pūtahi Kura Pūhou o Aotearoa
NZKF	New Zealand Kindergarten Federation
NZPC	New Zealand Playcentre
NZPF	New Zealand Playcentre Federation
NZQA	New Zealand Qualifications Authority
OECD	Organisation for Economic Co-operation and Development
OMEP	Organisation Mondiale pour l'Education Préscolaire
PAFT	Parents As First Teachers
PAT	Parents As Teachers
PIPEF	Pacific Island Polynesian Education Foundation
Playcentre	Te Whānau Tupu Ngātahi o Aotearoa – Playcentre Aotearoa
PCCF	Private Childcare Federation
PCNZ	Parents' Centre New Zealand (was FNZPC)
TTPOoA–NZCA	Te Tari Puna Ora o Aotearoa – New Zealand Childcare Association
VUW	Victoria University of Wellington
WCCA	Wellington Community Childcare Association
YWCA	Young Women's Christian Association

Note: Some organisations have changed their names and abbreviations over the years. The text tries to identify this. In the references archival collections are generally referred to by their current name.

GLOSSARY

aroha	love, compassion
awhina	to help, give assistance
hui	gathering
he kōrero Māori	speaking in Māori
kaiako	supervisor, caregiver
kaiarahi reo	language assistants
karakia	prayer
kaumātua	elder
Kaumātua Hui	Maori Elders' Conference
kaupapa	philosophy, principles
kōhanga reo	language nest
koroua	male elder
kuia	female elder
kura	school
manaaki	hospitality
marae	meeting place
mihi	greeting
Mana Motuhake	the spirit of Māori autonomy (also the name of a political party)
Nga Tamatoa	young warriors (also the name of an activist organisation)
poi	a light ball, dance
Ranginui and Papa	mother and father of creation
reo	language
roopu	group
rūnanga	assembly
tauiwi	foreigner
Tangaroa	god of the sea
tangata whenua	people first here
tamariki	children
tikanga	cultural practices
tino rangatiratanga	governance

tīpuna	ancestors
tu tangata	stand tall
waiata	song
wairua	sprirituality
wānanga	council
whakapapa	genealogy
whakatauira	hui for a specific purpose
whānau	extended family

INDEX